Perspectives in Economic and Social History
Series Editors: Andrew August and Jari Eloranta

The Nordic Economic, Social and Political Model
Challenges in the 21st Century
Edited by Anu Koivunen, Jari Ojala and Janne Holmén

North Eurasian Trade in World History, 1660–1860
The Economic and Political Importance of the Baltic Sea
Werner Scheltjens

A History of Cold War Industrialisation
Finnish Shipbuilding between East and West
Saara Matala

Social Cohesion and Welfare States
From Fragmentation to Social Peace
Edited by Christopher Lloyd and Matti Hannikainen

Agriculture and the Great Depression
The Rural Crisis of the 1930s in Europe and the Americas
Edited by Gérard Béaur and Francesco Chiapparino

Shadow Economies in the Globalising World
Smuggling in Scandinavia, 1766–1806
Anna Knutsson

National Brands and Global Markets
An Historical Perspective
Edited by Nikolas Glover and David M. Higgins

For more information about this series, please visit: www.routledge.com/Perspectives-in-Economic-and-Social-History/book-series/PESH

National Brands and Global Markets

Between Brexit, efforts to 'Make America great again', and ongoing appeals for patriotic consumption to boost economies, the intersection between national identity, marketing campaigns, and consumer choices has been brought to the fore. This book maps out this terrain and provides a framework for how research on 'Made in' campaigns and programmes in individual countries can be placed into a broader historical context. The book argues that the history of 'Made in' can be used to shed light on society at large: the actors that have promoted it, the institutions that have regulated it, and the cultural environments that have attributed it meaning. At times 'Made in' has been a basic, descriptive trade mark, while, in other periods, it has been a key component of carefully developed commercial brands, and in yet other instances it has been used in attempts to forge and redefine national identities. The book opens with an introduction to the three key factors which have featured prominently in 'Made in' campaigns – commercial logic, national economic policy, and its use as an instrument in political discourse, and it provides an overview of the evolution of 'Made in' from a marketing perspective. This is followed by country-specific discussions of 'Made in' with case studies including countries in Western Europe, the US, Japan, and the antipodes.

This book will be of significant interest to students and scholars of economic history, business history, and marketing.

Nikolas Glover is an associate professor and senior lecturer in the Department of Economic History, Uppsala University. His research has dealt with, among other things, public diplomacy, advertising history, and business history. His recent publications include 'Marketing Internationalism in an Era of Globalisation – The Swedish-South African Partnership Week, November 1999' in *Culture Unbound* (2021), and, with Andreas Mørkved Hellenes, 'A "Swedish Offensive" at the World's Fairs: Advertising, Social Reformism and the Roots of Swedish Cultural Diplomacy, 1935–1939' in *Contemporary European History* (2020).

David M. Higgins is a professor in the accounting and finance division at Newcastle University, UK. He has published numerous articles on the evolution of trade mark and merchandize mark protection from the nineteenth century, and he is the author of *Brands, Geographical Origin, and the Global Economy* (Cambridge University Press, 2018).

National Brands and Global Markets

An Historical Perspective

Edited by
Nikolas Glover and
David M. Higgins

Routledge
Taylor & Francis Group
LONDON AND NEW YORK

First published 2023
by Routledge
4 Park Square, Milton Park, Abingdon, Oxon OX14 4RN

and by Routledge
605 Third Avenue, New York, NY 10158

Routledge is an imprint of the Taylor & Francis Group, an informa business

British Library Cataloguing-in-Publication Data
A catalogue record for this book is available from the British Library

ISBN: 978-0-367-75497-6 (hbk)
ISBN: 978-0-367-76268-1 (pbk)
ISBN: 978-1-003-16618-4 (ebk)

DOI: 10.4324/9781003166184

Typeset in Bembo
by codeMantra

Contents

Figures

Tables

Contributors

Robin J.C. Adams is a Leverhulme Early Career Fellow at Queen's University Belfast. His doctoral research, completed at Oxford in 2019, was awarded the Economic History Society's Thirsk-Feinstein prize for the best dissertation in economic or social history and the Economic History Association's Alexander Gerschenkron prize for the best dissertation with a focus outside North America.

Felicity Barnes is a senior lecturer in History at the University of Auckland. A cultural historian, she has a particular interest in settler colonialism and imperialism. Her first book, *New Zealand's London: A Colony and Its Metropolis*, was based on her award-winning doctoral thesis and examined the impact of cultural links between New Zealand and London from the late nineteenth century till the 1980s. She also won the New Zealand History Association's Mary Boyd prize for the best article on New Zealand history for her work on colonialism and photography. Her second book, *Selling Britishness*, published by McGill-Queen's University Press in 2022, explores the connections between commodity marketing, colonialism, and the construction of whiteness in the former Dominions during the twentieth century.

Carlo Marco Belfanti is professor of economic history at the Department of Economics and Management, University of Brescia (Italy), where he also served as Dean and Chair. He is a member of the Faculty Board of the PhD Course 'Business and Law' at the University of Brescia. His main publications include articles in *Business History, Journal of Social History, Journal of Global History, Journal of Modern Italian Studies, Journal of Consumer Culture, Historical Research in Marketing, Investigaciones de Historia Economica*, and *Journal of Institutional Economics*.

Daniele Dalli is professor of marketing at the University of Pisa. His research area is consumer behaviour and his main research topics are consumer-brand relationships, consumption communities, consumer co-creation, and electronic word-of-mouth. He has published in many journals, including *Journal of Business Research, Marketing Theory, International Journal of Research* *in Marketing*, *Annals of Tourism Research*, and *Organization Studies*. He is the co-author of a textbook on consumer behaviour for undergraduate and master courses.

Pierre-Yves Donzé is a professor of business history at Osaka University (Japan) and a visiting professor at the University of Fribourg (Switzerland) and EM Normandie Business School (France). His research focuses on the global business history of creative industries (watches, fashion, and luxury), multinational enterprises, and medtech business. Website: https://sites.google.com/view/donze/home.

Oliver Kühschelm, Mag. Dr. PD, is an economic and social historian, and director of the Institute of Rural History (IRH) in St. Pölten, Lower Austria. He teaches history at the University of Vienna and Salzburg. His research interests include middle classes, migration and mobility, business history, consumption, advertising and propaganda, nation branding, and economic nationalism. His recent monograph is *Einkaufen als nationale Verpflichtung: Zur Genealogie nationaler Ökonomien in Österreich und der Schweiz, 1920–1980 [Shopping as a National Duty. On the Genealogy of National Economies. Austria and Switzerland, 1920–1980]*. Berlin: De Gruyter, 2022.

Nikolas Glover is an associate professor and senior lecturer in the Department of Economic History, Uppsala University. His research has dealt with, among other things, public diplomacy, advertising history, and business history. His recent publications include 'Marketing Internationalism in an Era of Globalisation – The Swedish-South African Partnership Week, November 1999' in *Culture Unbound* (2021), and, with Andreas Mørkved Hellenes, 'A "Swedish Offensive" at the World's Fairs: Advertising, Social Reformism and the Roots of Swedish Cultural Diplomacy, 1935–1939', *Contemporary European History* (2020).

David M. Higgins is a professor in the accounting and finance division at Newcastle University, UK. He has published numerous articles on the evolution of trade mark and merchandise mark protection from the nineteenth century, and he is the author of *Brands, Geographical Origin, and the Global Economy* (Cambridge University Press, 2018).

Jim McAloon is a professor of history at the Victoria University of Wellington. His research and teaching range widely across themes in the economic and political history of New Zealand (and elsewhere). With reference to New Zealand's natural resource-based economy, he has contributed to collective projects on that country's environmental history, and on the transformation of New Zealand's grasslands, as well as the recently published work on the export of kiwifruit and mussels. He has also had a long-standing interest in farming history, extending back to doctoral research on wealthy settlers in New Zealand's South Island. He is a past president of the New Zealand Historical Association and is currently secretary of the Economic History Society of Australia and New Zealand.

Audrey Millet is an MSCA postdoctoral fellow in history at the University of Oslo. She is a specialist in the ecosystem of fashion. She has recently published *Le livre noir de la mode. Creation, production, manipulation* (Les Pérégrines, 2021). Her current project is a comparison of sweatshops in Paris in the nineteenth century, in Shanghai and Prato around 2000 (European Union's Horizon 2020 MSCA Grant Agreement No. 101024003).

José Antonio Miranda is professor of economic history and a member of the Inter university Institute of Geography at the University of Alicante (Spain). He has been a visiting professor at the University of Padua and the University of Bari 'Aldo Moro' (Italy). He specializes in the industrial and business history of Southern Europe. His main lines of research are focused on the business of fashion, industrial districts, and business strategies. He has published widely on these subjects.

Véronique Pouillard is professor of modern international history at the Institute for Archeology, Conservation, and History (IAKH), University of Oslo. She is currently a Principal Investigator in the research project CREATIVE IPR: The History of Intellectual Property Rights in the Creative Industries (ERC CoG 818523). Her most recent book is *Paris to New York. The Transatlantic Fashion Industry in the Twentieth Century* (Harvard University Press, 2021).

Alba Roldán is a lecturer of economic history at the University of Alicante (Spain), and she has been a visiting scholar at the University of York, UK. She specializes in the monetary, industrial, and business history of Southern Europe. Her most recent publication is 'A Resilient Industry? Business Strategies in the Footwear Industry of Southern Europe, 1970–2007', with J.A. Miranda (*Enterprise & Society*, 23, 2022).

Simon Ville is senior professor of economics and business history at the University of Wollongong, Australia. He is a Fellow of the Academy of Social Sciences in Australia, and a recent member of the College of Experts at the Australian Research Council. He has published in leading journals including *American Economic Review*, *Economic History Review*, and *Journal of Economic History*. His major monographs include *The Big End of Town. Big Business and Corporate Leadership in Twentieth-Century Australia with Grant Fleming and David Merrett* (CUP 2004), and he jointly edited the *Cambridge Economic History of Australia*. He will be the Whitlam-Fraser Professor of Australian Studies at Harvard University in 2022–2023.

Acknowledgements

We are indebted to Andy Humphries, our commissioning editor. Particular thanks are due to Åke Wibergs Stiftelse and the Department of Economic History, Uppsala University, for funding and hosting the conference 'National Brands – International Markets A Symposium' held at Uppsala between 25 and 26 April 2019, at which many of the authors presented preliminary versions of their chapters.

Nikolas Glover gratefully acknowledges financial support from the Jan Wallander och Tom Hedelius stiftelse, project 2016–0044:1. Similarly, Véronique Pouillard and Audrey Millet appreciate funding from the European Research Council (ERC) under the European Union's Horizon 2020 research and innovation programme: Creative IPR: The History of Intellectual Property Rights in the Creative Industries, ERC CoG Grant Agreement No. 818523, and MISS: Made In SweatShops, Marie Skłodowska-Curie Grant Agreement No. 101024003.

Without the help of archivists and librarians, and government officials, many of the chapters in this volume could not have been written. It is appropriate, therefore, to record our thanks to Catherine Dale and colleagues, Law Library, Newcastle University, UK; Michael Funke; Amber Howe, Federal Trades Commission; Sveriges Allmänna Utrikeshandelsförening; and Richard Ward, House of Lords.

We are also grateful to those individuals and organisations who granted copyright permission, approved publication, and upgraded the technical specification of images to the required production standard. In this respect, we are pleased to record our thanks to: Lisa Crowe, Australian Made; Dublin City Library and Archive; Tracy Fairhall, Australian Chamber of Commerce and Industry; Irish Newspaper Archive; Steve Kershaw, York Digital Image; Pamela Lovis, Alexander Turnbull Library, New Zealand; Mijo Nikolic, Vienna Chamber of Commerce; and John Pearce, Made in Britain.

Finally, we wish to record our thanks to scholars who have commented on some of the chapters and helped in other ways, namely: Camilla Barbarossa, Dev Gangjee, Doug Irwin, Giada Mainolfi, George Tuttle III, and Geoff Tweedale.

Acknowledgements

1 Conceptualizing 'Made in' as a historical phenomenon[1]

Nikolas Glover and David M. Higgins

Introduction

In its simplest form, a mark of origin is a sign on a product identifying its geographical origin. Indications of national origin can be purely associative; an image of the Brazilian flag on a pair of flip-flops or an outline of the Taj Mahal on a jar of curry sauce. Such symbols are typically selected and designed by corporate marketing departments and brand agencies, and have historically been used in company logos, product designs, and official state-sponsored campaigns. Visual allusions to geographical origin need not be factually correct: The founders of Häagen Dazs and Frusen Glädjé chose (supposedly) 'Scandinavian' names for their respective ice cream brands, although both companies were founded in the US and had no links whatsoever to Northern Europe.[2] Marks of origin also include written legends such as 'Made in' or 'Country of origin' which, in contrast to the use of national symbols in logotypes, have been the subject of much regulation and legal consideration – even down to the exact choice of words. In the UK, the use of 'make' as opposed to 'Manufactured in', or 'Made in', was considered unsatisfactory in the 1930s because '"make" ... is capable of being misinterpreted as meaning no more than a style or fashion'.[3] The question was also raised whether 'Made in England' indicated something else than simply 'England'. This was the subject of much official wrangling between the Board of Trade and Her Majesty's Customs. Both departments operated on the assumption that the name of a country was a sufficient indication of origin if a UK trade mark, or the name of a UK firm, was used on imports. Thus, according to this interpretation, 'John Smith, Germany' was acceptable. But, where a UK place name appeared on imports, this had to be qualified by the use of a 'definite indication of origin', for example, 'John Smith, Sheffield: Made in Germany'.[4] As this example illustrates, geographical origins are open to interpretation. They are 'made' in several places, including in the minds of consumers and legislators. The present volume takes this fundamental insight as its point of departure.

This book provides a historical and multi-country perspective on 'Made in', focusing on national efforts to promote this legend, as well as its varied

DOI: 10.4324/9781003166184-1

commercial uses, in a number of economies. Although the term *branding* and the professional practice of designing, refining, and developing commercial brands are largely associated with the twentieth and twenty-first centuries, their antecedents have long historical roots. There are examples dating back thousands of years of how sellers used seals and other markings to show the origin of their goods in order to convey information to consumers and government authorities.[5] The primary emphasis in this collection, however, lies on the twentieth century, even if some chapters trace important developments back to the previous century and some follow the trajectory into the new Millennium.

As brands and branding have become ubiquitous in society since the late 1990s, geographers have begun to focus on the 'inescapable geography of brands'.[6] They have highlighted the ways in which places, nations, and products have tended to blur into each other through the increasing deployment of brands and branding.[7] The concrete processes and practices through which brands have actively been associated with geographic locations are what Andy Pike usefully conceptualizes as 'origination'. Such processes, Pike argues, should be studied by focusing on the 'varied actors involved in brands and branding' – the producers, circulators, consumers, and regulators – because 'This approach enables the identification of the actors involved and assessment of their roles, positions and claims within the broader spatial circuit within which they are related and animated'.[8]

Although Pike's expressed aim of focusing on processes of origination is to 'go beyond country of origin', we would argue that there still remains much historical work to be done on this phenomenon. Rather than focusing on the construction of meaning and value of brands *per se*, we argue that Pike's identification of the relevant actors – producers, circulators, consumers, and regulators – points to how the historicization of country-of-origin as international phenomena can be used as an entry point for studying twentieth-century economic history in a new light. Identifying these actors draws our attention to different intersections between state interests, (claims to) national identity, and commercial strategies *over time* and in *different national contexts*. An illustrative historical example of the interplay between consumers, circulators, and regulators can be found in Karl Gerth's *China Made*. Gerth argued that one consequence of Japanese aggression during the 1930s was that Chinese authorities sought to foster a general desire to buy more Chinese products and began harassing merchants selling Japanese wares.[9] Believing this was an attempt to obtain bribes, merchants simply offered officials bribe money and continued to sell Japanese products as Chinese products. Subsequently, Gerth argues, merchants *and* consumers participated in a facade of nationalistic consumption by referring to the disguised products as Chinese. The market became overstocked, prices collapsed, and merchants became bankrupt.[10] According to Gerth, the solution was the dissemination of a vocabulary in which 'national product' and 'foreign product' were clearly understood, which would help teach 'nationality' to Chinese consumers.[11]

The authors participating in the present volume have been involved in a growing field of research that, from different perspectives, has examined historical examples of 'origination', with a focus on individual firms, government bodies, and/or marketing specialists. A fundamental contribution of this volume is to show how individual commercial brands seeking to make use of a country-of-origin effect have evolved in an environment characterized by international regulations, political interventions, and societies ultimately dominated by a nation-centred worldview. In many cases, the contributions also suggest that such brands and the way they have been promoted and consumed have in turn contributed to the reshaping of that legal, political, and cultural environment.

Before we proceed, some of the limitations of this volume should be noted. First, each country-specific chapter covers a specific time period, during which a country was either developed in the sense that it possessed a mature economy with a technologically advanced infrastructure, such as the UK or the US, or a country was in the process of becoming developed, such as Australia, Ireland, and New Zealand. Most of the countries discussed in this volume were either sovereign states or became sovereign during the period under consideration.[12] To what extent these national examples can be generalized to other countries is an open question and one that deserves further research. Second, we have chosen to limit the scope of the volume by focusing on national indicators of origin, with a particular, but not exclusive focus on manufacturing. Consequently, regional and supranational indicators of geographical origin and the service sector remain to be treated in greater depth.

Introducing our framework

Our case studies advance the argument that the history of 'Made in' illuminates the dynamic relationships between the actors that have promoted this indication, the institutions that have regulated it, and the cultural environment that has attributed it meaning. We begin by sketching out a framework of how research on individual countries can be placed into a broader historical context.

Historically, 'Made in' had multiple functions and associations as they circulated and crossed national borders on the packaging of goods, in the pamphlets of official trade delegations, in the hype of mass media reporting, and through the subjective experiences of travelling consumers. This indication has been ascribed significance not only in markets but also in the realm of politics and society at large. For instance, in Greece, the commercial slogan 'Buy Greek' was injected with renewed political urgency and patriotic duty during the years of austerity after 2008.[13] 'Made in' has, at times, been a basic, descriptive trade mark, while, in other periods, it has been a key component of carefully developed commercial strategy. Consider Swiss Made as an example: with the growing importance of electronic technology rather than craftsmanship in the watch industry, in the twenty-first century, 'Made in' is no longer intended to indicate in which country Swatch watches are made, but rather it serves to regulate competition in a luxury segment dominated by global value chains.[14] In other instances, 'Made in' has been used in attempts to forge and redefine national identities. The decade after 1945, for instance, witnessed a 'trade mark war' of litigation between the East and West German branches of the Zeiss optical firm, as both sides claimed the technical prowess, workmanship, and national identity associated with Made in Germany.[15]

One way of refining these intersections between national politics, (inter) national regulation, and the constantly shifting flows of production, trade, and consumption is to begin with the framework illustrated in Figure 1.1. This figure illustrates that 'Made in' has been developed, deployed, and studied in three different contexts, each of which has been dominated by slightly different actors, interests and, with some exaggeration, different disciplines.

Marketing and advertising: branding origins

Originally, 'Made in' was studied from a marketing perspective, with a particular focus on how it was utilized by individual firms to increase sales and develop brands. The historical trajectory of this *commercial logic* is entwined with academic analysis of 'country-of-origin effect' (and later concepts) beginning in the mid-1960s.[16] This research grew into a rapidly expanding field of scholarship conducted primarily by business and marketing scholars as they sought to produce instrumental knowledge.[17] From the perspective of individual firms, the emphasis on 'Made in' has historically been optional and purely strategic: a device to use foreign consumers' perceptions of a certain country or its national character. The evolution of professional consultants

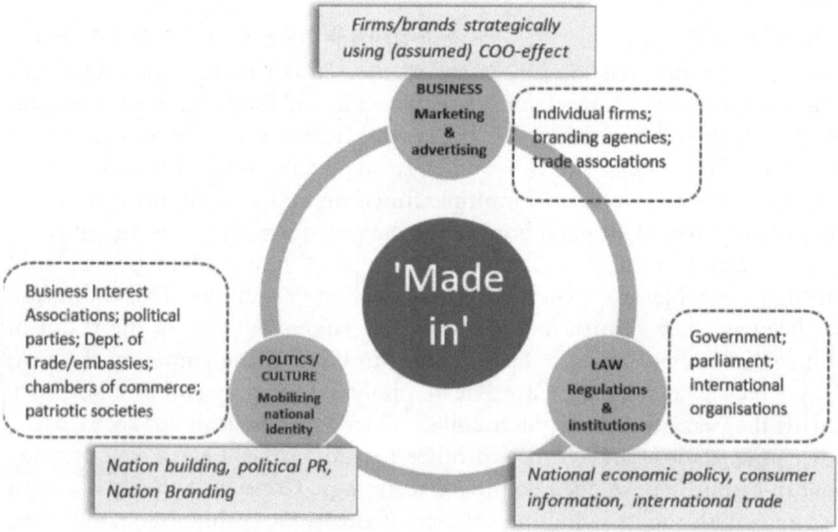

Figure 1.1 Conceptualizing 'Made in': main actors/contexts, dominant rationales

used in market research and branding strategies has shaped the why, where, and when firms have chosen to use 'Made in'.

In the last decades, a growing subfield of business history, and cultural history, has emerged which has focused on how firms sought to use national indicia in their advertising and branding strategies. For example, a body of literature documents how products and brands were promoted during times of war. In the Second World War, commercial advertisements explicitly sought to strengthen the domestic association between the consumption of specific products and the duty of consumers to be patriotic citizens.[18] Other studies have demonstrated how attempts to benefit from country-of-origin effects preceded the advent of the concept itself. Consider branding campaigns during the 1950s and 1960s, which emphasised the 'Americanness' of Jack Daniels' Whiskey, or the 'Canadianness' of Labatt lager, and the extent to which Star beer and Henkes gin were promoted as 'Nigerian' and 'Ghanian' beverages, respectively.[19] Conversely, there are examples of how companies have strategically sought to obscure or downplay geographic origin in their branding, with Spanish fashion brands Zara and Massimo Dutti, and the Catalan car manufacturer SEAT providing cases in point.[20] It has been argued that for high-tech industries with extensive international markets, company brands have been more important for marketing purposes than country of origin.[21] However, de-coupling a brand from its national origin is not always possible. 'Huawei' literally means 'China striving', and with the onset of the trade war between the US and China in 2018, this translation inevitably complicated matters for a firm whose founder was keen to downplay all geographical connotations: 'Huawei product is just a commercial product, use it if you like it, not if you don't, but do not politicise it'.[22]

From a branding perspective, studies of 'Made in' have provided an entry point for examining in what ways businesses are 'both embedded in and simultaneously creators of national identity and culture'.[23] 'Made in' has not only drawn on national myths of 'who we are', but it has also given customers the chance to experience, and participate, in the construction of those myths.[24]

Regulations and institutions: determining economic nationality

Looking beyond the firm, 'Made in' has also been used and regulated as a tool of *national economic policy*. Simply put, this legend has had two primary purposes: either to protect the domestic market from foreign products or to promote national products abroad. Consequently, 'Made in' can be viewed as the legal expression of government commitment to international trade conventions and, in a broader sense, expressions of a nationalistic, nation-state-centric, logic of economic policy. Developments within international law and shifting priorities in economic doctrine at the national level have determined the possible, preferable, and/or stipulated uses of 'Made in' in international trade.[25]

Historically, the main purpose of rules of origin has been to determine the *economic* nationality (or country of origin) of products; that is, where they have been produced or manufactured, as opposed to where they have been exported from. 'Made in' regulations have often been applied to imports to minimize consumer deception.[26] For example, when inscriptions affixed to products used a different language from the products' country of origin, the indication 'Made in Denmark' was necessary for Danish products imported to Australia and New Zealand.[27] In other circumstances, it was sufficient only to indicate the country of origin to comply with import protocols. Such regulations were generally applied in Argentina and the US, from 1923 and 1891, respectively.[28] For Australia, Canada, France, New Zealand, Spain, and the UK, imported products bearing the trade mark of a domestic manufacturer, or a place name similar to, or identical with, a place in the importing country, had to indicate their country of origin.[29]

For business historians, court cases offer insight into how 'Made in' has been historically regulated. An early reported case involved Jaeger Ltd, between 1896 and 1897. Jaeger manufactured woollen hosiery and underclothes, and it sourced its fabric from UK companies and the Berlin firm, Messrs. Benger Sohne. The company registered a trade mark with the UK Trade Mark Office in 1886. This mark showed an image of Dr. Jaeger with the surrounding text, 'Dr Jaeger's Sanitary Woollen System Co Lim'd, Sole Concessionaries' and 'Pure Warranted Wool'. One issue that was deliberated during court litigation was whether the company was permitted to apply its trade mark to products assembled from English and German textiles without any qualifying indication, such as 'Made in Germany', and whether such a practice would deceive the public. Ultimately, the Magistrate dismissed the prosecution's case, and Jaeger continued to apply its trade mark, without qualification, to its manufactures, even those sourced from Germany.[30]

In a completely open world economy, rules of origin are unnecessary because the countries from which articles originate are immaterial. Even in a partially free world economy, the significance of rules of origin is limited – provided they are applied on a non-discriminatory basis.[31] However, the growth of free-trade areas, such as the European Union, and the North American Free Trade Agreement, together with a multiplicity of bilateral trade agreements, has meant that rules of origin are imperative to ensure that imported products are properly accorded preferential or non-preferential treatment. Preferential treatment means that imports from a given country are either subject to zero tariffs or favourable, (preferential) tariffs; conversely, a non-preferential policy means that imports incur much higher duties.

The legal complexity surrounding rules of origin has necessitated intervention by the courts. The European Court of Justice (hereafter, ECJ), for instance, has had to determine whether untreated casein, imported from the Soviet Union and Poland, but cleaned, ground, and packaged in Germany, acquired EU origin. Similar considerations applied when the ECJ was asked to rule on unbleached cotton yarn imported from Egypt and the US but subject to a variety of processing treatments within the EU.[32] Court decisions involving gold chains from New Zealand, and alkaline batteries from Singapore were pivotal in the formation of Australian rules of origin.[33] In many of the above cases, and in others, determination of rules of origin was motivated by protocols governing anti-dumping.

Clearly, different actors have dissimilar perceptions of country of origin. Customs authorities are interested in economic nationality, whereas the exporting nation may be using 'Made in' to signal a much broader range of characteristics, for example, reliability, precision, and innovation (German motor cars and Japanese electronics); design and style (Italian and French textiles and luxury products), or tradition and heritage (British textiles and footwear). Viewed from this perspective, the legal regulation of 'Made in' is a complex area encompassing tangible factors that include both manufacturing processes (raw materials, and methods of assembly) and emotional cues (culture, geography, and heritage).

The politics of national identities: mobilizing the nation

Between the practices of individual firms and the outcome of politico-legal regulation, there is a strategic level where 'Made in' has been used for public relations and collective national identity construction initiated by constellations of individual actors, organizations, and social networks.[34] In the context of official and semi-official commercial and diplomacy drives, and comprehensive nation branding policies, a vital component was often the promotion of products, services, and firms under a common indication of 'Made in.'[35] This political dimension has been dealt with by historians of culture, nation-building, and international relations, since what a particular indication of 'Made in' signifies, and how individual firms can profit from it, has been open to negotiation between the historical actors using it. For instance, the spectacular World's Fairs during the second half of the nineteenth century consisted to a large extent of showcasing the products of the participating countries' industries. The fairs thus had the dual function of displaying goods as well as transmitting ideas about national identities.[36] At mega-events like these, associations were strategically strengthened between the brands and products on display and their national origin for both commercial and political reasons.[37] Building the pavilions and participating in the fairs required considerable resources which could originate from private donations, exhibitors' fees, or government support. Consequently, the precise way in which products were associated with their national origin was often a matter of negotiation between the executive committee responsible for the pavilion and its funders. Consider the Swedish pavilions during the interwar period. In the 1930s, the focus of the national pavilions was becoming more overtly political – a consequence of increased protectionism and looming competition between totalitarian states. The Swedish pavilion mirrored this shift from commerce to politics, and government funding became a more important source of funds than private donations. As a result, the products of participating Swedish firms were displayed in a setting that added new social and democratic values to the legend Made in Sweden, a dimension that had been completely absent only a few years earlier.[38]

Another development was the establishment in the late nineteenth and early twentieth centuries of private business associations dedicated to the promotion of patriotic consumption, and trade associations and chambers of commerce seeking to increase foreign trade and national exports. Motivated by patriotic concerns, these organizations were frequently involved in the promotion of 'Made in', investing them with commercial value and stirring debates about their necessity for the national economy. Such advocacy at once legitimized the organization's national credentials and provided a concrete means to mobilize members and attract government support.[39] For example, in 1904, the Victorian Chamber of Manufactures and Australian Natives Association initiated a Made in Australia movement, and in 1908, the South African Manufacturers Association launched a national buying campaign. During the 1930s, 'Buy Indian' campaigns sought to achieve the economic objectives of import substitution and economic self-sufficiency as a means to political independence.[40] In several countries, patriotic campaigns were launched in the protectionist interwar years by trade associations on the premise of economic nationalism.[41] Most of them went under slogans corresponding to that of the Buy American movement of 1933 in the US: 'American dollars for American-made goods'.[42]

During the first half of the twentieth century, foreign services and embassies became more commercialized. Prompted by intensified international competition and increased protectionism in world markets, this official reorientation tended to complement existing private initiatives. Civil servants were becoming more involved in conveying commercial information, organizing exhibitions, mediating contacts, and providing legal assistance to firms and merchants.[43] As more government resources became channelled towards official export promotion in the twentieth century, the field became a complicated mosaic of private, semi-private, and public actors, some of which had offices and representatives both at home and in overseas markets. Constantly battling with issues of how to most efficiently channel resources and coordinate a range of commercial interests, the field of export promotion constituted a fertile ground for defining, using, and reinventing 'Made in'. From the perspective of contemporary practices, this twentieth-century institutional development has been traced as 'the pre-history of nation-branding'.[44]

Thus, for government authorities, semi-official organizations, trade associations, and individual companies, uniting under a common 'Made in' logo at specific points in time and in specific markets could serve various purposes: gaining political legitimacy, attracting government support and influencing political debates. At this level of analysis, the focus is on the actors defining, adopting, and collectively promoting a particular form of 'Made in', and how these actions spanned both domestic and foreign markets and politics.

The effects of globalization: from 'Made in' to 'Made by'

Over the last two decades, the value of particular country-of-origin effects has gained attention as part of broader research into nation and place-branding programmes.[45] Contemporaneously, sociologists and human geographers have critically examined and questioned the relevance of country-of-origin in an era of globalization.[46] According to Andrew Pike:

> national identifiers such as country of origin have … been played down, reworked or even eradicated in specific cases … actors have tried to obscure historical associations or dissociate brands from specific national territories … apart from a few exceptions where specific sectors are strongly geographically associated, the real national brand is in decline.[47]

Thus, a glance towards the future of 'Made in' suggests a paradox: investments in national branding appear to increase the brand value of 'Made in', but the complex flows of global production and consumption render this logo increasingly irrelevant. Between 1995 and 2005, intermediate inputs accounted for 56 and 73% of total trade flows in goods and services, respectively.[48] In 2010, Pascal Lammy, former director of the World Trade Organisation, stated:

> … the concept of country of origin for manufactured goods has gradually become obsolete as the various operations, from the design of the product to the manufacture of the components, assembly and marketing have spread across the world, creating international production chains. Nowadays, more and more products are 'Made in the World' rather than 'Made in the UK' or 'Made in France'.[49]

Currently, when a final product is composed of multiple parts which have a different *geographic* origin, substantial transformation is used to determine economic nationality. Three criteria are used to determine substantial transformation.[50] First, when the manufacturing of a product in a particular country results in a change of tariff classification. For example, the tariff code for car parts is 8708. If the various components under this code are manufactured into a finished motor car, the finished product has a different tariff classification, which is 8703. Alternatively, an *ad valorem*, or minimum value-added test, can be applied. This test requires that the 'originating' state – the final country in which substantial transformation occurred – contributed a minimum percentage of the value added, typically 50%, to claim origin. Finally, there is the specific processing test: the country in which a particular manufacturing activity occurs qualifies it as the country of origin.

One consequence of these legal requirements is that 'Made in' is being replaced by 'Made by'. An exemplar of the need to demarcate between these terms is provided by Hong Kong. A study by Suzanne Berger and Richard

Lester noted that 'The scale of Hong Kong's manufacturing activity has greatly expanded, even as production within Hong Kong itself has shrunk. "Made *by* Hong Kong" has grown, even as "Made *in* Hong Kong" has declined'.[51] For Berger and Lester, 'Made by Hong Kong' refers 'to the products manufactured by Hong-Kong owned and/or managed enterprises wherever they are located'.[52] In this context, 'Made by Hong Kong' substitutes global chains of networked production for the geographical boundaries of the island. From a different perspective, studies which recognized the decline of the US manufacturing base sought to determine what needed to be done to secure and enhance this sector in the future so that 'Making in America' continued to be a valid description many years hence.[53]

The contributions to this volume

National Brands and Global Markets: An Historical Perspective is organized hence. There follows a chapter providing an overview and critique of developments in the 'Made in', or country-of-origin literature, which also refers to many of the case studies in this volume. The remaining chapters are a series of case studies which explore the evolution of 'Made in' across 11 countries. Seven of these chapters are based on European countries, while the remainder focus on Australia, Japan, New Zealand, and the US. Historical studies of 'Made in' lead to intersections between individual market actors, international regulations, and national political projects. 'Made in' can be approached as a legal construct, a political claim, or a promotional appeal, but each individual case must be unpacked and traced over time to see how these various dimensions have operated, reinforced each other, or come into conflict. In certain cases, the legal construct can be politically detrimental and commercially unattractive. In others, the promotional appeal can be politically problematic (Figure 1.2).

Daniele Dalli discusses the evolution of research on the country of origin (hereafter, COO) and its effects. This concept was originally developed by marketing scholars, and although it remains an active field of enquiry within the discipline of marketing, it has also been researched by scholars in other disciplines, especially international business. Dalli explains how accelerating globalization necessitated a re-assessment of COO as a concept. The rapid growth of global supply chains meant that reliance on a 'single cue' – country of origin – was misplaced. To address this issue, scholars had to deconstruct COO into multiple components, such as country of design and country of assembly, both of which indicate origin. Simultaneously, the growth of global brands further de-coupled the link between a product and its place, and necessitated further refinements, such as brand origin. The fundamental aim of COO research is to accurately determine, and quantify, the effect of various origin clues on consumer perceptions of a product. However, the precise effects of each origin clue are moderated by a diverse range of other factors, including ethnocentrism, and the sources (television, family, and personal contacts) from which consumers obtain information about the characteristics

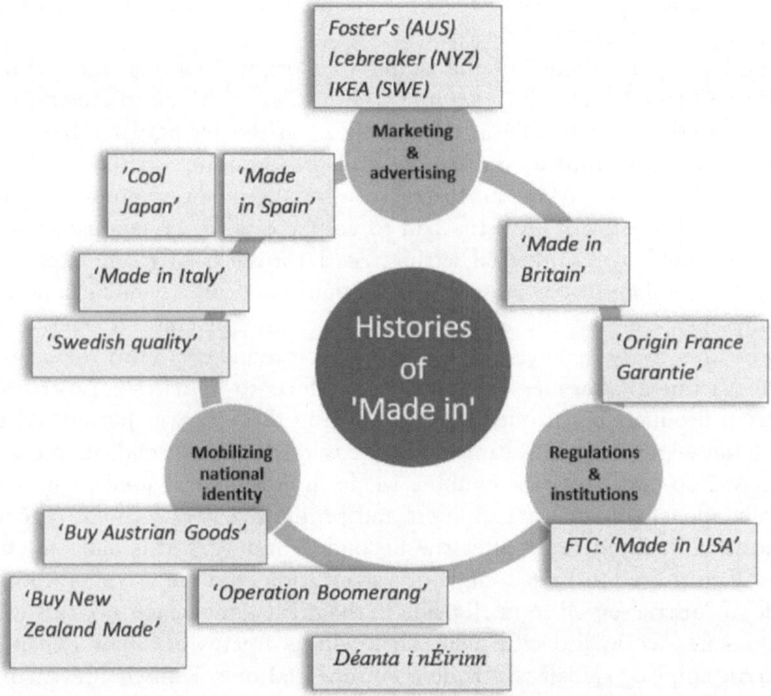

Figure 1.2 Labels and brands mapped out within the conceptual framework

(history, politics, geography, and culture) of other countries. After taking stock of these competing forces, Dalli concludes his chapter by offering a tentative model of how COO effects determine different actions by the key stakeholders in COO – businesses, consumers, and governments.

Robin Adams explores the Made in Ireland trade mark, *Déanta i nÉirinn*, which was created in 1907, adopted and promoted by the Irish Industrial Development Association (hereafter, IIDA), before its acquisition by the Irish Free State. A central theme of this chapter is how this trade mark, which denoted Irish origin, was used by Irish nationalists to determine the national identity of Ireland. This perspective is important because it indicates that, at least for 'small' nations, country-of-origin marking was indispensable for citizens' attachment to, and identification with, their country. In addition to promoting a sense of national identity, the *Déanta i nÉirinn* trade mark was also used to promote the export of Irish products, especially to the US in which resided a large Irish population. Unsurprisingly, the IIDA was alert and litigious when its trade mark was infringed, but it also adopted a robust stance when other indicia which might indicate Irish origin, for example, the Gaelic alphabet, or images of a Shamrock were used on non-Irish products.

Adams also reveals tensions between companies with renowned trade marks and their support of the *Déanta i nÉirinn* trade mark, a dichotomy which did not always follow political allegiances.

Developing the theme of the country-of-origin marking and national identity, Oliver Kühschelm examines the history of Made in Austria over the twentieth century. The analysis focuses on the triangular relationship between the government, the nation, and the economy. In the era of the Habsburg Monarchy, Made in Austria was initially used only in export markets, since domestically 'Austria' had to compete with the complex identities constituted by its imperial setting. As the English-language expression began to circulate in the press and was popularised in the public sphere, it became apparent that the legend had gained enough cultural traction for it to be effectively deployed also in domestic campaigns. With the support of the Viennese Chamber of Commerce, efforts to demarcate Austria and Austrian products began yielding fruit during the interwar period. As the social and economic elites came to terms with this new 'small state era' of the post-imperial Austrian republic, Made in Austria was used to simultaneously appeal to foreign customers and promote a new form of Austrian patriotism. In the decades after the Second World War, this dual function was still cultivated further: a range of organizations and initiatives promoting Made in Austria served to instil pride in the great achievements of this small nation-state, while also effectively channelling dreams of a new expansive Austrian empire – albeit this time a commercial one. Kühschelm's analysis thus provides a case study of how a 'Made in' legend may circulate in society and take on different connotations over time: in this case, it travelled from the sphere of imperial exports, via the cultural pages and debates of the domestic press, and into the coordinated nation-building (and branding) projects of a corporatist nation-state.

As a fellow small state characterized by what Peter Katzenstein termed 'democratic corporatism', Sweden shares a resemblance with Austria. In his chapter, Nikolas Glover highlights the historical processes by which the fluid notion of 'Swedish quality' has served the intertwined purposes of promoting exports abroad and instilling a national competitive culture at home. Glover argues that the meaning attributed to 'Swedish quality' shifted over time, in response to changes in the composition of the country's exports, international markets, and perceptions of 'Swedishness'. The long line of short-lived initiatives by individual firms, trade associations, government bodies, and marketing agencies to rally around 'Made in Sweden' and revive the value of the key concept 'Swedish quality', Glover argues, should not primarily be assessed in terms of their effect on Swedish exports, but rather as expressions of an extended, albeit disrupted, pedagogical project integral to maintaining an 'open economy'. These initiatives have continuously served to mobilize resources and raise awareness among key groups in Sweden, urging them to remain on the front foot, not to rest on their laurels, and always to aim for greater market shares. In this constant endeavour, different individual firms or brands, or different discourses about Swedish national character, have been brought into play over time.

Turning our attention to foreign buyers and customers, the relation between national myth and the international gaze is highlighted in Carlo Belfanti's analysis of Made in Italy. This chapter reveals the pronounced historical shift in the way this brand was constructed to appeal to foreign audiences. Originally, the mark was used simply to denote the origin of Italian exports. However, in the late nineteenth century, Italian entrepreneurs began to craft an image of Italy, and Italian products, that conveyed the Renaissance. This narrative had particular appeal to consumers in the US. Indeed, after 1945, leading fashion magazines such as *Vogue* reinforced the message that Made in Italy defined a set of characteristics – taste, refinement, sophistication – which were inherited from the Renaissance. In Belfanti's analysis, what mattered to the success of Made in Italy was not the ethnocentrism of Italian citizens, but US consumers' appreciation of Italy's cultural legacy. This 'myth of continuity', first invented to promote Italian fashion exports, would later be applied to other sectors too, such as interior design and furniture. The chapter also provides an important insight into the formative historical impact that individual actors and brands can have on the meaning and values attached to national 'Made in' labels.

The discussion of Made in France and Made in Paris, by Véronique Pouillard and Audrey Millet, assesses the strength of these marques in relation to luxury products, especially haute couture. Pouillard and Millet show that French entrepreneurs were more ambivalent about the US market than their Italian competitors. Thus, during the interwar period, such entrepreneurs appreciated that Made in Paris was admired as a brand in the US because it signalled creativity, taste, and virtuosity, but they were outraged that US manufacturers imported French textile designs and reproduced them on a substantial scale – a practice which threatened to undermine the cache associated with Made in France. In the post-1945 period, and particularly from the 1970s, manufacturers of luxury products sought to re-establish a stronger relationship between Made in France and French products, by defining the minimum proportions of value added, or labour costs that qualified a product to be labelled Made in France. This chapter provides an illuminating example of a 'Made in' label whose value has been curated and policed through a collaboration between government institutions and business organizations.

The issue of how to legally determine the national origin of a product constitutes the focus of David Higgins' chapter on Made in the USA. Higgins shows that the United States Customs and Border Protection (hereafter, USCBP) has permitted the import of products without an indication of origin, provided such products are 'substantially transformed' in the US. Marking imports with their country of origin was a 'soft' measure of protection predicated on the belief that US consumers preferred domestic manufactured products. However, when sold on the US market, substantially transformed products are assumed to be American. Higgins argues that this perception obscures the historic policy adopted by the Federal Trades Commission (hereafter, FTC), which only recognizes lawful claims to 'Made in the USA' when applied to products which are 'all or virtually all' made in the USA. Furthermore, the FTC's policy of allowing qualified 'Made in the US' claims, such as 'Assembled in the US', ensures that imported products which have been substantially transformed in the US are also entitled to make qualified 'Made in the USA' claims. Viewed from this perspective, it appears that there is scope for more regulatory alignment between USCBP and the FTC on 'Made in the US'.

José Miranda and Alba Roldán discuss the major dichotomy that continues to exist between Spain's leading clothing brands – *Pull & Bear, Massimo Dutti*, and *Zara* – and Made in Spain. As these authors note, from a global perspective, Spain is not renowned for manufacturing; instead, the popular image of Spain is based on its holiday resorts, nightlife, and tourism. Yet, its leading clothing brands have a global presence. This case study raises pertinent questions about the relationship between country of origin and company brands. Moreover, in marked contrast to the leading French and Italian fashion houses, Spanish clothing companies are focused on the low-medium price and quality segments of the market. Their competitiveness in this sector is based on 'fast fashion': replicating recent catwalk trends and high-fashion designs, mass-producing them at low cost, and bringing them to retail stores rapidly when demand is highest. Somewhat paradoxically, despite playing an active role in the government's export promotion campaigns on behalf of the Spanish economy, the leading Spanish fashion brands have themselves succeeded by downplaying or eschewing their Spanish credentials. A key finding of this chapter is that 'Made in' can simultaneously be ascribed with varying degrees of importance by the same firm: Made in Spain appears to have had little commercial value for firms such as Inditex, but from a political perspective the company clearly considered the brand valuable.

Tensions between the country of origin and company brands are also observed in Japan. However, in this case, as Pierre-Yves Donzé explains, this dissonance was not constant. Between the mid- and late-nineteenth century, the European and US bourgeoise had a strong affinity for Japanese decorative arts and products. During this period of *Japonisme*, the strong Japanese cultural identity associated with these products enabled Japanese manufacturers to penetrate foreign markets. Between the late nineteenth century and the 1930s, Japanese industrialization accelerated. Donzé argues that it was precisely for this reason that Made in Japan was attributed negative connotations in foreign markets: the growth of Japanese exports was associated with the government's imperial ambitions. In the immediate decades after 1945, too, Made in Japan was seen as a symbol of low quality. Large corporations such as Sony and Toyota, which were in the vanguard of the Japanese economic miracle, therefore tended to avoid references to their country of origin. In Donzé's analysis, Made in Japan provides an intriguing case in point, since the narratives and qualities associated with this legend have primarily been defined by outsiders. This explains the paradoxical observation that the periods in which Made in Japan has been attributed with positive values have coincided with Japanese industry being considered uncompetitive and non-threatening to foreign observers. Beginning in the 1990s, however, this pattern appears to have become less defined as the notion of 'cool Japan' has been embraced by successful Japanese exporters and eager foreign importers alike. This case study underlines the importance of historicizing the value ascribed to individual 'Made in' logos.

From a different perspective, the chapter on New Zealand by Felicity Barnes and Jim McAloon also highlights differences between domestic and foreign contexts. Their analysis follows two parallel trajectories of Made in New Zealand from the nineteenth to the twenty-first centuries: as a means to promote exports and as an instrument to increase domestic consumption of New Zealand products. For exports, the focus during the first half of the twentieth century was on promoting quality agricultural produce such as meat, wool, and dairy. For much of this period, such efforts were an intra-imperial project which required an appeal to the UK market. In contrast, campaigns and slogans aimed at the home market to 'Buy New Zealand Made' were linked to efforts to industrialize the home economy, and therefore tended to articulate the interests of the manufacturing sector. Towards the end of the twentieth century, the number of products being exported had broadened – wine, seafood, and fruits were becoming increasingly important – and export marketing now had to address geographically dispersed, discerning consumer groups and hone in on various niche markets. What was described as the concerns of the 'climate lobby' and related reputational issues were addressed by projecting a brand image of a remote country in close contact with nature, built on the values of sustainability and age-old Māori culture. However, the contemporaneous campaigns promoting New Zealand manufacturing in the home market do not seem to have used corresponding slogans about the nation's unique values and virtues but instead continued to emphasize consumers' opportunity to 'keep your country working'. Thus, Barnes and MacAloon conclude that the campaigns to sell 'Made in New Zealand' to the domestic market have overall been less long-lived, and their associated brand values far less coherent. Typically instigated in response to a looming economic crisis, they have been preoccupied with how consumers might help manufacturers, rather than with how buying domestic products would help New Zealand consumers.

Simon Ville explains how attempts to define and promote Made in Australia were constrained by its membership of the Commonwealth, the substantial presence of multinational companies, and a heavy reliance on primary produce, especially merino wool. Nonetheless, during the early twentieth century, a series of Made in Australia campaigns were launched to assert Australia's independence – which was accelerated by Britain's accession to the Common Market (subsequently, the European Union) and the decline of the sterling area. These exogenous economic and political events fostered more determined, nation-focused efforts to support local products, such as 'Operation Boomerang' and 'Australian Made'. However, such campaigns pale into insignificance when compared with Australia's long-term focus of becoming a successful exporter of primary products. In this regard, Australia is unusual: Ville argues that indirect indications of Australian origin – especially its close association with the international *Woolmark* – show that indications of national origin do not need to rely on 'Made in'.

In some respects, Made in Britain is the outlier in the case studies discussed in this book. At the national level, efforts to promote Made in Britain were devoid of government support with the exception of the interwar period. Historically, private attempts to promote such a marque were strongly opposed by major British companies which owned globally renowned trade marks. Moreover, since the 1980s, and possibly earlier, it is difficult to discern a close relationship between national identity and national consumption. And yet, in 2014, the organization *Made in Britain* succeeded in registering the trade mark 'Made in Britain'. David Higgins explains that the comparatively late development of 'Made in Britain' was not predicated on promoting the consumption of British products for its own sake. Market surveys conducted by this organization revealed that concerns about the climate were central to respondents and this, in turn, fostered greater efforts to purchase locally. Further, this organization sought to foster closer collaboration between its members – mainly small- and medium-sized enterprises – through the dissemination of commercial and technical information to help members compete in national and global markets. Instead of promoting provenance *per se*, 'Made in Britain' is the centre of a social capital network for its members.

Taken together, the contributions direct our attention towards how 'Made in' has historically been shaped by the interplay between domestic, transnational, and international factors. As the chapters on Italian and French fashion show, exporting firms have needed to respond to how 'their' countries are perceived abroad, but also to how their foreign competitors brand themselves and use their respective national origins. Legislation and national economic doctrine have continuously been shaped by major transnational economic and political shifts, with the (post-)imperial dimension to the histories 'Made in Australia' and 'Made in Austria' providing cases in point. Finally, the strategic collective actions of organizations have variously been aimed at domestic stakeholders (Japanese Export Trade Organization) and foreign consumers (Proyecto Marca España) – and sometimes both (such as the Made in Britain organisation). It is only by historically contextualizing their historical emergence, adaption, and variegated histories in this way that we can begin to fully account for why specific brands have been able to utilize their country of origin successfully, while many others have not.

Articulations of 'Made in' as a firm-level brand, object of legal regulation, and result of political mobilization have been closely related. In the US, the conditions governing Made in the USA have been directly influenced by business lobbying. Trade associations including the Alabama Textile Manufacturers,

American Hand Tool Coalition, American Textile Manufacturing Institute, and the National Knitwear & Sportswear Association, and companies such as Diamond Chain Co, Dynacraft Industries, Steel Technologies, and Summitville Tiles Inc, supported the FTC's long-established policy on Made in the USA.[54] Equally, as in the case of *Déanta i nÈirinn*, the way in which individual firms use geographic origin in their branding has been directly shaped by what the legal framework allows. Finally, as illustrated by the mobilizing capacity of the key national concept of 'Swedish quality', export campaigns on behalf of a country have been shaped by government economic policy as well as the existing marketing practices of successful participating firms.

Our comparative perspective provides further insights. First, the history of launching and marketing national 'Made in' logos was considered important under both relatively protectionist trade regimes (such as Australia and New Zealand) and more liberal ones (Austria and Sweden). In both contexts, they served to legitimize policy: in the former by emphasizing the shared interests between the nation's manufacturers and its citizen-consumers; in the latter by providing public national backing to manufacturers exposed to international competition. This prompts a second general point, brought home by many of the chapters in this book: 'Made in' has survived over time by circulating within and across national boundaries. Irrespective of their initial starting point, as a means to promote patriotic consumption, or as an attempt to secure international competitive advantage, they have been in constant motion and therefore been attributed variegated, and sometimes new meanings over time. For instance, the originally patriotic slogan 'Buy Austrian Goods' in the 1920s was reframed in the postwar era so as to appeal also to foreign consumers, while the narrative of 'Made in Italy', although largely constructed for representatives of the US fashion market, became internalized by Italian manufacturers and the broader public.

Additionally, the globalization of production chains and ownership structures since the 1990s appears to have led to a convergence between 'Made in' logos and corporate brand values pertaining to sustainability, creativity, and social responsibility. To these, a slew of differentiating attributes intended to communicate authenticity have been added: unique Japanese culture, French *terroir*, and defining *the* Italian lifestyle. This mobilization of essentialist nationalism often bears similarities with discourses articulated with respect to 'Made in' during the first globalization (as indicated by the chapters on Sweden and Ireland), even if the objectives have typically differed: attempting to strategically carve out a unique selling point in order to compete in global markets doubtlessly is something else than appealing to 'consumer ethnocentrism' at home. Nevertheless, the historical trajectories of these themes highlight how the history of 'Made in' has invariably involved mobilizing and negotiating national stereotypes for the purpose of monetizing them. In some cases this has been less than successful: Miranda and Roldán's chapter on Spain, and Donzé's contribution on Japan provide examples of how pervasive foreign stereotypes for a long time constituted 'headwind' when commercial actors sought to project alternative national self-representations that aligned with their interests. France, meanwhile, can be seen as an example of continuity, with the projection of national stereotypes becoming integral to domestic public policy. In their chapter, Pouillard and Millet highlight how the history of Made in France is intimately linked to the centralization of the French state which can be traced back to the days of absolute monarchy. New Zealand, on the other hand, provides an example of how the commercial value of certain national stereotypes has shifted significantly over the course of the twentieth century. Barnes and McAloon show how exporters emphasized New Zealand's fundamental 'Britishness' in the first decades of the twentieth century , but subsequently placed Māori heritage centre stage by the start of the new Millenium.

A final observation is that adopting a historical perspective clearly shows that the tensions between 'Made in' and 'Made by' have a history of their own. For permission to use the *Déanta i nÉirinn* trade mark it was decided that at least 50% of the cost of the product had to be represented by Irish labour. For the same reason, saxophones imported to the UK in the 1920s could be marked 'British made'. The interwar stipulations set out by the Chambre Syndicale de la Haute Couture in France chose a different method for determining the nationality of a product. According to its policy, garments had to be completely manufactured in-house by each individual Paris firm for them to be labelled as French haute couture. However, the origin of the textile raw materials was less rigidly regulated. In contrast, Holden automobiles were literally Made in Australia in the postwar decades, but the manufacturer was owned by the US-based multinational General Motors. In other instances, different interpretations of origin prevailed. In the US, a disjuncture developed between the USCBP and the FTC which meant that a product could be deemed to have been Made in the USA by the former (using substantial transformation criteria) but prohibited from using the legend 'Made in the USA', by the latter (because of consumer deception). In other words, the famous twenty-first-century iPhone legend 'Designed by Apple in California. Made in China' has a long history of precursors. This volume reminds us that even before the far-reaching globalisation of value chains, governments, firms, and trade associations found it necessary to determine often seemingly arbitrary thresholds that established a product's national origin.

Notes

1 The authors would like to thank Pierre-Yves Donzé for his helpful comments on this chapter. Nikolas Glover's research was funded by Jan Wallander och Tom Hedelius stiftelse, project 2016–0044:1.
2 http://www.todayifoundout.com/index.php/2013/03/haagen-dazs-and-frusen-gladje-are-both-american-companies/
3 The National Archives (hereafter, TNA). Public Notices (undated), BT 258/1135.
4 The National Archives, (hereafter, TNA). Public Notices (undated), BT 258/1135. Once the views of the departmental solicitors were obtained, it transpired that

the Board of Trade and HM Customs had misinterpreted the relevant legislation and had, in fact, been erroneously applying the relevant legislation for over 50 years. An indication of the name of the country hereafter was deemed sufficient when imports indicated the name of a UK manufacturer, UK trade mark, or UK place name. In the US, similar debates and court cases involving 'made in' evolved from the late nineteenth century. See Higgins' chapter in this volume.

5 See, for example, Viktorin et al., *Nation Branding*, p. 3; Pike, *Origination*, p. 60.
6 Pike, 'Introduction', p. 8.
7 See, for example, Ermann and Hermanik, *Branding the Nation.*
8 Pike, *Origination*, p. 54.
9 Gerth, *China Made.* The history of 'Buy Chinese' appeals dated back to the turn of the century, and had also been directed at products and firms of US and UK origin. Hou, *Foreign Investment*, pp. 150–151.
10 Gerth, *China Made,* p. 2.
11 Gerth, *China Made*, pp. 7, 10, 71, 74.
12 In our view, particularly interesting case studies worthy of further research would be China and Germany.
13 Lekakis, 'Economic nationalism'.
14 Donzé, 'National labels', p. 865.
15 Pence, 'Showcasing', p. 84.
16 See Dalli's chapter in this volume. Also, Dinnie, 'Country-of-origin'.
17 For overviews, see Phau and Prendergast, 'Conceptualizing'; Roth and Diamantopoulos, 'Advancing'.
18 Loxham, 'Profiting'; Clampin, *Advertising and Propaganda*; Broad, *A Small Price*, esp. chap. 4; Culver, 'For the sake'; Swett, 'Advertising'.
19 Holt, 'Jack Daniels'; Bellamy, 'The making'; van den Bersselaar, 'Who belongs'.
20 See for instance Miranda and Roldán's chapter in this volume; Ulldemolins, 'Barcelona'.
21 Donzé, 'National labels', 856.
22 Huawei's founder Ren Zhengfei quoted in Liu, 'Chinese multinational', p. 377.
23 Mordhorst, 'Arla', p. 117.
24 Holt, *How Brands*, p. 8.
25 Higgins, *Brands*, pp. 249–284.
26 Bower and Higgins, 'Litigation and lobbying'; Higgins and Mordhorst, 'Reputation'.
27 League of Nations, *Marks of Origin*, pp. 6, 10.
28 League of Nations, *Marks of Origin*, p. 25; US Tariff, 1890, Chap. 1244, p. 613.
29 League of Nations, *Marks of Origin*, pp. 26, 30–31, 37, 40–41, 47, 52.
30 We are grateful to Dr. Elena Cooper for supplying a transcript of this case. For a fuller discussion of the Jaeger litigation see: Cooper, 'The nineteenth century'.
31 Vermulst, 'Rules of origin', p. 61. For a recent study see, for example, Van den Bossche and Zdouc, *The Law*, pp. 418–463.
32 Waer, 'European community', pp. 109–112, 115–119.
33 Steele and Moulis, 'Country of origin', p. 221.
34 Kühschelm, 'Nationalizing consumption'; Hansen, *Danish Modern*, pp. 18–22.
35 See, for example, Hansen, *Danish Modern*; Tickner, 'Export Britain'; Head, *Made in Germany*. For a comprehensive overview of the international emergence of Nation Branding-programs, see Aronczyk, *Branding.*
36 Smits and Jansen, 'Staging the nation'. It was in fact not until the 1930s that all the national exhibits were completely housed in designated national pavilions.
37 See for instance, Bonell, 'Cheap and nasty', pp. 207–209.
38 Glover and Hellenes, 'A Swedish offensive'.
39 See, for example, Funke, 'Business associations'.

40 Thackeray, *Forging*, pp. 39, 102.
41 Kühschelm, 'Buy national'; Åström Rudberg, 'Selling the concept'; Thackeray, 'Selling the empire'.
42 Frank, *Buy American*, p. 64.
43 Badel, 'Conflicting identities'; Glover, 'Framtidsmarknader'; Kaufman, 'Organizational dimension'; Fisher, Pedaliu, and Smith, *The Foreign Office*.
44 Kühschelm, 'Promoting the nation'.
45 Ermann and Hermanik, *Branding the Nation*; Pike, *Brands and Branding*; Volaic and Andrejevic, *Commercial Nationalism*.
46 Moor, *The Rise*, chap. 6.
47 Pike, *Origination*, pp. 67–68.
48 Miroudot, Lanz, and Ragoussis, *Trade in*, p. 2.
49 https://www.wto.org/english/news_e/sppl_e/sppl174_e.htm. Accessed 9 September 2021.
50 For a further discussion see, Higgins, 'Made in Britain', and Higgins, 'Made in the USA', this volume.
51 Berger and Lester, *Made by Hong Kong*, p. xii.
52 Berger and Lester, *Made by Hong Kong*, p. xii.
53 Berger, *Making in America*.
54 Federal Trade Commission, *Proposed Guides for the use of U.S. Origin Claims*. Federal Register Notice, May, 1997, p. 8.

Bibliography

Aronczyk, M., *Branding the Nation: The Global Business of National Identity*. New York: Oxford University Press, 2013.

Åström Rudberg, E., 'Selling the concept of brands: the Swedish advertising industry and branding in the 1920s', *Journal of Historical Research in Marketing*, 9 (2017), pp. 535–542.

Badel, L., 'Conflicting identities: French economic diplomacy between the state and companies in the twentieth century', *Diplomacy & Statecraft*, 25 (2014), pp. 432–452.

Bellamy, M.J., 'The making of Labatt "Blue": the quest for a national lager brand, 1959–1971', *Business History*, 62 (2020), pp. 123–150.

Berger, S., and Lester, R.K., *Made by Hong Kong*. Hong Kong: Oxford University Press, 1997.

Berger, S., *Making in America*. Cambridge, MA: The MIT Press, 2013.

Bonell, A., '"Cheap and nasty": German goods, socialism, and the 1876 Philadelphia world fair', *International Review of Social History*, 46 (2001), pp. 207–226.

Bower, J., and Higgins, D.M., 'Litigation and lobbying in support of the marque: the scotch whisky association, c. 1945–c. 1990', *Enterprise & Society* (2021), pp. 1–31. https://doi.org/10.1017/eso.2021.33.

Broad, G., *A Small Price to Pay: Consumer Culture on the Canadian Home Front 1939–45*. Vancouver; Toronto: UBC Press, 2013.

Clampin, D., *Advertising and Propaganda in World War II: Cultural Identity and the Blitz Spirit*. London; New York: I.B. Tauris, 2014.

Cooper, E., 'The nineteenth century history of the Jaeger Trade Mark', in Bentley, L., and Bone, R. (eds), *Research Handbook on the History of Trade Mark Law*, Cheltenham: Edward Elgar, forthcoming.

Culver, A.A., 'For the sake of the nation: mobilizing for war in Japanese commercial advertisements 1937–1945', in Berghoff, H., Logemann, J., and Römer, F. (eds), *The*

Consumer on the Home Front: Second World War Civilian Consumption in Comparative Perspective, Oxford: Oxford University Press, 2017, pp. 145–174.

Dinnie, K., 'Country-of-origin 1965–2004: a literature review', *Journal of Customer Behaviour*, 3 (2004), pp. 165–213.

Donzé, Y.-P., 'National labels and the competitiveness of European industries: the example of the "Swiss made" law since 1950', *European Review of History*, 26 (2019), pp. 855–870.

Duguid, P., 'French connections: the international propagation of trademarks in the nineteenth century', *Enterprise & Society*, 10 (2009), pp. 3–37.

Ermann, U., and Hermanik, K.-J. (eds), *Branding the Nation, the Place, the Product*. Abingdon: Routledge, 2018.

Fisher, J., Pedaliu, E.G.H., and Smith, R., *The Foreign Office, Commerce and British Foreign Policy in the Twentieth Century*. London: Palgrave Macmillan, 2016.

Frank, D., *Buy American*. Boston, MA: Beacon Press, 1999.

Funke, M., 'Business associations and institutional development of Swedish post-war export advertising', *SSE Working Paper Series in Economic History*, Stockholm School of Economics, No. 2022:1 (2022). https://swopec.hhs.se/haechi/abs/haechi2022_001.htm.

Gerth, K., *China Made: Consumer Culture and the Creation of the Nation*. Cambridge, MA: Harvard University Asia Center, 2003.

Glover, N., 'Framtidsmarknader: Svensk ekonomisk diplomati i Asien och Afrika under avkoloniseringens era', *Historisk tidskrift*, 138 (2018), pp. 649–677.

Glover, N., and Hellenes, A.M., 'A "Swedish offensive" at the world fairs: advertising, social reformism and the roots of Swedish cultural diplomacy, 1935–1939', *Contemporary European History*, 30 (2021), pp. 284–300.

Hansen, P.H., *Danish Modern Furniture 1930–2016: The Rise, Decline and Re-emergence of Cultural Market Category*. Odense: University Press of Southern Denmark, 2018.

Head, D., *Made in Germany: The Corporate Identity of a Nation*. London and Sydney: Hodder & Stoughton, 1992.

Higgins, D.M., and Mordhorst, M., 'Reputation and export performance: Danish butter exports and the British market, c.1880–c.1914', *Business History*, 50 (2008), pp. 185–204.

Higgins, D.M., *Brands, Geographical Origin, and the Global Economy: A History from the Nineteenth Century to the Present*. Cambridge: Cambridge University Press, 2018.

Holt, D.B., *How Brands Become Icons: The Principles of Cultural Branding*. Boston, MA: Harvard Business School, 2004.

Holt, D.B., 'Jack Daniels' America: Iconic brands as ideological parasites and proselytizers', *Journal of Consumer Culture*, 6 (2006), pp. 355–377.

Hou, C.-M., *Foreign Investment and Economic Development in China 1840–1937*. Cambridge, MA: Harvard University Press, 1965.

Kaufman, B.I., 'The organizational dimension of United States economic foreign policy, 1900–1920', *The Business History Review*, 46 (1972), pp. 17–44.

Kühschelm, O., 'Buy national campaigns: patriotic shopping and the capitalist nation state', *Journal of Modern European History*, 18 (2020), pp. 79–95.

Kühschelm, O., 'Nationalizing consumption: products, brands, and nations', in Berger, S., and Fetzer, T. (eds), *Nationalism and the Economy*, Budapest: Central European University Press, 2019, pp. 163–187.

Kühschelm, O., 'Promoting the nation in Austria and Switzerland: a pre-history of nation branding', in Ermann, U., and Hermanik, K.-J. (eds), *Branding the Nation, the Place, the Product*, New York: Routledge, 2018, pp. 143–160.

League of Nations, *Marks of Origin*. Geneva: League of Nations, 1927.

Lekakis, E.J., 'Economic nationalism and cultural politics of consumption under austerity: the rise of ethnocentric consumption in Greece', *Journal of Consumer Culture*, 17 (2017), pp. 286–302.

Liu, X., 'Chinese multinational enterprises operating in Western economies: Huwaei in the US and the UK', *Journal of Contemporary China*, 30 (2021), pp. 368–385.

Loxham, A., 'Profiting from war: Bovril advertising during World War II', *Journal of Macromarketing*, 36 (2016), pp. 198–214.

Miroudot, S., Lanz, R., and Ragoussis, A. *Trade in Intermediate Goods and Services*. OECD Trade Policy Papers, No.93 (2009), OECD.

Moor, L., *The Rise of Brands*. Oxford: Berg, 2007.

Mordhorst, M., 'Arla and Danish national identity – business history as cultural history', *Business History*, 56 (2014), pp. 116–133.

Pence, K. 'Showcasing Cold War Germany in Cairo: 1954 and 1957 industrial exhibitions and the competition for Arab partners', *Journal of Contemporary History*, 47 (2012), pp. 69–95.

Phau, I., and Prendergast, G., 'Conceptualizing the country of origin of brand', *Journal of Marketing Communications*, 6 (2000), pp. 159–170.

Pike, A., *Origination: The Geographies of Brands and Branding*. Malden, MA: Wiley Blackwell, 2015.

Pike, A. (ed.), *Brands and Branding Geographies*. Cheltenham: Edward Elgar Publishing, 2011.

Pike, A., 'Introduction: brands and branding geographies', in Pike, A. (ed.), *Brands and Branding Geographies*, Cheltenham: Edward Elgar, 2011, pp. 3–24.

Rius-Ulldemolins, J., 'Barcelona and SEAT, a history of lost opportunity: corporate marketing, nation branding, and consumer nationalism in the automotive industry', *Enterprise & Society*, 16 (2015), pp. 811–846.

Roth, K.P., and Diamantopoulos, A., 'Advancing the country image construct', *Journal of Business Research*, 62 (2009), pp. 726–740.

Smits, K., and Jansen A., 'Staging the nation at expos and world's fairs', *National identities*, 14 (2012), pp. 173–188.

Steele, K., and Moulis, D., 'Country of origin: the Australian experience', in Vermulst, E., Waer P., and Bourgeois, J., *Rules of Origin: A Comparative Study*, Ann Arbor: University of Michigan Press, 1994, pp. 195–255.

Swett, P.E., 'Advertising and consumers in Second World War Germany', in Berghoff, H., Logemann, J., and Römer, F. (eds), *The Consumer on the Home Front: Second World War Civilian Consumption in Comparative Perspective*, Oxford: Oxford University Press, 2017, pp. 175–195.

Thackeray, D., *Forging a British World of Trade*. Oxford: Oxford University Press, 2019.

Thackeray, D., 'Selling the empire? Marketing and the demise of the British world, c. 1920–1960', *Journal of Imperial and Commonwealth History*, 48 (2020), pp. 679–705.

Tickner, L., '"Export Britain": pop art, mass culture and the export drive', *Art History*, 35 (2012), pp. 394–419.

van den Bersselaar, D., 'Who belongs to the "star people"? Negotiating beer and gin advertisements in West Africa, 1949–1975', *Journal of African History*, 52 (2011), pp. 385–408.

van den Bossche, P., and Zdouc, W., *The Law and Policy of the World Trade Organization*. Cambridge: Cambridge University Press, 2015.

Vermulst, E.A., 'Rules of origin as commercial policy instruments – revisited', *Journal of World Trade*, 26 (1992), pp. 61–102.

Viktorin, C., Gienow-Hecht, J.C.E., Estner, A., and Will, M.K. (eds), *Nation Branding in Modern History*. New York: Berghahn Books, 2018.

Volcic, Z., and Andrejevic, M. (eds), *Commercial Nationalism: Selling the Nation and Nationalizing the Sell*. Basingstoke: Palgrave, 2015.

Waer, P., 'European Community Rules of Origin', in Vermulst, E.P., Waer, P., and Bourgeois, J. (eds), *Rules of Origin in International Trade*, Ann Arbor: The University of Michigan Press, 1994, pp. 85–194.

2 Marketing perspectives on the country of origin[1]

Daniele Dalli

Introduction

The 'Made in' label is commonly used to emphasize special features of a product for the mere reason that it comes from a given place. Such features are often considered to be idiosyncratic. As the authors of this book have documented, country-of-origin (hereafter, COO) effects derive from complex historical, commercial, and political processes that involve several actors and institutions. These effects depend on multifaceted interpretation processes in which micro and macro-perspectives, and agencies, interact and constantly change the way in which the COO of a given product affects the perceptions of various publics.

Marketing scholars and professionals have often conceptualized, measured, and managed COO in such a way that the relationship between place, product, and final consumer appears linear, direct, and univocal. Thus, COO has been used to explain why consumers traditionally prefer cars from Germany or fashion products from Italy. These associations have been long-lasting. They enable companies to communicate the value of their products, help the government manage national and international trade, and facilitate consumer purchasing decisions because the COO serves as a proxy for quality and reliability.

It is therefore important that there is a discussion of the evolution of the marketing literature on COO, with particular reference to the measurement of COO effects, empirical evidence, and how these results might be translated into managerial and public policy. Additionally, it is also necessary to consider the criticisms that have been levelled at the COO, and how these might be used to develop new areas of research. Further, where appropriate, reference is made to the case studies discussed in this book.

This chapter proceeds as follows. The next section traces the general evolution of research on COO and summarizes some of the key themes in this literature with reference to a major meta-analysis. This is followed by a discussion of how definitions of COO have changed, largely in response to globalization, and how this has resulted in the development of new constructs in the COO literature. There then follows a review of theories that

DOI: 10.4324/9781003166184-2

have been advanced to explain differences in consumer perception of COO, moderating influences on COO effects, and the outcomes of this research. The penultimate section discusses some of the unresolved questions in COO research, and the final section presents a tentative model of how the fundamental themes in the COO literature may determine the perceptions of businesses, consumers, and governments – the key stakeholders in this concept.

Framework

The bulk of COO research is located in the disciplines of international business and marketing, and has sought to identify, and measure, how competitiveness depends on structural or contextual conditions at the product level. Often, this research is heavily slanted toward the commercial dimension, though adequate consideration for the economic and political/cultural dimensions is provided.

COO effects are usually defined and measured in terms of customer judgement and choice, such as brand attitude or purchase intention. If consumers prefer a product from one country compared to an identical product from another country, they are assumed to be influenced by a COO bias. Robert Schooler was probably the first scholar to empirically test this bias. Schooler reported that individuals from a given country or culture perceive differences in the same products originating from different countries.[2] Since then it became evident that COO effects are intrinsically dependent on individual or group interpretations, which can be affected by cultural, psychological, and social factors. Subsequently, scholars from different disciplines contributed to research on COO by applying this concept to food, international business management, and tourism,

In the last 50 years, research on COO has produced a voluminous literature[3] in which the following key themes can be identified:

- Initially, research was atheoretical and contingent: COO biases were assumed to exist but were not explained.[4] Thus, in COO research, why were German cars chosen? More recently, attempts have been made to develop more reliable and robust justifications for these biases, though a consensus is still lacking.[5]
- Scholars have sought to achieve greater accuracy in demarcating and measuring COO effects. Arguably the most important theoretical advance was the distinction between the country of origin, country image (hereafter, CI), and brand origin. The first concept is purely empirical and contextual (Germany *is* different from France), while the second depends on cultural interpretation (Germany can be *viewed* as being different from France). Brand origin developed when brands, especially global brands, became iconic and began to be de-coupled from the country in which they were born.

- COO effects are measured at the level of individual consumers: customers are asked if their preferences for particular products vary according to country of origin. Such an approach limits the reliability and generalizability of results because they depend on sampling criteria. Conversely, this method allows scholars to incorporate moderators and mediators for individual consumers and products. The former includes personal characteristics, cultural and ideological orientation, and experience, while the latter involves product category, positioning, and typology.
- The dependent variables used in COO research are largely derived from attitude theory and its methodological correlates. Thus, respondents indicate if they like a given country and/or its products. Questions can be presented in conative terms, for example, when respondents are asked if they would be willing to buy products originating from a specific country. However, both approaches are bounded to the same sampling criteria discussed above and are rarely compared with more objective measures, such as commercial sales or trade data.

COO effects can then be conceptualized as the outcome of the interaction between the ontological, objective nature of countries, and the cultural, subjective nature of individual interpretations, as exemplified in Figure 2.1.

Consumer perceptions of a specific country are based on that country's characteristics, such as its history, and politics; other socio-cultural elements, which include cultural distance; cognitive factors, like stereotypes; affective elements, namely animosity or affinity; and personal experiences, in particular, familiarity with a country. The interaction of all of the elements in Figure 1 leads to the development of a perceived (or subjective) CI, which can differ across consumers and cultures.

Consumer perceptions of individual countries are capable of generalization, but they remain heavily influenced by individual or group differences. They can change gradually or sometimes rapidly in response to critical events. Such perceptions are also elaborated through social discourse: in 2012, the dispute between Japan and China over the status of the Senkaku/Diaoyu Islands led to a 35% decrease in Japanese car sales in China.[6]

The interaction of cognitive (evaluation), affective (emotion), and conative (intention) factors determines actual behaviour, such as buying, or not buying. Because COO influences consumers' purchasing decisions, it has been used and manipulated in several contexts and for different purposes. See,

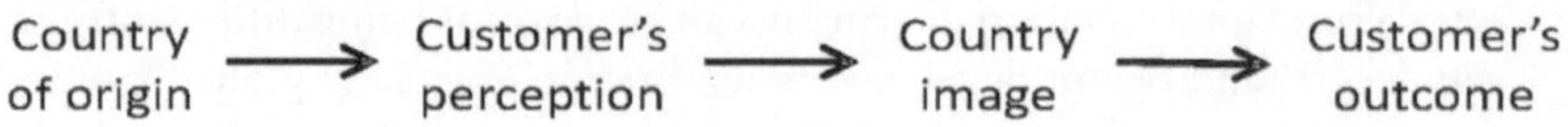

Figure 2.1 Stylised country-of-origin framework

for instance, the chapter on Made in Austria, by Oliver Kühschelm, which discusses the efforts of the Austrian government and industry associations to promote a national preference for Austrian products.

COO definition and related constructs

The original, and perhaps elementary, relationship between COO and consumer behaviour was defined and tested during the 1960s, a period in which international trade in intermediate products was much lower than the trade in fully-finished items. In this context, it was reasonable to associate products with the characteristics of particular countries, and, therefore, to make the claim that 'a product's country of origin can influence consumers' evaluative judgements of the product'.[7] The COO effect is typically operationalized and communicated through textual cues such as 'Made in', or images, for example, a national flag. In marketing terms, COO is an intangible product attribute, similar to other attributes – price, brand name, or warranty – that are used by customers to infer product quality. The ability of COO to affect consumer behaviour also depends upon cultural, historical, and – to some extent – mythical factors commonly associated with a given country.

The first literature review on COO effects identified moderating influences, which include demography and personality traits. One of the biggest weaknesses in early research was its reliance on single-cue studies. Frequently, scholars measured the association between COO and consumers' attitudes without considering the impact of other, competing factors, like price or brand, for instance.[8] As evidenced later in meta-analyses, multi-cue studies generate a more stable and reliable measure of the role of COO. On average, COO effects in multi-cue studies were around half the size of those reported in single-cue studies. Moreover, during the 1980s, and 1990s, substantial effort was directed to better explain COO effects.[9]

These later studies required scholars to redefine the basic constructs in this field of research. Three factors necessitated a more flexible, varied, and context-dependent definition of COO. First, production and distribution chains extended beyond national borders, which blurred the association between a product and its country of origin.[10] Increasingly, the products are designed, partly assembled, and 'finished' in multiple countries. Moreover, distribution, marketing, service, and transport logistics operate on a global basis. As Simon Ville notes in his chapter on 'Made in Australia', the subsidiaries of multinational companies were sometimes prominent in the development of 'Made in Australia' and may, paradoxically, have promoted a growing positive attitude toward domestic products.

The second factor was the development of global branding strategies by multinational enterprises. Companies from Coca-Cola to Unilever made substantial investments in their brands as 'drivers of value'. Product, service, and even country of origin have been replaced by the brand as the focal element that attracts consumer attention and promotes value perception. Such brands became icons,[11] targeted to a global population possessing a diverse culture and geography. Consequently, the narrative strategies that underpinned these brands became less dependent on the actual origin and characteristics of the product.

Finally, retailers and, especially, internet platforms are prominent in the marketing of products and services. Buying an item in a large chain store became a cultural experience in which the characteristics of the product were intertwined with those of the retailer. In some cases, using their own brands, large retailers were able to position their products as competitors of manufacturer's brands. Some retailers developed internationally and their country of origin became less significant as they integrated into local cultures. Similarly, E-commerce platforms such as Amazon and Alibaba, have been able to affirm their own brands, which has diluted the importance of country of origin.

Taken together, these factors have prompted a debate about 'Made in' versus 'Made by'.[12] In certain conditions, the development of global corporations paralleled and contributed to the growth of a positive CI, as evidenced by Pierre-Yves Donzé 's chapter on Made in Japan in this book. Contemporaneously, scholars developed new conceptualizations of COO.[13] Thus, the country of origin has been defined and measured not solely with reference to the geographical dimension. For example, many products are sold with *hybrid* traits in respect of origin, for example, 'Designed in Country X' and 'Manufactured in country Y'. This research has been extended to encompass 'Country of Assembly' and 'Country of Parts.[14] It is possible to summarize the results of empirical COO research using the findings of a recent meta-analysis (Table 2.1).

This meta-analysis is particularly useful because it provides an update of empirical research on COO following a gap of many years.[15] In this study, 64 papers were reviewed. The main findings of this review are that the COO exerts a moderate to large influence on consumer behaviour: 0.40 on a scale from −0.95 to +0.95. Second, the most important COO constructs are Country of Brand (0.32) and Country of Manufacturing (0.27). The Country of Design and the Country of Parts have the least impact on consumer behaviour. Additionally, the COO had the biggest impact on purchase intention (0.47), which is more than twice the values reported for product, and brand evaluation. The same study also reported that COO effects are moderated by the local culture of the participants in empirical studies: non-US participants manifested more intense COO effects compared to US respondents, and those who associated with cultural groups more oriented toward individualism, revealed less intense COO effects.

Other moderators require discussion, especially when dealing with product categories: socially relevant categories – automobiles, apparel, and personal accessories – induced more intense effects than non-relevant categories – consumer electronics, and industrial products. Similarly, compared to general

Table 2.1 A summary of partitioned COO effects

	Independent variables				
Dependent variables	*COO overall effect*	*Country of manufacturing*	*Country of brand*	*Country of design*	*Country of parts*
Product evaluation	.18	.05	.06	.04	.03
Brand evaluation	.20	.05	.06	.04	.04
Purchase intention	.47	.12	.15	.10	.09
Overall	.40	.27	.32	.21	.19
Moderators					
Non-US countries	+				
Individualistic culture	−				
Socially relevant categories	+				
Specific products/ categories	+				
Multiple cues	−	Brand name, price, product features, warranty			
Professional buyers	+				

Sources: Based on De Nisco, A., and Oduro, S., 'Partitioned country-of-origin effect on consumer behavior: a meta-analysis', *Journal of International Consumer Marketing*, Published online 4 January 2022. DOI: 10.1080/08961530.2021.2022062, Table 1, p. 11.

Note: Figures represent meta r, that is the mean effect size (correlation coefficient; −95% : +95%) in reviewed studies. Independent variables are listed in columns, and dependent variables, and moderators in rows.

stimuli, such as 'Product of France', specific product stimuli effects were more intense. This means that COO effects are significantly affected by the characteristics of product categories. The chapter on 'Made in Spain' by José Miranda and Alba Roldán, explains how the Spanish textile/clothing industry achieved rapid international exposure without any COO effects. On the contrary, Spanish companies and brands did not make any explicit or implicit reference to Spain

Greater use of multi-cultural samples revealed that COO effects varied according to the geographical location of consumers. Consequently, COO was then measured in a more subjective way using the concept of CI, which is defined as: 'the sum of beliefs and impressions people hold about places. … They are a product of the mind trying to process and pick out essential information from huge amounts of data about a place'.[16] CI has been used for products and services, consumer and industrial goods, tourist destinations, and to facilitate inward investment.

Conventional COO studies compared consumers' preferences for products, or brands originating from different countries. Analysing perceived images of countries allowed scholars to explain *why* these differences existed. To address the subjective nature of CI, and hence the variety of beliefs held by different individuals, it was necessary to increase the number of variables employed in its measurement. Moreover, scholars stressed the theoretical and empirical relevance of the interaction between country and product categories: COO effects are not equal for different categories from the same country. While Germany is renowned for its automobiles, the same does not apply to clothing and perfumes. Although consumers were well aware of this issue, it was some time before it was acknowledged by scholars.

In a seminal article, three distinct concepts of CI were recognized:[17]

- The general image of countries. Scholars measured CI using a combination of absolute and relative measures. The former includes economic environment, and international influence, while cultural affinity and similarity perceptions are included in the latter. The assumption underlying these measures is that the image of a given country is not affected by the products or services under consideration. In other words, the 'Made in' effect applies almost equally to every product category.
- The image of countries *and* their products (product-country images). Scholars measured CI with specific reference to the nature of the product and service. The assumption was made that CI varies across different product categories. To obtain a reliable measure of the 'Made in' effect, it was necessary to consider the specific product or service that could benefit from that effect and compare it with the relationship between country and product image.
- The image of products from a country (product image). Country and product image are considered together. For example, scholars measured the image of cars from Germany and compared it to French cars. In this research, the empirical evidence is strictly limited to the association between country X and product Y. The assumption is made that it is not possible to measure 'Made in' effects, *per se*, because these emerge only in association with a given product or service.

Subsequently, another important element in COO research emerged: country image management. Private and public institutions became interested in promoting products and services from a given country (including domestic *vs.* imports), and specific places and tourism destinations.[18] Growing empirical evidence in this field provided opportunities for using international segmentation to examine the impact of promotional activity.[19] As COO theories became more robust, the scope of this research moved from the purely corporate sphere into the political and regulatory field: public agencies, and even supranational entities began to actively engage in the process of 'origination'. Marco Belfanti's chapter on 'Made in Italy' describes the process through which the Italian public and private institutions actively promoted the transformation of 'Made in Italy' into a real brand.

One consequence of greater globalization and international sourcing practices was that CI researchers developed the concept of brand origin (hereafter, BO), which was used to represent the cognitive association between brands and the country they represent.[20] Crucially, CI does not take account of the locations involved in the design, manufacturing, and distribution of products.

BO is thus considered as a complementary, and even alternative, measure to COO. The former is the very essence of the cultural and geographic roots of the brand's firm. Thus, Apple and Toyota are considered to be US and Japanese brands, respectively, even though the components used in each company's products are sourced from many countries.[21] BO studies generated related concepts, such as brand foreignness, which refers to consumer perception that a brand is of foreign origin.[22]

Scholars working on brand origin report that consumers were frequently unable to correctly identify a brand's COO.[23] This particular finding demonstrated that consumers perceive international and global brands in subjective and idiosyncratic ways. Consequently, to develop reliable results with viable practical implications, it was necessary to study BO preferences using large-scale, multinational, and multi-cultural data.

In sum, there are three distinct perspectives on COO, each of which requires a different definition:

- CO (*country oriented*): scholars focus on the objective characteristics of the place from which the product originates;[24]
- CI (*product oriented*): scholars focus on the image that consumers associate with given countries, which depends on objective and subjective factors, and product characteristics;[25]
- BO (*brand oriented*): scholars focus on the origin of the brand, without taking account of where the product was designed, made, assembled, or distributed.[26]

Moving from CO to CI, and then BO, the importance of consumers' subjective perceptions increases. In the next section, the most important processes which determine these perceptions are discussed.

Consumers' perceptions: individual differences, evaluations, and outcomes

Original COO studies were based on the implicit assumption that the 'Made in' effect had the same global effect on products. Thus, the 'Made in' effect of German cars was identical in all countries. Subsequently, it became apparent that this belief was inaccurate for two fundamental reasons. First, perceptions of foreign products and foreignness are markedly dissimilar between different people in disparate countries. Second, there are relational properties in these perceptions: specific country-to-country relationships significantly influence consumers' perceptions and evaluations. These differences are not only contingent or casual but depend on historical conditions and cultural development, and were subject to manipulation by private and public institutions. As Robin Adams discusses in his chapter on Made in Ireland, the public, and a range of associations became involved in the development of cultural and political national awareness via the creation and protection of the *Déanta i nÉirinn* trade mark.

Individual differences (endogenous factors)

Individual traits affect consumers' perceptions and preferences. One of the first constructs applied to the analysis of COO effects was consumer ethnocentrism (hereafter, CET).[27] Originally, this concept was used to, 'represent the beliefs held by American consumers about the appropriateness, indeed morality, of purchasing foreign made products'.[28] In practice, ethnocentric consumers believe that purchasing imported products is 'wrong'. Conversely, non-ethnocentric consumers evaluate foreign products on their own merits, irrespective of their origin. Most empirical studies on ethnocentrism focused on the empirical verification of the negative influence of CET on various consumption outcomes, including purchase intention, attitude toward foreign products, and the willingness to buy them. These relationships have also been explained by reference to mediating variables, such as the perceived quality of the product.[29] In addition to CET, other socio-cultural constructs that may influence customers' perceptions include: animosity, cosmopolitanism, nationalism, patriotism, and xenocentrism.[30]

Unfortunately, as with other cultural constructs, ethnocentrism is heavily dependent on specific, 'relational' conditions. For instance, consumers may express more positive or negative attitudes toward products from particular countries. A recent study reported that consumers in Germany and China revealed different ethnocentric tendencies toward foreign organic products. This variation was explained in terms of trust. Chinese and German consumers were both affected by the same general issues of ethnocentrism, and product preferences, but they diverged on products from different countries: Chinese respondents preferred products from Denmark, Germany, and Australia, more than others, whereas Germans preferred products from Denmark, Austria and The Netherlands. More importantly, while Chinese consumers appreciated local products, they also manifested a degree of scepticism about their own country as a producer of organic food. In contrast, German consumers had a strong preference for domestic organic products because they strongly trusted domestic suppliers.[31]

CET has been employed as a moderator that affects the degree to which consumers like (or dislike) foreign as opposed to domestic products. One study compared ethnocentrism and national identity to demonstrate that these traits – even if apparently similar – are associated with different psychological factors. Motivated by fear and risk avoidance, ethnocentric consumers rejected foreign products. This finding holds even if they do not show high levels of national identification. Such consumers want to support domestic products because they are believed to possess superior quality and reliability.

Many studies demonstrate that the relevance and magnitude of COO effects depend largely on specific individual traits – openness toward foreign objects, people, and cultures – and specific 'relational' traits such as the proximity between specific dyads, or groups of countries because of cultural, historical, or political reasons. Thus, Austria, Germany, and German-speaking Swiss consumers share a common language and some cultural traditions, and their susceptibility to COO effects is biased accordingly. From another perspective, government agencies may reorientate their strategies to support domestic producers. In their chapter on New Zealand, Felicity Barnes and Jim McAloon argue that campaigns promoting New Zealand in the interwar period relied upon an affinity with the UK, the principal export market. Since the later twentieth century, campaigns have emphasized Maori culture and New Zealand's green credentials in order to better compete in a global marketplace, which was unconstrained by historical ties.

Information sources (exogenous antecedents)

In addition to assessing the social, cultural, and personal profile of consumers, it is important also to consider the sources from which consumers derive information about foreign countries. Information sources can be divided into two main categories: primary and secondary. The former refers to information obtained as a result of direct contact, such as visiting the country. Secondary sources can be induced, autonomous, and organic, and they are mediated by other actors.

Induced sources include communications provided by advertising, institutions, mass media, and newspaper reports.[32] An autonomous source is characterized by a greater awareness of, and willingness to acquire news and information on a given country by a foreign audience, and may involve books, films, and television.[33] Finally, organic information sources include word-of-mouth communication – information disseminated by acquaintances about their experiences with the country under evaluation. The influence exerted by this form of communication is inversely proportional to the degree of familiarity and knowledge of the foreign country. It therefore reflects the greater criticality of this information channel, which, although difficult to monitor, should not be underestimated within the broader analysis of CI. More recently, word-of-mouth information has encompassed online reviews which are an important factor affecting purchasing decisions, especially in the travel and tourism industries. The relationship between the COO and the role of reviews on buyers' evaluations and decisions has also been the subject of recent analysis.[34]

Evaluations and outcomes

The dependent variables employed in empirical analyses of COO effects include attitudinal factors such as evaluation and preference, as well as actual behaviour and, rarely, actual market data. An early meta-analysis reported that CI affects consumers' evaluations of product quality, perceived risk, and the likelihood of purchase, all of which are related to the attitudinal, or evaluative dimensions of consumers' decision processes, and are considered drivers of actual behaviour.[35]

Recently these variables have been classified according to four distinct dimensions: country cognition, country affect, country conations, and country norms. Country cognition and country affect are attitudinal variables used to directly measure CI, while country conations, even if attitudinal in nature, are employed to measure consumer behaviour toward products and brands from a particular nation. Country norms are usually employed as moderators because they can alter the magnitude of COO effects.[36]

Country cognition can be represented by the opinions consumers hold about given countries, their institutions, inhabitants, climate conditions, and even their products or brands. One study compared consumers' and retailers' perceptions of the products, country, and people of Argentina, Canada, Chile, and the US to explain buying behaviours. These perceptions were operationalized by including, *inter alia*, individual rights and freedoms, political stability, and quality of life.[37] Another study developed a scale to position countries in terms of human traits – agreeableness, wickedness, snobbism, assiduousness, conformity, and unobtrusiveness – all of which proved to be significantly associated with product-country attitudes, and attitudes toward countries as travel destinations.[38]

Country affect is represented as emotions and sentiments elicited by a particular country and its characteristics, culture, and history. Many studies employed scales used in the psychology of emotions literature but adapted to the specific context of study.[39]

Country conation consists of a consumer's behavioural intentions toward a country, such as the willingness to be a tourist in that country, or the desire to purchase products from that country. An important construct in some academic models is that of relationship: CI and its various dimensions can affect attitudes and behaviours when mediated by relational elements, such as attitudes toward immigration, and willingness to invest in, or accept investments from a country.[40] Other studies in this vein made extensive use of various forms of purchase intention measures.[41]

Categories: products, brands, and local contexts

Consumers' evaluations are strongly influenced by categories – the classifications of objects and concepts that individuals employ to simplify their evaluation processes. For instance, consumers evaluating a specific model of car are influenced by their knowledge about the 'category' of cars in general, and the way in which that category is associated with particular countries. This assessment is both a formal and informal process.

Empirical research on CI indicates that consumers are strongly influenced by a limited range of product categories:[42] consumer electronics, textile/apparel/shoes, cars, food, and beverages. Many studies have employed one, or a few categories to test CI effects on product evaluations. However, it is still unclear to what extent CI effects are specific to product categories, which raises some doubts about their generalizability. This is one reason why CI measurements are increasingly specified at the product level.

Scholars have tried to produce empirical evidence at a more general level, using conceptual categorizations such as product and brand nationality, and product type. These apparently simple constructs have become intractable: the globalization of production, marketing, and distribution has made it increasingly difficult to clearly identify so-called *uni-national* products or brands. For this reason, several scholars have employed *ad hoc* categorizations, such as bi-national, when products are manufactured in two countries, and multinational, when the locus of production is less relevant than the global dimension of brand image. Some scholars have argued that empirical evidence can be extended to other product categories with similar characteristics.[43]

Some studies have investigated how product class moderates COO effects on consumers' evaluations. One strand of research identified three product classes: utilitarian nature-based (fruits), utilitarian industrialized (home appliances), and hedonic industrialized (clothes), and reported that COO effects varied according to the product class in terms of significance, magnitude, and dependent variable.[44] Nonetheless, it is possible to affect the way in which these categories are perceived by consumers. Nikolas Glover's chapter on Made in Sweden demonstrates that the association between 'quality' and Swedish exports derived from specific product categories which were then transformed into a national trait following the involvement of government and trade associations.

Categories have been used in other aspects of COO research. The use of country categories implies that different countries or groups of countries possess specific properties that affect consumer evaluation. Scales have been developed to quantify an individual's subjective perceptions of a particular country and to define general country categories, both of which should produce more reliable results. For example, some scholars measured country positioning on a functional *vs.* emotional scale, while others reviewed a comprehensive literature on this topic to provide insights on the relevance of consumers' explicit and implicit stereotypes of foreign products.[45] Similarly, studies have shown that products from Japan or the United States benefit from a premium perception of quality which can be extended to categorize countries as developed or emergent.[46]

The previous studies originated from a recognition that consumers encounter difficulties when trying to identify the actual origin of products and brands.[47] One feature of this research was that scholars developed 'subjective' measures of localness and globalness, and other country categorizations that did not rely upon the intrinsic properties of countries, but on the perceptions of respondents.[48]

Assessment and future directions

As discussed above, the literature on COO effects developed over the previous 60 years, or so. The main advances in this research can be summarized as follows:

- Production and distribution chains extended and integrated beyond national borders making it difficult to identify and measure product-country associations. Consequently, scholars developed a more diversified and complex set of constructs, including brand origin, country of design, country of manufacture, country of assembly, and country image.[49]
- The association between global brands and a particular country became less relevant to consumers. To address this disjuncture, the literature evolved toward the comparative analysis of global and local brands.
- Retail platforms, especially E-commerce, benefited from explosive growth and further weakened the association between product and place. Currently, research on the impact of retail on COO is limited, but it promises to be a field of substantial enquiry.[50]

Nonetheless, there remain some unresolved issues. It remains difficult to determine the appropriate level of geographical scope to define and measure COO effects. There are no univocal, or widely accepted methodological approaches toward regions, nations, or continents, though supranational entities are beginning to receive attention.[51] Another problem is that of generalizability. Because research on consumer reactions to foreign products and destinations is grounded in surveys, the empirical results depend on the size and representativeness of the sample. Consequently, the generalizability of results depends on the characteristics of each sample. Many of the studies reviewed in this chapter employed national samples, hence their validity is limited to the populations actually represented in such samples.[52]

But samples, and populations, are heterogenous which means that COO effects are not uniform, they vary according to demography (young or old), gender, human capital (educated or not), and wealth. The practical implications of these issues need further investigation.[53] Similarly, it seems apposite to better understand COO effects among consumers in developed and emerging nations. Where comparisons have been made between these types of countries, it appears that consumer ethnocentrism and materialism have differed in the extent to which they moderated the COO effect.[54] Another neglected theme is whether COO effects are influenced by unusual market (and marketing) situations involving corporate or product crises. Even the decision to off-shore or re-shore can be observed in terms of COO effects.[55] Finally, the literature on services, especially product-service hybrids, is scant.[56]

A tentative model for future COO research

The literature on COO effects reviewed in this chapter is rooted in marketing and international business. A common trait in this research is that empirical evidence and its implications were designed to support professional decision-makers, such as managers and civil servants. The third category of stakeholders interested in COO effects are final consumers and consumers' associations.

Table 2.2 provides a classification of how the marketing literature on COO effects can be represented and employed according to different institutional perspectives. This framework describes how products and services are evaluated in 'different' markets by different actors.

The business management implications consist of recommendations for international marketing strategies that take account of COO effects. Companies engaged in business abroad (outgoing logic) should be aware of the general attitude (ethnocentrism and xenocentrism) of target customers toward foreign products, and their product/category-specific perceptions of these products. These considerations determine which countries are appropriate export markets. In certain conditions, and depending on corporate resources, it may be possible to counteract or change COO effects to better promote the company's products and brands.[57]

Simultaneously, domestic companies operating in their national market who are challenged by foreign competitors (incoming logic), also need to be aware of the preferences of domestic consumers: to what extent do they prefer domestic products, and would they be prepared to pay more for such products?

Because public bodies are responsible for regulating markets, they inevitably interact with corporate strategy. In this context, COO effects matter

Table 2.2 COO effects and their impact on different institutional perspectives

	Outgoing logic	*Incoming logic*
Companies	Foreign country-market selection and marketing strategy	Competition from foreign products and marketing strategy
Public agencies	Support domestic companies going abroad "Sounding" protection	Protection of domestic supply Selective barriers to trade
Consumers/citizens	Tourism Investments	Quality proxies Stereotypes

because the policies implemented by these bodies affect the export prospects of their domestic companies (outgoing logic). Such policies should consider the magnitude, valence, and specificities of COO effects for various cultures.

Turning to the domestic context (incoming logic), public agencies are often committed to the protection of domestic companies. The management of trade barriers should take into account the attitudes of local consumers toward foreign products. Moreover, public agencies are active in the protection of domestic products threatened by imports that are 'passed-off' as domestic.

Finally, consumers simultaneously participate in international markets, as tourists and investors (outgoing logic), and in their domestic market (incoming logic). The extent to which they are influenced by COO effects varies, but they often employ country stereotypes, or product-country associations which, even if they are incorrect, significantly affect their decisions.

Notes

1 I would like to thank Camilla Barbarossa (Toulouse Business School), and Giada Mainolfi (University of International Studies in Rome), for providing ideas and references as well as for friendly reviewing early versions of this chapter. I also thank the editors of this book for their support and suggestions.
2 Schooler, 'Product bias'.
3 Bilkey and Nes, 'Country-of-origin'; Dinnie, 'Country'; He, Wang, and Wu, 'Building'; Liefeld, 'Experiments'; Lu et al., 'An examination'; Magnusson and Westjohn, 'Is there'; De Nisco and Oduro, 'Effect'; Papadopoulos, 'What product images'; Peterson and Jolibert, 'A meta-analysis'; Pharr, 'Synthesizing'; Roth and Diamantopoulos, 'Advancing'; Samiee, ' Customer evaluation'; Samiee and Chabowski, 'Knowledge'; Samiee and Leonidou, 'Relevance'; Srinivasan and Jain, 'Country'; Al-Sulaiti and Baker, 'Country'; Verlegh and Steenkamp, 'A review'; Usunier, 'Relevance'.
4 Peterson and Jolibert, 'A meta-analysis'; Magnusson and Westjohn, 'Is there'; Lu et al., 'An examination'.
5 Diamantopoulos et al., 'Explicit'.
6 Antonetti, Manika, and Katsikeas, 'Why consumer'.
7 Pharr, 'Synthesizing', p. 34.
8 Bilkey and Nes, 'Country-of-origin'.
9 Peterson and Jolibert, 'A meta-analysis'; De Nisco and Oduro, 'Effect'.
10 Papadodopoulos and Heslop, *Product-country Image*; Jaffe and Nebenzahl, *National Image*.
11 Holt, *How Brands*.
12 See Glover and Higgins, 'Conceptualizing' in this volume.
13 Samiee and Chabowski, 'Knowledge'.
14 Chao, 'Partitioning'; Insch and McBride, 'The impact'.
15 Verlegh and Steenkamp, 'A review'.
16 Kotler, Haider, and Rein, *Marketing Places*.
17 Roth and Diamantopoulos, 'Advancing'.
18 See Véronique Pouillard and Audrey Millet's chapter in this book. They explain how entrepreneurs and business associations in the early development of the fashion industry promoted the 'Made in France' beyond this industry.
19 He, Wang, and Wu, 'Building'.
20 Samiee, Shimp, and Sharma, 'Brand origin'.

21 Balabanis and Diamantopoulos, 'Consumer'; Magnusson, Westjohn, and Zdravkovic, 'What?'.
22 Zhou, Yang, and Hui, 'Non-local'.
23 Magnusson, Westjohn, and Zdravkovic, 'What?'; Mandler et al., 'Brand'.
24 Chattalas, Kramer, and Takada, 'The impact'; Chao, 'Impact'.
25 Roth and Romeo, 'Matching'; Jaffe and Nebenzahl, *National Image;* Ahmed et al., 'Country-of-origin'; Nagashima, 'A comparison'.
26 Ahmed et al., 'Country-of-origin'; Thakor and Lavack, 'Effect'; Balabanis and Diamantopoulos, 'Consumer'; Sichtmann and Diamantopoulos, The impact'.
27 Shimp and Sharma, 'Consumer'; Sharma, Shimp, and Shin, 'Consumer'.
28 Sharma, Shimp, and Shin, 'Consumer', p. 280.
29 Kaynak and Kara, 'Consumer'; Vianelli, Reardon, and Guercini, 'Consumer'; Olsen, Biswas, and Granzin, 'Influencing'; Kim and Pysarchik, 'Prediction'.
30 Cleveland, Laroche, and Papadopoulos, 'Cosmopolitanism'; Riefler and Diamantopoulos, 'Consumer'; De Nisco and Oduro, 'Effect'; Balabanis and Diamantopoulos, 'Consumer'; Rybina, Reardon, and Humphrey, 'Patriotism'; Rawwas, Rajendran, and Wuehrer, 'The influence'.
31 Pedersen et al., 'Consumer'.
32 Hakala, Lemmetyinen, and Kantola, 'Country'; Gartner, 'Image'; Mainolfi, *Il modello.*
33 Frias et al., 'The formation'; Wu, 'Country'; Hahm and Tasci, 'Country'.
34 Tang, 'Mind your'; Stamolampros et al., 'Flying'; Phillips et al., 'The influence'.
35 Liefeld, ''Experiments'.
36 Roth and Diamantopoulos, 'Advancing'.
37 Heslop et al., 'Who controls'.
38 D'Astous and Boujbel, 'Positioning'.
39 Roth and Diamantopoulos, 'Advancing'.
40 Heslop et al., 'Who controls'.
41 See, for example, Wang and Yang, 'Does country-of-origin'; Pappu, Quester, and Cooksey, 'Consumer-based'; Garrett, Lee, and Chu, 'A store'.
42 Lu et al., 'An examination'.
43 Herz and Diamantopoulos, Country-specific'; Winit et al., 'Global'.
44 Costa, Carneiro, and Goldszmidt, 'A contingent'.
45 Herz and Diamantopoulos, 'Activation'; Diamantopoulos et al., 'Explicit'.
46 Schuiling and Kapferer, 'Real'; Hu and Wang, Country-of-origin'; Swoboda, Pennemann, and Taube, 'The effects'; Balabanis and Siamagka, 'Inconsistencies'.
47 Magnusson, Westjohn, and Zdravkovic, 'What?'; Mandler, Won, and Kim, 'Consumers'.
48 Mandler et al., 'Brand'; Gürhan-Canli, Sarial-Abi, and Hayran, 'Consumers'; Liu et al., 'Perceived'; Lu, Ma, and Xie, 'Foreignness'.
49 De Nisco and Oduro, 'Partitioned'.
50 Exceptions include Pegan, Vianelli, and De Luca, 'Online'; Maruyama, and Wu, 'The relevance'; Martinelli and De Canio, 'Country'.
51 García-Gallego and Mera, 'COO vs ROO'; Micevski, Halkias, and Herz, 'Multiple'.
52 Samiee and Chabowski, 'Knowledge'.
53 Chattalas, Kramer, and Takada, 'The impact'; Herz, Diamantopoulos, 'Activation'.
54 Sharma, 'Country'; Batra et al., 'Effects'; Auruskeviciene, Vianelli, and Reardon, 'Comparison'.
55 Grappi, Romani, and Bagozzi, 'Consumer stakeholder'; 'Reshoring'; 'Consumer reshoring'; Xu, Leung, and Yan, 'It is nice'; Barbarossa, De Pelsmacker, and Moons, 'Effects'; Barbarossa and Mandler, 'Not all'.

56 Vargo and Lusch, 'Evolving'; Javalgi, Cutler, and Winans, 'At your service'; Berentzen et al., 'Does "made in"'; Hauff and Nilsson, 'The impact'; Aruan, Crouch, and Quester, 'Relative'.

57 Magnusson, Westjohn, and Sirianni, 'Beyond'.

Bibliography

Ahmed, S., and d'Astous, A., 'Comparison of country-of-origin effects on household and organizational buyers' product perceptions', *European Journal of Marketing*, 29 (1995), pp. 35–51.

Ahmed, Z.U., Johnson, J.P., Ling, C.P., Fang, T.W., and Hui, A.K., 'Country-of-origin and brand effects on consumers' evaluations of cruise lines', *International Marketing Review*, 19 (2002), pp. 279–302.

Antonetti, P., Manika, D., and Katsikeas, C., 'Why consumer animosity reduces product quality perceptions: the role of extreme emotions in international crises', *International Business Review*, 28 (2019), pp. 739–753.

Aruan, D.T.H., Crouch, R., and Quester, P., 'Relative importance of country of service delivery, country of person and country of brand in hybrid service evaluation: a conjoint analysis approach', *Journal of Product & Brand Management*, 27 (2018), pp. 819–831.

Auruskeviciene, V., Vianelli, D., and Reardon, J., 'Comparison of consumer ethnocentrism behavioral patterns in transitional economies', *Transformation in Business & Economics*, 11 (2012), pp. 20–35.

Balabanis, G., and Diamantopoulos, A., 'Gains and losses from misperception of brand origin: the role of brand strength and country-of-origin image', *Journal of International Marketing*, 19 (2011), pp. 95–116.

Balabanis, G., and Diamantopoulos, A., 'Consumer xenocentrism as determinant of foreign product preference: a system justification perspective', *Journal of International Marketing*, 24 (2016), pp. 58–77.

Balabanis, G., and Siamagka, N.T., 'Inconsistencies in the behavioral effects of consumer ethnocentrism: the role of brand, product category and country of origin', *International Marketing Review*, 34 (2017), pp. 166–182.

Barbarossa, C., De Pelsmacker, P., and Moons, I., 'Effects of country-of-origin stereotypes on consumer responses to product-harm crises', *International Marketing Review*, 35 (2018), pp. 362–389.

Barbarossa, C., and Mandler, T., 'Not all wrongdoers are equal in the public eye: a moderated mediation model of country stereotypes, condemning emotions, and retaliatory intent in corporate crises', *Journal of International Marketing*, 29 (2021), pp. 26–44.

Batra, R., Ramaswamy, V., Alden, D.L., Steenkamp, J.B.E.M., and Ramachander, S., 'Effects of brand local and non-local origin on consumer attitudes in developing countries', *Journal of Consumer Psychology*, 9 (2000), pp. 83–95.

Berentzen, J.B., Backhaus, C., Michaelis, M., Blut, M., and Ahlert, D., '"Does 'made in ..." also apply to services? An empirical assessment of the country-of-origin effect in service settings', *Journal of Relationship Marketing*, 7 (2008), pp. 391–405.

Bilkey, W.J., and Nes, E., 'Country-of-origin effects on product evaluations', *Journal of International Business Studies*, 13 (1982), pp. 89–100.

Chao, P., 'Partitioning country of origin effects: consumer evaluation of a hybrid product', *Journal of International Business Studies*, 24 (1993), pp. 291–306.

Chao, P., 'Impact of country-of-origin dimensions on product quality and design quality perceptions', *Journal of Business Research*, 42 (1998), pp. 1–6.

Chattalas, M., Kramer, T., and Takada, H., 'The impact of national stereotypes on the country-of-origin effect: a conceptual framework', *International Marketing Review*, 25 (2008), pp. 54–74.

Cleveland, M., Laroche, M., and Papadopoulos, N., 'Cosmopolitanism, consumer ethnocentrism, and materialism: an eight-country study of antecedents and outcomes', *Journal of International Marketing*, 17 (2009), pp. 116–146.

Costa, C., Carneiro, J., and Goldszmidt, R., 'A contingent approach to country-of-origin effects on foreign products evaluation: interaction of facets of country image with product classes', *International Business Review*, 25 (2016), pp. 1066–1075.

D'Astous, A., and Boujbel, L., 'Positioning countries on personality dimensions: scale development and implications for country marketing', *Journal of Business Research*, 60 (2007), pp. 231–239.

Diamantopoulos, A., Florack, A., Halkias, G., and Palcu, J., 'Explicit versus implicit country stereotypes as predictors of product preferences: insights from the stereotype content model', *Journal of International Business Studies*, 48 (2017), pp. 1023–1036.

Dinnie, K., 'Country-of-origin 1965–2004: a literature review', *Journal of Customer Behaviour*, 3 (2004), pp. 165–213.

Fischer, P.M., Zeugner-Roth, Katharina P., Katsikeas, C.S., and Pandelaere, M., 'Pride and prejudice: unraveling and mitigating domestic country bias', *Journal of International Business Studies*, published online 7 February 2022, https://doi.org/10.1057/s41267-021-00496-1.

Frias D.M., Rodriguez, M.A., Casteneda, J.A., Sabiote, C.M., and Buhalis, D., 'The formation of a tourist destination's image via information sources: the moderating effect of culture', *International Journal of Tourism Research*, 14 (2012), pp. 437–450.

García-Gallego, J.M., and Chamorro Mera, A., 'COO vs ROO: importance of the origin in customer preferences towards financial entities', *International Marketing Review*, 34 (2017), pp. 206–223.

Garrett, T.C., Lee, S., and Chu, K., 'A store brand's country-of-origin or store image: what matters to consumers?' *International Marketing Review*, 34 (2017), pp. 272–292.

Gartner, W.C., 'Image formation process', *Journal of Travel & Tourism Marketing*, 2 (1994), pp. 191–216.

Glover, N., and Higgins, D.M., 'Conceptualizing the study of "made in" labels as an historical phenomenon', this volume.

Grappi, S., Romani, S., and Bagozzi, R.P., 'Consumer stakeholder responses to reshoring strategies', *Journal of the Academy of Marketing Science*, 43 (2015), pp. 453–471.

Grappi, S., Romani, S., and Bagozzi, R.P., 'Reshoring from a demand-side perspective: consumer reshoring sentiment and its market effects', *Journal of World Business*, 53 (2018), pp. 194–208.

Grappi, S., Romani, S., and Bagozzi, R.P., 'Consumer reshoring sentiment and animosity: expanding our understanding of market responses to reshoring', *Management International Review*, 60 (2020), pp. 69–95.

Gürhan-Canli, Z., Sarial-Abi, G., and Hayran, C., 'Consumers and brands across the globe: research synthesis and new directions', *Journal of International Marketing*, 26 (2018), pp. 96–117.

Hahm, J.J., and Tasci, A.D.A. 'Country image and destination image of Brazil in relation to information sources', *Journal of Hospitality and Tourism Insights*, 3 (2020), pp. 95–114.

Hakala, U., Lemmetyinen, A., and Kantola, S.P., 'Country image a nation-branding tool', *Marketing Intelligence & Planning*, 31 (2013), pp. 538–556.

Hauff, J.C., and Nilsson, J., 'The impact of country-of-origin cues on consumer investment behavior: the moderating influence of financial brand strength and investment management style', *European Journal of Marketing*, 51 (2017), pp. 1–21.

He, J., Wang, C.L., and Wu, Y., 'Building the connection between nation and commercial brand: an integrative review and future research directions', *International Marketing Review*, 38 (2021), pp. 19–35.

Herz, M.F., and Diamantopoulos, A., 'Country-specific associations made by consumers: a dual-coding theory perspective', *Journal of International Marketing*, 21 (2013a), pp. 95–112.

Herz, M.F., and Diamantopoulos, A., 'Activation of country stereotypes: automaticity, consonance, and impact', *Journal of the Academy of Marketing Science*, 41 (2013b), pp. 400–417.

Heslop, L.A., Papadopoulos, N., Dowdles, M., Wall, M., and Compeau, D., 'Who controls the purse strings? A study of consumers' and retail buyers' reactions in an America's FTA environment', *Journal of Business Research*, 57 (2004), pp. 1177–1188.

Holt, Douglas B., *How Brands Become Icons: The Principles of Cultural Branding.* Boston, MA: Harvard Business School Publishing, 2004.

Hu, Y., and Wang, X., 'Country-of-origin premiums for retailers in international trades: evidence from eBay's international markets', *Journal of Retailing*, 86 (2010), pp. 200–207.

Insch, G.S., and McBride, J.B., 'The impact of country-of-origin cues on consumer perceptions of product quality: a bi-national test of the decomposed country-of-origin construct', *Journal of Business Research*, 57 (2004), pp. 256–265.

Jaffe, E.D., and Nebenzahl, I.D., *National Image & Competitive Advantage: The Theory and Practice of Place Branding.* Copenhagen: Copenhagen Business School Press, 2006.

Javalgi, R.G.(R)., Cutler, B.D., and Winans, W.A., 'At your service! Does country of origin research apply to services?' *Journal of Services Marketing*, 15 (2001), pp. 565–582.

Kaynak, E., and Kara, A., 'Consumer perceptions of foreign products: an analysis of product-country images and ethnocentrism', *European Journal of Marketing*, 36 (2002), pp. 928–949.

Kim, S., and Pysarchik, D.T., 'Prediction purchase intention for uni-national and bi-national products', *International Journal of Retail & Distribution Management*, 28 (2000), pp. 280–291.

Kotler, P., Haider, D., and Rein, I., *Marketing Places: Attracting Investment, Industry, and Tourism to Cities, States and Nations.* New York: Free Press, 1993.

Liefeld, J.P., 'Experiments on country-of-origin effects: review and meta-analysis of effect size', in Papadopoulos, N., and Heslop, L.A. (eds), *Product-Country Image: Impact and Role in International Marketing.* New York: International Business Press, 1993, pp. 17–56.

Liu, H., Schoefer, K., Fastoso, F., and Tzemou, E., 'Perceived brand globalness/localness: a systematic review of the literature and directions for further research', *Journal of International Marketing*, 29 (2021), pp. 77–94.

Lu, I.R., Heslop, L.A., Thomas, D.R., and Kwan, E., 'An examination of the status and evolution of country image research', *International Marketing Review*, 33 (2016), pp. 825–850.

Lu, J.W., Ma, H., and Xie, X., 'Foreignness research in international business: major streams and future directions', *Journal of International Business Studies*, published online 15 September 2021, https://doi.org/10.1057/s41267-021-00465-8.

Magnusson, P., and Westjohn, S.A., 'Is there a country-of-origin theory?', in Jain, S.C., and Griffith, D.A. (eds), *Handbook of Research in International Marketing*, Northampton: Elgar, 2011, pp. 292–316.

Magnusson, P., Westjohn, S.A., and Zdravkovic, S., '"What? I thought Samsung was Japanese": accurate or not, perceived country of origin matters', *International Marketing Review*, 28 (2011), pp. 454–472.

Magnusson, P., Westjohn, S.A., and Sirianni, N.J., 'Beyond country image favorability: how brand positioning via country personality stereotypes enhances brand evaluations', *Journal of International Business Studies*, 50 (2019), pp. 318–338.

Mainolfi, G. (2010). *Il Modello Della Country Reputation. Evidenze Empiriche e Implicazioni Strategiche per le Imprese Del Made in Italy nel Mercato Cinese*. Torino: Giappichelli, 2010.

Mandler, T., Won, S., and Kim, K., 'Consumers' cognitive and affective responses to brand origin misclassifications: does confidence in brand origin identification matter?', *Journal of Business Research*, 80 (2017), pp. 197–209.

Mandler, T., Bartsch, F., and Han, and Min, C., 'Brand credibility and marketplace globalization: the role of perceived brand globalness and localness', *Journal of International Business Studies*, 52 (2021), pp. 1559–1590.

Martinelli, E., and De Canio, F., 'Country image dimensions and retail brand equity: a multi-cue analysis', *Sinergie Italian Journal of Management*, 39 (2021), pp. 17–36.

Maruyama, M., and Wu, L., 'The relevance of retailer country-of-origin to consumer store choice: evidence from China', *International Marketing Review*, 31 (2014), pp. 462–476.

Micevski, M., Halkias, G., and Herz, M., 'Multiple consumer identities and the crossover effect of the EU identity in predicting domestic and foreign product preferences', *Journal of Business Research*, 104 (2019), pp. 622–631.

Nagashima, A., 'A Comparison of Japanese and U.S. attitudes toward foreign products', *Journal of Marketing*, 34 (1970), pp. 68–74.

De Nisco, A., Mainolfi, G., Marino, V., and Napolitano, M.R., 'Effect of economic animosity on consumer ethnocentrism and product-country images: a binational study on the perception of Germany during the Euro crisis', *European Management Journal*, 34 (2016), pp. 59–68.

De Nisco, A. and Oduro, S., 'Partitioned country-of-origin effect on consumer behaviour: a meta-analysis', *Journal of International Consumer Marketing*. Published online: 4 January 2022. DOI: 10.1080/08961530.2021.2022062.

Olsen, J.E., Biswas, A., and Granzin, K.L., 'Influencing consumers' selection of domestic versus imported products: implications for marketing based on a model of helping behaviour', *Journal of the Academy of Marketing Science*, 21 (1993), pp. 307–321.

Papadopoulos, N., 'What product country images are and are not', in Papadopoulos, N., and Heslop, L.A. (eds), *Product-Country Image: Impact and Role in International Marketing*, New York: International Business Press, 1993, pp. 3–38.

Pappu, R., Quester, P.G., and Cooksey, R.W., 'Consumer-based brand equity and country-of-origin relationships', *European Journal of Marketing*, 40 (2006), pp. 696–717.

Pedersen, S., Zhang, T., Zhou, Y., Aschemann-Witzel, J., and Thøgersen, J., 'Consumer attitudes towards imported organic food in China and Germany: the key importance of trust', *Journal of Macromarketing*. Published online 10 February 2022. DOI: https://doi.org/10.1177/02761467221077079.

Pegan, G., Vianelli, D., and de Luca, P., 'Online channels and the country of origin', in Pegan, G., Vianelli, D., and De Luca, P. (eds), *International Marketing Strategy*, New York: Springer, 2020, pp. 149–180.

Peterson, R.A., and Jolibert, A.J., 'A meta-analysis of country-of-origin effects', *Journal of International Business Studies*, 26 (1995), pp. 83–900.

Pharr, J.M., 'Synthesizing country-of-origin research from the last decade: is the concept still salient in an era of global brands?', *Journal of Marketing Theory and Practice*, 13 (2005), pp. 34–45.

Phillips, P., Antonio, N., de Almeida, A., and Nunes, L., 'The influence of geographic and psychic distance on online hotel ratings', *Journal of Travel Research*, 59 (2020), pp. 722–741.

Rawwas, M.Y.A., Rajendran, K.N., and Wuehrer, G.A., 'The influence of worldmindedness and nationalism on consumer evaluation of domestic and foreign products', *International Marketing Review*, 13 (1996), pp. 20–38.

Riefler, P., and Diamantopoulos, A., 'Consumer cosmopolitanism: review and replication of the CYMYC scale', *Journal of Business Research*, 62 (2009), pp. 407–419.

Roth, K.P., and Diamantopoulos, A., 'Advancing the country image construct', *Journal of Business Research*, 62 (2009), pp. 726–740.

Roth, M.S., and Romeo, J.B., 'Matching product category and country image perceptions: a framework for managing country-of-origin effect', *Journal of International Business Studies*, 23 (1992), pp. 477–497.

Rybina, L., Reardon, J., and Humphrey, J., 'Patriotism, cosmopolitanism, consumer ethnocentrism and purchase behavior in Kazakhstan', *Organizations and Markets in Emerging Economies*, 1 (2010), pp. 92–107.

Samiee, S., 'Customer evaluation of products in a global market', *Journal of International Business Studies*, 25 (1994), pp. 579–604.

Samiee, S., Shimp, T., and Sharma, S., 'Brand origin recognition accuracy: its antecedents and consumers' cognitive limitations', *Journal of International Business Studies*, 36 (2005), pp. 379–397.

Samiee, S., and Leonidou, L.C., 'Relevance and rigor in international marketing research: developments in product and brand origin line of inquiry', in Jain, S.C., and Griffith, D.A. (eds), *Handbook of Research in International Marketing*, Northampton: Elgar, 2011, pp. 68–87.

Samiee, S., and Chabowski, B.R., 'Knowledge structure in product – and brand origin–related research', *Journal of the Academy of Marketing Science*, (2021). https://doi.org/10.1007/s11747-020-00767-7.

Schooler, R.D., 'Product bias in Central American common market', *Journal of Marketing Research*, 2 (1965), pp. 394–397.

Schuiling, I., and Kapferer, J.N., 'Real differences between local and international brands: strategic implications for international marketers', *Journal of International Marketing*, 12 (2004), pp. 97–112.

Sharma, P., 'Country of origin effects in developed and emerging markets: exploring the contrasting roles of materialism and value consciousness', *Journal of International Business Studies*, 42 (2011), pp. 285–306.

Sharma, S., Shimp, T.A., and Shin, J., 'Consumer ethnocentrism: a test of antecedents and moderators', *Journal of the Academy of Marketing Science*, 23 (1994), pp. 26–37.

Shimp, T.A., and Sharma, S., 'Consumer ethnocentrism: construction and validation of the CETSCALE', *Journal of Marketing Research*, 24 (1987), pp. 280–289.

Sichtmann, C., and Diamantopoulos, A., 'The impact of perceived brand globalness, brand origin image, and brand origin-extension fit on brand extension success', *Journal of the Academy of Marketing Science*, 41 (2013), pp. 567–585.

Srinivasan, N., and Jain, S.C., 'Country of origin effect: synthesis and future direction', in Jain, S.C. (ed.), *Handbook of Research in International Marketing*, Northampton: Elgar, 2003, pp. 458–476.

Stamolampros, P., Korfiatis, N., Kourouthanassis, P., and Symitsi, E., 'Flying to quality: cultural influences on online reviews', *Journal of Travel Research*, 58 (2019), pp. 496–511.

Al-Sulaiti, K.I., and Baker, M.J., 'Country of origin effects: a literature review', *Marketing Intelligence & Planning*, 16 (1998), pp. 150–199.

Swoboda, B., Pennemann, K., and Taube, M., 'The effects of perceived brand globalness and perceived brand localness in China: empirical evidence on Western, Asian, and domestic retailers', *Journal of International Marketing*, 20 (2012), pp. 72–95.

Tang, L., 'Mind your customers or mind your business: the moderating role of culture in online word-of-mouth reviews', *Journal of International Marketing*, 25 (2017), pp. 88–110.

Thakor, M., and Lavack, A.M., 'Effect of perceived brand origin associations on consumer perceptions of quality', *Journal of Product and Brand Management*, 12 (2003), pp. 394–407.

Usunier, J.C., 'Relevance in business research: the case of country-of-origin research in marketing', *European Management Review*, 3 (2006), pp. 60–73.

Vargo, S.L., and Lusch, R.F., 'Evolving to a new dominant logic for marketing', *Journal of Marketing*, 68 (2004), pp. 1–17.

Verlegh, P.W., and Steenkamp, J.B.E., 'A review and meta-analysis of country-of-origin research', *Journal of Economic Psychology*, 20 (1999), pp. 521–546.

Vianelli, D., Reardon, J., and Guercini, S., 'Consumer ethnocentrism, national identification, and cosmopolitanism', *Micro & Macro Marketing*, 2 (2015), pp. 181–198.

Wang, X., and Yang, Z., 'Does country-of-origin matter in the relationship between brand personality and purchase intention in emerging economies?', *International Marketing Review*, 25 (2008), pp. 458–474.

Winit, W., Gregory, G., Cleveland, M., and Verlegh, P., 'Global vs. local brands: how home country bias and price differences impact brand evaluations', *International Marketing Review*, 31 (2014), pp. 102–128.

Wu, G., 'Country image, informational influence, collectivism/individualism, and brand loyalty: exploring the automobile purchase patterns of Chinese Americans', *Journal of Consumer Marketing*, 28 (2011), pp. 169–177.

Xu, H., Leung, A., and Yan, R.N., 'It is nice to be important, but it is more important to be nice: country-of-origin's perceived warmth in product failures', *Journal of Consumer Behaviour*, 12 (2014), pp. 285–292.

Zhou, L., Yang, Z., and Hui, M.K., 'Non-local or local brands? A multi-level investigation into confidence in brand origin identification and its strategic implications', *Journal of the Academy of Marketing Science*, 38 (2010), pp. 202–218.

3 Making Ireland

The Made in Ireland trade mark and the delineation of national identity

Robin J.C. Adams

Introduction

It is ironic that the world's first self-regulated country-of-origin trade mark was established for a country without an official regulatory authority of its own. Exploiting the British Trade Marks Act of 1905,[1] the Made in Ireland trade mark was created in 1907, fully 15 years before the establishment of the Irish Free State. The purpose of this trade mark was not just to encourage consumers to 'buy Irish': It was also an attempt to strengthen the collective identity around which an Irish nation-state could be formed.

This chapter explores the efforts of Irish nationalists to define and regulate the national identity of Ireland through the vehicle of country-of-origin trade marking. Specifically, it charts the rise of the Irish Industrial Development Association (hereafter, IIDA), a voluntary organisation that between 1907 and 1927, regulated the use of an Irish country-of-origin trade mark, styled *Déanta i nÉirinn*. By analysing the products that used *Déanta i nÉirinn* it is possible to assess how contemporaries understood what it meant to be Irish. However, identities are negotiated phenomena based on agreed points of reference.[2] Consequently, there is also much to be learned about Irish identity from products fraudulently marketed as Irish. The IIDA prosecuted non-Irish producers that sold goods with Irish connotations, and thereby it effectively patrolled the boundaries of Irish branding and Irish identity.

The remainder of this chapter begins with an overview of the historical context in which the *Déanta i nÉirinn* trade mark was developed before documenting the establishment and growth of the trade mark and its place within the broader Irish industrial development movement. Next, there is a discussion of the sectoral and geographical characteristics of producers who used the *Déanta i nÉirinn* trade mark. In the penultimate section, misrepresentation of *Déanta i nÉirinn* and other forms of Irish imagery are reviewed and tentative inferences are drawn about the implications of such practices for Ireland's brand identity. Finally, the chapter explores the international reach and impact of the *Déanta i nÉirinn* trade mark.

DOI: 10.4324/9781003166184-3

Cultural nationalism and the first globalisation

To understand the *Déanta i* nÉirinn trade mark, it is crucial to appreciate the cultural and political context in which it emerged. The founders of this trade mark viewed it as a commercial manifestation of the broader cultural revival that had gripped Ireland from the 1880s.[3] The dominant animating force in late-nineteenth-century Irish politics was the Irish Parliamentary Party's pursuit of Home Rule – a form of limited self-government for Ireland while remaining part of the United Kingdom.[4] But, following the demise of nationalist leader Charles Stewart Parnell in 1889, the energy within Irish nationalism moved from the political to the cultural sphere. For example, the Gaelic Athletic Association was founded to engender a sense of national identity through sport, while the Gaelic League was established to revive the Irish language.[5] Meanwhile, the poet William Butler Yeats spearheaded a literary revival that romanticised Ireland's mythical Celtic past. Throughout urban Ireland, a new Catholic middle class emerged with expectations of becoming the ruling class of a self-governed Ireland.[6] Contemporaneously, in rural Ireland, the Irish Agricultural Organisation Society (hereafter, IAOS), was established to promote co-operative ownership and mutual credit societies, which were fundamental to the Irish dairy industry.[7] On the recommendation of IAOS leader, Sir Horace Plunkett, in 1899 a separate Department of Agriculture and Technical Instruction was created for Ireland.[8] Meanwhile, during the 1890s, there emerged the commercialisation of tourism in Ireland which promoted the rustic west coast's beauty spots to an international audience.[9]

It was during the late-nineteenth century that another nationalism emerged on the island of Ireland.[10] In the northern province of Ulster, Protestants, whose ancestors migrated from Scotland in the seventeenth century, reacted to calls for Irish self-government with their own nationalism: Ulster Unionism. Although they viewed themselves as Irish, they also identified themselves as British and were strongly in favour of a Union with Britain. While Irish nationalism was agrarian in ideal, Ulster's identity was industrial.[11] In broad terms, it was presentist rather than nostalgic and emphasised the economic benefits of the union with Britain. Some more narrow-minded Irish nationalists, conceiving Irish identity as essentially rural, went so far as to dismiss industrial Belfast as 'not an Irish city'.[12] While the emerging Catholic Irish middle class was largely composed of professionals and merchants, industry and large corporations were mainly the preserve of Unionists.[13] This was true of large corporations in Dublin but was especially pronounced in Ulster where business leaders were among the most active campaigners against Home Rule and independence.[14]

This late-nineteenth-century shift from political to cultural nationalism is a familiar trope to historians of Ireland.[15] However, as Graham Brownlow noted, it also happened against the backdrop of the 'first globalisation'.[16] This period, from 1870 to 1914, experienced unprecedented mobility of commodities, people, and capital.[17] But this acceleration in international trade also provided a fertile environment for the misuse of indications of geographical origin and this, in turn, fostered international protocols for the protection of all forms of intellectual property.[18] It was in this context that the Merchandise Marks Act of 1887, was enacted in Britain. This Act made it a criminal offence to apply misleading trade descriptions which referred to 'the place or country in which any goods were made or produced'.[19] This was followed by the Merchandise Marks Act of 1894, which empowered the UK Board of Agriculture to take action against the misrepresentation of agricultural products. The British government's Irish Department of Agriculture was particularly active in exploiting this legislation, aggressively pursuing those misrepresenting foreign eggs as Irish.[20]

Much like the recent resurgence in consumer ethnocentrism, the first globalisation engendered a popular reaction that was both commercial and cultural.[21] In Ireland, consumer ethnocentrism can be seen as a response to what the country's nationalists termed 'Anglicisation'. In their view, Britain's dominance of the Irish economy was just another manifestation of the cultural imperialism that threatened indigenous Irish culture, language, and identity.[22] Whatever the cause, Ireland's position as an economic laggard of the United Kingdom was not in question. Its economy had fallen behind the rest of the United Kingdom, with far fewer companies established per year than the comparable Kingdom of Scotland.[23] Similarly, in 1907, Ireland accounted for 10% of the UK population, but 4.2% of the industrial workforce and, indicative of lower productivity, only 3.2% of net output.[24] The country's poor economic performance was reflected in consumers' perceptions of Irish-made products. Notwithstanding the rising tide of nationalism, many Irish consumers viewed products made in Ireland as substandard. Reflecting this sentiment, some Irish companies chose to brand their products as foreign-made.[25] Conversely, the mass migration that accompanied the first globalisation created a large Irish diaspora with an appetite for Irish-branded products. This was particularly the case of the Irish diaspora in America, whose desire for goods representing their homeland was matched by a growing disposable income.[26]

Establishment of the IIDA and Déanta i nÉirinn

The cultural revival and growing concerns about Ireland's laggard economic performance provide the context in which the Irish industrial movement took shape as a regional organisation: the Cork Industrial Development Association (hereafter, Cork IDA), formed in 1903.[27] Its founders, older members of the cultural-nationalist Celtic Literary Society, were alleged by the Washington DC newspaper, the *Evening Star*, to be too old to learn the Irish language and therefore found an outlet for their nationalism in the economic sphere.[28] Yet, from its inception, the Cork IDA sought to transcend political and cultural divisions within Ireland. As stated by the association's secretary, its committee was, 'thoroughly representative of every shade of thought indulged in in Ireland and of every grade of society'.[29]

A founding member of the Cork IDA later recalled that many Irish businessmen and shopkeepers initially treated this organisation as a 'joke'.[30] The London *Saturday Review* derided it as, 'a body of Irishmen who talk industry to each other so industriously that they have no time to do anything industrial'.[31] Nevertheless, the establishment of the Cork IDA inspired the establishment of other Industrial Development Associations (hereafter, IDA), throughout the country. The largest regional IDA was the Dublin Industrial Development Association.[32] In 1905, a national association, the IIDA, was formed.[33] Registered with the Board of Trade in July 1906, its three objectives were: the promotion of Irish trade and commerce; the administration of the Irish National Trade Mark, and the initiation of legal action against anyone detected selling or misdescribing non-Irish goods as 'Irish'.[34]

The establishment of a trade mark for Irish-manufactured goods was the brainchild of Professor Sir Bertram A. Windle, former President of University College Cork.[35] His proposal was considered at the First All-Ireland Industrial Conference, held in Cork in November 1905. Following the proposition of William Wyndham-Quin, 4th Earl of Dunraven, and seconded by John Pious Boland, a former MP for the moderate nationalist Irish Parliamentary Party, the proposal was unanimously carried.[36] As noted by Boland in his speech, a Trade Marks Act containing provisions for collective trade marks had been passed in the previous session of parliament.[37]

The Trade Marks Act of 1905 was passed unopposed and appeared to have attracted little attention in the Irish press. However, not for the first time, secular Acts passed in Westminster found nationalistic applications in Ireland. Professor Windle chaired a committee of the All-Ireland Industrial Conference to discuss a national trade mark motion. Subsequently, a report was written, and the plan was enacted before the conference concluded.[38]

According to Boland, the Irish industrial movement had the official support of the moderate nationalist United Irish League as well as the cultural-nationalist Gaelic League.[39] As explained by John Strachan and Claire Nally, despite their differences on the national question, 'all parties – the Irish Parliamentary Party (IPP) nationalists, separatists and republicans, the southern Anglo-Irish elite and the northern Unionist alike – could stress the need to buy Irish goods.'[40] Nevertheless, members of the Gaelic League were among the most enthusiastic of the IIDA's supporters.[41]

The IIDA's place in the Gaelic revival was reflected in the design of the Made in Ireland trade mark (Figure 3.1). The League offered prizes for the best design, and the contract was awarded to William Buckley of Dublin.[42] Buckley's '*Déanta i nÉirinn*' trade mark was clearly influenced by the neo-Celtic design popular among Irish nationalists and cultural revivalists, but also owed something to the Arts and Crafts movement. The trade mark featured the Collar of Moran, a mythical Irish judge whose collar was placed around the neck of a witness. The collar would strangle the witness if he spoke falsely, but not if he spoke the truth.[43]

Figure 3.1 Déanta i nÉirinn trademark
Source: *Sinn Féin Weekly*, 16 October 1909.
Note: With thanks to Irish Newspaper Archive

Boland delivered the first application for the *Déanta i nÉirinn* trademark on 1st April 1906 – the day the Trade Marks Act of 1905 came into force.[44] However, the decision to grant legal status to the trade mark was the gift of the Board of Trade. The Act of 1905 stipulated:

> Where any association … undertakes the examination of any goods in respect of origin … and certifies the result of such examination by mark used upon or in conjunction with such goods, the Board of Trade may, if they shall judge it to be to the public advantage, permit such association … to register such mark as a trade mark in respect of such goods.[45]

However, the Board of Trade opposed the IIDA's proposed trade mark. One obstacle was whether a national trade mark should be entrusted to a government department. Boland countered that the government bureaucrats in Ireland were, 'English-nominated', and that, 'A *national trade mark* for Ireland controlled by English officials … would cease to be national'.[46] More vociferously, Boland argued:

> If it were suggested that Dublin Castle, manned by officials appointed by the English government, was to control an Irish National Trade Mark, it would not be necessary to summon Dean Swift from his grave to kill the idea with ridicule.[47]

Nevertheless, Lloyd George gave the Irish trade mark his approval on the spot, and the Board of Trade acceded to this decision. Ralph Griffin, Registrar of the Patents Office, was particularly helpful, and he suggested that the registration date should have some special association for Irish people. Boland chose 8th December, the Feast of The Immaculate Conception, and also a popular day for Christmas shopping.[48]

The IIDA started authorising the trade mark to Irish manufacturers in January 1907. Each application was assessed on its merits, but to qualify, Irish labour costs had to account for a minimum of 50% of the total cost of manufacture.[49] Every licence issued was renewable on an annual basis, subject to approval from the council. By the end of 1919, the IIDA had licensed the *Déanta i nÉirinn* trade mark to almost 700 products, of which only four had to be cancelled due to misuse.[50]

The made in Ireland directory

Fundamental to the IIDA's promotion of Irish-made products was the production and dissemination of directories listing products that carried the *Déanta i nÉirinn* trade mark. These were distributed to tens of thousands of households, both in Ireland and abroad.[51] For the historian, the directories provide a fascinating insight into the firms that deemed a brand association with Ireland to be a worthwhile investment. The following analysis is based on two such directories, for 1908 and 1921.

By 1908, within one year of its registration, there were 120 licensed users of the *Déanta i nÉirinn* trade mark. Some 42% of these early adopters were based in Dublin, 13% from Cork, and just 8% from the six counties that would later form Northern Ireland. By sector, 28% (34 companies) of the early adopters of the trade mark were creameries, of which 74% (25 companies) were co-operatives.[52] Two other co-operatives were among the early adopters: a carpet manufacturer and a lace manufacturer.[53] Textiles was the second largest sector adopting the trade mark, accounting for 19% of the total.[54] Among the most prominent brands adopting the *Déanta i nÉirinn* trademark in its first year were Boland's bakeries (belonging to the family business of John P. Boland), Eason and Son stationers, Fallon and Co publishers, M. H. Gill and Co publishers, and Gallagher's, the Belfast-based cigarette manufacturer.[55] Remarkably, only 24% of the early adopters of the trade mark had been registered as a joint stock company for more than ten years.[56]

Ireland's largest employers were conspicuous by their absence from the *Déanta i nÉirinn* register. Among the 120 early adopters of the trade mark, only three had more than 500 employees: Boland's bakery company, Gallagher cigarettes, and J. L. & F. Goodbody, a producer of jute textiles. Conversely, Dunlop (tyres), Jacob's (biscuits), and Guinness (stout) did not adopt the trade mark. There are two possible explanations for this. The first is particular to Ireland at the time: according to Frank Barry, of the 16 Southern Irish companies with more than 500 employees, 12 were Unionist in outlook.[57] The second possible explanation is more generalisable: firms with well-known brand identities have less to gain from the additional associations provided by a country-of-origin trade mark.[58]

Dwarfing the rest of the Irish business community, Guinness was Ireland's largest employer and the largest brewery in the world at this time.[59] Clearly, its adoption of the *Déanta i nÉirinn* trade mark would have been a triumph for the IIDA. However, when the Dublin IDA invited Guinness to use the *Déanta i nÉirinn* trade mark, the brewer rejected the offer, explaining that it, 'had invariably to decline such invitations'.[60] Subsequently, the Dublin IDA wrote to Guinness and, separately, its managing director C.E. Sutton. If necessary, the Dublin IDA considered appointing a deputation to wait on the firm.[61] But this was to no avail. Having registered its Harp trade mark in 1876, Guinness had no need to emphasise its 'Irishness'.[62] Indeed, by the turn of the twentieth century its brand had already become part of what it meant to be Irish.[63] Moreover, like Jacob's and Dunlop, Guinness was Unionist in outlook, so it may have been put off by the IIDA's links to radical nationalism. [64]

Among the IIDA's most prominent cheerleaders was Arthur Griffith, leader of the radical nationalist Sinn Féin party and editor of the newspaper of the same name. The *Sinn Féin* newspaper boasted that it was 'the only journal in Ireland entitled to use the Irish Trade Mark', which it displayed between the words 'Sinn' and 'Féin' on the front page of every issue.[65] Explaining its use of the *Déanta i nÉirinn* trade mark, *Sinn Féin* claimed, 'The Irish Trade Mark distinguishes what is Irish from what is spurious'.[66] Emphasising its status as the former, issues of *Sinn Féin* incorporated allusions to the *Déanta i nÉirinn* trade mark. For example, displaying a list of *Déanta i nÉirinn* users on its front page, or incorporating the *Déanta i nÉirinn* into cartoons that stressed the importance of domestic industry to national revival (Figure 3.2).[67]

The association between the *Déanta i nÉirinn* trade mark and Irish nationalist politics was particularly off-putting to the country's unionist northeast. As noted above, the Belfast business community was virtually unanimous in its support for the union with Britain.[68] A Belfast IDA was set up in 1909, but the nationalist connotations of the *Déanta i nÉirinn* trade mark made some business leaders apprehensive.[69] As one Belfast businessman recalled, 'For a little time it was looked upon with a certain amount of reserve, if not suspicion'.[70] However, once *Déanta i nÉirinn*'s popularity became apparent it was embraced by many businesses in that region.[71] The most prominent Ulster user of *Déanta i nÉirinn* was Gallagher's cigarettes, the largest independent tobacco producer in the world at that time. Although under Unionist ownership and management, Gallagher's had long used Irish nation branding as part of its marketing strategy, distributing cigarette cards that depicted

Figure 3.2 Representations of trademark in Sinn Fein cartoons

Source: Clockwise from top left: *Sinn Féin Weekly*, 16 October 1909, p. 3; *Sinn Féin Weekly*, 21 May 1910, p.1; *Sinn Féin Weekly*, 27 August 1910, p. 1; *Sinn Féin Weekly*, 19 March 1910, p. 1.

Note: With thanks to Irish Newspaper Archive.

scenes from all parts of Ireland.[72] Indeed, its founder, Tom Gallagher, was the founding President of the Belfast IDA.[73] The Belfast IDA's unionist complexion, at odds with other IDAs, was apparent in 1910, when the council adopted a motion to express its 'profound sorrow' on the death of King Edward VII.[74] Ultimately, the Belfast IDA did not survive the convulsions of Irish politics and ceased operations in 1914.[75] According to the *Irish Industrial Journal*, this was largely due to agitation over the 1912 Home Rule bill.[76] Then, from 1914, much of Belfast's industry focussed on war work, leaving little time or inclination for industrial development.[77]

Elsewhere, the Irish industrial movement's focus on economics over politics, albeit from a nationalist perspective, is clear from the minute book of the Cork IDA. Its executive committee's correspondence included mediation on the equipment of the nationalist paramilitary Irish Volunteers, as well as discussion on the equipment of the British army in Cork, urging the latter to use Irish suppliers.[78] Later in the war, the Cork IDA lobbied the War Office to increase Cork's share of munitions manufacturing.[79] Simultaneously, prominent members of its executive committee were actively campaigning against enlistment to the British army.[80]

Despite the conflict and ambiguities of Irish politics during the Great War, the IIDA's annual reports recorded a steady increase in the number of products carrying the *Déanta i nÉirinn* trade mark. From 397 in 1910, they grew to 625 in 1917.[81] By 1921, the IIDA could claim 448 users of its trade mark, which appeared on 912 products (Table 3.1).[82] The growth in users was accompanied by greater geographical diversity. Notwithstanding the demise of the Belfast IDA, the share of *Déanta i nÉirinn* users based in the six counties that would later become Northern Ireland almost doubled, from 8.3% of users in 1908 to 15.6% in 1921 (Table 3.2; Figures 3.3 and 3.4).

Among the *Déanta i nÉirinn* users in 1921 was Guinness's neighbouring brewery, Jameson, Watkins & Pim, which resulted from an invitation by the Dublin IDA. Initially, the brewer declined, explaining that it had no need for the trade mark, as it did little foreign trade. The Dublin IDA approached them again, however, and Watkins stout appeared in the directory in the following year.[83]

The well-known whiskey distillers, Jameson's and Power's, were also on the 1921 *Déanta i nÉirinn* list, despite the former's Unionist ownership and management.[84] The IIDA's involvement in the distilling industry is worthy of special note. As well as country-of-origin assurance, the IIDA also enforced product standards on distillers using its trade mark. Specifically, in addition to insisting that only Irish grain could be used in the production of Irish-branded whiskey, the IIDA only granted *Déanta i nÉirinn* status to distillers that used the pot-still method.[85] The IIDA's decision came one year after a British Royal Commission had declared that the term 'whiskey' could refer to either Coffey-still or pot-still whiskey.[86] By adopting the *Déanta i nÉirinn* trade mark, Jameson's and Power's were indicating that their product was Irish whiskey produced by the pot-still method. In its annual report for 1912, the IIDA proudly declared:

> We have learned that the Irish Trade Mark has been the deciding point in the giving of contracts for whiskey in the U.S.A.; that whiskey bearing this brand has been insisted upon by purchasers in Egypt, and that, generally speaking, it has greatly assisted in the sale of genuine Irish whiskey. Whiskey bearing the brand of the Irish Trade Mark is now being shipped to almost every country in the world.[87]

The IIDA also proved itself to be a valuable lobbyist representing the interests of Irish distillers. This even extended as far as the United States. In 1912, the IIDA was concerned that interstate variation in labelling regulations would harm the sale of Irish pot-still whiskey. With Boland acting as a conduit, the IIDA persuaded the Foreign Office in London to make an intervention on behalf of Irish whiskey exporters.[88] Closer to home, when a UK tax on the brewing and distilling industry was proposed in 1915, the Cork IDA demanded that leading nationalist and unionist Irish politicians in Westminster insisted on the exemption of Irish brewers and distillers.[89] The imposition of this tax was prevented, and the Cork IDA claimed credit.[90]

What is Irish and what is Spurious?

To reiterate the *Sinn Féin* newspaper's explanation of the success of the *Déanta i nÉirinn* trade mark, it was crucial to distinguish, 'what is Irish from what

Table 3.1 Product groups using the *Déanta i nÉirinn* trade mark, 1921

Product group	*Number of trademarked products*	*Share of trademarked products*	*Number of trademark users*	*Share of trademark users*
Food	99	10.86	54	12.05
Confectionary	38	4.17	17	3.79
Dairy	28	3.07	25	5.58
Beverages	37	4.06	22	4.91
Tobacco	32	3.51	17	3.79
Leather goods	37	4.06	22	4.91
Woollens	57	6.25	50	11.16
Other textiles	149	16.34	114	25.45
Homewares	66	7.24	25	5.58
Religious items	35	3.84	17	3.79
Paper, ink	88	9.65	31	6.92
Agricultural	45	4.93	20	4.46
Miscellaneous	201	22.04	34	7.59
Total	912	100.00	448	100.00

Source: IIDA, *A Directory of Users of the Irish Trade Mark*. Dublin: Corrigan and Wilson, 1921.

Table 3.2 Locations of firms using the *Déanta i nÉirinn* trade mark, 1908 and 1921

Location	*1908*	*1921*
Dublin	50 *(42%)*	171 *(38%)*
Cork	16 *(13%)*	63 *(14%)*
Northern Ireland counties	10 *(8%)*	70 *(16%)*
Other	44 *(37%)*	144 *(32%)*
Total	120 *(100%)*	448 *(100%)*

Sources: Porter's Guide, 1908, pp. 717-19; IIDA, *Directory of Users of the Irish Trade Mark* (Dublin, 1921).

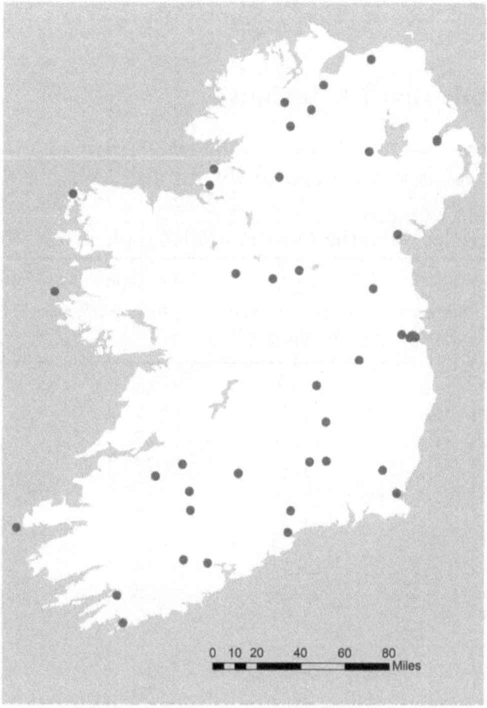

Figure 3.3 Déanta i nÉirinn users, 1908
Source: *Porter's Guide*, 1908, pp. 717–719.
Note: Some locations overlap.

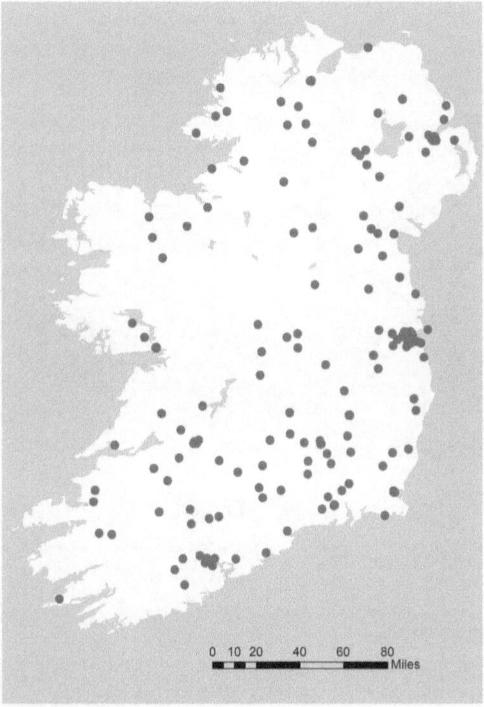

Figure 3.4 Déanta i nÉirinn users, 1921
Source: IIDA, *A Directory of Users of the Irish Trade Mark*. Dublin: Corrigan and Wilson, 1921.
Note: Some locations overlap.

is spurious'.[91] To guard against the latter, the IIDA actively sought out and prosecuted firms that fraudulently sold goods as Irish. Reduced transport costs, the proliferation of manufacturing technology, and the integration of markets created the perfect conditions for offshore production, and in 1911 the IIDA found that 'enormous quantities' of linen from Egypt were being fraudulently sold as Irish.[92] Libya and Syria also attracted the attention of the IIDA, as they were fast becoming centres of 'Irish lace' production for foreign markets. 'Irish' lace was also produced in Switzerland, the town of St Gallen leveraging its namesake's Irish origins.[93] As depicted in Figure 3.5, there was a sense in Ireland that the country was flooded with cheap imports fraudulently sold as 'Irish'. According to the cartoon, the IIDA was the remedy to this malpractice.

The average fine resulting from an IIDA prosecution was £8.55 – a largely nominal sum for most manufacturers.[94] The fine did not include legal costs which, in a case involving Marcus and Welham Poltzker selling 'Irish linen', amounted to £541.[95] Arguably the greater damage from prosecution was

Figure 3.5 'Showing them up'
Source: *Leprecaun*, 1914.
Note: It has not been possible to trace the exact date of this image.

reputational, as the IIDA was adept at gaining column inches by publicising their prosecutions.[96]

The IIDA's 'hit list' of successful prosecutions provides some insights into the brand identity of Ireland at the time. By examining the imagery used by the defendants, one can deduce the characteristics of national symbolism that were considered to be fraudulent. Philip Kotler and David Gertner have suggested that a country's imagery is comprised of its geography, history, proclamations, art and music, and famous citizens.[97] The IIDA's prosecutions fit this definition, including images of Blarney Castle, maps of Ireland, various shamrock designs, an image of a stereotypical Irishman, and a statue of Daniel O'Connell.[98] Most strikingly, the IIDA also took action against firms advertising non-Irish products using the Gaelic alphabet, effectively asserting monopoly power to sanction the use of that font.[99]

Apart from the word 'Irish' (25%), or specific Irish place names (22%), the word most frequently appearing in the IIDA's lists of objections between 1910 and 1919, was 'Shamrock', accounting for 22% of the total.[100] The association between Ireland and the shamrock was made binding in 1915 when the IIDA won a significant victory in the High Court of Chancery in London. When the Court ruled that the shamrock was indicative of the country of origin, the British Trade Mark office instituted a rule that it would not give anyone the exclusive right to use it as a trade mark in any class of goods. Nor would it permit the use of the shamrock in applications for trade mark registration if the trade mark was to be used on non-Irish goods.[101] Other recurring words in the IIDA's 'hit list' were Hibernian, Erin, Colleen, Gaelic, Erin-go-Bragh, and Faugh-a-ballagh.[102] Of course, as noted by Kotler and Gertner, most country images are stereotypes.[103] Nonetheless, the imagery and branding appropriated by manufacturers posing as Irish had a distinctively nostalgic flavour. In common with the *Déanta i nÉirinn* trade mark, they were firmly rooted in the Irish cultural revival. For a product to be viewed as Irish it had to be traditional, handmade, wholesome, and genuine: It was a guarantee not of dynamism or modernity, but of authenticity and heritage.

International reach

The majority of the IIDA's objections were directed towards firms in Britain. Out of a sample of 101 firms petitioned between 1911 and 1919, 61 were based in England, and seven were located in Scotland.[104] As explained by Strachan and Nally, 'In Great Britain, as in Ireland, the taxonomy of "Irishness" was now a valuable commodity'.[105] Yet the extent of the IIDA's trade mark registrations indicates that this taste was not confined to Britain and Ireland.

For the *Déanta i nÉirinn* trade mark to have legitimacy, the IIDA needed to guard against infringement and 'passing-off'.[106] In its 1911 annual report, the IIDA claimed that:

> owing to the perfect system we have entered into with our Trade Mark Solicitors, it is impossible for any person in any country of the world to register a Mark which resembles, or is a copy of, the Irish Trade Mark without our knowledge, or before we could enter an opposition to their application to register.[107]

By 1911, the IIDA had already registered *Déanta i nÉirinn* as a trade mark in France, Australia, and New Zealand. Simultaneously, it was contesting a rival application to register the *Déanta i nÉirinn* trademark in Indiana, USA, and the registration of a trade mark closely resembling *Déanta i nÉirinn* in Argentina.[108] By 1920, *Déanta i nÉirinn* was registered in Argentina, Australia, Canada, Chile, Egypt, France, New Zealand, and even Nigeria. In the case of Nigeria, by petitioning the Nigerian administration *via* the Colonial Office, the IIDA succeeded in reducing the price of registering its trademark from £202 to just £30.[109]

Of course, one of the most important markets for Irish goods was the United States. The growing prosperity of Irish-Americans coupled with the growth of consumer culture in America more generally, fed demand for distinctively Irish goods.[110] But registration of the *Déanta i nÉirinn* trade mark was not elementary in the US because this country did not have legislation equivalent to the British Trade Marks Act of 1905.[111] Boland addressed this omission by consulting Irish Parliamentary Party leader John Redmond on the matter, and Redmond took it upon himself to write to President Taft. Redmond reminded the President that a previous US administration had recognised the Red Cross trade mark. President Taft brought the matter before Congress, making specific reference to, 'articles of trade purporting to be made in Ireland' and called for legislation making it a misdemeanour to fraudulently claim any particular country of origin.

This interaction between Boland, Redmond, and President Taft reveals much about the place of the Irish in America at this time. The Irish-American community was large and had enough disposable income to constitute a significant market for Irish exporters. The affiliation that Irish-Americans had with their homeland was such that it was profitable to market Irish-branded products in the US. There was also a political dimension: Redmond approached President Taft in 1912 – the year of a tightly fought Presidential election. The share of the American electorate that identified as Irish was sufficient for the President and Congressmen to expect rewards at the ballot box for raising the issue.

Clearly, the IIDA's status as a pioneer in registering a trade mark denoting national provenance was a source of pride for its leadership,[112] and it encouraged them to foster similar initiatives abroad. When, in 1915, there were proposals to establish a Made in Britain trade mark, its proponents cited the success of *Déanta i nÉirinn* and sought advice from the IIDA.[113] The second self-regulated country-of-origin trade mark in which the IIDA was involved was the *Unis France* trade mark in 1917.[114] In 1918, when a bill was before Congress to establish a US country-of-origin trade mark, the US Consul at Queenstown, Co Cork, also wrote to the IIDA to seek its advice. Meanwhile, in Washington, advocates of this US trade mark cited the effectiveness of *Déanta i nÉirinn*.[115]

Conclusion

By regulating the use of *Déanta i nÉirinn* and prosecuting fraudulent advertisers, the IIDA policed the boundaries of Irish national identity before the creation of an Irish nation-state. The rise of the IIDA coincided with a radicalisation of Irish politics, with the majority of public opinion shifting away from the moderate nationalist Irish Parliamentary Party to the radical nationalist Sinn Féin party. This shift culminated in the 1918 UK general election when Sinn Féin won a landslide majority of the Irish seats in the House of Commons.[116] Following its abstentionist manifesto, Sinn Féin established its own parliament, *Dáil Éireann*, in Dublin. In the ensuing Irish War of Independence (1919–1921), the underground Dáil government continually asserted its right to speak as the, 'duly elected government of Ireland', essentially monopolising the brand of 'Government of Ireland'. This was particularly prominent in the Dáil's propaganda directed at the United States.[117]

The upheaval of the War of Independence provided opportunities for the industrial movement. In 1915, the Cork IDA had considered establishing an Irish Board of Trade 'under Governmental auspices for the furtherance of Irish industrial interests', but decided not to pursue this initiative because 'there was little or no chance of the English Government granting such facility'.[118] The establishment of the Dáil in 1919 presented a much more sympathetic authority, and following the establishment of a Dáil 'Department of Trade' the Cork IDA's secretary was appointed trade consul to New York.[119] However, the disturbance associated with the Irish War of Independence made the ordinary work of the industrial movement much more difficult. For example, a meeting of the Dublin IDA's council had to be cancelled after Crown Forces raided its offices, removed some correspondence, and scattered the remainder on the floor.[120] Simultaneously, the Dáil's attempt to instigate a boycott on goods produced in Belfast served further to alienate the business community in the northeast of Ireland.[121]

By the end of the Irish War of Independence, Ireland was divided into two jurisdictions. While the majority of the country gained independence as the Irish Free State, the six counties of the northeast remained part of the United Kingdom as Northern Ireland. Nonetheless, the IIDA regulated the use of its *Déanta i nÉirinn* trade mark with users on both sides of the border. As economic debates within the Free State turned to the merits or demerits of a protectionist trade policy, the IIDA was careful not to take sides and risk alienating its trade mark users in Northern Ireland.[122] Nevertheless, despite the persistence of these Northern Irish *Déanta i nÉirinn* users, in 1927, the Irish Free State parliament voted to take over regulation of the *Déanta i nÉirinn* trade mark from the IIDA.[123]

Notes

1 5 EDW.7. Trade Marks Act, 1905, s.62.
2 Stryker and Burke, 'The past'.
3 Boland, *Irishman's* Day, p. 35; Riordan, *Modern Irish*, p. 265.
4 Jackson, *Home Rule.*
5 Pašeta, *Before the Revolution*, p. 120.
6 Pašeta, *Before the Revolution*, ch. 6.
7 Doyle, *Civilising Rural Ireland.*
8 Maume, *The Long Gestation,* p. 18.
9 Furlong, 'Excavating', pp. 160–175.
10 Pringle, *One Island*; Townshend, *The Partition.*
11 Loughlin, 'Creating', p. 161.
12 Loughlin, 'Creating', p. 164.
13 Pašeta, *Before the Revolution,* p. 123; Barry, 'Business Establishment'.
14 Barry, 'Business establishment'; Brownlow, 'The political economy', p. 43.
15 Foster, *Modern Ireland*, p. 432.
16 Brownlow, 'The political economy'.
17 See, O'Rourke and Williamson, *Globalization and History.*
18 The most significant protocol was the formation in 1883 of the Paris Convention for the Protection of Industrial Property. Higgins, *Brands*, pp. 157–173.

19 50 & 51 Vict. Ch.28, Merchandise Marks Act, 1887, s.3.
20 Higgins, *Brands*, pp. 78–79.
21 Szlajfer, *Economic Nationalism*.
22 ÓConchubhair, 'The culture war', pp. 196–220.
23 Adams et al., 'The Wee divergence'.
24 Bielenberg, 'What happened', p.822.
25 Horgan, *Parnell to Pearse*, pp. 122–123.
26 Hotten-Somers, 'Relinquishing and reclaiming' pp. 227, 239.
27 Witness statement of Patrick Harris, National Archives of Ireland Bureau of Military History (hereafter BMH), WS80, p. 1.
28 *Evening Star*, 12 March 1911, p. 2.
29 Riordan, *Modern Irish*, p. 266.
30 Horgan, *Parnell to Pearse,* p. 122.
31 *Saturday Review of Politics, Literature, Science and Art*, 108/2810, 4 September, 1909, p. 288.
32 Daly, *Industrial Development*, p. 6.
33 Strachan and Nally, *Advertising*, p. 44.
34 *Fourteenth Annual Report* (1919) *of the IIDA*, p. 19.
35 *Fourteenth Annual Report (1919) of the IIDA*, pp. 25–26.
36 *Fourteenth Annual Report (1919) of the IIDA*, pp. 25–26. A large landowner in Adare, Co. Limerick, Dunraven was a conservative peer with a progressive, reform-focused unionist outlook. He was later a senator in the Irish Free State senate.
37 Boland, *Irishman's Day*, p. 36.
38 Boland, *Irishman's Day*, p. 36.
39 Boland, *Irishman's Day*, p. 34.
40 Strachan and Nally, *Advertising*, p. 140.
41 Boland, *Irishman's Day*, p. 34.
42 Boland, *Irishman's Day*, p. 36.
43 Strachan and Nally, *Advertising*, p. 46.
44 Boland, *Irishman's Day*, p. 36.
45 EDW.7. Trade Marks Act, 1905, s.62.
46 Boland, *Irishman's Day*, pp. 37–38.
47 Boland, *Irishman's Day*, p. 39. Dean Swift refers to Jonathan Swift, an Anglo-Irish satirist who became Dean of St. Patrick's Cathedral, Dublin.
48 Boland, *Irishman's Day*, p. 40.
49 *Fourteenth Annual Report (1919) of the IIDA*, p. 26.
50 *Fourteenth Annual Report (1919) of the IIDA*, p. 27.
51 Riordan, *Modern Irish*, p. 266.
52 *Porter's Guide*, 1908, pp. 717–719.
53 In 1910 there were discussions about establishing a separate trademark for Irish dairy products, either regulated by the IAOS or the British government. *Irish Industrial Journal*, 5 March 1910, p. 8; 2 April, 1910, p. 7.
54 *Porter's Guide*, 1908, pp. 717–719.
55 *Porter's Guide*, 1908, pp. 717–719.
56 Based on House of Commons Papers, Return of Joint Stock Companies, having Special Acts of Parliament, registered at Office of Registrar of Joint Stock Companies, 1863–1900.
57 Barry, 'Business establishment', p. 8.
58 Kotler and Gertner, 'Country as brand', p. 251. Guinness' refusal to adopt the *Déanta i nÉirinn* was not remarkable. Guinness, in common with many leading British companies owning renowned trade marks, opposed the registration of a 'Made in Britain' trade mark and the application by a French syndicate to

register a mark on behalf of the Union Nationale Inter-Syndicate des Marques Collectives (UNIS). See Higgins, this volume; Higgins, *Brands*, pp. 46–52.
59 Bielenberg, 'What happened', p. 830; Barry, 'Business establishment', p. 8.
60 Minutes of Dublin IDA council, 25 October 1920, National Library of Ireland (hereafter NLI), Ms.16,242/5/242.
61 Minutes of Dublin IDA council, 25 October 1920, National Library of Ireland (hereafter NLI), Ms.16,242/5/242.
62 Griffiths, *Guinness*, p. 132.
63 Griffiths, *Guinness*, p. 133.
64 Barry, 'Business establishment', p. 8.
65 *Sinn Féin,* 16 October 1909, p. 1.
66 *Sinn Féin,* 16 October 1909, p. 1.
67 *Sinn Féin,* 1 June 1907, p. 1; *Sinn Féin Weekly,* 16 October 1909; *Sinn Féin Weekly,* 16 October 1909; *Sinn Féin Weekly,* 27 August 1910; *Sinn Féin Weekly,* 19 March 1910.
68 Ollerenshaw, 'Industry', p. 66.
69 Carty, *Bibliography*, p. 2; *Irish Industrial Journal*, 21 May 1910, p. 9.
70 *Irish Industrial Journal*, 21 May 1910, p. 9.
71 *Irish Industrial Journal*, 21 May 1910, p. 9.
72 Loughlin, 'Creating', p. 179.
73 *Irish Industrial Journal*, 21 May 1910, p. 7.
74 *Irish Industrial Journal*, 28 May, 1910, p. 3.
75 Carty, *Bibliography*, p. 2.
76 *Irish Industrial Journal*, 4 September, 1920, p. 1.
77 The Great War also put a stop to IDAs in Limerick, Waterford, Dundalk, and Derry, as well as annual congresses that brought together representatives of the regional IDAs.
78 Minutes of Cork IDA committee, 31 August 1914, Cork City & County Archives (hereafter CCCA), B619/E/3; Minutes of Cork IDA committee, 25 January 1915, CCCA/B619/E/49.
79 Minutes of Cork IDA committee, 13 July 1915, CCCA/B619/E/99; Minutes of Cork IDA committee, 23 Aug. 1915, CCCA/B619/E/103.
80 Minutes of Cork IDA committee, 13 July 1915, CCCA/B619/E/99; Minutes of Cork IDA committee, 23 Aug. 1915, CCCA/B619/E/103. Witness statement of Patrick Harris, BMH/WS0080, p. 2.
81 *Sixteenth Annual Report (1921) of the IIDA*, p. 8.
82 IIDA, *Directory of Users of the Irish Trade Mark*. Dublin: Corrigan and Wilson, 1921.
83 Minutes of Dublin IDA council, 25 Oct. 1920, NLI/Ms.16,242/5/242; IIDA, *Directory of Users of the Irish Trade Mark*, 1921.
84 IIDA, *Directory of Users of the Irish Trade Mark*, 1921; Barry, 'Business establishment', p. 8.
85 *Fifth Annual Report (1911) of the IIDA*, p. 8.
86 *Final Report of the Royal Commission on Whiskey and other Potable Spirits*. Parliamentary Papers, XLIX.451, 1909.
87 *Sixth Annual Report (1912) of the IIDA*, p. 13.
88 *Seventh Annual Report (1913) of the IIDA*, p. 6.
89 Minutes of Cork IDA committee, 3 May 1915, CCCA/B619/E/80.
90 Minutes of Cork IDA committee, 23 August 1915, CCCA/B619/E/103.
91 *Sinn Féin,* 16 October, 1909, p. 1.
92 *Fifth Annual Report (1911) of the IIDA*, p. 8.
93 Boland, *Irishman's Day*, pp. 43–44.
94 Based on reports in the *Fourteenth Annual Report (1919) of the IIDA*.
95 *Irish Industrial Journal*, 22 January, 1910, p. 8.

96 *Irish Industrial Journal*, 1 February, 1919, p. 1.
97 Kotler and Gertner, 'Country as brand', p. 250.
98 *Annual Reports of the IIDA,* 1911–1919. Daniel O'Connell, was a leading Irish nationalist politician in the first half of the nineteenth century.
99 *Fourteenth Annual Report* (1919) *of the IIDA*.
100 Based on a sample of 103 prosecutions, in *Annual Reports of the IIDA,* 1911–1919.
101 *Tenth Annual Report* (1916) *of the IIDA*, p. 11.
102 *Annual reports of the IIDA,* 1911–1919.
103 Kotler and Gertner, 'Country as brand', p. 251.
104 *Annual Reports of the IIDA,* 1911–1919.
105 Strachan and Nally, Advertising, p. 45.
106 Boland, *Irishman's Day*, p. 41. In actions for infringement the plaintiff relies on his statutory title to the exclusive use of the trade mark, whereas passing-off is concerned with misrepresentation: the defendant is misrepresenting his products as those of the plaintiff.
107 *Fifth Annual Report* (1911) *of the IIDA*, p. 7.
108 *Fifth Annual Report* (1911) *of the IIDA*, p. 7.
109 *Fourteenth Annual Report* (1919) *of the IIDA*, pp. 28–29.
110 Hotten-Somers, 'Relinquishing and reclaiming', pp. 227–229.
111 Boland, *Irishman's Day*, p. 42. In the US, collective marks were not registrable to foreign and domestic associations until 1936 and 1938. Belson, *Certification*, p. 21.
112 *Twelfth Annual Report* (1917) *of the IIDA*, p. 7; *Sixth Annual Report* (1912) *of the IIDA*, p. 15.
113 *Ninth Annual Report* (1915) *of the IIDA*, p. 14. However, a Made in Britain trade mark did not exist until 2014. See Higgins, this volume.
114 *Twelfth Annual Report* (1917) *of the IIDA*, p. 7.
115 *Thirteenth Annual Report* (1918) *of the IIDA*, p. 6; *Irish Industrial Journal*, 1 February, 1919, p. 1.
116 de Bromhead, Fernihough, and Hargaden, 'Representation', pp. 886–925.
117 Adams, *Shadow*.
118 Minutes of Cork IDA committee, 8 February 1915, CCCA/B619/E/53.
119 Long, 'Fawsitt, Diarmuid'.
120 Minutes of Dublin IDA council, 13 June 1920, NLI/Ms.16,242/5/276.
121 See, D.S. Johnson, 'The Belfast Boycott', pp. 287–307.
122 Daly, *Industrial Development*, p. 23.
123 Seanad Éireann debate on Industrial and Commercial property (protection) bill, 23 March 1927, Vol. 8, No. 13.

Bibliography

Adams, R.J.C., *Shadow of a Taxman: Who Funded the Irish Revolution*? Oxford: Oxford University Press, 2022.

Adams, R.J.C., Coyle, C., Campbell, G., and Turner, J.D., 'The Wee divergence: business creation and political turmoil in Ireland, 1860–1900', QUCEH Working Paper (2022).

Barry, F., 'Business establishment opposition to Southern Ireland's exit from the United Kingdom', *Enterprise & Society* (forthcoming).

Belson, J., *Certification Marks*. London: Sweet & Maxwell, 2002.

Bielenberg, A., 'What happened to Irish industry after the British industrial revolution? Some evidence from the first UK Census of Production in 1907', *Economic History Review*, 61/4 (2008), pp. 820–841.

Boland, J.P., *Irishman's Day: A Day in the Life of an Irish M. P.* London: Macdonald, 1944.

Brownlow, G., 'The political economy of the ulster crisis: historiography, social capability and globalisation', in Boyce, D.G., and O'Day, A. (eds), *The Ulster Crisis, 1885–1922*, London: Red Glove Press, 2005, pp. 27–46.

Carty, J., *Bibliography of Irish History, 1912–1921.* Dublin: Stationary Office, 1936.

Daly, M.E., *Industrial Development and Irish National Identity 1922–1939.* Dublin: Gill and Macmillan, 1992.

De Bromhead, A., Fernihough, A., and Hargaden, E., 'Representation of the people: franchise extension and the "Sinn Féin Election" in Ireland, 1918', *Journal of Economic History*, 80/3 (2020), pp. 886–925.

Doyle, P., *Civilising Rural Ireland: The Co-operative Movement, Development and the Nation-state, 1889–1939.* Manchester: Manchester University Press, 2019.

Fanning, J., *The Importance of Being Branded: An Irish Perspective.* Dublin: Liffey Press, 2006.

Final Report of the Royal Commission on Whiskey and other Potable Spirits. Parliamentary Papers, XLIX.451, 1909.

Foster, R.F., *Modern Ireland, 1600–1972.* London: Penguin, 1988.

Furlong, I., 'Excavating the Emerald Isle: the use of the past in Irish tourism', in Dooley, T. (ed.), *Ireland's Polemical Past: Views of Irish History in Honour of R.V. Comerford*, Dublin: University College Dublin Press, 2010, pp. 160–175.

Griffiths, M., *Guinness Is Guinness: The Colourful Story of a Black and White Brand.* London: Cyan Books, 2004.

Higgins, D.M., *Brands, Geographical Origin, and the Global Economy: A History from the Nineteenth Century to the Present.* Cambridge: Cambridge University Press, 2018.

Horgan, J.J., *Parnell to Pearse: Some Recollections and Reflections.* Dublin: Browne and Nolan, 1949.

Hotten-Somers, D.M., 'Relinquishing and reclaiming independence: Irish domestic servants, American middle-class mistresses, and assimilation, 1850–1920', in Kenny, K. (ed.), *New Directions in Irish-American History*, Madison: University of Wisconsin Press, 2003, pp. 227–245.

Jackson, A., *Home Rule: An Irish History, 1800–2000.* London: Weidenfeld & Nicolson, 2003.

Johnson, D.S., 'The Belfast Boycott, 1920–1922', in Goldstrom, J.M., and Clarkson, L.A. (eds), *Irish Population, Economy and Society: Essays in Honour of the Late K.H. Connell*, Oxford: Clarendon Press, 1981, pp. 287–307.

Kotler, P., and Gertner, D., 'Country as brand, product, and beyond', *Journal of Brand Management*, 9/4 (2002), pp. 249–261.

Loughlin, J., 'Creating 'A social and geographical fact': regional identity and the Ulster question 1880s–1920s', *Past & Present*, 195 (2007), pp. 159–196.

Maume, P., *The Long Gestation, Irish Nationalist Life 1891–1918.* Dublin: Gill & Macmillan, 1999.

Ollerenshaw, P., 'Industry, 1820–1914', in Kennedy, L., and Ollerenshaw, P. (eds), *An Economic History of Ulster, 1820–1939*, Manchester: Manchester University Press, 1985, pp. 62–109.

Ó Conchubhair, B., 'The culture war: the Gaelic League and Irish Ireland', in Bartlett, T. (ed.), *The Cambridge History of Ireland*, Vol. 4. Cambridge: Cambridge University Press, 2018, pp. 196–220.

O'Rourke, K.H., and Williamson, J.G., *Globalization and History: Then Evolution of a Nineteenth-Century Atlantic Economy*. Cambridge, MA: MIT Press, 1999.

Pašeta, S., *Before the Revolution: Nationalism, Social Change and Ireland's Catholic Elite, 1879–1922*. Cork: Cork University Press, 1999.

Porter, F., *Porter's Guide to the Manufacturers and Shippers of Ireland*. Belfast: Davidson & M'Cormack, 1908.

Pringle, D.G., *One Island, Two Nations? A Political Geographical Analysis of the National Conflict in Ireland*. New York: Research Studies Press, 1985.

Riordan, E.J., *Modern Irish Trade and Industry*. New York: E.P. Dutton and Company, 1920.

Strachan, J., and Nally, C., *Advertising, Literature and Print Culture in Ireland, 1891–1922*. Basingstoke: Palgrave Macmillan, 2012.

Stryker, S., and Burke, P.J., 'The past, present, and future of an identity theory', *Social Psychology Quarterly*, 63/4 (2000), pp. 284–297.

Szlajfer, H., *Economic Nationalism and Globalization: Lessons from Latin America and Central Europe*. Leiden: BRILL, 2014.

Townshend, C., *The Partition: Ireland Divided, 1885–1925*. London: Allen Lane, 2021.

4 A genealogy of Made in Austria

Economic nationhood and imperial pretension

Oliver Kühschelm

Introduction

What does Made in Austria mean? An obvious answer is the registered word-picture mark that signals a product's Austrian origin, and which is in the possession of the Austrian Chamber of Commerce. This organisation represents all Austrian companies because membership is compulsory. The Chamber constitutes an essential part of the Austrian state machinery, the defining characteristic of which is its corporatist setup – sometimes referred to as a social partnership. Consequently, the Austria-mark can be viewed as promotional infrastructure in public hands.

The mark consists of a stylised A. From 1974, the crossbar of this capital letter carried the country's name spelled out in full while the two sides of the triangle that form the letter depict national colours. The label unmistakeably communicates the connection of a product with Austria. How does a product qualify? In brief guidelines on its website the Chamber points above all to the perspective of consumers who should not be misled about the product's origin.[1] But what is Austrian origin, really? The guidelines avoid specifying a percentage of Austrian inputs as a minimum requirement, they only explain that the activity of the Austrian company with regard to the product should go beyond minimal treatments such as packaging, dusting, or the mere assembling of component parts. Apart from that, they resort to technical terminology connected to tariffs.

For over 90 years there have existed in Austria collective marks signalling Made in Austria. In recent decades, a substantial literature has discussed country-of-origin effects, consumer ethnocentrism, the impact of buy national appeals, and more generally, the relationship between global and national/local consumer cultural identities.[2] Advertisers recognised, and then developed the semiotic potential of these marks from at least the nineteenth century.[3] A 'Made in' mark can possess the properties of a legally protected trade mark, but it also operates on a macro-level: 'Made in' is usually situated in the context of nation states; it is but one of many indicia connecting products with countries and, indeed, branding nations.[4] Although companies may include in their branding strategies references to their nation's history,[5] they

DOI: 10.4324/9781003166184-4

also have a substantial number of alternatives. However, 'Made in', can never escape history: the past bears heavily on what was, and is communicated. Even if we limit our discussion to the present, and to a narrow understanding of Made in Austria, its meaning and possible uses would be open to interpretation. Adopting a historical perspective adds many more layers of complexity; but it is the task of historians to determine how discourses on 'Made in' impacted historical political discourse, the formation of collective-national identity, and perceptions of a nation's economic performance.

Made-in labelling became prominent during the late nineteenth century. The exemplar of this practice was the British Merchandise Marks Act of 1887, which prohibited imports bearing the name or trade mark of any British manufacturer or dealer, unless accompanied by a definite indication of origin.[6] This Act soon became a cause celebre and it had the unintended effect of promoting 'Made in Germany'. Subsequent research established that 'Made in Germany' acquired symbolic meanings far beyond the realm of factual statements about the origin of products.[7] Similarly, Made in Austria, developed into a concept beyond a referential indication of the country of origin.

In Austria, as elsewhere, 'Made in' formed part of a hegemonic project that fostered a triangular relationship between state, nation (or, more generically, imagined community), and economy.[8] The Habsburg Empire, or 'Habsburgerreich', in German, was never considered a nation state, but its mix of feudal elements and modern institutions, of aristocratic privilege and citizenship, and of multinational arrangements and exclusionist ethnic nationalism was not that different from 'nation states' such as Britain, France, or Spain. However, under the pressure of competing nationalist ideologies, the Habsburg Monarchy was increasingly criticised as anachronistic. Its breakup as a result of World War I seemed an achievement from the viewpoint of those ethnic groups that dominated the new nation states.[9] The exception was German-speaking Austrians, especially those from the upper and middle classes, who had regarded the Habsburg state as theirs and found it hard to make peace with the small republican state they were left with. In 1938, the famous writer Joseph Roth explained Austria's annexation by Nazi Germany as the end of a road that German-speaking Austrians had already been walking along when they pursued imperialist ambitions vis-à-vis the other nations on Habsburg territory. An interesting detail to this analysis is the words Roth used to convey the pernicious attitude that Austrian Germans had adopted: 'Made-in-Germany-Hochmut [arrogance]'.[10]

In this chapter particular attention is devoted to the institutionalisation of joint advertising that bound business and state interests. It will thereby contribute to the discussion on the economic dimension of nationhood and the nationalist dimension of economic institutions and practices. For a long time, studies on nationalism have mostly ignored these topics while the economics literature has tended to reduce them to the analysis of protectionist measures.[11] The analysis is complemented by a discussion of 'Made in' in journalistic and political discourse. As an expression in English – a foreign language from the Austrian perspective – it carried a specific value for both labelling Austrian products and discussing the Austrian condition. One question is central to this chapter: How did Made in Austria relate to the country, imagined (national) community, and imperial ambitions that went by the name of Austria?

The rest of this chapter is organised as follows. First, it discusses the problems surrounding the creation of Made in Austria between the late nineteenth and early twentieth centuries. The next section examines the disintegration of the Austro-Hungarian empire after World War 1, with a particular focus on the economic imperative to develop export markets. It investigates the role played by state and business organisations in promoting Made in Austria, and Buy Austria, which reflected attempts to develop a distinctive national identity from Germany. The penultimate section explains how Austria re-fashioned its identity in the post-1945 period, which involved the creation of a narrative that emphasised small country, but great achievements, and then conclusions are presented.

Made in Austria in the late nineteenth and early twentieth centuries

In response to the British Merchandise Marks Act of 1887, firms in the Habsburg Monarchy applied the designation Made in Austria to their exports. This choice was less straightforward than one might think, but there were no plausible alternatives. Austria, or 'Österreich' was merely the informal name of a sizeable bundle of lands under Habsburg rule, officially, 'The Kingdoms and Lands Represented in the Parliament [Reichsrat]'. It is doubtful whether this lengthy name, which did not include a toponymical expression, would have had any value to consumers outside the Habsburg Empire; the same applies to Cisleithania, which referred to the river Leitha that formed part of the border with Hungary – the co-equal partner in the combined state of Austria-Hungary. However, it was not before World War I that Austria became the official designation of the Habsburg Monarchy's western half, which in itself was a federal state; its constitution granted basic rights to its citizens, and it shared a monetary and customs area with its Hungarian counterpart.

The Habsburg Monarchy was less integrated into international trade flows than other European powers: In 1900, merchandise trade as a percentage of gross domestic product (hereafter, GDP) was 22% for Austria-Hungary, 32% for Germany, and 49% for the United Kingdom.[12] Exports were less significant for the Habsburg economy compared to other major European states, excluding Russia.[13] The Hungarian government was nonetheless unhappy about the use of Made in Austria because it concealed the Magyar component of the Habsburg economy and did not contribute to the emancipation of Hungarian manufacturing from Vienna-based trading companies. Consequently, it became a matter of prestige to label exports 'Made in Hungary'.

Initially, the indication, Made in Austria, was devised solely to avoid aggravation by the British, and, following the McKinley tariff, 1891, US Customs.[14] It did not constitute a branding strategy – the systematic practice of persuasive communication to increase profits and sales. Although the Habsburg state had issued a law to protect trade marks in 1858,[15] several factors were unfavourable to the creation of Made in Austria for domestic consumers.

First, it did not help that there was a perceived lag in quality compared to Britain, and Germany – by far Austria-Hungary's most important trade partners.[16] This is in line with what we know about the dilemmas of producers from developing countries that are unsure about the benefits of using country-of-origin.[17] In 1900, it was reported to be common knowledge that in the Habsburg Monarchy, Austrian textiles were often sold as English made because customers perceived this to be a more prestigious indication of origin.[18] Some contemporaries did not object to the practice; on the contrary, it was considered evident that care should be exercised when regulating indications of origin. The same issue was debated 30 years later, when a contemporary argued that selling Austrian textiles as English, did not constitute fraud if the former were sold at a lower price than the latter. This argument was based on the premise that 'reasonable' consumers recognised that the 'English' textile was a fake since otherwise, it would be more expensive.[19]

Second, the use of Made in Austria as a non-tariff barrier was unnecessary because tariffs already provided protection. This observation was of crucial importance. Even producers in highly developed regions – Bohemia and Lower Austria – struggled to compete with industries located in the advanced European economies. Domestic firms relied on privileged access to the large market of the Habsburg Monarchy. For example, in the 1880s, Austrian textile manufacturers directed 65% of their exports to Hungary, which represented, on average, 95% of Hungarian textile and fibre imports during this decade.[20] While the dominance of Cisleithanian industry, and especially companies that were seen as German-Austrian proved controversial,[21] the co-dependence of Hungarian agricultural and Cisleithanian industrial interests prevented a breakup of the economic unit of the Dual Monarchy until World War I.

Admittedly, external tariffs during this period were not particularly high when compared to other major European countries, and when compared to the tariff levels during the interwar period.[22] Furthermore, not all industries benefitted from the same degree of insulation; consequently, some companies marketed their products as 'Österreichisches Erzeugnis' (Austrian product) to the German-Austrian public. An advert in 1905 informed consumers: 'If you want to buy a GOOD GRAMOPHONE, buy only an Austrian product'.[23] A manufacturer of sparkling wine used 'Austrian Product!' in advertisements – which also indicated that the source material was French.[24] However, it is important to distinguish between individual branding choices that spoke to German-Austrian nationalism/patriotism and labels that could be used on every product that was manufactured domestically. The Austrian origin of industrial goods consumed domestically was the norm and did not need to be emphasised.

On the contrary, the absence of origin marking served the interests of German-Austrian producers because it did not call unwanted attention to their dominance. This provides a third reason why use of Made in Austria was limited. The emerging Slavic nationalist movements sought to increase consumers' economic awareness. Consequently, they tried to carve out a privileged niche for their own national production. This trend was pronounced amongst the Czech population which benefitted from significant economic progress in the late nineteenth century, which promoted pride in Czech production.[25] However, Czech nationalists did not yet have control over their own nation state, unlike Hungarians, who in 1906 promoted the symbol of a tulip as an indication of the Hungarian origin of products. This enraged the German-speaking public of Cisleithania and the Viennese Chamber of Commerce petitioned the Austrian Minister of Trade to protect existing Austrian trade marks that depicted a tulip. Clearly, if the tulip was used to indicate Hungarian origin, its use on non-Hungarian products might create consumer deception.[26] However, in its annual report for 1906, the Viennese Chamber of Commerce reported that the initial furore over the tulip movement had subsided, and it claimed that such propaganda reflected an unnatural drive towards industrialisation which was not in the best interests of Hungary.[27] Such views indicated a patronising attitude towards non-German-Austrian ambitions of industrial development, and they demonstrated the tensions that would be created within the Habsburg Empire if Made in Austria was used.

If labelling products as manufactured in Austria entailed complications for internal and export markets, it also had unforeseen potential, both commercially and for identity building. Manufacturers soon recognised that 'Made in' was not a disadvantage when applied to products exported to the British Empire.[28] The press reported that such indicia enhanced the visibility of exports from Germany and the Habsburg Monarchy to foreign consumers who had been unaware of the precise origins of their imports.[29] Reports that consumers within the British Empire appreciated Austrian products could be reformulated into a narrative that cast Britain, the hegemon of the nineteenth century, as Goliath which failed to kill various 'Davids'.[30] Inserting 'Made in Austria' in any discussion about the Habsburg economy or products from its lands could thus serve as a call for self-confidence.[31]

Originally, 'Made in' was used on tangible products that were packaged and exported. But, after consumers became familiar with the denotative meaning of this phrase, it generated connotations. 'Made in' was even applied to human actors, for example, when people figured as products. In 1912, a Czech delegate complained in the Reichsrat that, in foreign countries, 'our industries and our trade' were rarely a known quantity. Instead, Austria was exporting people who were leaving their impoverished home regions: 'Made in Austria [English in the original,] is unfortunately the sought-after brand of the living commodity, the people's power [Volkskraft], which is our export commodity!'[32] This indicated a fundamental weakness of the Habsburg state. The delegate explained: 'If you want to be a great power, you have to be it in economic terms, too'. But the metaphor of people as Made in Austria was also used as an expression of pride when applied to consummate football players and artists, especially women. Treating female artists as an indigenous natural resource embedded Made in Austria in misogynist and racist discourse. An article about a revue remarked on the 'many delightful women of guaranteed European origin, made in Austria of best quality'.[33]

However, after Made in Austria gained recognition as an expression of pride in Austrian achievements, objects, customs, and people, the term was sometimes used in an ironic or critical sense. For example, one sports magazine commented that a sports association was, 'cheap and badly made! Made in Austria'[34]. In 1902, the *Neues Wiener Journal* observed that the German Reichstag was battling with obstructionism in ways which mirrored the history of the Cisleithanian Parliament: 'One could say of these latest manifestations of parliamentary life in the German Reichstag: "Made in Austria"'.[35] In the same year, a satirical magazine used the title Made in Austria; it recognised that this term inspired trust in, 'solid, always tasteful pieces of work'. Ironically, the magazine intended to denounce incidents that it considered possible only in Austria, and it called for the elimination of cultural and political practices that did not fulfil the ideals that Made in Austria was supposed to communicate.[36]

The unwelcome experience of 'smallness' in the interwar period

After World War I, the political and economic elites of the new Austrian Republic confronted the problem that Austria needed a market which was greater than that provided by its population of six million people, otherwise there would be considerable economic dislocation. The bourgeoisie was, at first, optimistic; they believed that other successor states would reintegrate into an economic sphere which was mutually advantageous. However, the newly independent states sought to prioritise their own economic interests – they had no desire to depend on the industries and services formerly provided by the centre of the empire.

One alternative was for Austria to become part of Germany. In October 1918, the provisional assembly named the new state Deutschösterreich – German Austria. Many Austrians considered an independent Austria to be a temporary phase. However, in 1919, the peace treaty forced the government to drop the attribute 'German'. The Allies were unsupportive of Austria joining Germany, and other successor states were also wary of this proposed union. The latter recognised the consequences they faced following an Austrian 'Anschluss': Austrian elites had presented themselves as experts on ruling Central Eastern Europe, and the unification with Germany was perceived as a strategy to regain power in the former Habsburg lands. Apart from the economic expediency of joining Germany, which was more doubtful than political discourse allowed, this option was consonant with how a large part of the population, especially the middle class and the ruling elite, viewed their nationality. Indeed, German-speaking Austrians considered themselves to be the southernmost tribe of the German people.

Another option for Austria was to emulate Switzerland, which appeared to provide a template for how small states could be prosperous.[37] Switzerland was not viewed as a political threat within Europe, and it had developed successful export-oriented industries. Overseas, Swiss companies profited from European imperialism while simultaneously avoiding its political and military costs.[38] However, there was a crucial difference between Austria and Switzerland in the 1920s: when the Austrian government adopted a liberal trade policy, it hoped in vain that the other successor states would follow suit. These states – Austria's most important export markets – were highly suspicious of its every move. It is unsurprising, therefore, that during the interwar period, their share in the Austrian merchandise trade decreased.

Nonetheless, during this period, exports became critically important to the fortunes of the Austrian economy. In 1913, exports as a percentage of the Habsburg Monarchy's GDP were 10%, but by 1925 the ratio was 19% for the Austrian Republic.[39] This trend enhanced the importance of institutions involved in promoting exports. During the last decades of the Habsburg Monarchy, a broad array of private and state-run organisations emerged that pursued this objective. However, the new Republic inherited only a small part of them, and, in any event, their international reach was much reduced. In this environment, the Viennese Chamber of Commerce became integral to the promotion of Austrian exports.[40]

During the early 1920s, conditions were not propitious for promoting Made in Austria. Nonetheless, by the mid-1920s, Austria had adjusted to its new situation, and Made in Austria was now utilised for economic propaganda. For example, the trade journal *Die neue Wirtschaft* labelled its international edition, *Made in Austria*, to inform foreigners about the Austrian economy, while businesses also sought to promote sales in their domestic market. In 1927, a new organisation, 'Buy Austrian Goods', was founded under the auspices of the Ministry of Trade. Its purpose was to persuade domestic consumers that whenever feasible they should purchase Austrian products. As in the interwar years, economic nationalism reached a high point; the Buy-Austrian campaign was aligned with similar initiatives in other countries.[41]

Although joint advertising of business interest groups and political propaganda became more conspicuous,[42] there was still no provision in Austrian trade mark law for distinctive labels that signalled membership of an association. This omission was all the more glaring as Austria was a signatory to the Paris Convention for the Protection of Industrial Property, which introduced protection for collective marks in 1911.[43] In 1929, the government finally decided to act.[44] After circulating a draft law among business organisations for comment, a bill was submitted to the parliamentary committee. In its report, this committee alerted the government to the need for a clear designation of Austrian products to facilitate their sale on the domestic market. It also recommended the adoption of the bill, which in April 1930 was duly enacted.[45] The Buy Austrian Goods organisation immediately arranged a competition to determine the visual design of a trade mark for products of Austrian origin. It was initially to be accompanied by the legend 'Austria-Österreichisches Erzeugnis' (Austrian product). After the public became acquainted with the label, it was envisaged that it could be used without the accompanying text.[46] The competition attracted 1,422 submissions, from which the judges chose a design that used the letters in Austria to form the wings of an eagle (Figure 4.1). Variants of this logo were used after World War II.

Which companies were allowed to use the Made in Austria trade mark? The easiest answer to this question is when a product is 'wholly obtained' within a country; that is when domestic workers use domestically sourced

Figure 4.1 The new trademark for Austrian products, 1931
Source: Archive of the Viennese Chamber of Commerce E 27.468/3.
Reproduced by permission of the Vienna Chamber of Commerce.

products to manufacture products for a company that has its headquarters in the same country. Frequently, organisations that promoted economic nationalism demanded that a minimum of 50% of the added value should be attributed to domestic inputs. However, the Buy Austrian Goods organisation never published quantitative specifications. In fact, any domestic company was permitted to use the new label if at least a 'substantial' part of the production process occurred within Austria. The determination of this matter was devolved to the appropriate regional Chamber of Commerce. In 1934, about three years after its introduction, 1,369 companies had registered for the Made in Austria trade mark.[47]

Promoting Austrian products on the home market, together with demanding displays of patriotism from consumers, were attempts at identity building that centred on the Austrian state. Although the government and the media always took pains to emphasise the German character of Austria, the propaganda on behalf of Austrian products formed part of a process that worked towards establishing and fostering a separate collective identity. This laid the foundations for a new round of nation-building after 1945.

Pride in smallness and imperial ambition in the *Trente Glorieuses*

If Switzerland appeared to offer lessons for the First Austrian Republic, these were even more pertinent to Austria's Second Republic. During the interwar period, Austrian elites were not enthusiastic about emulating Switzerland because this entailed renunciation of great-power status, but this changed after World War II.[48] The feeling of having escaped disaster made the small Second Austrian Republic more palatable to its citizens. Austria celebrated its independence from Nazi Germany and Allied occupation in 1945 and 1955, respectively, and not being encompassed by the Iron Curtain. Furthermore, the liberalisation of global trade enshrined by the General Agreement on Trade and Tariffs, 1947, offered the possibility that access to large markets did not require the forfeiture of state sovereignty.[49]

In 1956, the government set the 26th of October as Flag Day, to be celebrated especially by schools and the army. There were often complaints that this date lacked meaning and content; a tradition had to be invented. The Austrian Chamber of Commerce – the new umbrella organisation of the regional chambers of commerce – cast this day as a celebration of Austrian economic prowess. In 1958, the Chamber organised an Austrian Week, a promotional event to honour the achievements of Austrian business and to raise citizens' awareness as consumers and workers that they had contributed to Austrian economic success. In a planning meeting, one participant stressed that the event should not be too nationalistic; instead, it should emphasise 'Austrian taste' and 'Austrian quality'.[50] Organisers of this event did not seek a break with the past, but wanted to substitute one imagined past for another: the recent past of Nazi Germany, which was framed as quintessentially non-Austrian, for the non-nationalist Habsburg Empire that supposedly lacked the aggressiveness of other empires.

In the immediate aftermath of World War II, when Austria was an occupied country, its place in the world was of intense concern to its citizens. Made in Austria framed this concern in terms of the characteristics that Austrian products possessed and how these would be communicated to the global market. 'Taste' was one facet that was emphasised. The concept of Viennese taste was based on memories of aristocratic culture and the grandeur of the imperial residences. However, the Habsburg court no longer existed and, after two wars, hyperinflation, genocide, and massive destruction, Vienna lacked the economic and social base needed to cultivate luxury production. Nonetheless, the promotional brochure, *Made in Austria*, published by the Vienna Trade Fair Company in 1949, contained fashion items and artisanal products manufactured in Austria. The most salient feature of *Made in Austria* was its depiction of Austrians as harmless and charming people; Austrian participation in Nazi crimes was discounted.

Made in Austria was also the title of a brochure published by the Chamber of Commerce in 1962 as educational material for young Austrians. Its subtitle celebrated 'the big adventure of export', and 250,000 copies were distributed to schools and the military. The booklet was authored by the influential journalist, Herbert Krejci, who became general secretary of the Federation of Industry in the 1980s. In the first chapter, Krejci informed his readers of the Austrian dichotomy: a small country with great accomplishments. The loss of great-power status was again recast as a virtue, using the image of a rocket launch.[51] Krejci explained that Austria had neither the means nor the desire to compete with the major powers in the conquest of space. What could have been a source of frustration – that Austria had not conquered space – was presented as the virtue of restraint: 'Made in Austria – that is the motto for this great adventure of a small country'.[52] The adventure was rooted in Austria's past, and Krejci reminded the young of the 'long tradition of interacting with other people'.[53] One objective of the booklet was to explain why businesses needed to relinquish any belief that Austria's imperial past provided a path to future prosperity:

> Austria's historical mission was once to open up the vast areas of Eastern and South-Eastern Europe economically and culturally. This mission has been interrupted by historical developments. Today, our country must seek tasks in other areas. Other small, also neutral states, such as Switzerland and Sweden, have been following this path for a long time.[54]

In 1967, a new annual publication, also with the title *Made in Austria*, was launched in German, French, and English, which provided a List of Goods Produced by Austrian Crafts and Industries. Included in the text was the statement: 'In addition to its topographical, historical, artistic and humanitarian merits, Austria can also point with rightful pride to its economic development'. *Made in Austria* had become shorthand for expressing belief in the potential of the small Austrian state to achieve economic greatness which complemented its artistic and cultural achievements.[55]

Jupiter, the publishing house that edited *Made in Austria* also owned the *West-Ost-Journal*. This bimonthly periodical was the magazine of the Danube European Institute (Donaueuropäisches Institut), which provided a forum for diplomats, entrepreneurs, and politicians from Austria and socialist countries.[56] This institute promoted trade with the socialist bloc *and* sustained the imperial fantasy. Its activities testified to a continuing ambivalence that shaped trade policies and nationalising discourse.

The economic success of Switzerland also influenced Austrian economic propaganda. In 1968, the Swiss journalist Lorenz Stucki published a book about Switzerland's hidden empire.[57] He argued that because the entrepreneurial Swiss nation had built a commercial empire, it was not affected by decolonisation. Herbert Krejci was enthusiastic about adapting this concept for Austrian economic propaganda. Consequently, in 1969, activities surrounding the national holiday were held under the motto 'The Greater Austria'. In the year of the first moon landing, space was no longer considered beyond the reach of Austrian business: 'Austrians hold key positions in NASA, and we supply the metal alloys they [the Americans] need as heat shields for space travel'.[58]

Events during the 1970s ended the *Trente Glorieuses*,[59] but not in Austria. On-going economic growth inspired admiration from foreign observers.[60] Austria had revealed its economic viability, Austrian exports had moved up the value chain, and Austrian society was growing wealthy. Austrians were now convinced that the small state was the vessel of an Austrian nation. According to a survey in 1979, 68% of respondents believed that Austria constituted its own nation;[61] by 2008, this figure had increased to 80%.[62] Clearly, Austrian citizens were becoming more willing to acknowledge Austria as their nation. This trend confirmed the success of the nation-building project: Most Austrians overcame their attachment to Germany and were rehabilitated from the loss of the Habsburg Empire.

From 1977, Austrian Week used a label that indicated Austrian origin on exports. Apparently, the organisers of this event no longer feared that a general call for pride in the Austrian origin of products would be viewed as chauvinistic propaganda. Previously, Austrian Week used a symbol that consisted of the interlocked letters Ö and Q, the initials of Österreich and Qualität, to emphasise that high quality was an inherent characteristic of Austrian manufacturing. Interviews with a sample of 100 consumers conducted in 1978, supported the decision to change the logo: 95% of interviewees preferred the Austria sign, and criticised the ÖQ symbol for lack of clarity. The marketing research company attributed the preference for the A symbol to its capacity to embed 'technocratic' associations of consistently high quality in a patriotic environment.[63]

By the mid-1970s, negative trade balances were prominent in debates on Austria's economic performance. A new tax was imposed on luxury products, especially cars, to reduce imports. This measure was complemented by government support to increase the patriotic sentiment of consumers, and in 1978, the Chamber of Commerce, and the Chamber of Labour founded a new organisation, *Made in Austria*, symbolised by the Austria label, to achieve this objective. This body was a corporatist arrangement that represented the interests of business and labour/consumers; it replicated the 'Buy Austrian Goods' campaign of the interwar years, but in an era of more cooperative international trade policies it was considered unwise that a buy domestic imperative appeared in the title. To be effective, the promotional effort required a compelling slogan: 'Ja zu A', – 'Yes to A[ustria]'. One consequence of this initiative was that buying Austrian products instead of imports was a means by which Austrian consumers could prove their identification with the Austrian nation. During the 1980s, the most conspicuous promotional activity of *Made in Austria* was an eponymous quiz show on national television. The presenter asked questions which were so simple that participants were bound to give the correct answer and win Austrian products as prizes. The show was often derided for its awkward patriotism, but in contemporary Austria, it is an emblematic memory of the 1980s. Indeed, a survey in 1996, found that 93% of respondents knew the Austria sign, and the majority were able to provide a pertinent explanation of the message it communicated.[64]

The late 1970s and early 1980s were decades in which an emotional inward turn culminated with citizens' satisfaction with the achievements of their small nation state. Made in Austria gained a new visibility, and Austrians believed they were living a blessed existence. Moreover, the Austrian economy was becoming increasingly integrated into European and global markets: Exports had grown steadily since the 1950s, in nominal and real terms, and as a percentage of GDP. For example, exports as a percentage of GDP were 27% and 31%, respectively, in 1970 and 1980.[65] These figures are substantial when compared with the 1920s. This achievement is even more remarkable when it is recognised that GDP grew by more than threefold since 1929. For the more recent period there are indications that this progress has been maintained: the relevant percentages for 2000 and 2007 were 40% and 51%, respectively.[66]

The meaning of Made in Austria has been affected by foreign direct investment (FDI), which may be a consequence of the successful external projection of the nation, or represent a problematic intrusion by foreign companies. Either way, FDI has the potential to dilute or obscure the meaning of 'Made in'. From today's vantage point, FDI was not a prominent feature of the post-1945 period. In the 1970s, passive and active FDI reached their highest point in 1971. Net inflow was only 0.8% of GDP and the net outflow was even less: 0.2%. In the 1990s, the latter figure was 0.45% at its lowest, and reached 2.8% in 2000.[67] Trends in FDI during this period were aligned with geopolitical changes: Austria had pledged everlasting neutrality. The end of the Cold War and the subsequent disintegration of the communist bloc opened up new investment opportunities in a region that Austrian elites still considered to be theirs. Simultaneously, the government began seeking membership in the European Economic Community, which was achieved in 1995.

Conclusion

This chapter has provided a reconstruction of how Made in Austria evolved from an expression applied to products exported to Britain and its empire, into a concept that was used in multiple ways. However, it was not until the interwar period that the legend 'Österreichisches Erzeugnis' (Austrian product) was designed and subsequently registered as a protected trade mark. This trade mark was used after 1945, but it was eventually superseded by Made in Austria and *Made in Austria*; the former was used to promote Austrian exports, while the latter persuaded Austrians to buy domestic products.

Made in Austria appeared to support an unequivocal identification with a small nation state. However, during the 1990s, it was common parlance to refer to countries in central and eastern Europe (hereafter, CEE) as forming part of Austria's enlarged home market. In CEE countries, the recent history of Soviet hegemony and German economic dominance overshadowed the more distant memory of Habsburg rule, or cast it in a more favourable light. This changed environment provided new business opportunities to Austrian companies – a hidden (commercial) empire in the Austrian hinterland. Made in Austria, therefore, provides an instructive example of the interdependency that can arise between imperial projection and national identity, and of how the cultural imagination of empire, and nation, interacted with economic and political consequences.

Notes

1 https://www.wko.at/Content.Node/service/aussenwirtschaft/fhp/Ursprung/Made_in_....html. Accessed 10 November 2021.
2 Strizhakova and Coulter, 'Consumer'; Pekkanen and Penttilä, 'The responsibility'.
3 Brühwiler, *Zeichenform*; da Silva Lopes and Guimaraes, 'Trademarks'. For examples from the 1920s, see: Lauterer, *Lehrbuch*, p. 287; Paneth, *Grundriss*, pp. 109–112.
4 Kühschelm, Eder, and Siegrist, *Konsum und Nation*; Viktorin et al., *Nation Branding*.
5 Miranda and Ruiz-Moreno, 'Selling', p. 3; Belfanti, 'History'. For Austrian brands and companies as sites of memory, see Kühschelm and Pfoertner, *Unternehmer, Firmen*.
6 This Act also stipulated similar restrictions on imports bearing place names identical with, or similar to, British locations. 50 & 51 Vict, Ch. 28, Merchandise Marks Act, 1887, s16 (1), (4).
7 Umbach, 'Made in Germany', pp. 405–418.
8 Kühschelm, *Einkaufen*.
9 Judson, *The Habsburg Empire*, pp. 442–452.
10 Csáky, *Das Gedächtnis*, p. 348.
11 Berger and Fetzer, *Nationalism*.
12 Figures for Austria are based on own calculation. Figures for Germany and the UK were obtained from Müller, 'Internationale Verflechtung', p. 347.
13 Eddie, 'Economic policy', p. 828.
14 Claims that British Customs were harsh in their administration of the Merchandise Marks Act, 1887, were made in the *Report from the Select Committee on Merchandise Marks Act*, 1887, Parliamentary Papers, XV.19, 1890.

15 Reichsgesetzblatt für das Kaiserthum Österreich (Imperial Law Gazette for the Austrian Empire), 1858, no. 230.
16 In 1900, 37% of Austrian imports, and 52% of Austrian exports, by value, were accounted for by Germany. *Austrian Statistical Yearbook* 19 (1900), p. 241.
17 Papadopoulos et al., 'Of countries', p. 738.
18 *Agramer Zeitung*, 6 September 1900, p. 1.
19 Reif, 'Die Frage', pp. 123–125.
20 Eddie, 'Economic policy', p. 837.
21 Jaworski, 'Zwischen ökonomischer', pp. 257–268.
22 *World Trade Report*, 2007, p. 41.
23 *Wiener Caricaturen*, 29 January 1905, p. 7.
24 *Allgemeine Sport-Zeitung*, 6 June 1903, p. 683.
25 Albrecht, 'Pride', pp. 101–118.
26 *Neues Wiener Tagblatt*, 16 May 1906, p. 16; *Prager Tagblatt*, 23 May 1906, p. 9.
27 *Österreichische Fahrrad- und Automobil-Zeitung*, no. 45, 10 June 1907, not paginated.
28 *Wiener Zeitung*, 15 February 1893, p. 9.
29 *Welt-(Neuigkeits-)Blatt*, 1 December 1894, p. 12; *Bregenzer Tagblatt*, 8 May 1896, p. 1.
30 *Neues Wiener Journal*, 5 May 1906, p. 1.
31 *Pester Lloyd*, 17 April 1897, p. 1.
32 *Neues Wiener Journal*, 30 March 1912, p. 2.
33 *Die Stunde*, 23 March 1934, p. 4.
34 *Allgemeine Sport-Zeitung*, 7 May 1899, p. 508.
35 *Neues Wiener Journal*, 9 November 1902, p. 1.
36 *Der Floh*, no. 46/47, 23 November 1902, p. 10.
37 See, for example, Layton and Rist, 'The economic', p. 43.
38 Purtschert, Lüthi, and Falk, *Postkoloniale Schweiz*.
39 Own calculations based on data from Jobst and Scheiber, 'Austria-Hungary'.
40 Meyer, *Exportförderungspolitik*, p. 132.
41 Kühschelm, 'Buy national'.
42 Reinhardt, *Von der Reklame*, pp. 148–168.
43 Article 7bis, Paris Convention for the Protection of Industrial Property (Revision Conference of Washington in 1911). *Actes de la Conférence.*
44 Zimbler, 'Entwurf'.
45 Stenographic minutes of the Austrian parliament (Nationalrat) session V, 1927–1930, report 471; Bundesgesetzblatt (Federal Law Gazette) 1930, no. 109.
46 Archive of the Viennese Chamber of Commerce, E 27.468/3. Working group: 'Buy Austrian Goods', Annual Report for 1930, letter to regional chambers, 1 October 1930.
47 Graf, *'Kauft österreichische*, p. 100.
48 Rathkolb, *The Paradoxical*, p. 22.
49 On the policy options available to small states see Müller and Myllyntaus, *Pathbreakers.*
50 Archive of the Austrian Chamber of Commerce, Vienna (hereafter, ACC), Austrian Week, meeting, 24 September 1956, p. 3.
51 ACC, Wirtschaftsförderunginstitut, minutes of the advertising committee, 25 May 1962, p. 4.
52 *Made in Austria, Das große*, p. 4.
53 *Made in Austria, Das große*, p. 5.
54 *Made in Austria, Das große*, p. 5.
55 *Made in Austria, List of Goods.*
56 Danubian Europe was another term for the geographical area governed by the Habsburg Monarchy. Kühschelm, 'Den 'Osten' öffnen', pp. 109–132.
57 Stucki, *Imperium*.

58 *Wir und unsere Welt*, October 1969, p. 3.
59 *Trente Glorieuses* refers to the rapid economic growth of France between the end of World War II and the mid-1970s.
60 Katzenstein, *Small States,* p. 77.
61 Bruckmüller, *The Austrian,* p. 62.
62 S. Tributsch and P. Ulram, '1918, 1938, 2008: Geschichte im Spiegel der Forschungsergebnisse von GfK Austria', 2008, https://docplayer.org/74714745-1918-1938-2008-geschichte-im-spiegel-der-forschungsergebnisse-von-gfk-austria-mag-svila-tributsch-und-univ-doz-dr-peter-a.html. Accessed 7 December 2021.
63 ACC, Fessel & GfK, 'Austrian consciousness: Psychological consumer study', Autumn, 1978, p. 43.
64 ACC, Austrian Gallup Institute, Made in Austria, January/February 1996, pp. 2–4.
65 Exports of goods and services (% of GDP), https://data.worldbank.org. Accessed 11 February 2022.
66 Exports of goods and services (% of GDP), https://data.worldbank.org. Accessed 11 February 2022.
67 Foreign direct investment, net outflows and net inflows (% of GDP), https://data.worldbank.org. Accessed 11 February 2022.

Bibliography

Actes de la Conférence de Washington. Bureau International de l'Union, Berne, 1926.

Albrecht, C., 'Pride in production: the Jubilee Exhibition of 1891 and economic competition between Czechs and Germans in Bohemia', *Austrian History Yearbook*, 24 (1993), pp. 101–118.

Belfanti, C.M., 'History as an intangible asset for the Italian fashion business (1950–1954)', *Journal of Historical Research in Marketing*, 7 (2015), pp. 74–90.

Berger, S., and Miller, A., 'Building nations in and with empires – a reassessment', in Berger, S., and Miller, A. (eds.), *Nationalizing Empires*. Budapest: CEU-Press, 2015, pp. 1–30.

Berger, S., and Fetzer, T. (eds.), *Nationalism and the Economy: Explorations into a Neglected Relationship*. Budapest: CEU Press, 2019.

Bruckmüller, E., *The Austrian Nation: Cultural Consciousness and Socio-political Processes*. Riverside, CAL: Adriadne, 2003.

Brühwiler, W., *Zeichenform und Warenverkehr: eine Formatgeschichte der Marke, 1840–1891*. Konstanz: Konstanz University Press, 2020.

Csáky, M., *Das Gedächtnis der Städte. Kulturelle Verflechtungen – Wien und die urbanen Milieus in Zentraleuropa*. Köln: Böhlau, 2010.

da Silva Lopes, T., and Guimaraes, P., 'Trademarks and British dominance in consumer goods, 1876–1914', *Economic History Review*, 67 (2014), pp. 793–817.

Eddie, S., 'Economic policy and economic development in Austria-Hungary, 1867–1913', in Mathias, P., and Pollard, S. (eds.), *The Cambridge Economic History of Europe from the Decline of the Roman Empire Volume 8: The Industrial Economies: The Development of Economic and Social Policies*, Cambridge: Cambridge University Press, 1989, pp. 814–886.

Gellner, E., *Nations and Nationalism, New Perspectives on the Past*. Ithaca, NY: Cornell University Press, 1983.

Graf, M., '*Kauft österreichische Waren!' Gemeinschaftswerbung in der Zwischenkriegszeit*. Unpublished thesis, University of Vienna, 2009.

Hörnigk, P.W., 'Austria Supreme (if it so wishes) (1684)', in Rössner, P.R. (ed.), *Austria Supreme (if it so wishes) (1684): A Strategy for European Economic Supremacy*. London: Anthem Press, 2018, pp. 143–214.

Jaworski, R., 'Zwischen ökonomischer Interessenvertretung und nationalkultureller Selbstbehauptung: Zum Wirtschaftsnationalismus in Ostmitteleuropa vor 1914', *Zeitschrift für Ostmitteleuropa-Forschung*, 53 (2004), pp. 257–268.

Jobst, C., and Scheiber, T., 'Austria-Hungary: from 1863 to 1914', *South-Eastern European Monetary and Economic Statistics from the Nineteenth Century to World War II*. https://www.oenb.at/en/Publications/Economics/south-east-european-monetary-history-network-data-volume.html.

Judson, P.M., *The Habsburg Empire: A New History*. Cambridge, MA: Belknap Press, 2016.

Katzenstein, P., *Small States in World Markets: Industrial Policy in Europe*. Ithaca, NY: Cornell University Press, 1985.

Kühschelm, O., and Pfoertner, A. (eds.), *Unternehmer, Firmen, Produkte, Memoria Austriae*, vol. 3. Vienna: Böhlau, 2005.

Kühschelm, O., Eder, F.X., and Siegrist, H. (eds.), *Konsum und Nation. Zur Geschichte nationalisierender Inszenierungen in der Produktkommunikation*. Bielefeld: Transcript, 2012.

Kühschelm, O., 'Den 'Osten' öffnen. Das Donaueuropäische Institut als Schnittpunkt von Politik und Unternehmerexpertise, von pragmatischen Kalkülen und großen Erzählungen', in Brait A., and Gehler, M. (eds.), *Grenzöffnung 1989. Innen- und Außenperspektiven und die Folgen für Österreich*. Vienna: Böhlau, 2014, pp. 109–132.

Kühschelm, O., 'Buy National Campaigns: Patriotic Shopping and the Capitalist Nation State', *Journal of Modern European History*, 18 (2020), pp. 79–95.

Kühschelm, O., *Einkaufen als nationale Verpflichtung: Zur Genealogie nationaler Ökonomien in Österreich und der Schweiz, 1920–1980*. Berlin: De Gruyter, 2022.

Kumar, K., *Empires: A Historical and Political Sociology*. Cambridge: Polity, 2020.

Lauterer, K., *Lehrbuch der Reklame. Einführung in das Werbewesen*. Vienna: Barth, 1923.

Layton, W.T., and Rist, Ch., *The Economic Situation of Austria. Report Presented to the Council of the League of Nations*. Geneva: League of Nations, 1925.

Made in Austria. Das große Abenteuer des Exportes. Vienna: Wirtschaftsförderungsinstitut, 1962.

Made in Austria. List of Goods Produced by Austrian Crafts and Industries. Vienna: Jupiter, 1967.

Meyer, C., *Exportförderungspolitik in Österreich. Von der Privilegienwirtschaft zum objektiven Förderungssystem*. Vienna: Böhlau, 1991.

Miranda, J.A., and Ruiz-Moreno, F., 'Selling the Past. The Use of History as a Marketing Strategy in Spain, 1900–1980', *Business History*, (2020), DOI: 10.1080/00076791.2020.1717473.

Müller, M., and Myllyntaus, T. (eds.), *Pathbreakers: Small European Countries Responding to Globalisation and Deglobalisation*. Bern: Lang, 2008.

Müller, M., 'Internationale Verflechtung', in Halbeisen, P., Müller, M., and Veyrassat, B. (eds.), *Wirtschaftsgeschichte der Schweiz im 20. Jahrhundert*. Basel: Schwabe, 2012, pp. 339–465.

Osterhammel, J., *The Transformation of the World: A Global History of the Nineteenth Century*. Princeton, NJ: Princeton University Press, 2009.

Paneth, E., *Grundriss der kaufmännischen Reklame und des Reklamerechts in Deutschland und Oesterreich*. München: Oldenbourg 1927.

Papadopoulos, N., Cleveland, M., Bartikowski, B., and Yaprak, A., 'Of countries, places and product/brand place associations: an inventory of dispositions and issues relating to place image and its effects', *The Journal of Product and Brand Management*, 27 (2018), pp. 735–753.

Pekkanen, T.L., and Penttilä, V., 'The responsibility of an ethnocentric consumer – nationalistic, patriotic or environmentally conscientious? A critical discourse analysis of "buy domestic" campaigns', *International Marketing Review*, 38 (2021), pp. 300–320.

Purtschert, P., Lüthi, B., and Falk, F. (eds.), *Postkoloniale Schweiz. Formen und Folgen eines* Kolonialismus!!! *ohne Kolonien*. Transcript, Bielefeld, 2012.

Raissig, W., *Das Schweizer Produkt. Die wirtschaftliche und rechtliche Bedeutung des Ursprungshinweises*. Zürich: Buchdruckerei zum Gutenberg, 1939.

Rathkolb, O., *The Paradoxical Republic: Austria 1945–2005*. New York: Berghahn, 2021.

Reif, H., 'Die Frage der obligatorischen Ursprungsbezeichnung', *Gerichts-Zeitung*, 81 (1930), pp. 123–125.

Reinhardt, D., *Von der Reklame zum Marketing: Geschichte der Wirtschaftswerbung in Deutschland*. Berlin: Akademie-Verlag, 1993.

Strizhakova, Y., and Coulter, R., 'Consumer cultural identity: local and global cultural identities and measurement implications', *International Marketing Review*, 36 (2019), pp. 610–627.

Stucki, L., *Das heimliche Imperium. Wie die Schweiz reich wurde*. Bern: Scherz, 1968.

Umbach, M., 'Made in Germany', in François, E., and Schulze, H. (eds.), *Deutsche Erinnerungsorte*, vol. 2. München: Beck, 2001, pp. 405–418.

Viktorin, C., Gienow-Hecht, J.C.E., Estner, A., and Will, M.K. (eds.), *Nation Branding in Modern History*. New York: Berghahn, 2018.

World Trade Report. Geneva: World Trade Organization, 2007.

Zimbler, O., 'Entwurf für ein Verbandsmarkengesetz', *Juristische Blätter*, 58 (1929), pp. 386–388.

5 The long life of 'Swedish quality'

Promoting exports and keeping Swedes competitive, c. 1900–1990s[1]

Nikolas Glover

Introduction

In 1928, the Swedish Minister for Commerce, Felix Hamrin, informed international visitors to the Swedish Industries Fair in Gothenburg that 'Wherever there is a demand for goods of high quality there is no doubt but that the Swedish products will come to their own'. In Hamrin's opinion, Swedish producers of matches, ball bearings, and telephone apparatus, 'represent the most typical characteristics of Swedish industry: genuineness and a continuous endeavour to accomplish the best and most durable which is possible at present'.[2] The Minister's dual claims were that Swedish products were characterised by their quality *and* that producing quality products was typically Swedish. Variations of this proposition were repeated throughout the twentieth century. For example, in 1965, it was claimed, 'Next time you consider accepting a concept or buying a product you'll ask yourself if it's the best. If it is, Swedish skill probably played a major role in creating it. And that's your assurance of top value'.[3] Similarly, during the World's Fair in Seville, in 1992, the official magazine distributed by the Swedish Trade Council was entitled *Made in Sweden*, because 'Made in Sweden has always had a special meaning for Swedes, who understand that quality is the very heart and soul of a nation of traders'.[4]

This chapter takes as its point of departure that 'quality' was a persistent value used to promote Made in Sweden throughout the twentieth century. Inspired by Oliver Kühschelm's work on the 'nationalisation of product communication', it sets out to analyse this *nationalisation of quality* in Swedish policy initiatives and export promotions.[5] It traces how that process was shaped by the interplay between two analytically distinct, but closely related components. On the one hand, it explains how the changing structure of the economy and consequent shifting of 'flagship' export industries over the course of the twentieth century shaped the domestic construction of Swedish national identity. On the other hand, it elucidates how a series of collective, export-promotion initiatives endeavoured to define and promote Made in Sweden, and imbue it with marketing value. By tracing these parallel

DOI: 10.4324/9781003166184-5

processes, the chapter shows how different notions of 'Swedishness' and definitions of 'quality' over time led to 'Swedish quality' becoming intergral to the value of Made in Sweden.

Per Hansen argued that brand management depends not only on corporate brands but, 'also on the nation image of the brand's home country and on the cultural context of foreign consumers'.[6] This chapter's focus on collective narratives about Swedish quality, rather than claims made by specific firms, is in line with Hansen's argument. However, instead of focusing on the cultural context of foreign consumers, the analysis here is concerned with the cultural contexts in which domestic producers and promoters defined and projected what Hansen calls 'the nation image' of Sweden.

Adopting such a focus, this contribution heeds Stefan Berger's appeal to economic historians to study the place of market processes in historical articulations of nationalism and national identity.[7] Indeed, previous research suggested that an emphasis on quality was a crucial component in the formation of Swedish consumer society. In a study of public debates about mass culture in Sweden, Orsi Husz argued that quality, 'should be seen as a key concept in the attempts at shaping and reinterpreting mass consumerism in order to make it compatible with … the emerging Swedish welfare state'. Husz viewed the Swedish 'obsession with quality' as a means of coupling mass culture with democratic popular culture: 'the issue of quality was turned into a way of moralising about, or taming and reforming mass (consumer) culture'.[8]

'Quality' is a notoriously elusive concept.[9] Husz' analysis demonstrates that its meaning evolved over time in Swedish debates. Husz shows that the original descriptive meaning, which referred to the different *qualities*, or characteristics of things, was increasingly supplanted by a normative meaning, referring to a degree of excellence. Husz also identified another shift in how the concept was used: from alluding to the objective characteristics of durability and level of craftsmanship, to including subjective, relational dimensions such as customer satisfaction, and emotional attachment.[10] These trajectories mirror definitions of quality that evolved simultaneously within the professional field of quality management over the twentieth century.[11] The present chapter shows how business organisations, exporters, and advertisers adapted the slogan of 'Swedish quality' accordingly.

The rest of this chapter is organised as follows. The next section establishes how the notion of Swedish quality became attached to Made in Sweden as the country became an industrial society, with the rise to prominence of a number of successful manufacturers. The discourse alluded to both the characteristics of the raw materials and the ascribed national technical genius of company founders. The following section deals with how the understanding of Swedish quality shifted in the post-war era, as exports of consumer products grew in importance. 'Quality' was now the product of efficient organisation rather than natural endowment, while essentialist notions of Swedishness became less pronounced, and were rather linked to the modern, welfare-capitalist society. The penultimate section shows how accelerated globalisation beginning in the 1970s led to yet another shift: While 'quality' became the object of international standardisation and management trends, Swedishness was adopted as a corporate brand that could enhance the competitiveness of the Swedish economy. Conclusions are then presented.

The breakthrough of industrial society: establishing the concept

Sweden's economic growth accelerated in the 1890s, and for the next 60 years, it would remain among the highest in the industrialised world. This leap was largely based on advanced engineering.[12] Between 1890 and 1930, the composition of Swedish exports changed substantially. The share of timber and food, once dominant, declined by 50%, while manufacturing, including pulp and paper, grew in importance. Thus, the share of exports accounted for by engineering increased from 1–2% at the beginning of the period, to around 10% by 1930.[13] Inventions, or refinements of new developments in the mechanical and motor engineering industries, enabled several Swedish manufacturers, which included ASEA (electrical engineering), AGA (machinery and appliances), LM Ericsson (telephone systems), Separator (machinery), and SKF (ball bearings), to become leaders in their respective industries – positions which they maintained for more than half a century. All of these companies were associated with Swedish innovators.[14] Their technical genius and practical mindset established them as public heroes in nationalist myth; they were hailed as the founders of modern Sweden.[15]

As Liz Moor observed, the creation of values associated with mass-produced, branded products that began during the first half of the twentieth century, was intimately connected with the forging of links between brands and national projects.[16] Against this background, the concept of Swedish quality became predominantly associated with two national traits. The first referred to the unique characteristics of Swedish raw materials: the origin of Sweden's propensity to produce quality goods was traced to the centuries-long tradition of iron production, and then steel manufacture.[17] Swedish steel, it was argued, was widely recognised to be of exceptional quality, when measured against objective criteria, such as strength and durability. [18] This focus on raw materials was evident in 1944 when the Swedish General Export Association (hereafter, Export Association) and the Stockholm branch of the Swedish Advertising Federation jointly arranged a poster competition for Made in Sweden. Virtually all of the contributions played on the quality of timber and steel; the winning entry included the literal caption 'Swedish steel bites' which appeared between the open tips of a heavy-duty bolt cutter.[19] Making such direct links between Sweden's natural resources and the industrial products manufactured with them, was a recurring theme. It was claimed that Swedish separators, generators, ball bearings, and telephone exchanges manufactured with Swedish materials, were making the nation universally famous as its exports peacefully 'conquered the world'.[20]

Second, the quality of Swedish products was commonly associated with the national genius they embodied. The fact that the most dynamic industries depended on technical solutions produced by Swedish inventors significantly shaped the Swedish nationalist narrative: It was claimed that the Swedes were particularly adept at mechanical inquiry and technical invention.[21] Consequently, it was the mechanical industries that ensured Made in Sweden became 'an international stamp of quality'.[22] Such culturally orientated representations of Swedish enterprise were documented in the marketing materials of the Export Association, which was dominated by firms in the ascendant engineering industry. In 1912, a publication marking the Association's first 25 years 'quite impartially' (in its own words) observed that it was, 'mainly Swedish engineers and technicians … that have created Sweden's modern export industry as well as its successful commercial exploitation in foreign countries'.[23] References to Swedes' inventive genius, and their technical bent appeared in the Association's publications aimed at foreign customers.[24] The Conservative statistician and MP, Gustaf Sundbärg, claimed in 1911 that, because of their national psyche, Swedes were completely uninterested in the thoughts and emotions of their fellow humans. Consequently, they were 'unwilling to compete with foreigners' and were inadequate at 'carefully calculated economic dealings', and 'convincing and persuading others'.[25] The upside to this apparent deficiency was that the Swedes conveyed their technical skills via the products they manufactured. Effectively, Swedish products were so good that they sold themselves. It was in this spirit that Minister Hamrin referred to the 'genuineness' of Swedish products. Similarly, international merchants visiting the Swedish Industries Fair in 1929, were informed that it was the Swedes' 'predilection for genuine, *honest* goods', and their technical skills that had, 'made high quality a trade mark of industrial products'.[26]

Drawing on claims about the uniqueness of Swedish raw materials, and national character, the patriotic myths that surrounded Swedish quality during the early twentieth century were translated into commercial presentations for foreign customers:[27]

> The Swedish engineers are admittedly very efficient in their profession, and the Swedish mechanics rank as highly skilled in their trades to which they bring an unrivalled sence [sic] of accuracy and conscientiousness. This personal equation in conjunction with excellent raw materials has resulted in high class products, and it safe to say that Swedish goods in general are sold on their reputation for high quality alone.[28]

Such claims to high quality, and others made by ministers and businessmen, were never substantiated or questioned: Swedish companies manufactured quality products *because* they were Swedish. The advertising industry played a part in formulating and projecting these patriotic truisms in national campaigns, exhibitions, and 'Swedish weeks'. As Elin Åström Rudberg argued, 'the combination of the nationalistic movement and a strong belief among advertising professionals that advertising (and thus also brands) was a crucial component in a market society makes it understandable that the advertising agencies drew the conclusion that national brands must be beneficial for Sweden'.[29] However, it was not until the post-1945 period that the advertising industry played a more active role in the overseas promotion of 'Swedish quality'.[30]

The Golden Age of industrial society: marketing the concept

After 1945, Swedish quality began to be associated with social, rather than natural factors. This change mirrored the shifting composition of exports and the simultaneous professionalisation of export promotion.[31] During the 1950s and 1960s, engineering products became increasingly important in Swedish exports: They doubled their share, and accounted for more than 40% by the early 1970s. In the same period, motor vehicles became the single most important exported product.[32] This expanding segment of technically advanced consumer-oriented goods included cars (Volvo and Saab), mechanical office appliances (Addo/Facit), cameras (Hasselblad), and kitchen appliances (Electrolux). Several of these brands referenced their Swedishness when marketed abroad, which reaffirmed the established association between Sweden and advanced engineering, technical precision, and reliability.[33]

Increasingly, quality was attributed to the rational organisation of Swedish manufacturing, rather than Sweden's natural resources.[34] According to the Swedish president of the European Advertising Association, foreign experts agreed that Swedes had 'a way of getting things organized more thoroughly and sensibly than most other people. And frequently a lot faster'.[35] This conceptualisation of quality as the outcome of efficient organisational capabilities did not utilise national-psychological traits but drew on the economic theory of comparative advantage.[36] The Stockholm Chamber of Commerce confidently declared that Made in Sweden was 'a symbol of quality' because 'quality products find markets everywhere'.[37] Sweden's limited domestic market meant it was imperative that its manufacturers competed in international 'buyer's markets' even though their prices were often considerably higher than those of competitors. Other reports concluded that Swedish manufacturers were, 'doomed to produce quality goods'.[38] Because Swedish products were successful, *ipso facto*, they were high quality.

In the competitive trading environment from the 1960s, it was the moral duty of exporters to overcome the national traits once described by Sundbärg. Because good customer relations are indispensable to export success, it was crucial that potential buyers were actively alerted to the quality of Swedish products. Hans Swedberg, of the Export Association, observed that the 'practical English' possessed a unique capacity to handle people: by observing the motto 'enterprise is fiction in action', the English were able to build good business relationships.[39] Swedberg proclaimed that in the new world of competition, the Swedes' lack of insight into the psychology of others was unacceptable.[40] On the basis of interviews with commercial representatives, one trade journal in 1949 reported that Swedish businessmen needed to be absolutely resolute if they wished to overcome their 'psychological limitations'. This journal issued 'ten commandments' to Swedish exporters that included: 'Thou shalt pay attention to quality, the finest argument in favour of Swedish exports', and 'Thou shalt adapt to the market, even if it requires a certain reorganisation'.[41] Swedish products might be globally respected, declared one exporter, but that was not sufficient: 'the most important thing is that we also can SELL them – FAST, OFTEN and with MINIMAL EXPENSE!'[42] Whereas Sundbärg considered Swedish reticence indicative of laudable 'honesty', it was now portrayed as an example of immoral passivity in the face of fierce competition.

As quality became defined in terms of competitive organisation, natural links to the specific Swedishness of products became weaker. Theoretically, efficient organisations anywhere on the globe could deliver quality. Balancing economic theory with claims for a unique national character presented a challenge for the expanding advertising industry. With the right branding, customers could learn (not to forget) that Swedish products were not only of high quality but uniquely so, precisely because they were Swedish. Lars Ekengren of the Advertising Agency AB Svenska Telegrambyrån, proposed the introduction of the trade mark 'Swedish Quality' (Figure 5.1). This trade mark was to verify that *any* export product was of a specified, government-guaranteed, *Swedish* high standard.[43] Ekengren's grand vision was not realised, but the notion of a single brand representing Swedish quality continued.

Figure 5.1 'Swedish quality': Proposed government-controlled guarantee for exports

Source: Lars Ekegren, "Svenskt kvalitetsmärke för export?", *Den svenska marknaden,* 5 (1949), p. 176. Artist unknown. Reproduction: Lina Löfström Baker, The Royal Library (Stockholm).

Note: Every effort has been made to trace the copyright holders; apologies are offered for any omission, and the publisher will be pleased to add any necessary acknowledgement in subsequent editions.

In 1953, the Swedish Advertisers' Association invited William Honneus, former chair of The International Advertising Association, to give a lecture. Honneus argued that through their overseas advertisements, US companies often sought to sell ideas, rather than individual products *per se*. By 'exciting the imagination' of foreign consumers, they created and expanded their markets.[44] This reasoning resurfaced when a group of Swedish advertising managers drew up plans for co-ordinated export advertising by Swedish exporters.[45] One conclusion they reached was:

> most products that are being manufactured or will be manufactured in Sweden can be produced in other countries, probably as well and at comparable prices ... Undocumented, spontaneously voiced statements about Swedish quality etc. we thus do not see as appropriate, especially not since the word 'quality' has been worn down and lost much of its original meaning.[46]

This statement signalled a significant deviation from the received view. This group determined that they should focus on attaching meaning to Swedish products by which a personal bond would be formed with customers: marketing campaigns should first and foremost be angled towards the emotional value of "Sweden".[47]

Consequently, in 1958, an export symbol was introduced: it consisted of a stylised Viking ship with an 'S' as a sail and the word 'Sweden' on its side. Later, the slogan 'Where Quality is Tradition' was added to the symbol.[48] Appealing to consumers' emotions was not new, but the explicit way it was discussed in relation to Sweden, and Swedish products, deviated from earlier debates. There was a clear difference between Ekengren's proposition in 1948, and the export symbol: the former sought to objectively guarantee Swedish quality, whereas the 1958 initiative utilised brand value. Nonetheless, the export symbol did not represent a clean break from the past: Even if Swedish quality was no longer conceived as a measurable characteristic, it is unclear to what extent its ascribed 'emotional value' extended beyond Sweden's borders.[49] Although well-received within Swedish advertising circles, there is little evidence that consumers naturally responded to the link between Sweden, quality, and Vikings. Although the intention was to actively replace nineteenth-century nationalist discourses with professional advertising know-how, the two in fact remained closely entwined.

In the post-1945 era of global economic growth, the production of quality goods and their active marketing were claimed to be inseparable.[50] Rather than providing patriotic evidence of the nation's essential greatness, Swedish quality now represented the country's modern, capitalist credentials: efficient, dynamic, and market-oriented. References to the quality of Swedish raw materials and national technical genius continued – but as deftly integrated components in outwardly-directed promotion campaigns. Simultaneously, the traditional emphasis on the objective quality of Swedish manufacturing, and the newer appeal of quality as an emotional value remained juxtaposed, though not always in harmony. In 1967, for instance, a new Volvo assembly plant was to be inaugurated in Malaysia. The Export Association instructed the local Swedish Trade Commissioner to organise a commercial 'Sweden-manifestation' with a display of products bearing the motto, 'quality products of modern Swedish engineering'. The Commissioner, with a background in export management at Facit-Addo, dissented. A 'new national profile' would introduce Swedish consumer goods, and lifestyle products to the expanding middle classes in Singapore and Malaysia: 'Why not for once abandon all the reasoning about Swedish quality, Swedish engineering etc. and instead use *softer strings*?' The Commissioner proposed a department store campaign for Swedish products with the slogan 'Enjoy Swedish Lazy Living'.[51] These proposals resulted in conflict with the Export Association's offices in Stockholm. Any attempt to associate Swedes with laziness was unacceptable, 'out of consideration for the [general] opinion at home. Unfortunately it is the case that one often must adapt to it, and describing a Swede as lazy is worse than blasphemy'.[52] In its view, the technical pledge of 'quality products' was an acceptable slogan for promoting Sweden, but not the emotive 'quality of life'.

Adapting to globalization: recalling the concept

In the 1970s, Sweden's growth rate slowed, and its GDP per capita decreased markedly when compared with international levels. Lennart Schön claimed that by the 1980s, Sweden had lost its position as 'a first-rank industrial country'.[53] The traditional core of the economy was severely affected by decreased global demand and increased competition from low-wage countries. Contemporaneously, industrialists declared that Sweden had become a 'cross-national society', which was heading towards a 'multinational future'.[54] As early as the 1940s, the marketing departments belonging to the foreign subsidiaries of major Swedish manufacturers were largely autonomous from company headquarters in Stockholm,[55] but it was in the 1960s and 1970s that the internationalization processes accelerated. By 1985, Volvo, Sandvik, Electrolux, and Saab-Scania could be described as 'international marketing organisations with a specialised range of products'.[56] The Swedishness of their products, and therefore their inherent quality, was becoming less obvious.[57]

The decline of the 'Swedish model', and growing multinational activity by Swedish firms reduced the appeal of adopting a shared national slogan. The trade press reported that 'Swedish quality was no longer unique'.[58] In public debates, Made in Sweden was referred to in the past tense; this legend had lost its sales value.[59] Even the Swedish King admonished the export industry: 'The expression "Made in Sweden" is unfortunately stuck in the 1950s, [it is] a remnant from when Swedish products practically sold themselves'.[60] The general sense of demoralisation was palpable; the confidence of the 1960s had dissipated. In 1986, a report by the Royal Swedish Academy of Engineering Sciences declared that there was little value in using Made in Sweden as a brand, because:

> We have been able to establish that there is a significant identity problem for Swedish industrial companies in several markets. … Others have even researched what is known about Sweden abroad. The results of these studies quite clearly show that such knowledge is very limited. In the case people do know about Sweden, perceptions are not necessarily only positive. Using what in these cases is obviously a value-charged concept is thus a risk that most international companies will not be willing to take.[61]

At this point, Made in Sweden as an imprimatur of quality had to be reinvented to incorporate the growing importance of the tertiary sector.[62] In 1986, the National Committee for Swedish Quality, a corporatist initiative which comprised government, trades unions, and employer representatives, was founded, and the same year it launched a National Quality Offensive, using the legend 'Swedish Quality – the Right Way' (Figure 5.2). This campaign was designed to raise general awareness of the importance of Swedish quality – which provided the country with 'a traditional competitive advantage'.

According to the Committee:

> If our rate of improvement is lower than our competitors', we will lag behind. If it instead is higher, our competitiveness will be strengthened. That is the objective. … The demands of quality therefore affect all businesses and the whole public sector.[63]

Figure 5.2 'Swedish quality – the right way', symbol of the National Quality Offensive organised by the National Committee for Swedish Quality

Source: Nationalkommittén för svensk kvalitet, *Svensk kvalitet - rätt sätt* (Stockholm, 1986). Reproduction: Anna Guldager, The Royal Library (Stockholm).

Note: Every effort has been made to trace the copyright holders; apologies are offered for any omission, and the publisher will be pleased to add any necessary acknowledgement in subsequent editions.

In this campaign, quality was presented as being essential not only for manufacturing but also services. Importantly, the level of quality could not be determined without taking into account the cost of production and the expectations of customers.[64] The Swedish high-street fashion chains, Hennes & Mauritz, and Lindex, adopted these criteria when they began expanding abroad. Their business models were the antithesis of promising durability: instead, they offered 'the latest fashion at low prices at an *acceptable* quality', and no claim was made that the garments were produced in Sweden.[65] Similarly, IKEA, the rapidly expanding furniture store, sold products of *the right* quality; prices should not be dissociated from what customers were willing to pay. In 1984, this company stated: 'Our aim is not to increase the quality of individual products but to limit the number of deviations from our *kvalitetsnorm* [quality norm]'.[66] In contrast to the previous era, 'too much' quality was now defined as a problem. From 1992, the foreword to the book *Quality: Made in Sweden*, underlined this relativistic interpretation: quality 'is judged by how a product is described and how this description is interpreted'.[67]

In the early 1990s, the economy experienced a severe recession which prompted further enquiries into 'quality'. The Swedish Institute for Quality, a national centre for business excellence founded in 1990, announced that quality management was not merely a project but a continuous process: 'Only then can we once again be world class. Only then will we reclaim our most effective competitive edge: Swedish quality'.[68] This aim, similar to the 1986 National Quality Offensive, sought to inject the corporate mindset of quality management into Swedish society as a whole: 'The concept of quality and its applications are of great importance for the development of quality on a national level'.[69] Aligning businesses, civic organisations, and public agencies behind a shared value of 'quality', coincided with an all-encompassing understanding of brands and corporate values that emerged in the 1990s.[70] In mature capitalist economies, 'a previously diffuse set of practices – product design, retail design, point-of-purchase marketing, among others – became consolidated into an integrated approach to marketing and business strategy known as branding'.[71] This holistic strategic approach was increasingly applied to all types of organisation – not only businesses – and it could even be used by entire nations.[72]

It was against the ever-broadening application of branding throughout society that the commercial value of Swedishness was revived in the last decades of the twentieth century. The free-market Think Tank, Timbro, published a book which called on firms and agencies to use 'Swedishness' as a corporate strategy.[73] The author of this book distilled and evaluated the essential traits of the Swedish national psyche in a way that bore a clear resemblance to Sundbärg's approach. Later, marketing entrepreneurs launched 'Sweden brands' that could be used by companies, and even government bodies in their overseas promotions. In 1992, one PR consultant created the logo 'Natural Sweden', which fused nineteenth-century natural romanticism with the 'softer strings' suggested in the 1960s. Illustrated by a green wave, the logo was submitted to the Tourist Council, Swedish Trade Council, and Ministry for Foreign Affairs, with the claim that:

> Once 'Made in Sweden' stood for unique quality. That is no longer the case. But Sweden is one of Europe's last wildernesses, Europe's green corner … Swedish business has a great opportunity to profile itself with 'natural' arguments.[74]

A few months later, a competing initiative – 'Qualities of Sweden' – was launched in which the Viking ship was once again used as the main motif. The intention was that an organisation would be created to hold the rights to the brand, which would be available on subscription to 'Swedish industry, trade unions, cultural organisations and sports associations'.[75] The promoters of this initiative feared that Sweden's image as a 'quality-leading pioneer' was being erased, and that, 'Sweden and its different qualities have to be impressed on all international investors if we are not to become completely forgotten'.[76] Although Natural Sweden, and Qualities of Sweden, were never adopted, both projects indicated how 'Swedish quality' remained a potent concept in the face of far-reaching economic change.

During the 1980s and 1990s, quality was standardised and relativised. On the one hand, the widespread adoption of ISO certification reduced quality to a number of technical, measurable criteria, independent of the type of organisation (firm or public agency), or the product (manufacture, or service). On the other hand, customer satisfaction and the 'right price' were fully integrated into the definition of quality, which fundamentally challenged the concept of 'absolute' or inherent quality. Durable components and rational organisation did not represent quality; this could only be affirmed by satisfied customers. Since both standardisation and relativisation decouple 'quality' from the national origin, the communication industry sensed a market opportunity: initiatives such as 'Natural Sweden', and 'Qualities of Sweden' were attempts to define and market the brand value of 'Swedishness'.[77] The most striking example of this development was IKEA. In the early 1980s, when Swedish companies seemed to be abandoning Made in Sweden, IKEA introduced its blue and yellow logo, and its entire corporate identity was rebranded as quintessentially Swedish.[78] In this case, the claim being made was not that the products were made in Sweden, but that the firm's values and its products represented *what had come to be seen* as Swedish: democratic, innovative, and rational. In its promotional materials, this multinational company explicitly fused these established cultural and political narratives to explain the specific Swedishness of its range of globally sourced products:

> Swedish and Scandinavian design have been famous ever since the beginning of the twentieth century. The Swedish model has also become synonymous with good value, functionality and quality together with an ambition to achieve widespread accessibility.[79]

By the end of the twentieth century, the long history of marketing narratives surrounding Sweden and its products provided a ready-made package of distinct associations for marketing consultants and branding agencies, irrespective of whether they were contracted by global companies such as IKEA or Volvo, or by government departments including the Swedish Foreign Service and the Ministry for Trade.[80]

Conclusion

The concept of Swedish quality was first attached to Made in Sweden during the first decades of the 1900s. Embedded in broader nationalist narratives of Swedish engineering greatness, Swedish quality offered a conceptual link between the emerging industrial economy and established narratives of national character and natural geography: Technically gifted, honest Swedes were conquering the world with their quality products derived from the nation's natural resources.

In the decades after 1945, this narrative was subtly revised, adapted, and marketed by advertising specialists. In this period, Swedish quality represented the outcome of organised, efficient Swedish industrial society, and was proof of the nation's ability to compete in world markets. 'Quality' was not merely an objective characteristic of Swedish products, but it was also identified as a unique selling point that needed to be actively promoted. Following the economic downturn of the 1970s, Swedish quality was simultaneously declared dead and used as a domestic rallying cry to revive past glories. As the internationalization of Swedish firms intensified, and quality control and quality management became increasingly professionalized, links to specific Swedish conditions were irrevocably severed. Simultaneously, marketing consultants, trade organisations, and government bodies rediscovered and revived the concept of Swedish quality for specific purposes. By such means, nineteenth-century essentialist narratives of the Swedish national character became newly relevant. Consonant with the worldview promoted in Michael Porter's *The Competitive Advantage of Nations,* nationalising quality was a means for Sweden to promote its economic prosperity in an era of global competition.[81]

From one perspective, the history of collectively promoting Made in Sweden is a history of failures. The Viking ship logo introduced in 1958 was used by some firms, and trade commissioner offices for a few years, but then seems to have disappeared. Ekengren's vision of a 'Swedish quality trade mark', and the project 'Swedish qualities', never became ascendant. The ambitious, government-backed National Quality Offensive in 1986 – 'Swedish Quality – the right way' – left few traces. However, the fact that 'Swedish quality' kept resurfacing, strengthens the argument that it is an articulation of a broader national narrative which has mobilised varying coalitions of Swedish advertisers, exporters, public authorities, and trade unions to the nation's service.

In Peter Katzenstein's seminal comparative study of the industrial policy of Western European countries, Sweden belonged to the group characterised by 'small state democratic corporatism'. Such countries effected policies of trade openness and international liberalisation, and their centralised corporatist institutions allowed economic flexibility and provided democratic legitimacy.[82] As noted by other scholars, this institutional capacity to deal with economic exposure was often based on a strong sense of national identity.[83] Political and economic elites tended to frame the need to adapt and respond to structural change as a *national* challenge, as they mediated the shifting contours of international markets to employers, workers, and government bodies.[84] Consequently, the lesson that national economic interests are best served by being internationally competitive, 'has been easy to teach and learn.'[85] The history of collective initiatives to promote Made in Sweden can be viewed as integral to that institutionalised pedagogical project. Whatever their short-term effects on export sales, these initiatives served the long-term purpose of sustaining awareness among industrialists, businesses, trades unions, and the broader public, of the imperative to remain internationally competitive. The cultural debates about quality that Husz analysed concerned the relationship between mass consumption and democracy. In contrast, the history of 'Swedish quality' discussed in this chapter concerns the capitalist logic sustaining this national 'obsession'.

The historical trajectory of the elusive but potent notion of Swedish quality draws attention to the dynamic nature of national narratives which imbue 'Made in' with meaning. In the process of cobranding nations and products, it might seem intuitive to view the latter as variable, and the former as constant: different products, the same national stereotypes. However, this chapter suggests that these roles may be reversed. Sectoral changes in the national economy determined which industries were the most visibly successful: first steel, then motor cars and advanced consumer durables, and, finally, flatpack furniture. Such developments affected the collective identity of the nation. For a small, open economy, such as Sweden, the national 'us' was constantly being negotiated in relation to foreign opinions and external interactions, many of which were commercial. If a significant number of producers and advertisers use national narratives to brand products, this can lead to a reinterpretation and reformulation of these narratives within society.

Notes

1 This research was funded by Jan Wallander och Tom Hedelius stiftelse, project 2016-0044:1.
2 'Swedish Export Industries', *Svenska Varor,* 3 (1928), p. 3.
3 'Who can match the Swedes for good ideas?' Full page advertisement published in the journals, *Business Week, Fortune, Saturday Review,* and *Time* in 1965, as part of the three-year Swedish export-promotion campaign, *Meet Modern Sweden,* aimed at the US market (undated in the archives). The Swedish National

Archives (Riksarkivet, RA), The Swedish-American News Exchange (Svensk-amerikanska nyhetsbyrån).
4 The Swedish Trade Council, *Made in Sweden* (1992), p. 3.
5 Kühschelm, 'Nationalizing consumption', pp. 166–167.
6 Hansen, 'Co-branding', p. 80.
7 Berger, 'Historians, nationalism', p. 37.
8 Husz, 'The morality', p. 179.
9 See, for example, Strannegård (ed.), *Den omätbara kvaliteten*; Berg, 'Why quality'.
10 These subjective/objective dimensions of the meaning of 'quality' were recognised by Shewhart, *Economic Control*, p. 53. See also, Garmin, 'What does'.
11 For an overview of the historical paradigms of quality management, see Weckenmann, Akkasoglu and Werner, 'Quality management', pp. 281–293.
12 Schön, *An Economic History*, p. 147.
13 Schön, *An Economic History*, p. 147.
14 Schön, *An Economic History*, p. 134.
15 Bergwik et al., 'Inledning', p. 15.
16 Moor, *The Rise*, p. 19.
17 On the long history of marking the origin of Swedish steel, see Evans and Rydén, 'Iron marks'.
18 For example, 'Något om utvecklingen av svensk järn- och stålexport under de senaste 50 åren, and 'Svensk bilexport', both in the jubilee publication The General Export Association of Sweden, *Svensk Exports jubileumsnummer*, pp. 69, 98; The General Export Association of Sweden; *What Sweden*, p. 19; 'Sweden as a steel producer', *Swedish Export*, February (1922), p. 17.
19 '267 affischer "Made in Sweden"', *Svenska Dagbladet* 3 June 1944, p. 9. In fact, the alloying metals necessary to produce quality Swedish steel were sourced from abroad. Vikström, Högselius, and Avango, 'Swedish steel'.
20 De Geer, *Sveriges*, pp. 7–8.
21 Bergwik et al., 'Inledning', p. 9.
22 Advertisement for Skandinaviska Banken, *Aftonbladet*, 29 December 1941, p. 5.
23 The General Export Association of Sweden, *Sveriges Allmänna Exportförening 1887–1912*, p. 17.
24 On the firms dominating the Association, see affiliations of board members listed in The General Export Association of Sweden, *Svensk Exports jubileumsnummer*, pp. 7–9; The General Export Association of Sweden, *Industrial Sweden*, p. xxiv; The General Export Association of Sweden, *What Sweden*, pp. 19, 23.
25 Sundbärg, *Det svenska,* pp. 81, 84.
26 'Sweden on the World Market', *Svenska Varor*, 3 (1929), p. 3.
27 For example, the representations of Sweden in four different languages that appeared in the annual *exportnummer* ('special export issues') of the trade journal *Svenska varor*, produced each year for the Swedish Industries Fair in Gothenburg in the 1920s and 1930s.
28 The General Export Association, *Svensk industri-*, p. 28; Houltz, 'Myten', pp. 138–139.
29 Rudberg, 'Selling', p. 499.
30 This process began in the context of the Swedish pavilions of the World's Fairs immediately prior to the Second World War. See Glover and Hellenes, '"A Swedish offensive"'.
31 Funke, 'Business associations'.
32 Schön, *An Economic History*, p. 242.
33 For examples, see Addo's magazine *Figures: House Magazine of Addo* (1951–1965). Also, 'Volvo means products of superb Swedish engineering', which appeared on

the back of *Volvorama 1958* (1958), a magazine published by The Volvo Group. Both promotional publications were aimed at the US market.

34 AB Svenska Telegrambyrån, *Att sälja*, p. 3. See also 'Exportförsäljningen i brännpunkten', *Svensk utrikeshandel*, 16 (1951), p. 12.

35 Cited in the special English-language issue of the advertising journal *Den svenska marknaden: kvartalstidskrift,* 'Key words in Sweden: Practical organization', *The Swedish Market 1966–1967*, p. 5.

36 Maze, *Creative*, pp. 63–65.

37 Stockholm Chamber of Commerce, *Invest in Sweden*; The General Export Association of Sweden, *What Sweden Can Do*, p. 19.

38 'Skjuter på reklamchefen', *Industria*, 7–8 (1954), p. 59.

39 'Några praktiska exportsynpunkter', *Svensk utrikeshandel*, 16 (1951), p. 11.

40 'Exportförsäljningen i brännpunkten', *Svensk utrikeshandel*, 11 (1952), p. 13.

41 'Budord för exportörer', *Industria*, 4 (1949), pp. 28–29.

42 'Hur går det med exportutbildningen?', *Svensk Export*, 2 (1961), p. 8.

43 'Svenskt kvalitetsmärke för export?' *Den svenska marknaden*, 3 (1949), pp. 175–178.

44 'Annonsörkväll med exportprogram', *Annonsören*, 8 (1953), p. 23.

45 'Sverigereklam', *Info*, 6 (1957), p. 31.

46 'Förslag till Sverige-propaganda', 14 October 1957, Archives of *Annonsörföreningen* (the Advertisers' Association), Stockholm. On this group, and its report, see Funke, 'Business Associations', pp. 16–17.

47 'Förslag till Sverige-propaganda', p. 2; p. 7. See also 'Svensk exportreklam och turistpropaganda går hand i hand', *Info*, 10 (1956), p. 23.

48 Funke, 'Business associations', p. 19.

49 US perceptions of Swedish quality products are reported by Reierson, 'Are Foreign Products', pp. 33–40.

50 See 'Kvalitetsbegreppet – inget svenskt monopol' and 'Kvalitet säljer kvantitet', *Svensk Export*, 2 (1970), pp. 3–5, 6.

51 Wellfelt to Zarelius, 17 March 1967, The Swedish National Archives (Riksarkivet, Arninge, RA), The General Swedish Export Assocation (Sveriges Allmänna Exportförening, SAE), Series F1J, vol. 42.

52 Palm to Wellfelt, 19 May, 1967, RA, SAE, FIJ:42.

53 Schön, *An Economic History*, p. 300.

54 'Morgondagens Sverige – det tvärnationella samhället', *Svensk Export*, 13 (1970), pp. 2–3; 'Vår multinationella', *Vår industri*, 9 (1976), pp. 17–19.

55 Minutes from the meeting of "exportreklamkommittén", 12 April 1945. RA, Svenska annonsörers förenings arkiv, Series F9, vol. 8.

56 Eliasson, *De svenska*, p. 51; Andersson, Fredriksson and Svensson, *Multinational Restructuring.*

57 'Handeln köper svenskt om det är bäst', *Köpmannen*, 41 (1980), p. 1.

58 'Inga genvägar till framgång', *Dagens industri*, 2 March 1978, p. 22. See also 'Allt färre fördelar minskar er mark', *Dagens industri*, 3 November 1977, p. 8.

59 'Blågule säljarens misstag: locka med "svensk kvalitet"' , *Veckans affärer*, 8 January 1976, p. 39.

60 'Kungen om exportindustrin: Svenska företag, ta er i kragen!', *Expressen*, 6 March 1981, p. 7. See also 'Nu satsar företagen på reklam för industriprodukter', *Dagens industri*, 2 April 1981, p. 13.

61 The Royal Swedish Academy of Engineering Sciences, *IVA om design*, pp. 76–77.

62 For an explicit attempt to broaden the concept of quality, see 'Svensk kampanj i Holland för att sälja på säkerhet', *Dagens industri*, 16 September 1982, p. 10.

63 Nationalkommittén för svensk kvalitet, *Svensk kvalitet*, p. 7.

64 Nationalkommittén för svensk kvalitet, *Svensk kvalitet*, p. 2.

65 'Detaljhandel över gränserna', *Affärsvärlden*, 22–23 (1985), p. 15. Italics added.

66 'Våra ambitioner har en prislapp', *Tomorrow*, 1 (1984), p. 8; 'We are to avoid "over-quality" [överkvalitet]", according to IKEA's internal quality management guidelines *Kvalitetssäkring*, undated, ca 1985, unpaginated. Accessed at the Royal Library, Stockholm, collection of varia (*vardagstryck*).
67 Hedin, *Quality*, p. 5.
68 'Svensk kvalitet skall bli världsklass!', back page of supplement for 'World Quality Day 1991' in *Dagens industri*, 14 November, 1991.
69 Hedin, *Quality*, p. 9.
70 Broberg, Gianneschi and Jonsson, *Svensk reklam*, pp. 144–148.
71 Moor, *The Rise*, p. 3.
72 Aronczyk, *Branding the Nation*, chap. 2.
73 Laine-Svejdby, *Svenskhet*. See also Hellenes, *Fabricating*, pp. 306–311.
74 'Symbolskiftet', *Dagens industri*, 12 January 1992, p. 40.
75 'Ett skepp kommer lastat med Sverige', *Svenska dagbladet*, 16 March 1992, p. 2.
76 'Ett skepp kommer lastat med Sverige', *Svenska dagbladet*, 16 March 1992, p. 2.
77 For a case study on how international PR framed multinational firms as 'Swedish' during this era, see Glover, 'Marketing'.
78 Kristoffersson, *Design by IKEA*, p. 67.
79 Marketing material from 1994, cited in Kristoffersson, *Design by IKEA*, p. 67.
80 Kristoffersson, *Design by IKEA*, pp. 84–87; Glover, 'Marketing', pp. 41–65; Hellenes 'New Gustavians', pp. 90–113.
81 Porter, *The Competitive*. Porter's influence on the history of nation branding is discussed in Aronczyk, Branding, pp. 43–47.
82 Katzenstein, *Small States*.
83 Campbell and Hall, 'National identity', pp. 547–572; Kettunen, 'Globalisation'.
84 Kettunen, 'Globalisation', p. 54.
85 Kettunen, 'Globalisation', p. 51.

Bibliography

AB Svenska Telegrambyrån, *Att sälja med modern exportreklam*. Stockholm: AB Svenska Telegrambyrån, 1956.

Andersson, T., Fredriksson, T., and Svensson, R., *Multinational Restructuring, Internationalization and Small Economies: The Swedish Case*. London: Routledge, 1996.

Aronczyk, M., *Branding the Nation: The Global Business of National Identity*. New York: Oxford University Press, 2013.

Åström Rudberg, E., 'Selling the concept of brands: the Swedish advertising industry and branding in the 1920s', *Journal of Historical Research in Marketing*, 9 (2017), pp. 535–542.

Berg, A., 'Why quality in education – and what quality? A linguistic analysis of the concept of quality in Swedish government texts', *Education Inquiry*, 2 (2011), pp. 709–723.

Berger, S., 'Historians, nationalism studies, and the economy', in Berger, S., and Fetzer, T. (eds), *Nationalism and the Economy*, Budapest: Central European University Press, pp. 23–41.

Bergwik, S., Godhe, M., Houltz, A., and Rodell, M., 'Inledning', in Bergwik, S., Godhe, M., Houlz, A., and Rodell, M. (eds), *Svensk snillrikhet? Nationella föreställningar om entreprenörer och teknisk begåvning 1800–2000*, Lund: Nordic Academic Press, 2014, pp. 9–26.

Broberg, O., Gianneschi, M., and Jonsson, S., *Svensk reklam: Annonser, varumärken och marknadskommunikation 1975–2012*. Stockholm: Dialogos förlag, 2016.

Campbell, J.L., and Hall, J.A., 'National identity and the political economy of small states', *Review of International Political Economy*, 16 (2009), pp. 547–572.

De Geer, G., *Sveriges andra stormaktstid*. Stockholm: Albert Bonniers Förlag, 1928.

Eliasson, G., *De svenska storföretagen: En studie av internationaliseringens konsekvenser för den svenska ekonomin*. Stockholm: Industrins utredningsinstitut, 1985.

Evans, C., and Ryden, G., 'Iron marks as early brand names: Swedish iron in the Atlantic market during the eighteenth century', in Müller, L., and Ojala, J. (eds), *Information Flows: New Approaches in the Historical Study of Business Information*, Helsinki: Suomalaisen Kirjallisuuden Seura, 2007, pp. 193–211.

Funke, M., 'Business associations and institutional development of Swedish Post-War export advertising', *SSE Working Paper Series in Economic History, Stockholm School of Economics*, 2022:1 (2022). https://swopec.hhs.se/haechi/abs/haechi2022_001.htm.

Garvin, D.A., 'What does "product quality" really mean?', *MIT Sloan Management Review*, 15 October 1984, pp. 25–41.

Ghobodian, A., and Woo, H.S., 'Characteristics, benefits and shortcomings of four major quality awards', *International Journal of Quality & Reliability Management*, 13 (1996), pp. 10–44.

Glover, N., 'Marketing internationalism in an era of globalization: the Swedish-South African partnership week, November 1999', *Culture Unbound*, 13 (2021), pp. 41–65.

Glover, N., and Hellenes, A.M., 'A "Swedish Offensive" at the world fairs: advertising, social reformism and the roots of Swedish cultural diplomacy, 1935–1939', *Contemporary European History*, 30 (2021), pp. 284–300.

Hansen, P.H., 'Co-branding product and nation: Danish modern furniture and Denmark in the United States, 1940–1970', in da Silva Lobes, T., and Duguid, P. (eds), *Trademarks, Brands and Competitiveness*, New York; London: Routledge, pp. 77–101.

Hedin, G., *Quality: Made in Sweden*. Stockholm: Informationsförlaget, 1992.

Hellenes, A.M., *Fabricating Sweden: Studies of Swedish Public Diplomacy in France from the 1930s to the 1990s*, unpublished doctoral thesis, University of Oslo, 2019.

Hellenes, A.M., 'New Gustavians: Sweden, Europe and the return of the 18th century during the 1990s crisis', *Culture Unbound*, 13 (2021), pp. 90–113.

Houltz, A., 'Myten om snilleindustrin: SKF, Volvo och den eviga återkomsten', in Bergwik, S., Godhe, M., Houltz, A., and Rodell, M. (eds), *Svensk snillrikhet? Nationella föreställningar om entreprenörer och teknisk begåvning 1800–2000*, Lund: Nordic Academic Press, 2014, pp. 127–150.

Husz, O., 'The morality of quality: assimilating material mass culture in twentieth-century Sweden', *Journal of Modern European History*, 10 (2012), pp. 152–181.

Katzenstein, P.J., *Small States in World Markets: Industrial Policy in Europe*. Ithaca, NY: Cornell University Press, 1985.

Kettunen, P., 'Globalisation and the criteria of 'us': a historical perspective on the discussion on the nordic model and new challenges', in Fleming, D., Kettunen, P., Søborg, H., and Thörnqvist, C. (eds.), *Global Redefining of Working Life – A New Nordic Agenda for Competence and Participation?*, Copenhagen: Nordic Council of Ministers, 1998, pp. 33-80.

Kristoffersson, S., *Design by IKEA: A Cultural History*. London; New York: Bloomsbury, 2014.

Kühschelm, O., 'Nationalizing consumption: products, brands, and nations', in Berger, S., and Fetzer, T. (eds), *Nationalism and the Economy*, Budapest: Central European University Press, 2019, pp. 163–187.

Laine-Svejdby, K., *Svenskhet som strategi*. Stockholm: Timbro, 1987.

Maze, E., *Creative Sweden*. Stockholm: Geber, 1965.

Moor, L., *The Rise of Brands*. Oxford: Berg, 2007.

Nationalkommittén för svensk kvalitet, *Svensk kvalitet: Rätt sätt*. Stockholm: Nationalkommittén för svensk kvalitet, 1986.

Porter, M., *The Competitive Advantage of Nations: Creating and Sustaining Superior Performance*. London: Macmillan, 1990.

Reierson, C., 'Are foreign products seen as national stereotypes? A survey of attitudes in college students', *Journal of Retailing*, 42 (1966), pp. 33–40.

Schön, L., *An Economic History of Modern Sweden*. Stockholm: SNS förlag, 2012.

Shewhart, W., *Economic Control of Quality of Manufactured Product*. New York: D. van Nostrand Co, 1931.

Strannegård, L. (ed.), *Den omätbara kvaliteten*. Lund: Sudentlitteratur, 2013.

Sundbärg, G., *Det svenska folklynnet: Aforismer*, 4th ed. Stockholm: P.A. Norstedt & Söner, 1911.

The General Export Association of Sweden, *Industrial Sweden: Edited for publication on the occasion of The Gothenburg Tercentenary Exhibition in 1923*. Gothenburg: Wal. Zachrisssons Boktryckeri, 1923.

The General Export Association of Sweden, *Svensk Exports jubileumsnummer*. Stockholm: Sveriges Allmänna Exportförening, 1937.

The General Export Association of Sweden, *Svensk industri- och exportkalender 1925*. Stockholm: Sveriges Allmänna Exportförening, 1925.

The General Export Association of Sweden, *Sveriges Allmänna Exportförening 1887–1912*. Stockholm: Norstedt & Söner, 1912.

The General Export Association of Sweden, *What Sweden Can Do*. Stockholm: Sveriges Allmänna Exportförening, 1919.

The Royal Swedish Academy of Engineering Sciences, *IVA om design*, IVA-meddelande 258. Stockholm: Ingenjörsvetenskapsakademin, 1987.

The Stockholm Chamber of Commerce, *Invest in Sweden*. Stockholm: The Stockholm Chamber of Commerce, 1960.

The Swedish Trade Council, *Made in Sweden: Politics, Investment Climate, Products, Management*. Stockholm: Sveriges exportråd, 1992.

The Volvo Group, *Volvorama 1958*. Gothenburg: Volvo (1958).

Vikström, H., Högselius, P., and Avango, D., 'Swedish steel and global resource colonialism: Sandviken's quest for Turkish chromium, 1925–1950', *Scandinavian Economic History Review*, 65 (2017), pp. 307–325.

Weckenmann, A., Akkasoglu, G., and Werner, T., 'Quality management – history and trends', *Quality the TQM Journal*, 27 (2015), pp. 281–293.

6 Made in Italy

A history of storytelling

Carlo Marco Belfanti

Introduction

The factors which are thought to be important in the construction of Made in Italy often derive from a simplistic representation of Italian culture and society, and are based on a superficial reconstruction of the historical development of the country. The most frequent theories adopted to explain this image have relied upon a seemingly inexhaustible Italian creative vein which is centuries old; a tradition of refined craftsmanship, and an infinite history of excellence in the artistic field.[1] One consequence of the interplay of these forces was that Italy became a great museum; through constant exposure to fine arts, citizens were educated to appreciate artistic beauty.[2] A recent publication stated:

> Our long historical-cultural stratification seems to have given us an unlooked for competitive advantage. Many of the quality products for which we are known at international level may boast of authenticity linked to solid cultural traditions, whose traces are lost in time … And it is precisely when we are able to credibly elaborate our cultural roots that Made in Italy is able to generate that irresistible fascination which attracts multitudes of consumers. The reason why we are able to build a rapport between past and present, offering much more than a product, albeit one of excellent manufacture is also because we are dealing with a cultural experience that concerns the production process as much as the context of the use of the product.[3]

The efficacy of Made in Italy is such that it is applied to many consumer goods: 'Italy has become a style setter by creating a synergy between luxury and craftmanship – deeply rooted in the Italian Renaissance – and entrepreneurial creativity'.[4] Consequently, Made in Italy became an integral part of global consumer culture.

Table 6.1 indicates the frequency with which Made in Italy appeared in the articles of the major Italian newspaper, *Corriere della Sera*. It is apparent that the 1980s was the decade in which Made in Italy enjoyed an explosion of media interest.

DOI: 10.4324/9781003166184-6

Table 6.1 Number of times in which the term Made in Italy recurs in the articles in the *Corriere della Sera*

Years	*Recurrence*
1945–1950	2
1951–1960	54
1961–1970	98
1971–1980	402
1981–1990	2,212
1991–2000	2,455

Sources: *Corriere della Sera*.

Note: An electronic search of 'Made in Italy' was conducted using the entire online archive of the Coriere della Sera.

The above trends can be viewed from an international perspective. Using the Books Ngram Viewer from Google,[5] it is evident that Made in Italy was becoming more 'visible' during the 1950s and 1960s. Following a decline in the 1970s, the prominence of Made in Italy began to increase; this trend is pronounced after 2000 (Figure 6.1).

This chapter traces the evolution of Made in Italy from a mark of origin to a brand. The remainder of this chapter proceeds as follows. In the next section, the discussion focuses on the immediate post-1945 era. During this period, it was recognised that creativity in Italy's fashion and design industries would be crucial to post-war reconstruction, and the mark Made in Italy could be used to accelerate development by signalling the origin of exports from these important industries.[6] The next section explains how, from 1951, when Italian fashion debuted on the international market, storytelling created a narrative in which Italian fashion houses were presented as legitimate descendants of the Renaissance. Among the industries within the ambit of Made in Italy,[7] fashion was especially relevant because it was integral to the evolution of the brand, Made in Italy.[8] In fact, fashion was almost *the* symbol of this brand.[9] As noted, it was from the 1980s that media coverage of Made in Italy exploded. The penultimate section of this chapter discusses the consolidation of Made in Italy as a brand communicating good taste and creativity, and then conclusions are drawn.

Building a reputation

In the first half of the twentieth century, Made in Italy was used exclusively to denote the origin of Italian exports.[10] For example, on the rare occasions when this mark was used in *Corriere della Sera*, it was in reference to the favour accorded Italian straw hats in North and South America,[11] or the opportunities offered to Italian products embossed with the Italian flag, in China.[12]

Nonetheless, the specialist press, especially in America, recognised Italy as the source of refined taste, and this became the leitmotiv of Made in Italy

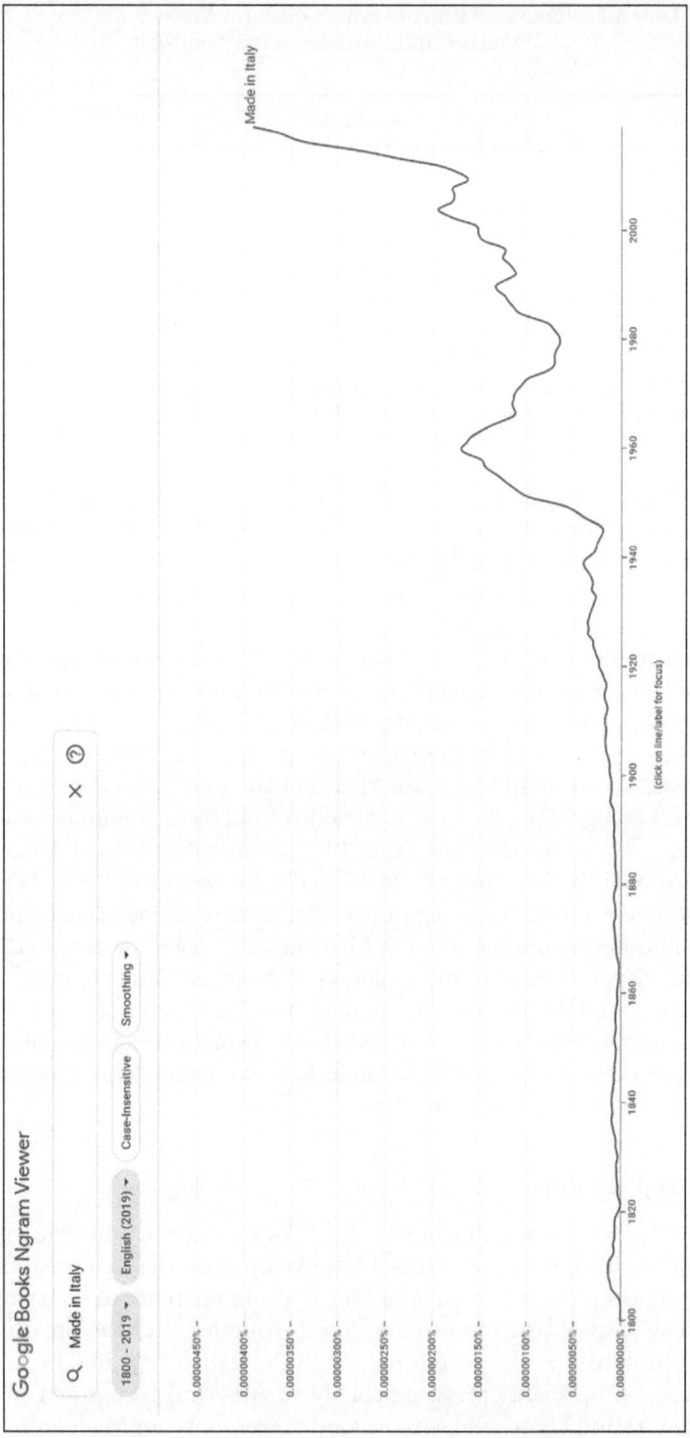

Figure 6.1 International diffusion of the term 'Made in Italy', 1800–2020

Source: https://books.google.com/ngrams.

storytelling: the Renaissance was the source of artistic inspiration in Italy. From the mid-nineteenth century, this passion for the Renaissance – the golden age of artistic taste centred on Italy – enthused élites in the US.[13] It is, therefore, unsurprising that *Women's Wear Daily*, the retailer's daily newspaper, offered diverse examples of how the Renaissance provided creative stimuli to fashion houses.[14] Italy was a country of fascinating contradictions; its folklore captured the imagination of American designers. Indeed, images of Venetian fishing boats inspired decorative motifs.[15] In 1937, *Vogue* described Italy – and Tuscany in particular – as 'a new field for shop-hounds – full of new faces, new ideas, and new shops to investigate'.[16] One year before the end of the Second World War, Anis Mead, *Vogue's* correspondent in Rome, reported on 'smartly dressed women' and 'shops filled of things you really want to buy', and named Gabriella di Robilant as among the most creative designers: 'She hasn't tried inventing drastic new fashions. She has just made pretty dresses'.[17]

During this period, Italian design demonstrated its vivacity with the Milanese *Triennali* exhibitions, and with the publication of magazines such as *Casabella* or *Domus*.[18] In 1949, *Vogue* claimed that architecture and design were central to Italian economic recovery. The success of Milan, and the 'Milanese school', in Italian architecture, was also attributed to the Renaissance: 'The Renaissance tradition lives among these Milanese artists for its universal and humanistic vision'.[19] The same article illustrated the efficacious synergy between the Milanese architects, and the furniture making industry which had been located in Lombardy for centuries. The result of such collaboration would be consolidated during the 1970s when leading producers abandoned traditional 'reproduction furniture' in favour of a more modern and original taste.[20]

After 1945, Italy became a democracy. The country benefitted from the European Recovery Plan (Marshall Plan), which generated significant commercial opportunities for Italian producers.[21] The fashion sector rapidly gained international visibility because some Italian fashion designers were much appreciated by American consumers. In 1947, the image of Italian creativity was re-launched when Salvatore Ferragamo received the prestigious *Neiman Marcus Award*. However, Emilio Pucci was probably the best-known and most appreciated Italian fashion designer in the US. Pucci was 'discovered' in 1947, and he was brought to the notice of the American public by an article which appeared in *Harper's Bazaar* in 1948. Pucci's designs were produced by the sportswear company White Stag and sold by the department store Lord and Taylor. The aristocratic Florentine designer captivated the American public with his brightly coloured printed silks, and his designs for tight-fitting trousers.[22] Contemporaneously, this Italian appeal extended to film production. The Roman studios at Cinecittà began hosting American cinema productions, often referred to as 'Hollywood on the Tiber'. Actresses from Hollywood arrived in Rome where they began to appreciate the creativity and taste of the Roman fashion houses, of which the Fontana Sisters were pre-eminent.[23]

The American Press described the reawakening of creativity that characterised the Italian economic recovery in the second half of the 1940s, as a new Renaissance. An article on Italy published in *Fortune* stated, 'Today the inventive, productive tradition is still lively. It may once again bring rebirth to the land of the Renaissance'.[24] In March 1950, Alice K. Perkins, a correspondent for *Women's Wear Daily*, reported the creations of diverse Italian fashion houses to American retailers; the former were represented as heirs to a craft tradition 'of skilled workers since the great days of the Renaissance'.[25] This statement commenced the storytelling that entwined Italian affinity for refined taste with the Renaissance;[26] a narrative that emphasised the continuity between Renaissance craftsmanship and contemporary Italian fashion designers.

By the late 1940s, Italian craftsmanship was becoming increasingly visible to the American public. Among the most active intermediaries promoting such products was Giovanni Battista Giorgini, a well-established supplier of ceramics and Maiolica ware, leather goods, embroidery, artistic glassware, objects in alabaster, furniture, and articles of antiquarian interest, to major department stores.[27] Giorgini also advocated and promoted the itinerant exhibition, *Italy at Work. Her Renaissance in Design Today*, which, after its inauguration at the Brooklyn Museum, travelled throughout the US between 1950 and 1953, and reminded American citizens of their fascination with the Renaissance. This exhibition, which promoted the image of Italian craftsmanship and design, was sponsored by the Chicago Art Institute and 11 American museums.[28] In fact, Giorgini had suggested to the directors of the New York department store, B. Altman & Co, that they sponsor the event, but they refused because the costs were judged too high. Nonetheless, the concept of bringing Italian fashion into the international spotlight remained valid.[29]

Not only fashion

Giovanni Battista Giorgini launched the first Italian fashion show in 1951. This event is generally considered to mark the birth of Italian fashion.[30] As noted, Giorgini began his professional career in the 1920s, selling the best Italian products to department stores. The war interrupted his promotional activity, but he was adamant that Made in Italy had great potential in the US. In the immediate post-war period, Giorgini invited US buyers and the specialist American press – already in Europe attending Paris fashion shows – to prolong their stay by attending a similar show in Florence. To be successful, this initiative had to address considerable obstacles, of which the two most important were American perplexity about the need to view the Florence show (which did not boast great credentials), and securing the collaboration of Italian fashion houses (many of whom failed to comprehend the potential importance of the planned event). Ultimately, thanks to his excellent personal contacts, Giorgini convinced a respectable number of American representatives, and the most important Italian fashion houses, to attend the Florence show.

The first event was scheduled for 12 February 1951 at Villa Torrigiani – Giorgini's own home. The fashion houses that displayed their creations were Carosa, Fabiani, Simonetta Visconti, Emilio Schuberth, the Fontana Sisters, Jole Veneziani, Vanna, Noberasko, Germana Marucelli, Emilio Pucci, Avolio, La Tessitrice dell'Isola, and Mirsa. Also present were four Italian journalists, including Elisa Massai, special envoy of the authoritative American publication *Women's Wear Daily*, and, most importantly, buyers representing US stores, for example, B. Altman & Co., Bergdorf Goodman, I. Magnin, Henry Morgan, and Leto Cohn.[31]

Giorgini fully exploited the Florentine context: literature distributed to journalists and buyers stated: 'the Italian collections, for the first time brought to the attention of the world, recall in their line, in their cut, and in their ease of wear the legacy of the artistic tradition of the Renaissance'.[32] The Renaissance was presented not only as the golden age of Italian civilisation, but also as the period in which artistic genius placed itself at the service of elegance, thereby allowing Italy to dictate fashion to Europe. Viewed from this perspective, the fashion houses which participated in the show were the inheritors of such supremacy. By creating the show, Giorgini was suggesting that Italian fashion descended from a Renaissance culture, the product of such brilliant artists as Leonardo da Vinci and Michelangelo. Although such suggestions contained a minimum of historic truth, they were, nonetheless, powerful marketing devices.

The Florence show was a success. The creative freshness of the products and the relatively low prices of the designs – less than half the price of articles shown in Paris – led to foreign buyers purchasing everything. Consequently, it was not difficult for Giorgini to suggest a repetition of the event. The following July the show was held at the Grand Hotel. This event was attended by the big names of the American specialist press, Bettina Ballard from *Vogue*, and Carmel Snow from *Harper's Bazaar*, who later raved about Italian fashion. Applause and enthusiastic comments were repeated at the January 1952 show. Building on this success, the event was transferred to the prestigious Sala Bianca in the Medici palace of Palazzo Pitti in July 1952. Subsequent shows, with complementary events which evoked the splendours of Italy's history, reinforced the ties between Renaissance taste, and Italian fashion.[33]

Giorgini had revived the idea that the Renaissance, the golden age of Italian creativity, was reincarnated in Italian fashion in the 1950s. Giorgini promoted Italian fashion as being the result of creativity that descended directly from the Renaissance; it was a brilliant invention, subsequently elaborated by the myth of continuity: the idea that Italian fashion had descended directly from the Renaissance, an age in which interaction between the most able craftsmen, the most genial artists and the most elegant aristocrats had produced a historic event, the birth of fashion, which had then been spread throughout Europe.

But, what impact was created by these shows? To address this question, there follows an analysis of the reaction of the international press, especially in the US, which was an important market for Italian fashion.[34] The specialist press reported the boom in Italian fashion, and it appears to have accepted the 'myth of continuity'. The day after the second fashion show, held in July 1951, Carmel Snow stated:

> But after all there is another very simple explanation for this tremendous vitality and inventiveness. They might well be due to the fact that the Italian people have such a rich heritage of visual beauty. What goes to make up the life of this lovely land seems to have been handed down from generation to generation and the habit of living in beautiful surroundings tends to give every Italian an instinctive talent for harmonious design.[35]

One theme which the more attentive journalists emphasised increasingly was the felicitous period that Italian creativity enjoyed during the 1950s. The achievements of Italian fashion during this decade were contrasted with the dark decades of Fascism and the War. Many American periodicals during this decade claimed that Italy was benefiting from a second Renaissance. *Vogue*, for example, compared Italy to a phoenix, reborn from its own ashes, which was living through, 'the latest of the Italian Renaissances'.[36] *Women's Wear Daily* described an exhibition of Italian products at Macy's, in New York City, as a 'Second Renaissance Italian Craftsmanship'.[37] This perspective was adopted by *Time*, with the article 'Italy's Renaissance', which reported Giorgini's fashion show, and used the word Renaissance to indicate the prolific creative movement enveloping Italian fashion and Italy: 'Not only in Florence, but in Rome, Milan and other major cities the Italian Renaissance of fashion is in full swing'.[38] In 1952, journalist Florence de Santis wrote an article for *Fashions of Italy Today*, with the title, 'After Four Centuries Italy Is Back in Fashion'; it included the subtitle '*Alta Moda* Shares in Italian Post-War Renaissance'.[39] Finally, in 1954, *Vogue* endorsed the narrative of continuity in Italian creativity:

> These six pages chronicle an extraordinary and exciting development: the influence of post war Italian design .... Its influence has steadily grown and strengthened .... Italy's architects and designers, backed by the centuries-old skills of Italian craftsmen and artisans, have attacked with brio the designing of everything from a teaspoon to an office building, somehow combining a crisply modern approach with the warmth and richness of Italy's past.[40]

In the following two decades, the industrial structure underpinning the Italian 'fashion system' underwent numerous radical changes.[41] For example, small-scale artisanal production became less prominent, and production vaunted a new type of fashion designer, the stylist, who combined creative innovation with large-scale production. One result of these changes was that

Florence lost its role as Italian fashion capital to Milan – capital of the *prêt-à-porter* – and to Rome, the seat of high fashion.[42] By the 1970s, Italian fashion had established an enviable international reputation; it was no longer necessary that the accompanying narrative focused on Renaissance origin:

> Italian fashion conjures up the myths of ancient history, but also those of its own history, equally glorious ..., and of recent history. We might describe it as 'double vintage'. From the romanticization of a glorious remote past emerges the idea of craftsmanship and creative workshop, combined with a feeling of leadership in taste.[43]

During the same period, design furniture also became representative of Italian creativity – though without recourse to elaborate storytelling. In common with clothing, the furniture industry possessed a long tradition of craftsmanship, largely dedicated to the production of articles that imitated traditional styles. However, the international market for modern furniture was dominated by Scandinavian countries. Nonetheless, and again comparable with clothing, a promotional initiative projected Italian design furniture onto the international scene. The *Salone del Mobile* (Furniture Fair) was created in 1961 to facilitate collaboration between designers and furniture makers.[44] A key turning point in the activities of the *Salone del Mobile* occurred in 1965, when a sector of the fair, dedicated exclusively to design furniture, was opened to reveal the most innovative designs.[45] The specialist international press provided considerable and complimentary coverage of this event, which continued in later years. For example, in 1966, an article in *Furnishing World* stated: 'Modern Italian furniture has succeeded in overtaking and distinguishing itself from the Scandinavian style that dominates furniture in other countries'.[46]

Definitive international endorsement of Italian furniture designers occurred in 1972, with the exhibition 'Italy: the New Domestic Landscape' hosted by the Museum of Modern Art in New York, and directed by the Argentinean architect, Emilio Ambasz. At this event, important trends in Italian design were reflected in the creations of Ettore Sottsass, Joe Colombo, Afra and Tobia Scarpa, and Gae Aulenti.[47] A review of Italian furniture design published in *Vogue* referred to 'some of the leading creative talents who have put Italy ahead in the field of new forms' and 'It's a shocker, an eye-opener, and an informative, beautifully conceived show that defines the aesthetic of the space age for the future'.[48]

Is it a brand?

In the 1970s, Italian fashion, and design furniture occupied premier positions on the international market. However, Made in Italy was not part of the common vocabulary, and nor was it a synonym for the creativity and culture represented by Italian products. Subsequently, Made in Italy evolved from an indicator of the country of origin to a brand label which signalled to global consumers Italian refinement, taste, and manufacturing quality.[49] It was during this latter period that organisational changes in the Italian fashion sector reirnforced strategies that promoted Made in Italy.

During the late twentieth century, the Italian fashion industries replaced craft character with an industrial physiognomy characterised by a 'system' centred on Milan. These industries included clothing, shoes, textiles, and the manufacture of other accessories that completed the 'total look' of Italian brands and styles from the 1980s.[50] Increasingly, interaction between architects and designers, and business enterprises began to characterise design furniture. Although Milan was also the focal point for the fashion industries, many companies located in this city adopted a strategy of internationalisation by recruiting foreign designers and attracting external investment which accelerated and then consolidated the reputation of Made in Italy.[51]

Simultaneously, Made in Italy began to signal a particular organisational set-up – the industrial district – in which were located companies active in the fashion industries.[52] Prominent in Central and Northern Italy, these districts, characterised by a network of small and middle-sized businesses, were adept at flexible production which was crucial for success in the continuously changing fashion industries. Further, such districts offered an alternative industrial model to Fordism which was experiencing a period of crisis.[53] A publication in 2017 by the *Istituto per il Commercio Estero* (Italian Foreign Trade Institute, hereafter, ICE) to celebrate 30 years of its *Rapporti* (Reports) identified these industrial districts as the key factor in the success of Made in Italy on the international market.[54]

In 1986, in one of its first annual reports, the ICE acknowledged the communicative value represented by Made in Italy that had been acquired by that date – which extended beyond that of a mark of origin. The ICE established a budget for 'testing the image of Made in Italy' on export markets and it launched promotional initiatives.[55] In fact, the promotional activities of the ICE began some 20 years earlier, and analysis of advertisements referring to the Italian fashion sector which appeared in *Women's Wear Daily* permits a discussion of the progressive enrichment of the sense attributed to Made in Italy.

One of the first advertisements, published in 1962, was a simple black and white image which depicted a mother and her young son sitting in a small model car with the Ferrari logo. This image promoted children's clothing to retailers with the generic message: 'For instant customer appeal in every corner of your store, check all the possibilities offered you by the label: Made in Italy'.[56] Much more elaborate and refined advertisements appeared in the 1970s. One example is a portrait of a woman by the contemporary artist Domenico Cantatore, with the title, 'New, Now, Contemporary Italy. Here the artistry of fashionable lifestyle begins', accompanied by the caption:

> There's the whole fashionable elegance of Italy in women's fashions ... Springing from the beauty of this creativity comes spirited design that is far-flung in influence. Colors to enchant the eye. Superior workmanship. Intriguing detailing. Luxury of fine fabrics ... And there's so much more to Italy – furs, accessories, fashion fabrics, men's and children's fashions and home furnishing fabrics.[57]

Similar advertisements which appeared in later years also sought to convey the excellent quality embodied in Made in Italy. Thus, in the 1990s, a full-page advertisement devoted to women's fashion adopted a reproduction of a detail from a Renaissance painting accompanied by the legend: 'The essence of Italy'.[58] In 2002, a campaign entitled 'Italia: life in "I" style', was launched which sought to disseminate a broader affinity to the Italian lifestyle:

> One of the primary goals of this campaign is to introduce consumers to the best of the Italian lifestyle, particularly through its rich assortment of fine products. Since U.S. metropolitan areas have more exposure to 'things Italian', the key target is to reach further into the American heartland and spread '*la dolce vita*'.[59]

Concurrently, the narrative surrounding Made in Italy achieved full cultural legitimation with a great exhibition in the *Palazzo della Triennale*, Milan, which celebrated the 50th anniversary of Made in Italy – which began with the first Italian fashion show in Florence. This Milan exhibition focused on fashion and design furniture because these industries held, and hold a primary role in Italian fashion exports, and both represent, 'the highest product of our culture', notwithstanding that Made in Italy also includes, '*La dolce vita*, Parmesan cheese, Solaia wine and those bright red cars from Maranello'.[60]

Conclusion

According to the important Italian economic newspaper, *Il Sole 24 Ore*, 'If Made in Italy were really a brand it would be the third best known one in the world, coming only after Coca Cola and Visa'.[61] In the strictest sense, Made in Italy may not be considered a brand because it is not accompanied by a logo. Nonetheless, this mark is perceived to be a brand because it communicates a much broader message than the country of origin. This perception appears to be strongest in the US:

> Something's happening at this moment, and that's a remarkable- unmistakable – presence of things Italian in the U.S. and in our lives. Whether it' s the Italian way of dressing, or way of eating, a fine Italian stamp, now in wine, or the most modern furniture design, there's an ease, and humour, and simple common sense that we find in the best of Italy that's obviously right for us.[62]

The previous quotation marks the culmination of the Made in Italy narrative. This story commenced after 1945 with two design-driven sectors, fashion, and design furniture. Italian fashion 'arrived' on the international scene in 1951, when the first fashion show was held. Subsequently, Italian fashion designers created a narrative around the Renaissance to achieve cultural legitimation, which enabled them to compete with Parisian *Haute Couture* on the international market. Global endorsement of Italian design furniture as an accredited competitor to Scandinavian furniture was achieved with the 1972 exhibition at the Museum of Modern Art.

The transformation of Made in Italy from mark to brand occurred during the 1980s. The process involved other industries, for example, food, but above all, the transition integrated heterogeneous aspects of Italian culture associated with the 'Italian lifestyle', best exemplified by *La dolce vita*. This evolution was fostered by a global market in which 'Made in' was a source of competitive advantage for countries with a favourable image.[63] Michael Storper and Robert Salais have observed that: 'The development of international specialisation moves away from mass production to be based today on the uniqueness of every product. Such uniqueness means that both producer and/or consumer have conferred an identity to the product and that they are able to recognise it.[64]

It is plausible that debates on 'Made in' have been stimulated by a growing recognition that brands are more important than products. According to Naomi Klein, 'A single, seemingly innocuous idea [was] developed by management theorists in the mid 1980's: that successful corporations must primarily produce brands, as opposed to products'.[65] Similar changes have been noticed with respect to the country of origin effect and the relaunching of branding strategies involving luxury products. According to Luc Boltansky and Arnaud Esquerre:

> These 'made in X' goods can then be sold under a brand name whose marketing emphasizes a national identity; this gives them added value and also often plays on the supposedly artisanal, 'old style' character of their manufacture, which is intended to single them out and support their claim to exceptionality.[66]

Currently, for these authors, at least, it seems that Made in Italy is losing its image as a brand for high-end products (*haut de gamme*), which it had acquired in the twentieth century. This image was vital to international competitiveness. Increasingly, Made in Italy is being used as a mark to protect Italy's domestic market from the invasion of products Made in China, especially those products that exploit 'Italian sounding' terms, thereby undermining the traditional image of Made in Italy.

Notes

1 See, for instance, Fortis, *Il Made in Italy*, p. 8. See also Fortis and Curzio, *Il Made in Italy oltre il* 2000; Ross, 'Made in Italy'.

2 'Most country images are in fact stereotypes, extreme simplifications of the reality that are not necessarily accurate'. Kotler and Gertner, 'Country as brand', n. 4–5, p. 251. See also Randa and Rao, 'The effect'.
3 Bettiol, *Raccontare il Made in Italy*, pp. 57–65. See also Corbellini and Saviolo, *La scommessa*, pp. 2–8; Fortunati and Danese, *Manuale di comunicazione*, pp. 51–56; Morace and Santoro, *Italian Factor*.
4 Bertoli and Resciniti, 'Introduction', p. 7.
5 The Google Books Ngram Viewer displays a graph showing how selected phrases have occurred in a corpus of books over a selected period. https://books.google.com/ngrams/info. Accessed April 2022.
6 The principles established by the Paris Convention for the Protection of Industrial Property (1883), and the Madrid Agreement for the Repression of False or Deceptive Indications of Source of Goods (1891), were formally recognised in Italy by the law n.676/1967. However, the adoption of the label 'Made in Italy' to advertise Italian products was practiced only from the early 1950s. See, the video produced by the Istituto Luce by appointement of the Italian Governement in 1953 with the title "Made in Italy" (Archivio Storico Istituto Luce, La Settimana Incom 00925, "Made in Italy", 2 April 1953 - https://patrimonio.archivioluce.com/luce-web/detail/IL5000025850/2/made-italy-fabbricato-italia.html?startPage=0).
7 See, for instance, Bucci, Codeluppi, and Ferraresi, *Il Made in*.
8 Or 'metabrand'. Barile, 'Made in Italy'.
9 Fortis, *Il made in Italy*, pp. 12–13.
10 Higgins, *Brands*, pp. 1–28.
11 *Corriere della Sera*, 13 February, 1926, p. 4.
12 *Corriere della Sera*, 28 June 1938, p. 5.
13 Belfanti, *Storia culturale*.
14 'Bright red the dominant note in display of Italian Renaissance boudoir gowns', *Women's Wear Daily*, 11 December 1918; Exquisite modern fashion ideas from early Italian masterpieces', *Women's Wear Daily*, 28 August 1920; Fashion significances: Agnes takes millinery inspiration from the Italian Renaissance', *Women's Wear Daily*, 17 May 1935; 'Boston stores promote fashions reflecting colors of Renaissance period', *Women's Wear Daily*, 22 July 1935.
15 'Lido-Bragozzo styles in debut tomorrow', *Women's Wear Daily*, 13 April 1938.
16 'Shop-hound in Italy', *Vogue*, 15 October 1937, pp. 158–159.
17 *Vogue*, 1 September, 1944, p. 142.
18 Vitta, *Il progetto della bellezza*, pp. 209–215.
19 'Milan, design Renaissance'. The author of this article, Ernesto R. Rogers, was amongst the innovative architects of this period. *Vogue*, 15 September 1949, pp. 152–156.
20 Giannola, 'Design', pp. 100–103; Pasca, 'Italian design', pp. 104–107; Pinchera, *La moda*, pp. 27–79.
21 White, *Reconstructing*, pp. 19–31; Paris, *Oggetti* cuciti, pp. 83–91, 190–197.
22 White, *Reconstructing*, pp. 40–41.
23 Capalbo, *Storia della moda*, pp. 128–135.
24 Malossi, 'Paesaggio con rovine', p. 175.
25 'Florence Source of Individual Italian Accessories', *Women's Wear Daily*, 24 March 1950; 'Reports from Italy on Dressmaker Showings', *Women's Wear Daily*, 28 March 1950.
26 Belfanti, 'History'.
27 Pagliai, *La Firenze*.
28 Rogers, *Italy*. See also Sparke, 'The Straw Donkey'.
29 Vergani, 'Italian'; Pinchera, *La moda*.

30 Vergani, 'Italian fashion', pp. 130–141; Giannola, 'Design and fashion'; Pinchera and Rinallo, 'The emergence'.
31 Vergani, 'Italian'; Pinchera, *La moda*, pp. 27–79.
32 Landini, 'Sala Bianca'.
33 Belfanti, 'History'.
34 White, *Reconstructing*; Paris, 'Orígenes'.
35 Belfanti, 'Marketing', p. 63.
36 Belfanti, 'History', p. 85.
37 *Women's Wear Daily*, 11 September 1951, p. 57.
38 Belfanti, 'Marketing', p. 63.
39 Alta Moda is the Italian term for haute couture. Belfanti, 'History', p. 85.
40 *Vogue*, 15 October 1954, pp. 116–117.
41 Paris, 'Fashion'; Paris, 'Orígenes'.
42 Prêt-à-Porter, refers to designer clothes which are sold ready-to-wear, rather than made to measure. Carloni, 'Milan', pp. 142–148; Paris, *Oggetti cuciti*, pp. 456–493; Merlo and Polese, 'Turning Fashion'.
43 Reinach, 'If you speak'. It has been claimed that, 'American advertisements (...) epitomize our national tendency to lump together all monuments of all periods of Italian history into one dark backward and abysm of time. With the exception of Rome and the Renaissance, those two great clichés, the distinct stages of Italian history are forgotten'. Casillo, *Dirty gondola*, p. 341.
44 Giannola, 'Design'; Pasca, 'Italian design'; Lazzaroni, 'From exhibit', pp. 118–127.
45 Lazzaroni, 'From exhibit'.
46 Lazzaroni, 'From exhibit', p. 120.
47 Pasca, 'Italian design', p. 107; Vitta, *Il Progetto,* pp. 279–281.
48 *Vogue*, July 1972, p. 28.
49 Ross, 'Made'.
50 Merlo and Polese, 'Turning Fashion'; Paris, 'Fashion'; Merlo, 'Italian'; Merlo, 'The Ascendance', pp. 137–154.
51 Pasca, 'Italian design'.
52 Fortis, *Il made in Italy*, pp. 48–60, 86–113.
53 Sabel, and Zeitlin, 'Stories, strategies', pp. 1–33; Blim, *Made*. For a critical view on the rhetoric of of small-scale industrialisation, see Ross, 'Made'.
54 Iapadre and Salvati, 'L'Italia nell'economia', p. 26.
55 *Rapporto sul commercio estero* 1987. Rome: Istituto per il Commercio Estero, (now the Italian Trade Agency), 1988, p. 160.
56 *Women's Wear Daily*, 29 March 1962, p. 24.
57 *Women's Wear Daily*, 27 November 1978, p. 16a.
58 *Women's Wear Daily*, 2 September 1998, p. SII1.
59 *Women's Wear Daily*, 1 February 2002, p. 17.
60 Settembrini, '(Pre)Conceptions', p. 20.
61 Il Sole 24 ore, 27 August 2014, p. 16.
62 *Vogue*, October 1981, p. 266.
63 Ross, 'Made'; Castro and Sáiz, 'Cross-cultural'.
64 Salais, and Storper, *Les mondes*, p. 12.
65 Klein, *No Logo*, p. 3.
66 Boltanski and Esquerre, *Enrichment*, p. 31.

Bibliography

Barile, N., 'Made in Italy: da Country of Orign a Metabrand', in Colaiacomo, P. (ed.), *Fatto in Italia. La cultura del Made in Italy, 1960–2000*, Rome: Meltemi, 2006, pp. 132–157.

Belfanti, C.M., 'History as an intangible asset for the Italian fashion business', *Historical Research in Marketing*, 7 (2015), pp. 74–90.

Belfanti, C.M., 'Marketing Italian fashion through history', *Journal of Modern Italian Studies*, 20 (2015), pp. 53–66.

Belfanti, C.M., *Storia culturale del Made in Italy*. Bologna: Il Mulino, 2019.

Bertoli, G., and Resciniti, R., 'Introduction', in Bertoli, G., and Resciniti, R. (eds), *International Marketing and the Country of Origin Effect: The Global Impact of 'Made in Italy'*, Cheltenham: Edward Elgar, 2013, pp. 1–20.

Bettiol, M., *Raccontare il Made in Italy: Un novo legame tra cultura e manifattura*. Venice: Marsilio, 2015.

Blim, M., *Made in Italy: Small-scale Industrialization and Its Consequences*. New York: Praeger Publishers, 1990.

Boltanski, L., and Esquerre, A., *Enrichment: A Critique of Commodities*. Cambridge: Polity Press, 2020.

Bucci, A., Codeluppi, V., and M. Ferraresi, M. (eds), *Il Made in Italy*, Rome: Carocci, 2011.

Capalbo, C., *Storia della moda a Roma*. Rome: Donzelli Editore, 2012.

Carloni, M.V., 'Milan, the laboratory of Italian Style', in Settembrini, L. (ed.), *Made in Italy, 1951–2001?*, Milan: Skira, 2001, pp. 142–148.

Casillo, R., 'Dirty gondola: the image of Italy in American advertisements', *Word & Image*, 1 (1985), pp. 330–350.

Castro, R., and Sáiz, P., 'Cross-cultural factors in international branding', *Business History*, 62 (2020), pp. 1–25.

Corbellini, E., and Saviolo, S., *La scommessa del Made in Italy e il futuro della moda italiana*. Milan: Etas, 2004.

Fortis, M., *Il Made in Italy*. Bologna: Il Mulino, 1998.

Fortis, M., and Quadrio-Curzio, A. (eds), *Il Made in Italy oltre il 2000: Innovazione e comunità locali*. Bologna: Il Mulino, 2000.

Fortunati, L., and Danese, E., *Manuale di comunicazione, sociologia e cultura della moda: Il made in Italy*. Rome: Meltemi, 2005.

Giannola, R., 'Design and fashion: driving forces of Italy', in Settembrini, L. (ed.), *Made in Italy, 1951–2001?* Milan: Skira, 2001, pp. 100–103.

Higgins, D.M., *Brands, Geographical Origin, and the Global Economy*. Cambridge: Cambridge University Press, 2018.

Iapadre, L., and Salvati, I. (eds), 'L'Italia nell'economia internazionale: trasformazioni e persistenze. Un viaggio attraverso i Rapporti annuali dell'ICE', in *L'Italia nell'economia internazionale. Rapporto ICE. Edizione celebrativa 1986–2016*. Rome: Istituto per il Commercio Estero, 2017, pp. 9–46.

Klein, N., *No Logo*. London: Flamingo, 2001.

Kotler P., and Gertner, D., 'Country as brand, product and beyond: a place marketing and brand management perspective', *Brand Management*, 9 (2002), pp. 249–261.

Lazzaroni, L., 'From exhibit to event: the Salone del mobile "case"', in Settembrini, L. (ed.), *Made in Italy, 1951–2001?* Milan: Skira, 2001, pp. 118–127.

Malossi, G., 'Paesaggio con rovine: L'immagine dell'Italia descritta dai media americani', in Malossi, G. (ed.), *La Sala Bianca: Nascita della moda italiana*, Milan: Electa, 1992, p. 175.

Merlo, E., and Polese, F., 'Turning fashion into business: the emergence of Milan as an international fashion hub', *Business History Review*, 80 (2006), pp. 415–448.

Merlo, E., 'Italian fashion business: achievements and challenges, 1970s–2000s', *Business History*, 53 (2011), pp. 344–362.

Merlo, E., 'The ascendance of the Italian fashion brands, 1970–2000', in Segreto, L., Bonin H., Manera, C., and Pohl, M. (eds), *European Business and Brand Building*, Brussels: Peter Lang, 2012, pp. 137–154.

Morace, F., and Santoro, B., *Italian factor: Moltiplicare il valore di un paese*. Milan: Egea, 2014.

Orsi-Landini, R., 'Sala Bianca', in Vergani, G. (ed.), *Fashion Dictionary*, New York: Baldini-Castoldi-Dalai, 2006, pp. 679–687.

Pagliai, L., *La Firenze di Giovanni Battista Giorgini: Artigianato e moda tra Italia e Stati Uniti*. Florence: Edifir, 2011.

Paris, I., *Oggetti cuciti: L'abbigliamento pronto in Italia dal primo dopoguerra agli anni Settanta*. Milan: Franco Angeli, 2006.

Paris, I., 'Fashion as a system: changes in demand as the basis for the establishment of the Italian fashion system, 1960–1970', *Enterprise & Society*, 11 (2010), pp. 524–559.

Paris, I., 'Orígenes del Made in Italy: Moda italiana y mercado internacional en la segunda posguerra, 1951–1969', *Revista de Historia Industrial*, 19 (2010), pp. 121–154.

Pasca, V., 'Italian design: elements of history', in Settembrini, L. (ed.), *Made in Italy, 1951–2000?* Milan: Skira, 2001, pp. 104–117.

Pinchera, V., *La moda in Italia e in Toscana*. Venice: Marsilio, 2009.

Pinchera, V., and Rinallo, D., 'The emergence of Italy as a fashion country: nation branding and collective meaning creation at Florence's fashion shows, 1951–1965', *Business History*, 62 (2020), pp. 151–178.

Randa, S., and Rao, C.P., 'The effect country-of-origin related stereotypes and personal beliefs on product evaluation', *Psychology and Marketing*, 14 (1997), pp. 689–702.

Reinach, S.S., 'If you speak fashion you speak Italian: notes on a present day Italian fashion identity', *Critical Studies in Fashion and Beauty*, 1 (2010), pp. 203–215.

Rogers, M., *Italy at Work: Her Renaissance in Design Today*. Rome: Compagnia Generale Artigiana, 1950.

Ross, A., 'Made in Italy: the trouble with craft capitalism', *Antipode*, 36 (2004), pp. 209–216.

Sabel, C., and Zeitlin, J., 'Stories, Strategies, structures: rethinking historical alternatives to mass production', in Sabel, C., and Zeitlin, J. (eds), *World of Possibilities: Flexibility and Mass Production in Western Industrialization*, New York: Cambridge University Press, 1997, pp. 2–36.

Salais, R., and Storper, M., *Les mondes de production. Enquête sur l'identité économique de la France*. Paris: Editions de l'EHESS, 1993.

Settembrini, L., '(Pre)Conceptions of an exhibition', in Settembrini, L. (ed.), *Made in Italy, 1951–2001?*, Milan: Skira, 2001, pp. 15–28.

Sparke, P., 'The straw donkey: tourist Kitsch or pro-design? craft and design in Italy, 1945–1950', *Journal of Design History*, 11 (1998), pp. 59–69.

Vergani, G., "Italian fashion is born: not even Mussolini succeeded in accomplishing as much'", in Settembrini, L. (ed.), *Made in Italy, 1951–2001?* Milan: Skira, 2001, pp. 130–141.

Vitta, M., *Il progetto della bellezza. Il design fra arte e tecnica, 1851–2001.* Turin: Einaudi, 2001.

White, N., *Reconstructing Italian Fashion: America and the Development of the Italian Fashion Industry.* Oxford: Berg, 2000.

7 Made in France and Made in Paris

Luxury branding in the *longue durée*[1]

Véronique Pouillard and Audrey Millet

Introduction

This chapter explores the history of branding the city of origin, and country of origin, in French consumer goods, especially luxury goods such as ceramics and haute couture. We consider how important Made in France was in relation to indications of regional origin, and other forms of intellectual property, especially industrial designs, and copyright. Particular importance is attached to informal mechanisms, for example, the entente of entrepreneurs that created and maintained standards of production.

Previous studies examined the symbiotic relationship between the image of France and the products of its terroir, especially champagne, foodstuffs, and wines,[2] and documented the important contribution that business lobbies and trade associations made to legislation governing trade marks and appellations. This chapter focuses on the French luxury goods industry, and the ways in which its composite firms created specific national images and labels that associated their products with France, and French quality. The identity of this industry developed symbiotically with French national and urban landscapes.

This chapter contextualizes the evolution of this identity within the history of French protectionism from the late seventeenth century. Indeed, Made in France was intimately linked to the centralization of the French state under absolute monarchs. The last years of the Ancien Régime were a crucial period during which French taste, and the reputation of its products, were formed. The second territorialization of French taste emerged during the eighteenth century, and this was associated with Made in Paris. These dual applications of 'Made in' were supported by economic policies oriented towards the arts, specific manufactures, and the training of craftsmen. The latest phase in the evolution of Made in France began in the late nineteenth century and concluded with the offshoring of production. This relocation attracted official interest during President Hollande's government, which created the Ministry of Productive Recovery (Ministère du Redressement Productif) led by Arnaud Montebourg. These recent discourses are viewed from a long-term perspective to demonstrate that support for 'French' manufacturing has a considerable lineage underpinned by civil servants, entrepreneurs, and politicians on both sides of the political spectrum.

DOI: 10.4324/9781003166184-7

This chapter proceeds as follows. The next section explains how France became renowned for manufacturing excellence in the 'luxury' industries. This is followed by sections on how Alexandre Brongniart sought to protect the reputation that Sèvres had established in the production of porcelain, and the growth of haute couture from the mid-nineteenth century. The penultimate section discusses how the temptation to offshore production threatened France's reputation in luxury products before conclusions are presented.

From Made in France to Made in Paris

Debates on French supremacy in luxury products can be traced to the eighteenth century. Contemporaries lauded the eminently artistic character of French manufactures, which captured the aura of the high arts and represented '*French genius*'.[3] This favourable image was imposed via French culture and language, and, to varying degrees, technological superiority, notably in the decoration applied to products.

In 1765, the British mercer, Ashburner, gave evidence before the London Select Silk Committee, and claimed that English brocades failed to incorporate the new designs inspired from France, or 'à la française'.[4] British manufacturers tended to distinguish themselves by evoking their relation to France. For example, Irishman Édouard Duras settled in Bordeaux. Initially, Duras designated his wallpaper designs as 'London', but subsequently emphasized their Parisian origins:[5]

> The ambition to earn the title of the French manufacture (Manufacture Française), has determined the latter (the manufacturer) to only execute French drawings, and to apply to give them the grace and elegance that characterize all the French works.[6]

An indication of French manufacture practically became a label of quality. With the important concentration of manufacturers in Paris and Lyon, the two cities quickly distinguished themselves from other manufacturing regions. The aura of the French court, and the success of Rose Bertin (1747–1813), hatmaker (*modiste*) to Marie-Antoinette, helped create a narrative on the unparalleled quality of French manufacture.[7] During the nineteenth century, products made in Paris were known as 'la Fabrique de Paris', and following in the footsteps of Bertin, its manufacturers became renowned for the diverse range of fashion accessories they supplied: Umbrellas, fans, pins, shawls, and gloves were offered for sale at every conceivable price.[8] During the seventeenth century, Paris gradually became the capital of the French luxury goods industry. A skilled artisanal workforce was readily available to serve a demanding clientele.[9] Consequently, around 1800, Made in France essentially denoted Made in Paris.

Jean Zuber, a wallpaper manufacturer in Rixheim, in the region of Alsace, often referenced Paris in his letters: 'What new are we undertaking in the

Paris manufactures? Don't you have a person who can instruct you about what happens & give us samples of the novelties from the main manufacturers, there is an absolute need that you find a way to realize this'.[10] In his journal, Henri Lebert (1792–1864), a draughtsman from Colmar, in Alsace, described the feminine elegance of Madame Jurienne, a bourgeois woman used to the Parisian social evenings:

> Beautiful, graceful and spirited, doing the honors as a Sylph, she possessed to the highest degree the so Parisian art to trace her own circle of admirers that made as many people happy as guests were. If you remember a description of Mad. de Staël on the Parisian society, read it again, to complete my opinion.[11]

By the early nineteenth century, the superiority of Parisian elegance was established. Honoré de Balzac stated in 1830: 'The person that does not come often to Paris will never be elegant'.[12] For this reason, Zuber hired Parisian draughtsmen, such as Darmancourt, or, Saint Georges, 'in the capital 2 or 3 months to get his ideas shaped a bit'.[13] The brands *Made in France,* and *Made in Paris* were becoming embossed on products originating from these areas.

The premier position of Paris in the production of luxury goods affected the training of French craftsmen and influenced the education of artisans in other European capitals and French cities. The ascent of Paris began in the seventeenth century, under the guidance of Jean-Baptiste Colbert, First Minister of State between 1661 and 1683.[14] The French government concentrated on leading artisans' workshops, such as the Gobelins Manufactory, in Paris, to facilitate the dissemination of technical knowledge – which underpinned the excellence of luxury goods made in this city. This geographical density was complemented by support for 'modern' education in drawing. To improve talent, artisans were educated in the 'French taste'.[15] State-funded communal courses in drawing ensured French mastery in this skill continued for many generations. Such drawing schools were the ancestors of the great Paris schools of the nineteenth century, such as the Arts décoratifs de Paris. Moreover, craftsmen were sent to other towns and cities to improve their drawing and technical skills in particular manufactures, for example Aubusson, or Felletin, (tapestry), Amiens, or Rouen (porcelain and embroidery), Lyon (silk textiles), and Mulhouse (printed fabrics). Considerable effort was devoted to the identification of the most competent teachers. In many private workshops, education in the crafts became an obsession.[16] The fundamental aim of this training was to produce outstanding results from the marriage of art and industry.

It is apparent, therefore, that during the seventeenth century, the benefits of commercial drawing became increasingly recognized and valued. The growth of this type of drawing demonstrated a growing interchange of ideas between art schools, the world of business, and the state – all of which shared common concerns. Drawing helped determine the boundaries of good taste and this made it imperative that the best workers were trained to become exceptionally proficient. The artistic and technical capabilities of French craftsmen were crucial to the emergence of a culture which valued Made in France.

Draughtsmen were at the centre of a production network. Their drawings defined the design, shape, technical characteristics, and decoration of products. Subsequently, the ability of artisans to anticipate changes to drawings also contributed to the prestige of Made in France. The evolution of artistic and technical conventions, understood by workers with diverse skills, developed in performative activities such as formatting, assembling, and surfacing.[17] Consequently, in addition to the skills learned by craftsmen during their training, Made in France was also shaped by technical 'sub-consciousness'. The beauty of the object – its colours and motifs – and its intrinsic quality, were essential to attract customers who wished to purchase items of good taste.

Art might be represented by unique objects of unassailable quality, which commanded high prices that only the elite could afford. Conversely, mass-produced articles, of lower quality, were attractive to poorer consumers. Nonetheless, Made in France was defined by the marriage between art and industry; it was this complementarity that enhanced the French reputation.[18] Indeed, by 1800, the brands Made in France, and Made in Paris, were universally adopted by French craftsmen.

Protecting the origin of products during the long nineteenth century

During the nineteenth century, the defence of high-quality French products became a political issue. The government was subjected to intense lobbying from producers' associations who wanted state protection against misrepresentation, and other forms of unfair competition that were being practiced in domestic and export markets.[19] In Europe, and especially France, protection of geographical indications (hereafter, GIs) has a long history, and they continue to be fiercely defended.[20] Recognition of the importance of terroir was fundamental to GIs in foodstuffs and wines. For these products, wine growers, merchants, and politicians collaborated to secure national, and then international recognition of this form of intellectual property. Nonetheless, other sectors of the French economy – l porcelain, luxury leather goods, and haute couture – were also subject to similar campaigns for protection.

In 1800, Alexandre Brongniart (1770–1847) became the administrator of porcelain manufacture in Sèvres. Brongniart founded his artistic-economic policy on the principle of creating 'a trade mark per trade mark' (d'une marque par la marque). In this context, 'Made in Sèvres' was part of the evolution of Made in France. Brongniart sought to affirm the reputation of Sèvres by making its products remarkable and, therefore, attractive to consumers. Imitation was a key component of this policy. For Brongiart, Sèvres had a duty to ensure that existing artistic designs ('modèles') were made freely available to private manufacturers. Consequently, he gave private manufacturers the right to make overcasts of older designs and drawings. Over time, the brand Made in Sèvres had a dual function: it indicated the geographical origin of the product, and that it was made according to the 'French' manner.[21] Eleven signs placed on a piece of porcelain were necessary to assert the superiority of 'Sèvres' manufacture. Two of the marks indicated that the product was finished: one mark was the manufacturing trade mark in chrome green, while the other was for the setting of the background (pose de fonds'). The other marks belonged to the spinner, draughtsman, outliner ('décalqueuse'), calibrator, cutter, and enameller. Taken together, these marks created the 'Sèvres' brand.

To extend the appeal of the Sèvres brand, Brongniart promoted the manufacture of cheaper porcelain which was produced to less exacting artistic and technical standards compared to the porcelain that had made the reputation Sèvres.[22] Effectively, Brongniart was 'extending' the brand from the luxury category into the realm of common use ('choses banales').[23] The cheaper products were copies of the Sèvres luxury artefacts and were also embossed with the traditional Sèvres brand. However, cheaper porcelain was sometimes produced in independent Parisian workshops which specialized in decoration. Simultaneously, Brongniart increased the number of sales depots and shops selling Sèvres porcelain. For example, a new shop was opened at Lignereux in 1808, and a new warehouse on the count de St. Didier, 23 boulevard des Italiens, in 1818.[24]

Brongniart's management policy is reminiscent of the *Good luxuries* or *English luxury* as described by the anglophile, Montesquieu.[25] According to Montesquieu, the variety, novelty, and pleasure of 'physical forms' and their creative 'imitation' bring taste and distinction to a large group of consumers. Imitation was viewed as indispensable to innovation. Despite legislation to protect copyright, imitation of books and other literature persisted during the eighteenth and the nineteenth centuries, because such practices signalled creativity.[26] Nonetheless, such imitations were always inaccessible to the majority of the population; replication did not result in demi-luxe or *populuxe*, manufacturers – quite the contrary.[27] Even though reproduction porcelain was not manufactured to the onerous standards traditionally associated with Sèvres, it nonetheless helped to enhance the visibility of Sèvres as a brand and, thereby, the general reputation of French manufacture.[28] Indeed, in the short term, the process of decalcomania became much less expensive than hand decoration, and it facilitated the diffusion of styles and brands associated with Sèvres. Brongniart's policies were designed, first, to increase the geographical significance attached to French products , and, second, to disseminate in overseas markets the repute attached to products marked Made in France.

Brongniart's ambition was to make Sèvres the archetype of European taste. For example, the Caron and Lefebvre factories hired decorators from Sèvres to imitate this style to perfection. These factories employed Jacques François Swebach, a Sèvres-based manufacturer between 1803 and 1813, to imitate the style of Sèvres by representing on a vase the passage through Mont-Saint-Bernard.[29] Under Brongniart's direction, imitations of Sèvres porcelain became prolific as it assumed its role as a champion of French taste.[30] The administration never filed a complaint: imitation meant dissemination.[31] The diffusion of the Sèvres style acted as an advertisement and reinforced the primacy of the manufacturer's taste.

Country-of-origins and World Fairs

During the later nineteenth century, World Fairs and exhibitions organized by commercial associations and colonial governments showcased inventions and new products that were attributed to 'national genius'. Competition between a diverse range of manufacturers accentuated international economic rivalry. Exhibitions were a means of demonstrating national artistic and technical ingenuity, and revealing national know-how by way of patented inventions that were oftendisplayed for the first time at such events. This tension was best exemplified by the French clothing and garment firms that attended exhibitions.[32]

From the mid-nineteenth century, French firms that informed the development of style in the clothing and textile industries became known as *haute couture.*[33] It is plausible that some of the fashion trends emerged from a broader group of firms, including textile manufacturers, negociants, and artisans that produced many types of fabric.[34] Nonetheless, haute couture established domination in this field of manufacture and contributed to the development of a strong brand, first as Made in Paris, and, following *Unis France* in the early twentieth century, Made in France. Haute couture, therefore, became synonymous with French expertise.[35]

Haute couture firms emerged in the mid-nineteenth century as a cosmopolitan trade, in which many workers, entrepreneurs, and clients had international backgrounds. Although the luxury industries are symbolic of France, they have always been characterized by an openness to international networks and migrants.[36] This industry was characterized by small to medium-sized firms that produced exclusive garments for women in very small quantities. Innovative in cut, colour, and materials, haute couture garments often set the tone for fashionable clothes produced by large-scale manufacturers. From 1868, haute couture firms were represented by a professional syndicate, the Chambre Syndicale de la Haute Couture, which organized the trade and lobbied the government for better trading conditions.[37] Couturiers assembled in the Chambre Syndicale to determine rules for the trade, and to decide which firms were worthy of membership. Subsequently, members of the Chambre Syndicale agreed to supply two types of client: the private customers, and foreign corporate buyers, who were admitted to the seasonal haute couture shows. Foreign buyers paid 30 or 50% more than private customers for each garment purchased. This premium was considered to be the fee for authorized reproduction in overseas markets.

Towards the end of the nineteenth century, however, concerns emerged about the marketing of haute couture. The problem was the growth in counterfeiting, and imitation, which became a source of nationalist discourse. According to the contemporary sociologist, Gabriel Tarde, French luxury products were relying upon imitation because consumers wished to adopt the new trends launched by the elites.[38] New lines were communicated via the press, though it is doubtful whether the drawings and descriptions therein were always of French origin.[39] Numerous studies in art, and art history, document that some who worked in haute couture felt that their Paris shops were being undermined by competition from other fashion cities, especially Vienna and New York.[40] French entrepreneurs and journalists had misgivings about imitators working in Berlin, Brussels, Vienna, New York, and other cities. Sometimes, this discourse became nationalistic, as for example, towards Austrian and German manufacturers during the First World War.[41] Such nationalistic overtones were not only directed to Germanic producers: research has revealed that the couturier Paul Poiret, was equally antagonistic towards US imitators.[42]

After 1918, haute couture firms sought greater international exposure for their products, even though they did not have the capacity to manufacture their designs on a substantial scale. Indeed, only a few haute couture firms had foreign retail outlets before the First World War, and this number dwindled during the interwar era.[43] For example, Marcel Rochas, who was not a member of the Chambre Syndicale, opened a New York branch in 1937. Rochas produced dresses in Paris that were sold in New York, but he encountered difficulties with US Customs and eventually closed the American branch.[44] In any event, during this period, the Chambre Syndicale developed a policy that haute couture should only be produced in Paris. The justification for this initiative was that everything had to be made within the haute couture house located in Paris, in order to provide employment to workers in the city. In practice, complementary products – perfumes, boxes, and wrappings –were often made elsewhere in France. And, for the majority of consumers, textiles were sourced in France, though researchers have recently demonstrated that this declined during the post-1945 era.[45]

Some of those involved in the trade, and in local politics, embraced the defence of haute couture. In the late 1920s, Yves Georges Prade, head of redaction at *L'Officiel de la Couture et de la Mode*, a luxury magazine that represented haute couture on domestic and international markets, started campaigning for the safeguarding of French industries. Prade was a staunch advocate of the French luxury business, and a pen for *L'Officiel*. A connoisseur of fine wine, and automobiles, Prade thought that haute couture was a product of terroir to be preserved and protected from copying. However, the simplification of designs by firms not engaged in haute couture was a source of concern to Prade. This journalist campaigned for the French automobile industry in *L'Officiel*: 'that standard taste of Detroit is not the norm in Paris',[46] and alerted the public to the threat posed to French automobile brands by the craze for American cars. Prade expressed similar sentiments for haute couture.

In June 1929, Prade, who was a Conservative, had almost attained the age of political majority (25 years), which allowed him to be elected. Prade campaigned in the fourteenth arrondissement, and became the youngest *conseiller municipal* in France, when he was elected *conseiller municipal* of Paris, and *conseiller général* of the Department of the Seine. The couture profession welcomed his election as a significant step in the defence of luxury industries because it expected Prade to be a major propagandist.[47] Prade encouraged domestic citizens to buy French cars[48] and fostered the development of glittering competitions at which famous Parisians and international socialites displayed their motor cars while wearing the latest designs in haute couture, and millinery. In November 1929, Prade published a flattering portrait of entrepreneur, Louis Renault, which saluted his, 'admirable offensive' towards US automobile production. Prade also urged the female readership of *L'Officiel* to resist the appeal of mass-produced motorcars: to be consistent in their preferences, such readers, who preferred their shoes to be made-to-measure, should buy personalized French automobiles.[49] In 1933, *L'Officiel* created the *Coupe des Dames* (Ladies Cup), for the Monte Carlo rally, which gathered the elite of the European and American automobile industries.[50]

During the Great Depression, Prade recognized the importance of invisible exports and called for the rescue of tourism in France.[51] Prade also worked on initiatives such as the *Grande Semaine* of Paris, a week in June dedicated to various festivities, which attracted an international crowd of socialites to horse races, motorcar shows, and elegance competitions.[52] In the summer of 1930, Prade visited the US with trips to Niagara Falls, Detroit, Chicago, Washington, D.C., Philadelphia, and New York. He had recently read books by Paul Morand, enthusiast Americanophile, and future biographer of Chanel, and Georges Duhamel, author of *Scènes de la vie future*, an essay that became one of the first anti-American manifestos. For Prade, Duhamel, 'enjoyed himself suffering like a French genius whose habits have been overturned.'[53] Prade was won over by America, especially New York, but did not mention the Depression. Citing figures at length to demonstrate American gigantism to his French readership, he added that 'presently America has three masters: Costes, Maurice Chevalier, and the Chic Parisien'.[54] Prade claimed that Americans were discovering individual creativity, taste, virtuosity, and artistic and aesthetic sense in France, and that Made in Paris was admired as a brand. Throughout the US, he argued that couture and millinery were unmistakably identified as French.

While in the US, Prade witnessed the effects of counterfeiting and imitation, and commented:

> this advertisement which, the day before my departure, was announcing in a popular store, *the success dress of Augustabernard for 30 dollars, the famous Agnès beret for 8,5 dollars*. Such prices … show well that the most modest customer also demands a little bit of the French taste. As his purchasing power is important, one seeks to give him satisfaction, sometimes even

> in cheating him, and I have seen designs audaciously baptized with the name of our major brands, which would make our Parisian masters ebullient with indignation.[55]

According to Prade, 'Paris' dresses were everywhere in New York, and they included cheap, knock-off garments in lower-end department stores, in addition to high-end, quality designs, legally imported from France by luxury enterprises which included Saks-Fifth Avenue.

After this outburst, Prade became more critical of counterfeiting. In February 1931, he commented on the successful protection of the French automobile industry from American competition, which followed an initiative by Louis Renault. Prade feared that US manufacturers might overtake the French fashion industry: the former were becoming more independent of Paris, and they had launched a systematic propaganda campaign against French prestige. Essentially, US companies were using Paris haute couture as a creative office; they purchased designs for reproduction on a mass scale and reaped the fruits of French creativity. According to Prade, the consequences of this American activity were that the brands belonging to haute couture houses were tarnished, and there was a general decline in French creativity. The solution to this problem was to respond to the manner in which US manufacturers conducted their business.[56]

Labels of origins: towards a clearer policy in the 1940s

During the 1920s, the majority of cases heard in the Paris small crimes court concerning authenticity involved alcoholic beverages. Additionally, there were a number of lawsuits for counterfeiting in the fashion industry, especially the lawsuits waged by members of the Chambre Syndicale de la Couture Parisienne, to which could be added the occasional non-member, such as Chanel.[57] However, the protection of Made in France or Made in Paris did not feature in these cases. Nonetheless, examination of these small crimes court cases shows that entrepreneurs in all industries sought to protect their intellectual property against substitute products. It was during this decade that defending authenticity became more prominent in French society.[58]

Most couturiers continued to produce only in Paris. In 1943, decisive legislation was introduced by the Vichy regime to protect the term *haute couture* from unauthorized use. This staute also prohibited the use of associated symbols, or similar brand names, such as representations of the Eiffel tower, or *Paris couture*, respectively. Potentially, this legislation was important to the French haute couture profession. However, the archives of the Chambre Syndicale are inconclusive as to why this legislation – which became effective only in 1947 – was introduced during this decade. It is also debatable whether this legislation was enforceable. From a different perspective, French protection of its haute couture needs to be considered in a broader context: this industry was isolated from the international market during the German occupation of France. As far as we can determine from the archives, the 1943 legislation was used to protect the French haute couture trade.[59]

After 1945, the production of luxury goods was revitalized. There was increased recognition that French manufacture of these products was characterized by tacit knowledge which generated artefacts of substantial value, and benefitted employment, both of which were important in the reconstruction period. This belief was very old: it echoed the defence of luxury goods proposed in eighteenth-century writings, including that of Bernard Mandeville in *Fable of the bees*, a satire describing the social goods that vices bring somehow inadvertently to society, notably by way of the luxuries in which criminals may indulge. France had to endure considerable hardship during the immediate post-1945 era. Nonetheless, as Claude Rouzaud argued, craftsmanship allowed France to add high value to its limited raw materials; this, in turn, would accelerate French growth in subsequent decades.[60]

De-localization and re-localization

France continued to develop its high reputation in the manufacture of luxury goods in the postwar era. A pertinent question that arose was the extent to which Made in France, or equivalent indicia mattered to the strategies of firms in this industry. As previously discussed, during the interwar period, the majority of French entrepreneurs believed that the production of luxury goods had to remain in France. But how did this belief change in the post-1970 era – the last phase of globalization? Would the association between quality and France remain intact if there was a partial or complete relocation of production to another country?[61]

For wines and many foodstuffs, the strict enforcement of appellations d'origine contrôlée, means that relocation of production is impossible. For some foods, though, such as Gruyère cheese, origin remains contested.[62] The answer to the previous question is far less certain for perfumes, couture garments, couture designer ready-to-wear, and accessories. For the latter products, two interrelated issues need to be considered. First, large luxury firms have invested considerable sums overseas in the training of craftsmen who are becoming increasingly adept in the production of high-quality products. This investment, complemented by growing international technology transfer, meant that the benefits from relocation were likely to grow. Second, as the international demand for French luxury goods increased, it was expected that production would relocate to satisfy such markets. Rarity would still play a role in the definition of luxury, but the precise origins of this characteristic could change. In a milestone study on luxury, management experts, Vincent Bastien and Jean-Noël Kapferer, suggested that a product was no longer a luxury product if its production was relocated. Instead, such a product should be classified as a 'simple premium product'.[63]

The legend 'Made in' has struggled to reconcile the competing demands of national prestige and the increased complexity of global value chains.

Consequently, 'Made in' has fragmented to indicate either, place of production, or place of design, or source of raw material. Made in France indicates that products received their last substantial transformation in France. This legend continues to be important to French producers of luxury goods: the organization Comité Colbert, which was established in 1954, promotes luxury products, and its members export 80% of their production.[64]

In recent decades, the government was preoccupied with the current state, and likely future of Made in France. In the 1990s, Dominique Taddéi and Benjamin Coriat provided an analysis of Made in France within the context of global competition. Their research was funded by the French government which sought to define and measure the impact of *Made in France* on the French economy.[65] According to Taddei and Coriat, the aftermath of the 1970s oil shock, the advent of the last phase of globalization, and the challenge of remaining competitive justified the need to assess the importance of Made in France. Taddei and Coriat reiterated current debates on competition: the world had become dangerous ("*le monde est devenu dangereux*"), in the authors' italics.[66] Ultimately, the objective of improved competitiveness was to maintain high levels of employment.[67] Consumer demand for high-quality products was another factor advanced by the authors to justify the use of country-of-origin labels.[68]

Currently, debates on Made in France share common features with debates in the seventeenth and eighteenth centuries. Rather than buying imports which results in an outflow of currency, contemporary debates emphasize the benefits of relocating manufacturing to France to foster reindustrialization. During the 1990s and 2000s, improved transportation and access to a cheaper overseas workforce led to offshoring by many French firms.[69] The Covid-19 pandemic has partly offset this trend: fear of shortages attracted the attention of consumers, industrialists, and the government. Since the 1980s, regions in the East and North of France have not benefitted from plans to reignite the economy. Imported counterfeit articles and substitutes of poorer quality have been the subject of considerable critical commentary.[70] The tendency to retract the provenance of such products has been influenced by nationalism fuelled by the economic and social crisis that has been endemic since the late 1970s. Within the framework of the last phase of globalization, there have been growing demands for a redefinition of Made in France.[71]

The above trends have resulted in subterfuge: labelling a product 'designed in France' may mislead consumers by creating the impression that the article was manufactured entirely in France. To address such problems, new labels have been developed. Thus, the logo *France terre textile* provides several guarantees: at least 75% of the manufacturing occurs in the five 'cradles' of the French textile industry. Certified firms may use the mark 'Berceaux Textiles Français' (AGR), This logo also certifies a high level of quality, and that production is environmentally friendly. Products with this label are subject to random inspection, and they must be declared on the platform of traceability *EColTex-TerreTextile*.[72]

Similarly, the certification trade mark, Origine France Garantie, was created in 2010 following a report by Yves Jégo on the brand 'France'.[73] This trade mark differs from similar marks, such as Made in France, 'conçu en France', and 'Fabriqué en France', because the latter are self-declared by the producer. Origine France Garantie certifies the French origin of a product. It may be applied to any product, and the right to use this mark is subject to independent verification. To obtain certification, applicants must satisfy two cumulative criteria. First, no less than 50% of the unit production price must occur within France. One consequence of this requirement is that Made in France became synonymous with re-territorialization. The second criterion is to determine whether workers with specific know-how will be available and, if so, if they will accept work in the certified factory. Funding schools to provide education in handwork and the new technologies is essential to this phase; but it is also challenging considering that the division of labour can suffer from a negative cultural image.[74]

Conclusion

This chapter has argued that France's image did not depend solely on Made in France. The protection of country-of-origins in France appears to be an on-going which sometimes generates heated political and economic debates. Numerous economists, politicians, and groups of entrepreneurs have for a long time advocated a reinforcement of 'Made in France', especially for exported products.

The only French products that have been effectively and continuously protected are appellations, for which it is not possible to de-couple product and place. In France, the terroir, or the regional denomination of origin appears as a protective mechanism that also had the effect of reinforcing the identity and presence of the nation on international markets. Yet, the growth of licensing arrangements enabled numerous luxury products, including haute couture, to be successfully off-shored, which also contributed, indirectly, to the prosperity of the French economy.

Currently, *official* promotion of Made in France is illegal under European Union trade rules. In contrast, GIs for food and alcoholic beverages have been accepted for over 100 years.[75] But such indications are founded on the region, not the nation. This distinction is particularly apposite for France: ever since Napoleon Bonaparte, French history was characterized by the centralization of institutions, government, and power in Paris, and, therefore, the erasure of regional languages and dialects in favour of a unified version of the French language. While dialects and regional languages were forbidden in the Nation's schools, terroir became the legal basis for the defence of French wines and foods throughout the world.

Can consumers realistically pay for products marked Made in France? The relocation of some luxury goods production to Southeast Asia led to a decline in retail prices. Moreover, social and environmental laws in Western Europe are much more demanding than those in developing countries. In the current economic crisis, few consumers can afford an increase in price. Moreover, if the supply of products labelled Made in France did not increase, it might signal a new divergence between the rich and poor. Some economists, inspired by David Ricardo and Milton Friedman, believe that the solution is to lower employers' charges and free up labour.[76] However, it has been widely demonstrated during the numerous crises of the last 40 years, that free labour is linked to forced labour.

Notes

1 This chapter is part of two projects that have received funding from the European Research Council (ERC) under the European Union's Horizon 2020 research and innovation programme: Creative IPR: The History of Intellectual Property Rights in the Creative Industries, ERC CoG Grant agreement No. 818523, and MISS: Made In SweatShops, Marie Skłodowska-Curie Grant agreement No. 101024003.
2 Guy, *When Champagne*; Vabre, *Le sacre du Roquefort*; Stanziani, *Rules.*
3 Joubert de l'Hiberderie, *Le dessinateur pour les fabriques.* Leroudier, 'Les dessinateurs', 1908, pp. 13–31 and *Les Cahiers d'Étienne Benoit*, 1930.
4 Miller, 'Designers', p. 1.
5 Blanc-Subes, 'Le marché', p. 16.
6 *Mercure de France*, 1 January, 1775, p. 204.
7 In 1770, Bertin opened her first hats shop under the brand "Le Grand Mogol", in the rue du Faubourg-Saint-Honoré, in Paris. Her creativity and her sense of business helped her develop the firm very fast, soon employing 30 people and working with 120 suppliers. Her clientele was solely aristocratic. Sapori, *Rose Bertin*, pp. 112–127.
8 Sougy, 'La Fabrique'. Another popular cliché still alive influences the studies: some believe that Paris, capital of luxury and good taste, was born at the end of the nineteenth century, and more precisely with the installation in 1858, rue de la Paix, Charles Frederick Worth (1825–1895), English, "inventor of haute couture. Fashion historians make it the date of the birth of haute-couture. What is the difference between the milliner and the designer? The first would not be a force of proposal, while the second would impose his style, the right tone, the good taste to his customers. It is hard to believe in this opposition which minimizes the work of the milliner and transforms the couturier into a dictator. Krick, 'Charles Frederick Worth', http://www.metmuseum.org/toah/hd/wrth/hd_wrth.html; Cole, 'Patrimoine'; Zajtmann, "L'organisation'.
9 Jacqué, *De la manufacture*, p. 68.
10 Musée du Papier Peint, Rixheim, France, Zuber, Z 108, 28 prairial an VIII (17 juin 1800); 14 vendémiaire an VIII (6 Octobre 1799); Jacqué, *De la manufacture*, pp. 66, 69.
11 Bibliothèque Municipale de Colmar, France, Henri Lebert, Journal, vol. 2, 13 avril 1813 et vol. 4, 10 novembre 1818; Millet, *Vie et destin.*
12 Balzac, *Traité de la vie élégante*, p. 56.
13 Musée du Papier Peint, Rixheim, France, Zuber, Z 108, 4 complémentaire an VIII (21 septembre 1800); Jacqué, *De la manufacture*, p. 69.
14 P. Minard, *La fortune du colbertisme: état et industrie dans la France des Lumières.*
15 Millet, 'La manufacture'.
16 Millet, 'Transmettre', pp. 273–284.

17 Becker, *Les mondes*, p. 49; Hilaire-Pérez, *La pièce et le geste.*
18 Celina Fox has shown that there was an attempt to separate the two distinct spheres from the seventeenth century onwards, but this was above all intellectual and corresponded to academic discourse that did not reveal much about practices. Fox, *The Arts.*
19 V. Pouillard, 'Intellectual property rights and country-of-origin labels', p. 403.
20 V. Pouillard, "Intellectual property rights and country-of-origin labels,", p. 403.
21 The imposition of the brand of the manufacture is imposed well before that of the designer. The artist or draftsman imposes his signature when the art market takes off. It was not until the end of the nineteenth century that drawings were systematically signed.
22 Such products, just as the ceramics manufactured by Josiah Wedgwood, however remained costly.
23 Millet, 'La manufacture'. Roche, *Histoire.*
24 Archives de la Manufacture de Sèvres, Sèvres, France, U 4, dépôts de vente, liasses 1–4 (Magasin de Paris rue Grammont, 1815; Pérès, Jamas, Irlande et Cie, 1816–1817; Dépôt rue Sainte Anne, 1817; Projet de dépôt au Bengale, 1827; Dépôt rue de Rivoli, Paris, 1828–1840; chez M. Bury, 1848–1849; Dépôt rue d'Enfer n°7, 1848–1853; Dépôt Sallandrouze à Londres, 1849–1853, n°2 rue Voltaire, Paris, 1853–1857.
25 de Montesquieu, *De l'esprit*, pp. 341–345; Berg and Eger, *Luxury*; Berg, *Luxury & Pleasure.*
26 Blanc and Beaumont, *Code General.*
27 J.-F. de Saint-Lambert, 'Luxe', in D. Diderot, J. Le Rond D'Alembert, *Encyclopédie ou Dictionnaire raisonné des sciences, des arts et des métiers*, 1751, t. IX, p. 763. Maxine Berg and Hélène Clifford have also shown that imitations were not demi-luxe replicas of the originals. Berg, 'New commodities', pp. 63–87.
28 Grenier, 'Une économie'; Millet, 'la manufacture'.
29 Archives de la Manufacture de Sèvres, Sèvres, France, Vase en forme fuseau, cartel peint par Swebach : Passage du Mont Saint Bernard, fond brun, décor camaïeu d'or, Swebach Jacques François Joseph (1769–1823), 1806, porcelaine, manufacture Caron et Lefebvre (1806–1812). AMS, Oa 1, 1800–1815, État des personnes attachées à la manufacture nationale de Porcelaine de Sèvres ou employées momentanément en l'an X, en l'an XII, en l'an XI, en 1806, en 1810.
30 Slitine, *Samson.*
31 Guillerme and Sebestik, *Les commencements*, pp. 92–93; Vérin, 'La technologie', pp.137–139; Beckman, *Entwurf ;* Dieterich, cited in Hilaire-Pérez, *La* pièce, p. 12.
32 Pouillard, *Paris*, pp. 22–42.
33 Simon, *Monographie*; Grumbach, *Histoires.*
34 Maillet, *Histoire*; Blaczszyk and Wubs, *The Fashion.*
35 For a recent discussion of the *UNIS* trade mark, see Higgins, *Brands*, pp. 49–52.
36 This topic was addressed in Saillard, *Mode d'Ici.*
37 Grumbach, *Histoires.*
38 de Tarde, *Les lois.*
39 Schweitzer, 'American fashion', pp. 130–149.
40 Troy, *Couture Culture.*
41 Pouillard, *Paris*, pp. 33–40.
42 Troy, *Couture Culture.*
43 Grumbach, *Histoires*; Green, *Ready-to-Wear*; Pouillard, 'Managing fashion'.
44 Pouillard, *Paris*, pp. 110–112.
45 Dubé-Sénécal, *La mode francaise*, pp. 249–261.
46 *L'Officiel*, 87, 15 November 1928, p. 9.
47 *L'Officiel*, 94, 15 June 1929, p. 13; 15 November 1928, p. 9.

48 *L'Officiel*, 95, 15 July 1929, pp. 11–15.
49 *L'Officiel*, 99, 15 November 1929, p. 17.
50 *L'Officiel*, 142, 15 June 1933, pp. 19–20.
51 *L'Officiel*, 105, 15 May 1930, pp. 13–15.
52 *L'Officiel*, 108, 15 August 1930, p. 11.
53 *L'Officiel*, 110, 15 October 1930, pp. 11–12.
54 *L'Officiel*, 110, 15 October 1930, pp. 11–12.
55 *L'Officiel*, 110, 15 October 1930, pp. 11–12.
56 *L'Officiel*, 114, 15 February 1931, p. 15.
57 Pouillard, *Paris*, pp. 49–57.
58 Green, *Ready-to-Wear*; Green, *The Limits*; Pouillard, *Paris*, chapter 2.
59 Chambre Syndicale de la Couture Parisienne archives, Compte-rendu de la réunion du Comité de la Chambre Syndicale de la Couture Parisienne, 13 May 1945, p. 10; and General Assembly, report, year 1959, pp. 3–4. Also, see Pouillard, *Paris*, p. 186.
60 Rouzaud, *Un problème*; Mandeville, *La fable*.
61 Koromyslov, 'Le Made in France'.
62 Jenny Gross, 'Is Gruyère still Gruyère if it doesn't come from Gruyères?', *New York Times*, 12 January 2022, Is Gruyère Still Gruyère if It Doesn't Come From Gruyères? – *The New York Times* (nytimes.com). Accessed 15 January 2022.
63 Bastien and Kapferer, *Luxe Oblige*, p. 226.
64 Koromyslov, 'Le Made in France', p. 111; p. 119; 'Marquage d'origine pour les produits industriels', *Bulletin de l'office des douanes*, numéro 6567, 'Protection de l'origine française' (8 March 2003).
65 Taddéi and Coriat, *Made in France*, p. 10.
66 Taddéi and Coriat, *Made in France*, p. 11.
67 Taddéi and Coriat, *Made in France*, p. 14; Stanziani, *Rules*.
68 Taddéi and Coriat, *Made in France*.
69 Millet, *Le livre*, pp. 62–63, 188; Hoskins, *Stitched Up*, pp. 79–80.
70 Courtecuisse, *Réindustrialiser*.
71 'Made in' must be analyzed in the context of European lobbies. Van Schendelen, *More Machiavelli*.
72 http://www.franceterretextile.fr/dossier-de-presse-terre-textile/
73 Y. Jégo, *En finir avec la mondialisation anonyme. La traçabilité au service des consommateurs et de l'emploi*, Rapport public, République Française: 2010. https://www.vie-publique.fr/rapport/31065-en-finir-avec-la-mondialisation-anonyme-la-tracabilite-au-service-des.
74 Birnbaum, *Source-it*; Jégo, *En finir*; Banaji, *Theory*.
75 https://www.euractiv.fr/section/elections/news/le-made-in-france-peu-efficace-et-anti-europeen/
76 Ricardo, *Des principes*; Friedman, *Capitalism*.

Bibliography

Banaji, J., *Theory as History: Essays on Modes of Production and Exploitation*. Leiden and Boston: Brill Academic Publishers, 2010.

Bastien, V., and Kapferer, J.N., *Luxe Oblige*. Paris: Eyrolles, 2008.

Becker, H., *Les mondes de l'art*. Paris: Flammarion, 2006.

Berg, M., 'New commodities, luxuries and their consumers', in Berg, M., and Clifford, H. (eds), *Consumers and Luxury: Consumer Culture in Europe, 1650–1850*, Manchester: Manchester University Press, 1999, pp. 63–87.

Berg, M., and Eger, E. (eds), *Luxury in the Eighteenth Century: Debates, Desires and Delectable Goods*. Basingstoke: Palgrave Macmillan, 2003.

Berg, M., *Luxury & Pleasure in Eighteenth-Century Britain*. Oxford: Oxford University Press, 2005.

Bergeron, L., *Les industries du luxe en France*. Paris: Odile Jacob, 1998.

Birnbaum, D., *Source-it. Global Material Sourcing for the Clothing Industry*. Genève: International Trade Centre, UNCTAD/WTO, 2005.

Blaczszyk, R.L., and Wubs, B., *The Fashion Forecasters: A Hidden History of Color and Trend Prediction*. London: Bloomsbury, 2018.

Blanc, E., and Beaumont, A., *Code général de la propriété industrielle littéraire et artistique comprenant les législations de tout le pays et les traités internationaux*. Paris: Imprimerie et Librairie générale de la jurisprudence, 1854.

Blanc-Subes, F., Le marché du papier peint à Bordeaux à la fin du XVIIIe siècle. *Le port des Lumières*, Bordeaux: MAD, 1989.

Cole, D.J., 'Patrimoine et innovation: Charles Frederick Worth, John Redfern ou la naissance de la mode modern', *Mode de recherche*, Centre de recherche Institut français de la mode: June 2011, https://d2mulcrgfv1yq5.cloudfront.net/documents/Patrimoine-et-innovation-D-J-Cole-juin-2011.pdf?mtime=20181024093800&focal=none.

Courtecuisse, M., *Réindustrialiser c'est possible!* Paris: Belin, 2020.

Dubé-Sénécal, V., *La mode francaise. Vecteur d'influence aux Etats-Unis (1946–1960)*. Laval: Presses de l'Université Laval, 2020.

Fox, C., *The Arts of Industry in the Age of Enlightenment*. New Haven, CT: Yale University Press, 2010.

Friedman, M., *Capitalism and Freedom*. Chicago: University of Chicago Press, 1962.

Green, N., *Ready-to-Wear and Ready-to-Work: A Century of Industry and Immigrants in Paris and New York*. Durham, NC: Duke University Press, 1997.

Green, N., *The Limits of Transnationalism*. Chicago: University of Chicago Press, 2019.

Grenier, J.-Y., 'Une économie de l'identification : Juste prix et ordre des marchandises dans l'Ancien Régime', in Stanziani, A. (ed.), *La qualité des produits en France (XVIIIe-XXe siècles)*, Paris: Belin, 2003, pp. 25–53.

Grumbach, D., *Histoires de la mode*. Paris: Editions du Regard, 2008.

Guillerme, J., and Sebestik, J., *Les commencements de la technologie*. Paris: Presses Universitaires de France, 1966.

de L'Hiberderie, J., *Le dessinateur pour les fabriques d'étoffes d'or, d'argent et de soie*. Paris: Sébastien Jorry, 1765.

Higgins, D.M., *Brands, Geographical Origin, and the Global Economy*. Cambridge: Cambridge University Press, 2018.

Hilaire-Pérez, L., *La pièce et le geste: artisans, marchands et savoir technique à Londres au XVIIIe siècle*. Paris: Albin-Michel, 2013.

Hoskins, T.E., *Stitched Up: The Anti-Capitalist Book of Fashion*. London: Pluto Press, 2014.

Jacqué, B., De la manufacture au mur: pour une histoire matérielle du papier peint (1770–1914). Unpublished PhD thesis, University of Lyon 2, 2003.

Koromyslov, M., 'Le Made in France en questions: Pratiques et opinions des professionnels francais du luxe', *Revue francaise de gestion*, 19 (2011), pp. 107–122.

'Marquage d'origine pour les produits industriels', *Bulletin de l'office des douanes*, numéro 6567, Protection de l'origine française (8 March 2003).

Leroudier, E., 'Les dessinateurs de la fabrique lyonnaise au XVIIIe siècle', *Revue de l'histoire de Lyon*, 1908, pp. 13–31.
Leroudier, E., *Les Cahiers d'Étienne Benoit (1761–1771): Livre de Raison d'un Dessinateur de la Fabrique lyonnaise*. Lyon: M. Camus et Carnet, 1930.
Maillet, T., *Histoire de la médiation entre textile et mode en France: des échantillonneurs aux bureaux de style (1825–1875)*. Unpublished PhD thesis, Paris, EHESS, 2013.
Mandeville, B., *La fable des abeilles, première partie*. Paris: Vrin, 2007.
Miller, L., *Designers in the Lyon Silk Industry, 1712–1787*. Unpublished PhD thesis, Brighton Polytechnic, 1988.
Millet, A., 'La manufacture de Sèvres ou les stratégies de l'imitation: Entre acquisition d'un savoir-faire et marqueur d'identité (18e-19e siècles)', *Entreprises et histoire*, 1 (2015), pp. 36–48.
Millet, A., 'Transmettre le dessin de fabrique: Matérialité et immatérialité du livre technique en manufacture (18e-19e siècles)', in Hilaire-Pérez, L., Nègre, V., Spicq, D., and Vermeir, K. (eds), *Le livre et les techniques avant le 20e siècle. À l'échelle du monde*, Paris: CNRS Éd., 2016, pp. 273–284.
Millet, A., *Vie et destin d'un dessinateur textile, d'après le Journal d'Henri Lebert, 1794–1862*. Seyssel: Champ Vallon, 2018.
Millet, A., *Le livre noir de la mode: Création, production, manipulation*. Paris: Les Pérégrines, 2020.
Minard, P., *La fortune du colbertisme: état et industrie dans la France des Lumières*. Paris: Fayard, 2014.
de Montesquieu, C., *De l'esprit des lois*. Geneva: Barillot & Fils, 1748.
Pouillard, V., 'Managing fashion creativity. the history of the Chambre Syndicale de la Couture Parisienne during the interwar period', *Investigaciones de Historia Economica/Economic History Research*, 12 (2016), pp. 76–89.
Pouillard, V., 'Intellectual property rights and country-of-origin labels in the luxury industry', in Pierre-Yves, D., Pouillard, V., and Roberts, J. (eds), *The Oxford Handbook of Luxury Business*, Oxford: Oxford University Press, 2020, p. 403.
Pouillard, V., *Paris to New York: The Transatlantic Fashion Industry in the Twentieth Century*. Cambridge, MA: Harvard University Press, 2021.
Ricardo, D., *Des principes de l'économie politique et de l'impôt*. London: John Murray, 1817.
Roche, D., *Histoire des choses banales: naissance de la consommation dans les sociétés traditionnelles, XVIIe-XIXe siècle*. Paris: Fayard, 1997.
Rouzaud, C., *Un problème d'intérêt national: les industries du luxe*. Strasbourg: Librarie du Recueil Sirey, 1946.
Saillard, O., *Mode d'Ici, Créateurs d'ailleurs*. Paris: Flammarion, 2014.
Sapori, M., *Rose Bertin, la couturière de Marie Antoinette*. Paris: Perrin, 2010.
Schendelen, R.V., *More Machiavelli in Brussels: The Art of Lobbying the EU*. Amsterdam: Amsterdam University Press, 2013.
Schweitzer, M., 'American fashion for American women: the rise and fall of fashion nationalism', in Blaszczyk, R.L. (ed.), *Producing Fashion: Commerce, Culture and Consumers*, Philadelphia: University of Pennsylvania Press, 2008, pp. 130–149.
Simon, P., *Monographie d'une industrie de luxe: la haute couture*. Unpublished PhD thesis, Paris: Presses Universitaires de France, 1931.
Slitine, F., *Samson, génie de l'imitation*. Paris: Massin, 2002.
Sougy, N., 'La Fabrique de Paris au XIXe siècle. Qualités de produits et formation des fabricants', in Lembré, S., and Millet, A. (eds), *Entre art et industrie: les enjeux*

de la formation technique. XVIIIe-XXe siècles. Artefact. *Techniques, histoire & sciences humaines*, 2 (2014), pp. 89–100.

Stanziani, A., *Rules of Exchange: French Capitalism in Comparative Perspective, Eighteenth to Early Twentieth Centuries*. Cambridge: Cambridge University Press, 2012.

Taddéi, D., and Coriat, B., *Made in France: l'industrie francaise dans la compétition mondiale*. Paris: Libraire Générale française, 1993.

de Tarde, G., *Les lois de l'imitation*. Paris: F. Alcan, 1890.

Troy, N., *Couture Culture. A Study in Modern Art and Fashion*. Cambridge, MA: The MIT Press, 2003.

Vabre, S., *Le sacre du Roquefort. L'émergence d'une industrie agro-alimentaire*. Tours: Presses Universitaires Francois-Rabelais, 2015.

Vérin, H., 'La technologie: science autonome ou science intermédiaire', *Documents pour l'histoire des techniques*, actes de la journée d'études doctorales en histoire des techniques, n°14, (2007), pp. 134–143.

Zajtmann, D., 'L'organisation professionnelle comme source de légitimité. Le cas de la Fédération de la couture, du prêt-à-porter des couturiers et des créateurs de mode', *Mode de recherche*, Centre de recherche Institut français de la mode, 11 (2011), https://d2mulcrgfv1yq5.cloudfront.net/documents/Lorganisation-professionnelle-D-Zajtmann-juin-2011.pdf?mtime=20181024093031&focal=none.

8 It's Made in the USA, but it can't be branded 'Made in the USA'

David M. Higgins

Introduction

The title of this chapter raises a beguiling question: why is it that a product that is made in the USA cannot be marked 'Made in the USA'? The answer to this problem is that different regulatory bodies – primarily the United States Customs and Border Protection (hereafter, USCBP) and the Federal Trades Commission (hereafter, FTC) – have different responsibilities and employ separate tests to determine when a product is made in the USA.[1] The former department relies heavily on the concept of 'substantial transformation' to determine whether products need to indicate their country of origin *after* importation.[2] In contrast, the FTC is primarily responsible for ensuring that US consumers are not deceived by misleading advertisements claiming that products are 'Made in the USA' (hereafter, MUSA). To be eligible to use MUSA without qualification, products need to be 'all, or virtually all' made in the USA.[3]

The first US tariff to mandate that imports should indicate their country of origin emerged from the McKinley Report, 1890. This report recognised the importance of origin marking for tariff purposes *and* consumer protection:

> The admitted superiority of certain lines of American goods has induced the importation of foreign imitations of inferior quality, with American brands, to be put on our market as the superior goods of American manufacture ... A practice has also grown up of importing goods under invoices authenticated in a country other, and in a currency of less value, than of the country of manufacture
>
> Section 23 [of the McKinley Tariff] forbids entry to merchandise not plainly marked, stamped, branded or labeled with the name of the country in which it is manufactured, with the purpose of protecting both our own people from the importation of inferior goods and the revenue from possible loss through undervaluation.[4]

Subsequent tariff legislation retained this marking requirement but provided for certain exemptions.[5] During the twentieth century, court cases involving substantial transformation emphasised the importance of marking which

DOI: 10.4324/9781003166184-8

enabled domestic consumers to exercise a preference for US products, and thereby protect US jobs. This reasoning appears to have been first applied in *United States v. Friedlander*, when the court ruled that the intention of Congress was to ensure that, 'at the time of purchase the ultimate purchaser may, by knowing where the goods were produced, be able to buy or refuse to buy them, if such marking should influence his will'.[6]

Implementation of the substantial transformation criterion by the USCBP is becoming increasingly important because for many US industries, such as electronic products and computers, machinery, and transportation, the proportion of imported intermediate products to final products has steadily increased, and in 2016, this ratio averaged 23% compared to 8% for all other US manufacturing.[7] In other words, for such industries, almost a quarter of their output *might* be sold in the USA without any indication of foreign origin. Furthermore, because the bar set by the FTC for unqualified use of MUSA, is very high, some US industrialists have recently argued that the FTC should adopt the USCBP substantial transformation rule for unqualified claims and/or establish a policy similar to that of California which stipulates a minimum value percentage that must be attributable to US inputs to justify unqualified MUSA claims.[8]

It is apparent that determination of US origin by the USCBP has considerable importance to debates on MUSA. Under USCBP regulations, any imported product that is substantially transformed in the USA is considered to be a domestic product that does not need to indicate origin.[9] This premise dates to the famous Gibson-Thomsen case, which involved the import of toothbrush handles and their processing into toothbrushes. The United States Court of Customs and Patent Appeals held that:

> … as a result of such manufacturing processes, the imported toothbrush handles and wood brush blocks lose their identity as such, and become new articles having, respectively, a new name, character, and use; that *as such new articles are produced in the United States they are products of the United States.*[10]

It is important, therefore, to understand how the USCBP applied the substantial transformation test to permit imports to be sold without indicating their foreign origin.

As noted above, the USCBP determines when a product must be marked to indicate its country of origin, but it is the FTC that is responsible for determining lawful use of MUSA. FTC guidelines concerning the 'all or virtually all' criterion for unqualified MUSA claims have remained unchanged since the 1940s.[11] The most recent FTC consultation on Made in the USA, which occurred in 2019, re-affirmed this policy:

> … these studies and discussions do not form a basis to update the Policy Statement. Specifically, they do not provide any evidence to challenge

> the past findings that at least a significant minority of consumers expect a MUSA [Made in the USA]-advertised product to be "all or virtually all" made in the United States. Accordingly, without evidence that consumer perception has changed, the staff finds that the Policy Statement continues to represent the most current advice to marketers on how to comply with Section 5 of the FTC Act.[12]

Nonetheless, the FTC's enforcement of the 'all or virtually all' criterion for MUSA has recently been subject to a number of criticisms. Of particular relevance to this chapter are the interrelated charges that the FTC's policy undermined the legitimate claims of US companies that used *de minimis* quantities of imported content, and that it encouraged US firms to be excessively conservative even when they made qualified claims that their products were MUSA. These criticisms, in turn, have generated repeated demands that the FTC adopts the substantial transformation criterion employed by USCBP. In any event, imports that have been subjected to substantial transformation are eligible to have qualified MUSA claims applied to them. Consequently, the latter products may be perceived by US consumers as equivalent to products that have been produced in the USA, largely with domestic inputs, but which cannot lawfully be described as MUSA.

One theme which has been common to both the USCBP and the FTC is that the different tests they used to determine MUSA were not capable of precise quantification; consequently, they differed from a series of official initiatives designed to promote US business. The Buy American Act of 1933, stipulated that the federal government procured products defined as being made within the USA; part of this regulation defined a US-made product as one in which the cost of US-made components accounted for more than 50% of the overall cost of the product. Similarly, the 'Buy America' provision of the American Recovery and Reinvestment Act (hereafter, ARRA) of 2009, mandated that no funds would be appropriated for building projects or public works unless all the iron and steel and other necessary manufactured products were made in the USA.[13] Nonetheless, economic analysis has indicated that the impact of the above initiatives on 'Buy America' was negligible; without domestic content requirements, such policies would have exercised a *bigger* positive effect on US jobs.[14]

From a broader perspective, the challenges confronting the USCBP and the FTC about Made in America raise broader questions about what is an American product and, therefore, the extent to which US companies derive an advantage over their foreign competitors simply because they are located in the USA. Concerns about the strength of the US firm–US country relationship have been raised by the globally renowned marketing specialist, Simon Anholt:

> … for the first time in history, at least in a couple of business sectors, and at least for the moment, 'Made in America' confers negative equity.

> American industry finds itself all at once in a strange and hostile world … It's a world where 'Made in America' is suddenly not the only offering, nor automatically the most exciting, nor the best; it's just one choice among many.[15]

The remainder of this chapter is organised as follows. The next section discusses some of the early legal cases involving substantial transformation which created the benchmark for future judicial decisions. This is followed by a review of the fundamental issues which determined substantial transformation – value added, and the complexity of post-import processing. The following section then explains why the concept of 'ultimate purchaser' was fundamental to court decisions on origin marking. The penultimate section examines the possible conflict between the FTC and USCBP, and the enduring pressures which have confronted the FTC as it balanced the competing demands of consumer protection with manufacturers' clamour for greater relaxation of the 'all or virtually all' requirement for unqualified MUSA claims. Conclusions are then presented.

USCBP and substantial transformation

Early cases involving the USCBP and substantial transformation involved 'drawback': a refund of the duties paid or assessed against imported merchandise upon re-exportation.[16] These actions provided the fundamental criteria which guided the USCBP and jurists. One of the earliest and most famous cases to address substantial transformation involved Anheuser-Busch, which sought to recover $27,000 in drawback on corks imported from Spain which were used by the company to bottle beer prior to export. The US Court of Claims rejected this claim because, 'There must be transformation; a new and different article must emerge, "having a distinctive name, character or use". This cannot be said of the corks in question. A cork put through the claimant's process is still a cork'.[17] In this quotation, the key words are, 'new and different article' possessing 'distinctive name, character or use'. Such terms were fundamental to the landmark Gibson-Thomsen case which 'has been the traditional basis for evaluating the country of origin for marking processed articles'.[18]

The Gibson-Thomsen case involved the importation of toothbrush handles and wood brush blocks from Japan which were subsequently manufactured into toothbrushes, and hairbrushes, respectively. The court had to consider two interrelated issues. First, was the US manufacturer the 'ultimate user'? Second, did US manufacture substantially transform the imported items? According to the 1930 Tariff Act, the ultimate purchaser was, 'the last person in the United States who will receive the article in the form in which it was imported'.[19] However, this concept is potentially ambiguous: a manufacturer who processes imported products may be the ultimate user *provided* the manufacturing results in a substantial transformation. But, if the processing is only minor, the ultimate purchaser is the consumer who buys the product after processing.[20]

If the manufacturer was adjudged to be the ultimate user because they substantially changed the imported item, there was no need for the final product to indicate its origin when the manufacturer sold it to another buyer.[21] In Gibson-Thomsen, the court ruled that the US manufacturer was the ultimate purchaser and therefore there was no need for the transformed article to indicate its Japanese origin after import. Of particular importance, it was acknowledged that considerable confusion would arise when 'an article manufactured in the United States [had to] bear the marking legend of several countries; and that such confusion of markings could not have been intended by the Congress'.[22] Further, the court determined that the imported items were substantially transformed in the USA, 'having a new name, character, and use'.[23] Indeed, in the manufacture of toothbrushes, 60% of the total cost of manufacture was attributed to the cost of the bristles and US labour; for hairbrushes, the bristles accounted for between 60 and 70% of the total cost.[24]

At this juncture, it is appropriate to explain that USCBP employs the term 'substantial transformation' in a variety of contexts, including drawback, application of the Generalised System of Preferences, and to enforce country of origin marking. However, the justification for applying this test varied according to each of these contexts: Substantial transformation was employed to foster US manufacturing exports, to encourage industrialisation in less developed countries, and to facilitate the making of informed purchasing decisions by US consumers, respectively.[25]

Nonetheless, the consistency with which the USCBP subsequently applied its interpretation of substantial transformation was opaque and this generated considerable criticism from academic lawyers. David Silverstein claimed, 'Different customs statutes have different objectives, and different policy approaches may be required to effect these objectives'.[26] David Palmeter asserted:

> … the definitions of the term 'substantial transformation' that appear in regulations and rulings of the Customs Service, and in court decisions, differ slightly from one substantive legal area to another: a 'transformation' apparently may be 'substantial' enough for one purpose but not for another. Some substantial transformations, the United States Customs Service says, sometimes must be more 'substantial' than others.[27]

The fundamental problem is that there does not exist any statutory or regulatory provision explaining exactly when a substantial transformation has occurred.[28] Even the US Court of International Trade acknowledged that 'Our court and its predecessors have struggled valiantly to determine what processing will result in a substantial transformation'.[29] Consequently, ever since *Gibson-Thomsen*, the courts have treated each case on its merits – with sometimes apparently bizarre results.

What constitutes substantial transformation?

The Anheuser-Busch and Gibson-Thomsen cases established the importance of 'name', 'character', and 'use' when determining substantial transformation. But what, precisely, do each of these terms mean? Providing a simple and convincing answer is not easy for a variety of reasons. One problem is that each case depends on its particular facts, which will vary between firms and industries. Another problem is what constitutes a 'substantial transformation'? For example, is 'substantial manufacturing' necessary to produce the required transformation? Conversely, can substantial transformation occur by an insubstantial process?[30] Of relevance also, does the complexity of operations determine the necessary transformation, and what importance is attached to the proportion of value-added in pre- and post-importation processes?

Case law suggests that a change in name is the least convincing criterion to determine substantial transformation. Of fundamental importance in this context is that the change in name applies to a name having general commercial usage different from that of the pre-existing material or articles.[31] For example, a change in name from 'concentrated orange juice for manufacturing' to 'frozen concentrated orange juice' and 'orange juice from concentrate' did not indicate the required transformation because 'they merely refer to the same product, orange juice, at different stages of production'.[32] In other cases, the courts held that substantial transformation had not occurred if post-import processing did not alter the names of the constitutive components. Thus, in *National Hand Tool Corp*, the court found that 'the name of each article as imported has the same name in the completed tool', and in *Energizer*, the court ruled: 'The constitutive components of the Generation II flashlight do not lose their individual names as a result of post-importation assembly ... no such name change occurred'.[33]

A change in character must involve a material change in the original article, for example, a change in its chemical or physical identity. Processing which did not change the identity or essence of the article would not produce the required transformation.[34] In *Uniroyal*, imported footwear uppers from Indonesia were sold to Stride Rite which attached outsoles and sold the finished article as Sperry Topsiders. The plaintiff argued that this post-import processing constituted a substantial transformation which negated the need to mark Made in Indonesia on the uppers. However, this claim was dismissed on the following grounds. First, as imported, and in the absence of an outer sole, the uppers were a complete shoe (almost like a moccasin). Second, the attachment of an outsole was no more than a combining process, or minor assembly operation, equivalent to, 'attaching buttons to a man's dress shirt or attaching handles to a finished piece of luggage'.[35]

Sometimes, when determining whether a substantial transformation has occurred, the courts have considered the contribution of pre- and post-import processing to the value of the finished product, or the complexity of these processes. Thus, in *Uniroyal*, the court found that manufacturing the uppers required considerably more time than attaching the outsoles to the uppers. Further, the cost of direct labour to produce the uppers was about eight times greater than that of attaching the outsole to the upper.[36] Similarly, in *National Juice*, which involved imported orange concentrate, it was reported that the US processing contributed less than 2% to the value of the final product.[37] Determining the *method* by which to calculate value added has proved contentious. In *National Hand Tool*, the plaintiff argued that its costs and profits should be considered as value added, which would have demonstrated that the enhanced value of the finished product was substantial compared to the value of the imported components. However, the court rejected this argument because it led to inconsistent marking requirements for importers performing identical processing, but selling at different prices.[38]

A related theme was the complexity of post-import processing. This topic is pertinent because it presents a conundrum: is it possible to effect a substantial transformation if the processing itself is not substantial? In *Carslon*, parts of wooden chairs were imported and then assembled with adhesives before sanding, lacquering, and polishing. The USCBP argued that the assembly of *finished* wooden parts did not constitute substantial transformation, in contrast to the assembly and finishing of chair parts. However, the court ruled that the fundamental issue at stake was that the imported items, whether finished or not, were not going to be sold in the USA as an article of commerce:

> The imported articles are not chairs in unassembled or knocked down condition. They are at best the wooden parts which go into the making of chairs … even if all of the chair parts were … surface finished at the time of importation … additional work would have had to be performed and materials added to them to create with them a functional article of commerce.[39]

In contrast, technically complex processing was not always sufficient to substantially transform a product. In *National Hand Tool*, some of the components used to manufacture mechanics' tools were imported to the USA and subject to further processing, which included: heat treatment which strengthens the steel by increasing its carbon content; cleaning with sand blasting, and/or chemical vibration; electro-plating, and final assembly. Nonetheless, the court ruled that post-import processing did not result in substantial transformation because the use of the imported components was predetermined at the time of importation: there was no change in use as a result of the processing.[40]

Who are the ultimate users of the imported product?

Assessing whether a manufacturer or retail consumer is the ultimate purchaser has also determined the necessity for origin marking and, therefore, whether this marking can act as a 'soft' trade barrier. As noted above, it is not always clear who is the ultimate purchaser. This uncertainty becomes apparent in some of the relevant court cases which are discussed below.

In *Grafton Spools*, empty ribbon spools were imported from England. The containers were marked with an indication of origin, but the individual spools were not so marked. Customs officials argued that American manufacturers of ribbons which were wound on the empty spools were not the ultimate purchasers of the spools; consequently, individual spools had to be marked with an indication of origin. The court admitted the possibility that there were two ultimate purchasers – ribbon manufacturers, who wound the ribbon onto empty spools, and manufacturers of business machines, who purchased full spools from the former – and the court determined that both were, in fact, ultimate purchasers. This ruling was justified as follows: spools lost their identity as an imported article when they became an integral part of business machines. Turning to ribbon manufacturers, the court recognised that winding ribbon onto empty spools was a skilled task, and that business machine makers were only interested in buying full spools from ribbon manufacturers.[41]

Similarly, in *Diamond Match*, wooden spatulas were imported from Japan and used in the manufacture of ice cream on a stick. When imported, bundles of spatulas were enclosed in paper strips indicating their country of origin. However, individual spatulas were not marked; these reached the ultimate purchaser in an unbound condition and so it was thought necessary that each spatula indicated its origin. It was also claimed that as the spatulas had multiple uses, including in arts and crafts, it was nonsensical to believe that only ice cream manufacturers were the ultimate users. However, the court ruled that, when used by manufacturers of ice cream on sticks, the imported spatulas were component parts; they lost their identity, in a tariff sense, as independently usable spatulas. Consequently, the ultimate users of the spatulas were the ice cream manufacturers.[42]

A long-running and controversial dispute on the ultimate purchaser began with *Midwood* in 1970 'when the court made a distinction between producers' and consumers' goods. In this action, the plaintiff claimed that the steel forgings it imported from England, Italy, and West Germany, were substantially transformed by its manufacturing division, Tube Line Manufacturing Co, which therefore negated the need for the imported items to indicate their country of origin. In finding for the plaintiff, the court placed particular emphasis on the distinction between producer and consumer goods.

Evidence given during this trial indicated considerable agreement between the parties on the post-importation processing of the forgings, which consisted primarily of removing scale and rust; trimming excess material from the ends of fittings; bevelling and machining the ends, and drilling bolt holes. After processing, the products were sold to oil and petroleum companies, chemical refineries, and other industries requiring high-pressure piping systems. The USCBP argued that such processes did not substantially transform the imported products because they did not result in the manufacture of a different article with, 'a new name, character, or use'.[43] The court, however, indicated that this processing did lead to a substantial transformation because it created a new range of producers' goods – flanges and fittings; although the dimensions of the imported forgings were very similar to the ultimate finished product, yet:

> they nevertheless, remain forgings unless and until converted by some manufacturer into consumers' goods, i.e., flanges and fittings. And as producers' goods the forgings are a material of further manufacture, having, as such, a special value and appeal only for manufacturers of flanges and fittings. But, as consumers' goods the flanges and fittings produced from these forgings are end use products, having, as such, a special value and appeal for industrial users and for distributors of industrial products.[44]

The key implication of the court's decision was that Midwood were 'ultimate users' because they transformed the imported items into a form capable of use by other manufacturers – who were the consumers of the finished product.

Subsequently, the USCBP became concerned at the problems caused by this ruling and, on the basis of later court decisions involving substantial transformation, it acknowledged that *Midwood* would have been decided differently.[45] To resolve the problems generated by *Midwood*, USCBP indicated it would no longer rely on the distinction between producer and consumer goods when determining country of origin marking requirements.[46] To gauge public opinion on this proposal, interested parties were invited to submit their views by 26 May 1998.

This consultation revealed that a substantial majority favoured the USCBP's proposal.[47] Evidence provided by the respondents indicated a number of fundamental problems generated by *Midwood*. One complication was that recent court cases either did not use the producers' good-consumers' good distinction, or it was held that such a distinction was not determinative of substantial transformation. Another concern was that *Midwood* threatened to abrogate country of origin marking because it, 'exempts from marking virtually any product that was imported in unfinished form and finished prior to sale'.[48] The corollary of this was that any product which was transformed from a producers' to a consumers' product, must have been substantially transformed. Crucially, was it possible for a producers' good to be used by a consumer? If not, at what stage in manufacture did a producers' good become a consumers' good? In economic terms, the adverse consequences of this ruling were that it had 'caused artificial distinctions within the pipe fitting industry, confusion [and did] not accurately indicate the origin to consumers'; consequently, 'certain industry members [had] suffered lost sales and price suppression because of unmarked foreign flanges.'[49] The USCBP was especially alert to the fact that the impact of *Midwood* was not uniform on all firms: much depended on whether the tubes were imported from countries belonging to the North American Free Trade Agreement (hereafter, NAFTA).[50]

Following the consultation, USCBP issued a final interpretation: 'This notice advises the public that Customs does not intend to rely on the distinction between producers' goods and consumers' goods in making country of origin marking determinations'.[51] However, the actions of USCBP were subsequently judged by the US Court of International Trade to be 'arbitrary, capricious, an abuse of discretion, and otherwise not in accordance with law', and this Court did not sustain Customs' recommendations in the final interpretation.[52] In finding for Boltex, the Court made the following observations. First, reliance on the producers' goods-consumers' goods distinction was complementary to the Court's reliance on the Gibson-Thomsen criteria. Second, even if *Midwood* were decided differently in the future, it was not the prerogative of USCBP to make this determination.

MUSA and the Federal Trades Commission

Previous sections of this chapter have demonstrated that USCBP relies on substantial transformation to determine whether imported products needed to indicate their country of origin after importation. However, only the FTC was empowered to decide the veracity of MUSA claims. For almost 30 years, US manufacturers sought to persuade the FTC to liberalise the regulations governing the unqualified use of MUSA. Such appeals often involved the request that the FTC aligned its policy with that of the USCBP. On every occasion, demands for liberalisation have been rebuffed.

Ever since its formation in 1914, the FTC was required to prohibit, 'unfair or deceptive acts or practices in or affecting commerce'.[53] There are two categories of MUSA claims: qualified and unqualified. The FTC maintained that it has always, 'permitted marketers to use appropriately qualified claims where their products would not meet the standard for an unqualified "Made in USA" claim'.[54] However, even qualified claims have been judged to be misleading, and for this reason, the FTC provided guidelines on appropriate nomenclature. Companies were advised not to make qualified claims unless the product had a 'significant amount of US input or US processing'. For example, if US parts accounted for a negligible proportion of the total cost of an item, the claim 'Made in USA of U.S. and Imported Parts' would be ruled deceptive, whereas 'Made in U.S. from Imported Parts' or 'Assembled in U.S.A' were permitted. Irrespective of the precise terms used in a qualified claim, they must be truthful and substantiated.[55] For products subject to unqualified MUSA claims, the FTC relied on the 'all or virtually all' standard: only a *de minimis* quantity of foreign content was permitted in such products. Unqualified claims were considered most beneficial because they were wholly consonant with the views of US consumers. Specifically, '…consumer commentators … generally supported an "all or virtually all" standard or advocated a specific percentage, usually 90% or, more often, 100%'.[56]

At first sight, it appears that the FTC might be in conflict with the USCBP: an imported product which has been substantially transformed is not required to indicate its country of origin, but this does not mean it is eligible to indicate MUSA. Indirectly, both departments share a common objective – the preservation of American jobs. As discussed above, ever since the McKinley Tariff, origin marking was justified because it enabled US consumers to exercise a preference for US products. Similarly, in response to the views of consumers and manufacturers, the FTC acknowledged that any dilution of its *de minimis* criterion would adversely affect US jobs and the manufacturing sector. It may be argued that one of the most pronounced differences between the USCBP and the FTC is how they preserve employment. The USCBP's requirement for substantial transformation ensures that the competitiveness of imported products which have been transformed are not undermined by an indication of the country of origin, and the FTC's insistence on the *de minimis* criterion ensures that US consumers can accurately express a preference for MUSA products.

In response to two high-profile cases, the FTC launched its first major consultation on MUSA between 1995 and 1997. Following this hearing, the FTC decided to alter its MUSA criterion, and two 'safe harbours' were proposed that would permit US manufacturers to make unqualified MUSA claims that would not be considered deceptive.[57] This proposal provoked an outcry from consumer groups, manufacturers, and politicians, and the FTC decided not to deviate from its traditional policy.[58]

The issue of unqualified MUSA claims re-emerged in 2019 when the FTC again held a public workshop and invited comments. The fundamental objective of this enquiry was to determine whether consumer perceptions of MUSA were the same as those expressed in the 1990s. It was recognised that the commercial environment had changed considerably during the intervening period. Greater globalisation had increased brand confusion: *Levi's* is a major US brand, even though US consumers understood that its products were no longer produced in the USA. Conversely, US consumers also recognised that imported products marked 'Made in China', contained a significant amount of US content.[59] Another concern was that it was becoming more difficult for companies to determine how the FTC might respond to unqualified MUSA claims. Some observers claimed that the FTC had been very lax in its treatment of Patriot Puck, Element Electronics, and New Balance, all of whom had flagrantly breached the *de minimis* standard. This slipshod behaviour meant some surveys reported that 23% of respondents did not trust Made in the USA claims.[60] Other commentators claimed that the FTC's reliance on 'significant minority' to determine misleading claims was so strict that many manufacturers decided the costs of making qualified origin claims were not outweighed by the benefits.[61] Finally, the growth of direct selling to consumers via e-commerce, made it more difficult for the FTC to monitor misleading origin claims. It was estimated that such sales accounted for 22% of total US sales.[62]

On the basis of the limited survey evidence presented to this enquiry, the FTC concluded that 'at least a significant minority of consumers are likely to be deceived by an unqualified MUSA claim for a product incorporating more than a de minimis amount of foreign content. Accordingly, neither workshop participants nor commenters offered any evidence to support changing the "all or virtually all" guidance'.[63] In fact, the FTC acknowledged that only one variable would permit a relaxation in its enforcement policy: a change in consumer perceptions about the meaning of unqualified MUSA claims.[64]

If consumer perceptions were to change, it is possible that USCBP's reliance on substantial transformation would be adopted by the FTC to justify unqualified MUSA claims. Calls for greater regulatory alignment between the FTC and the USCBP have featured in every public consultation on MUSA initiated by the FTC.[65] But even this solution is not without problems. One difficulty is that the onus of preventing consumer deception would simply be transferred from the FTC to the USCBP. A second problem is that substantial transformation cannot be defined with any precision. This amorphous term has been subject to protracted court rulings, the parameters of which depend on each specific case. Finally, adoption of this criterion raises a contentious issue: should determination of the economic nationality of a product take precedence over consumer deception? Alternatively, what guarantee exists that consumers are less likely to be deceived by unqualified MUSA claims that rely on substantial transformation rather than the *de minimis* rule?

Conclusion

This chapter has tried to resolve the paradox: why is it that a product that is made in the USA cannot be labelled 'Made in the USA'? The explanation is that if USCBP determines that a product has been substantially transformed in the USA, it does not need to indicate its country of origin. In economic terms, the transformed product is American. However, because the FTC applies a *de minimis* rule, any claim that this product is MUSA would be false. US consumers believe that MUSA means that a product is 'all or virtually all' made in the USA. Consequently, for the FTC, economic nationality is of secondary importance to the prevention of consumer deception.

Traditionally, the decisions of the USCBP and the FTC on origin marking, and MUSA claims, respectively, have been the preserve of trade lawyers. But these issues deserve more attention from business historians. To the extent that US consumers have exercised a preference for domestic products, it is imperative that MUSA claims are accurate to support US employment. Similarly, USCBP decisions on economic nationality can affect consumer perceptions of a product: those which have been substantially transformed in the USA contribute to employment, and it is likely that consumers view unmarked products more favourably compared to products which indicate their country of origin.[66] Perhaps the only way to resolve this issue is to compare the relative proportions of US manufactured products that are 'all or virtually all Made in the USA', with those which have been substantially transformed within the USA.

Although recent business history literature comprises many studies on the protection of regional appellations, it seems odd – to this author at least - that much less attention has been devoted to indications of the country of origin.[67] This oversight seems all the more remarkable because MUSA has been described as 'The Mother of all Brands'.[68] Many leading global brands – *Apple, Boeing, Coca-Cola, Microsoft*, and *Nike* – are owned by companies with headquarters in the USA, even though their products (or inputs) are manufactured in many countries. Thus, Nike trainers are sold in the USA with the legend 'Made in Vietnam'. This observation suggests that for many US consumers, the company brand is the more (most?) important indication of origin. If the dislocation between the company brand and country of origin was to increase, searching questions would be raised. For example, what *is* an American product? And, is it more important that domestic consumers buy American products, or products marked 'Made in the USA'?

Notes

1 US Customs was formed in 1789. In 2003, it was renamed the Bureau of Customs and Border Protection.

2 It is appropriate at this juncture to indicate that this chapter is not concerned with USCBP's use of substantial transformation for tariff and quota purposes.

3 Qualified claims include the terms 'Assembled in the United States' and 'Made in the United States from Imported Parts'. However, there are concerns that consumers remain sceptical of qualified claims. Federal Trade Commission, *Made in the USA*, p. 14.

4 House of Representatives, 51st Congress, 1st Session, Report No. 1466, 1890, pp. 6–7.

5 See, for example, Section 304 of Tariff Act, 1930, as amended.

6 *United States v. Friedlander*, 27 United States Court of Customs and Patent Appeals, 26 February 1940, p. 302.

7 Imported intermediate products refers to the total value of the imports of foreign produced intermediate products used in US final production. Total intermediate products refers to the sum of imported intermediate products and US-produced intermediate products consumed in the production of final products (excluding US-made intermediate products which are exported). Calculated from United States International Trade Commission, 'Intermediate goods imports in key US manufacturing sectors', Table ST1. https://usitc.gov/research_and_analysis/trade_shifts_2017/specialtopic.htm.

8 Federal Trade Commission, *Made in the USA*, pp.13–14. Downloaded from: https://www.ftc.gov/system/files/documents/plain-language/bus03-complying-made-usa-standard.pdf.

9 US firms may prefer substantial transformation because it removes indications of origin which might harm their competitiveness because US customers may view some countries more favourably than others. Clarke III, Owens, and Ford, 'Integrating', p. 118. These authors appear to confuse the activities of US Customs and the FTC. Imports which are substantially transformed in the USA do not have to indicate their country of origin; but it is the Federal Trade Commission which determines the validity of claims that a product is 'Made in America;' or 'Made in the USA'. 15 U.S.C., section 45a.

10 Emphasis added. *United States v. Gibson-Thomsen Co, Court of Customs and Patent Appeals*, 1940, p. 270. This case is discussed in more detail in the next section. 19 C.F.R. s.134.35.

11 For a history of Federal Trade Commission policy on Made in the USA, see, Higgins, *Brands,* pp. 260-276.
12 Federal Trade Commission, *Made in the USA*, pp. 8–9.
13 There were exceptions to these regulations, and other loopholes. For example, the 1933 Act did not require that the products must be made and extracted by US nationals. The ARRA regulations were not applicable if the policy was not in the public interest, or if inclusion of US products increased the cost of the overall project by more than 25%. Jones, and Martin, 'International trade', p. 17. Subsequently, the two Acts were promulgated in 2017 by the Executive Order, 'Buy American and Hire American'.
14 Dixon, Rimmer, and Waschik, 'Evaluating'.
15 Anholt, and Hildreth, *Brand America*, p. 132. Imports as a proportion of US GDP increased from 6.2 to 15.0%, between 1970–1974 and 2015–2019. Calculated from: https://www.macrotrends.net/countries/USA/united-states/imports.
16 Glick, *Guide,* p.55. Drawbacks were designed to foster US manufacturing.
17 *Anheuser-Busch Brewing Association v. United States*, 207 U.S., 1908, p. 562.
18 Bade, 'Beyond marking', p. 185.
19 Tariff Act, 1930 19 U.S. Code § 1304 (a) (H). As amended, 19 CFR §134.1 (d).
20 For a further discussion of this concept see, for example, Glick, *Guide*, pp. 49–50.
21 In this case, the goods were correctly marked to indicate their Japanese origin at the time importation. However, marking was not required when, 'An ultimate purchaser, by reason of the character of such article or by reason of the circumstances of its importation, must necessarily know the country of origin of such article even though it is not marked to indicate its origin'. 19 U.S. Code § 1304 (a) (H).
22 *United States v. Gibson-Thomsen Co*, United States Court of Customs and Patent Appeals, 1940, p. 270.
23 *United States v. Gibson-Thomsen Co*, p. 273.
24 *United States v. Gibson-Thomsen Co*, pp. 269–270.
25 *National Juice Products et al. v. United States et al.*, p. 988.
26 Silverstein, 'Country-of-origin', p. 289.
27 Palmeter, 'Rules of origin', p. 4.
28 Galfand, 'Heeding the call', p. 472.
29 *Boltex Manufacturing Co, et al. v. United States of America*, 140 *Federal Supplement*, 1339, p. 973.
30 Palmeter, 'Rules of origin', pp. 46, 55.
31 Foote, 'The Caribbean', p.324.
32 *National Juice Products Association et al., v. United States*, 1986, United States Court of International Trade, p. 989.
33 *National Hand Tool Corp. v. United States*, 1992, p. 311; Energizer Battery Inc, *v.* United States, United States Court of International Trade, 2016, p. 1322.
34 Foote, 'The Caribbean', p. 324.
35 *Uniroyal, Inc. v. United States*, Federal Supplement, 542, 1026, United States Court of International Trade, 1982, p. 224.
36 *Uniroyal, Inc. v. United States*, Federal Supplement, 542, 1026, United States Court of International Trade, 1982, p. 222.
37 *National Juice Products Association et al., v. United States*, 1986, United States Court of International Trade, p. 990.
38 *National Hand Tool Corp. v. United States*, United States Court of International Trade, 1992, p.312. Put in fn: Customs changed its views.
39 *Carslon Furniture Industries v. United States*, 65 United States Customs Court (1970), p. 482.
40 *National Hand Tool Corp. v. United States*, United States Court of International Trade (1992), pp. 311–312.

41 *Grafton Spools Ltd v. United States*, 45 *United States Customs Court*, 16 (1960).
42 The evidence given in this case indicates that less then 1% of imported spatulas were used firms not involved in ice cream manufacture. *The Diamond Match Co. v. The United States*, 49 *United States Court of Customs and Patent Appeals*, 52 (1962).
43 *Midwood Industries Inc, v. United States*, United States Customs Court, 1970, pp. 502–504.
44 *Midwood Industries Inc, v. United States*, United States Customs Court, 1970, p. 507.
45 *Federal Register*, 63, Thursday, 26 March 1998, p. 14751.
46 *Federal Register*, 63, 26 March 1998, p. 14751.
47 Fourteen replies were received of which nine supported a change in policy. Three replies objected to change, and two of the replies indicated indifference. *Federal Register*, 65, 14 March, 2000, p.13827.
48 *Federal Register*, 65, 14 March 2000, p. 13828.
49 *Federal Register*, 65, 14 March 2000, p. 13830.
50 *Federal Register*, 65, 14 March, 2000, p. 13830. One of the provisions of the NAFTA Implementation Act of 1993 was that substantial transformation occurs when there is a tariff shift, which can be easier to demonstrate compared to establishing a change in name, character, or use.
51 *Federal Register*, 65, 14 March 2000, p.13827.
52 *Boltex Manufacturing Co v. United States of America and United States Flanges and Fittings Marking Coalition*, *Federal Supplement*, 140, 8 September 2000, p. 987.
53 Federal Trade Commission Act, 15 USC, 45,1914, section 5.
54 *Federal Register*, 62, No. 231, 2 December 1997, pp. 63766, 63770.
55 Federal Trades Commission, *Complying with the Made in US Standard*, pp. 9–10.
56 *Federal Register*, 62, No. 231, 2 December 1997, p. 63758.
57 *Federal Register*, 62, No. 88, 7 May 1997, p. 25020.
58 *Federal Register*, 62, No. 231, 2 December 1997.
59 Federal Trade Commission, *Made in the USA*, *Transcript of evidence*, pp. 22–23: Made in the USA: An FTC Workshop | Federal Trade Commission.
60 Federal Trade Commission, *Made in the USA*, *Transcript of evidence*, pp. 54–57: Made in the USA: An FTC Workshop | Federal Trade Commission.
61 Federal Trade Commission, *Made in the USA*, *Transcript of evidence*, pp. 11, 39: Made in the USA: An FTC Workshop | Federal Trade Commission.
62 Federal Trade Commission, *Made in the USA*, *Transcript of evidence*, p. 65: Made in the USA: An FTC Workshop | Federal Trade Commission.
63 Federal Trade Commission, *Made in the USA*, pp. 6–7.
64 Federal Trade Commission, *Made in the USA*, *Transcript of evidence*, p. 34: Made in the USA: An FTC Workshop | Federal Trade Commission.
65 See, for example, Federal Trade Commission, *Proposed Guide for the Use of U.S. Origin Claims*, pp. 29–33; Federal Trade Commission, *Made in the USA*. *Transcript of Evidence*, p. 64: Made in the USA: An FTC Workshop | Federal Trade Commission.
66 US consumers might be prejudiced toward products emanating from countries with an undesirable international reputation on account of human rights abuse. Conversely, it is also conceivable that the same consumers view products from other countries more favourably than unmarked products, especially if the former are considered superior to products made in the US. For example, French haute couture, Italian fashion, and Swiss watches.
67 See, for example, Mollanger, 'The effects'; Simpson, 'Selling'; and Stanziani, 'Wine reputation'. Studies on the emergence of national indications of origin include Higgins and Mordhorst, 'Bringing'; Barnes and Higgins, 'Brand image'; and Bower and Higgins, 'Litigation'.
68 This is the subtitle of Anholt and Hildreth, *Brand America*.

Bibliography

Anholt, S., and Hildreth, J., *Brand America*. London: Cyan Books, 2004.

Bade, D.L., 'Beyond marking: country of origin rules and the decision in CPC International', *John Marshall Law Review*, 31 (1979), pp. 179–205.

Barnes, F., and Higgins, D.M., 'Brand image, cultural association and marketing: "New Zealand" butter and lamb exports to Britain, c. 1920–1938', *Business History*, 62 (2020), pp. 70–97.

Bower, J., and Higgins, D.M., 'Litigation and lobbying in support of the Marque: the Scotch Whisky Association, c. 1945–c. 1990', *Enterprise and Society*, (2021), pp. 1–31. DOI: 10.1017/eso.2021.33.

Clarke III, I., Owens, M., and Ford, J.B., 'Integrating country of origin into global marketing strategy', *International Marketing Review*, 17 (1999), pp. 114–126.

Dixon, P.B., Rimmer, M.T., and Waschik, R.G., 'Evaluating the effects of local content measures in a CGE model: eliminating the US Buy America(n) programs', *Economic Modelling*, 68 (2018), pp. 155–166.

Foote, F.W., 'The Caribbean basin initiative: development, implementation and application of the rules of origin and related aspects of duty-free treatment', *George Washington Journal of International Law and Economics*, 19 (1985), pp. 245–394.

Federal Trade Commission, *Proposed Guide for the Use of U.S. Origin Claims*. Washington, DC: Federal Trades Commission, 1997.

Federal Trades Commission, *Complying with the Made in US Standard*. Washington, DC: Federal Trade Commission, 1998.

Federal Trade Commission, *Made in the USA*. Washington, DC: Federal Trade Commission, 2020.

Galfand, C.E., 'Heeding the call for a predictable rule of origin', *University of Pennsylvania Journal of International Law*, 11 (1989), pp. 469–493.

Glick, L.A., *United States Customs and Trade Laws after the Customs Modernization Act*. The Hague: Kluwer Law international, 1997.

Higgins D.M., and Mordhorst, M., 'Bringing home the "Danish" Bacon: food chains, national branding and Danish supremacy over the British Bacon market, c. 1900–1938', *Enterprise & Society*, 16 (2015), pp. 141–185.

Higgins, D.M., *Brands, Geographical Origin, and the Global Economy*. Cambridge: Cambridge University Pres, 2018.

Jones, V.C., and Martin, M.F., 'International trade: rules of origin', Congressional Research Service, 5 January, 2012.

Mollanger, T., 'The effects of producers' trademark strategies on the structure of the cognac brandy supply chain during the second half of the nineteenth century: the reconfiguration of commercial trust by the use of brands', *Business History*, 60 (2018), pp. 1255–1276.

Palmeter, N.D., 'Rules of origin or rules of restriction? A commentary on a new form of protectionism', *Fordham International Law Journal*, 11 (1987), pp. 1–50.

Silverstein, D., 'Country-of-origin marking requirements under section 304 of the tariff act: an importer's map through the maze', *American Business Law Journal*, 25 (1987), pp. 285–300.

Simpson, J., 'Selling to reluctant drinkers: the British wine market, 1860–1914', *Economic History Review*, 57 (2004), pp. 80–108.

Stanziani, A., 'Wine reputation and quality controls: the origin of the AOCs in 19th century France', *European Journal of Law and Economics*, 18 (2004), pp. 149–167.

9 Spanish fashion without the country-of-origin effect

José Antonio Miranda and Alba Roldán

Introduction

Since the Middle Ages, indications of geographical origin have informed consumers about the provenance of foodstuffs and manufactured products.[1] Until the second globalisation, from approximately the last third of the twentieth century, 'Made in' usually coincided faithfully with the country in which a manufactured product was made. Such indicia signalled a range of characteristics about a particular country and thereby influenced consumers' purchasing decisions. However, the growing integration of international markets, especially the filamented nature of global supply and value chains, meant that many products do not have a single, or evident country of origin. Many products are designed in advanced countries but produced in developing countries which have lower labour costs – and a less favourable international image. Consequently, companies have downplayed the country of manufacture and emphasised where the product was designed, or the country to which the brand belongs.

As a result of these trends, some marketing scholars have questioned the impact that 'Made in' – or country of origin – had on consumer behaviour,[2] while others emphasised the need to differentiate between the different types of geographical indication, which include, 'country of design', 'country of manufacture', 'country of assembly', and 'country of brand origin'. Research on which indication has the greatest effect on consumers has proved inconclusive.[3] It appears that the country with which the product is associated is decisive, and this usually coincides with the brand's country of origin. Thus, an *Armani* shirt is associated with Italian fashion, even though it is made in China.[4]

Nonetheless, many recent empirical studies indicate that country of origin continues to influence consumers.[5] Recognition of this sway partly explains why the federal government enacted regulations which determine when 'Swiss Made' can be applied to watches and clocks manufactured in Switzerland.[6] Similarly, in the United States, the Federal Trades Commission has investigated cases where Made in the USA has been wrongly applied to domestic products.[7] Some scholars have argued that it is precisely because of globalisation, the increased internationalisation of companies, and the global

DOI: 10.4324/9781003166184-9

consumption of standardised products that business associations and central governments have promoted the use of country of origin. [8]

A product's association with a country which is renowned for manufacturing excellence is especially important for consumers of fashionable clothes. A garment, or brand which is synonymous with France, or Italy will secure a price premium. To what extent does 'Spain' generate positive connotations for firms in its textile industry? Until recently, Spanish fashion was practically unknown in other countries. However, since the late twentieth century, Spanish clothing companies have achieved rapid growth in the international market, and opened stores in the principal shopping centres and streets throughout the world, on the basis of their well-known and highly-valued brands which include *Zara*, *Mango*, *Bershka*, *Massimo Dutti*, and *Desigual*. The most prominent company is Industria de Diseño Textil SA (Inditex), owner of many famous Spanish brands, and, since, 2008, the global leader in 'fast' fashion.

The leading Spanish fast fashion companies succeeded in creating global brands even though Made in Spain would not be regarded as a mark of distinction when applied to textiles. This lacklustre image has persisted despite official campaigns to improve the international appearance of the country and its products. In fact, we argue that Spanish fashion companies which enjoyed the most international success adopted a marketing strategy that minimised references to their country of origin. This strategic decision was fundamentally important to the development of these companies, but it meant that there was no enhancement of Spain's image in the fashion sector.

This chapter proceeds as follows. In the next section, we provide a brief literature review of the country-of-origin effect on the fashion industry. The following section discusses how Spain's external image has evolved, and the official policies that were implemented to improve this image. In the penultimate section, we explain why Spain's leading fashion companies were successful in overseas markets, before presenting our conclusions.

Fashion and country-of-origin effect

The country-of-origin effect is generated by the reputation of a country's products, 'country image', which comprises stereotypes of the country, and a mental map composed of cognitive, affective, and normative elements. The cognitive aspects of the country image – how consumers view the economic, social, political, and cultural characteristics of a country – act as indicators of quality, while the affective aspects of this image – whether consumers' have positive or negative feelings towards a country – have symbolic and emotional connotations. Simultaneously, normativity introduces social and personal values into consumption decisions, for example, when to refuse to buy products from countries with questionable political regimes. Moreover, the image of a country is also affected by its historical evolution. Consequently, this image may not be constant; it can be modified by activities which promote it in a more favourable light.[9]

The influence of country of origin on consumers' attitudes seems to be particularly pronounced for clothes, cosmetics, and perfumes.[10] A recent study analysed advertisements by selected countries in *Cosmopolitan* to quantify the proportion of brands that used nationality indicators.[11] This study reported that more than a third of advertisements contained nationality indicators, the most important of which were the name of the city, or country, followed by the text written in the language of the country of origin. However, this study also found that 'Made in' was rarely used – probably because the country in which the product was manufactured did not coincide with the country that the company wished to associate with the product. Another pertinent conclusion from this study was that many brands were defined as 'global' brands: they did not refer to a specific country, and only the English language was used in the advertisement. [12] This last finding is referred to as 'global consumer culture positioning',[13] a strategy by which brands are linked to a series of symbols which are recognised globally.

London, Milan, New York, and Paris are recognised as the world's fashion capitals. Clothes and related products associated with these countries have global appeal,[14] and their fashion brands have a substantial competitive advantage over brands from other countries. Particularly noteworthy are France and Italy, which account for more than half of the world's luxury fashion brands.[15] In both countries, there exists a strong symbiotic relationship between the fashion industry and the external image of the country. This synergy affects the large luxury brands and the brands associated with small and medium-sized companies. It is likely that the brands of the latter companies obtain a greater benefit from the positive images associated with their country.

Because consumers are often unaware of the country in which fashion articles are manufactured, they rely on the country with which a brand is associated when making their purchasing decisions. A study by Zoran Krupka, Durdana Ozretic-Dosen, and Jozo Previsic, reported that the mere association of a brand with Italy or France mitigated the potential negative effects of consumers learning about the country of manufacture: consumers still perceived the brand to be luxurious, and remained willing to pay a price premium. Consequently, many brands simulate an association with the premier countries in high fashion even though they are not connected to these countries.[16]

The image of Spain and Spanish products

Immediately after the Second World War, Spain's international standing was unenviable: the dictatorial regime had collaborated with the defeated fascist countries, and it was initially excluded from principal international organisations such as the United Nations, International Monetary Fund, and the

World Bank. To rehabilitate Spain's image, Franco's government launched campaigns to attract American tourists and Hollywood film shoots to Spain and made a significant investment in the Spanish pavilion at the 1964–1965 New York World's Fair. The Dictatorship also worked to generate favourable media coverage in the United States by hiring public relations specialists. Further, it defused criticism from American Protestants and Jews by allowing more religious freedom for non-Catholics in Spain. The progressive reintegration of Spain into the Western block accelerated in the 1960s when the Dictatorship allowed greater trade liberalisation and the general opening-up of the Spanish economy. These policies were complemented by tourism promotion campaigns, supporting North American film companies operating in Spain, and substantial international propaganda.[17]

The momentum behind these policies weakened at the beginning of the 1970s, because of Franco's political weakness. However, the death of Franco in 1975, and the subsequent democratisation, led to a substantial improvement in Spain's international image. This progress was consolidated when Spain joined the European Community, in 1986, by favourable economic conditions, and the rapid modernisation of the country's institutions in the second half of the 1980s. Throughout this period, successive governments continued to promote Spain's image with a variety of initiatives, including hosting the 1992 Olympic Games in Barcelona.[18] Similarly, the tourism promotion campaigns of the 1960s and 1970s were rejuvenated with the slogan: 'Spain. Everything under the sun' which was accompanied by a logo that symbolised Spain's modernity.

Although Spain's image was likely affected in the short term by the economic crisis of 1993, this was subsequently repaired by becoming a member of the Eurozone in 1999. During the 1980s and 1990s, Spain continued to modernise, and it became an example of successful country branding.[19] A study conducted by the Ortega y Gasset Institute in 1996, revealed that 84% of sample respondents in four European countries had a very positive opinion of Spain.[20] In 2009, the *Country Brand Index* calculated by *Futurebrand*, ranked Spain tenth in the world.[21]

However, the positive external image of Spain was closely linked to tourism. Spain was perceived to be a joyful, open, and culturally interesting country; it was associated with leisure, fun, and sport. In the 1960s, under the slogan, 'Spain is different', the romantic archetype of an exotic and backward country was promoted, and in subsequent decades tourism promotion campaigns highlighted Spain's climate, beaches, festivals, and gastronomy. These policies were very successful, and Spain quickly established itself as a leading holiday destination. Unfortunately, such positive images did not extend to other sectors of the Spanish economy: many Spanish brands were unknown overseas; there was no comparable promotion of Spain's manufacturing capacity, its technology, or the quality of its products.

Despite the growth in Spanish exports and foreign direct investment during the 1980s and 1990s, respectively, the general image of Spanish manufacturing was weak. An academic study reported that in the early 1980s, Spain was associated with economic backwardness, and international consumers were largely unaware of the country's products and brands.[22] Furthermore, the survey conducted by the Ortega y Gasset Institute in 1996, confirmed the weakness of Made in Spain: 70% of respondents did not identify Spain with any specific products or skills.[23] In 2000, the marketing multinational Young & Rubicam reported that in Europe and the United States, Spanish products were considered to be deficient in terms of innovation, price competitiveness, and quality.[24] Surveys of directors in overseas Spanish companies, and sales offices, by Foro de Marcas Renombradas Españolas (hereafter, FMRE), in 2003, 2004, and 2006, found that Spain was perceived to be a developed, stable country, with a good standard of living. Conversely, it was also viewed as a country that did not possess well-known brands or leading technological research. Unsurprisingly, perhaps, it was only respondents in Latin America and the Maghreb who valued products embossed with Made in Spain.[25]

During the 1990s, several countries developed national branding strategies[26] to boost the competitiveness of their products and services, support tourism, and attract foreign investment and skilled workers.[27] The Spanish government enacted similar policies with the creation of the *Proyecto Marca España* (Spain Brand Project). This initiative was promoted by the Ministry of Foreign Affairs, the Spanish Institute of Foreign Trade (hereafter, ICEX), the Elcano Royal Institute (a private foundation, supported by the Spanish State, dedicated to international and strategic studies), the FMRE, and the Association of Communication Managers. In 2003, a conference on the Spain brand endorsed the need for an official policy to improve Spain's external image so that the country appeared modern, competitive, and dynamic. Other recommendations were the creation of an institution dedicated to promoting the image of the country, a Strategic Plan to improve this image, and a Permanent Observatory to monitor Spain's external image.[28]

However, when the Socialist Party won the 2004 general election, there was a temporary suspension of the Spain Brand Project. The new government, headed by Rodríguez Zapatero, initially opted to apply sectoral marketing plans and to support companies seeking to consolidate their brands in overseas markets. Rapid economic growth, and the substantial international expansion of Spanish companies in the 2000s, enhanced the country's image: the Country Brand Index of 2006 ranked Spain seventh in the world and fourth in Europe. A report by the Reputation Institute in 2009, confirmed the elevated image of the country but indicated that this was based on a favourable natural environment and tourism. Although Spain had excellent tourist attractions, its companies, and their brands and products, received the lowest rating compared to other European countries included in the survey.[29]

The financial crisis of 2008 exacerbated the weak international perception of Spanish brands and undermined the image of the country. The effects of the crisis were particularly pronounced in Spain which endured high levels of unemployment and needed official intervention to protect its financial sector. Other consequences of the crisis were the accentuation of social inequality and increased impoverishment for many of its citizens. In September 2012, the *New York Times* published the article 'Spain Recoils as Its Hungry Forage Trash Bins for a Next Meal' – an accurate reflection of the deterioration suffered in the country's image.[30] In the *Country Brand Index*, Spain fell from seventh to twenty-third position between 2007 and 2014.[31]

Part of the government's response to this crisis was to prioritise export growth and to support the promotional campaigns of ICEX. The latter's strategy focused on the use of Made in Spain and Made by Spain, to improve the external image of certain products. This project was particularly keen to enhance US consumers' perception of Spanish products; between 2009 and 2010, 44 million Euros was devoted specifically to the US market. This plan was partly co-financed by a select group of large Spanish companies possessing a strong international presence, but more than 2,500 companies participated in the different parts of the plan. The socialist government also developed a 'Made in Spain' and 'Made by Spain' campaign for the Russian market, and a budget of 38 million Euros was devoted to this particular scheme between 2011 and 2012.[32]

The triumph of the Popular Party in the 2011 general election marked the rebirth of the Spain Brand Project. In June 2012, the High Commissioner of the Government for the Spain Brand was appointed.[33] The Commissioner had a rank equal to the secretary of state, but this department did not have its own budget and it was supported by a limited staff. The first holder of this post was Carlos Espinosa de los Monteros, a businessman with senior managerial experience in major Spanish companies, including Inditex. The Commissioner was responsible for three tasks: the Spain Brand Observatory was created to engage in the systematic analysis and monitoring of Spain's image – the Observatory was hosted by the Elcano Royal Institute, a think-tank foundation supported by major government departments and leading Spanish companies; the coordination and stimulation of public and private actions to promote Spain abroad, and, finally, the dissemination of Spain's positive attributes.[34]

However, the High Commission was not truly operational until 2013, after which many of the activities of this office were limited to signing agreements with companies and institutions, launching a communication programme through a website and social networks, and organizing conferences. The Commissioner did not have adequate resources to effect a substantial campaign, or a specific and differentiated mission within the government's foreign action structure. In a 2018 report, The Court of Auditors reported that the lack of resources was a major impediment to the Commissioner's activities. Furthermore, some of the initiatives launched by the Commissioner's office were financed as a result of agreements with private companies; agreements that sometimes conflicted with the regulations governing public bodies. Another criticism raised by the auditors was the failure to assign specific functions to the Commissioner, some of which were replicated by other departments. Finally, the auditors attributed some culpability to the Commissioner for only addressing general objectives which made it impossible to assess the effectiveness of the organisation.

Following a vote of no confidence in the Popular Party, the Socialist Party formed a government in June 2018, and quickly dismissed De los Monteros as High Commissioner for the Spain Brand. He was dismissed because his management had been highly criticised by the left-wing parties and the nationalist parties in Catalonia and the Basque Country. In addition, the new government wanted to substantially modify Spain's foreign image policy. Three months later, *España Global* was created. This new institution, hosted within the Ministry of Foreign Affairs, replaced the Spain Brand Project. Unfortunately, at the same time, the international image of Spain was being undermined by the rebellion for independence in Catalonia. This protest led to a redefinition of the objectives of foreign promotion in which Spain's democratic virtues were emphasised.

Indicators of Spain's external image show that deterioration stopped in 2013, after which a timid recovery began, culminating in its zenith in 2017. The slight decline in 2018 may be attributed to the political instability generated by the independence movement in Catalonia (Figure 9.1). Nonetheless, Spain's image remained heavily reliant on 'soft' attributes, such as the kindness and friendliness of its people, or the exceptional tourism and leisure facilities on offer. Conversely, 'hard' attributes, such as innovation, product quality, and research and development remained weak. This was also the case for the brands owned by Spanish companies. Although there was some improvement in the standing of Spanish brands between 2017 and 2018, they remained well below those of France, Germany, and Italy (Figure 9.2).

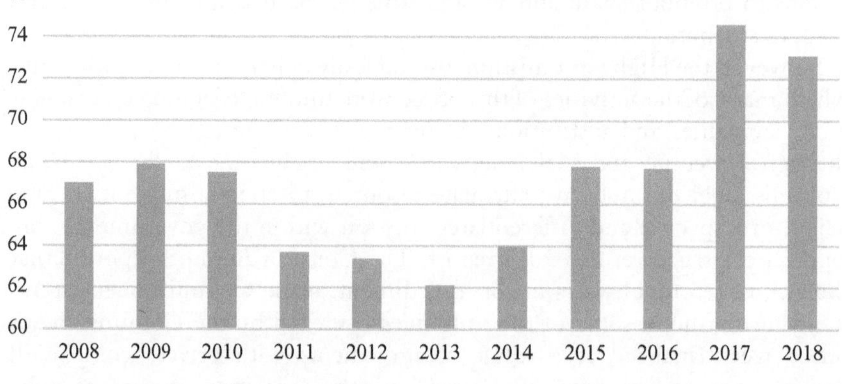

Figure 9.1 Reputation index of Spain, 2009–2018
Source: Reports of the Reputation Institute.

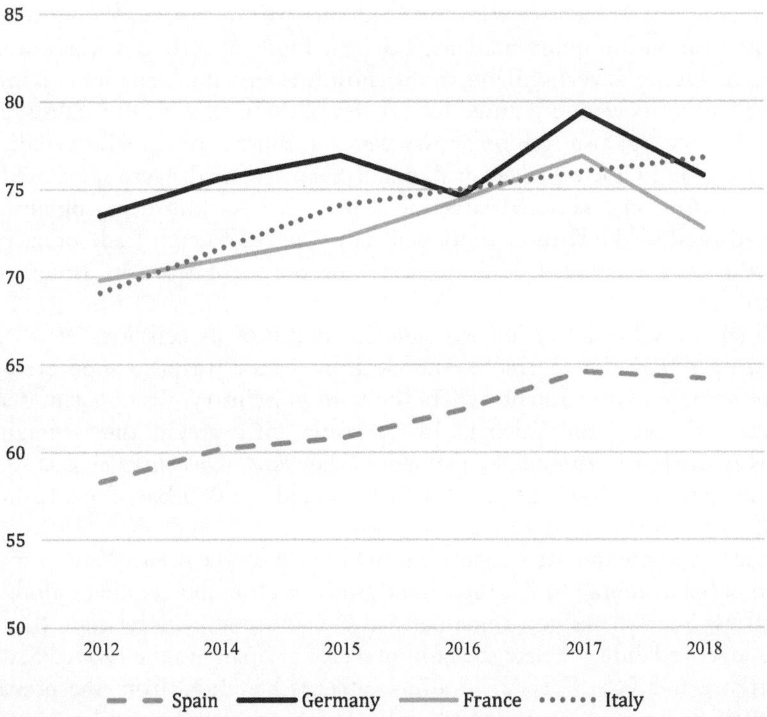

Figure 9.2 Index of recognition of companies and brands of each country, 2012–2018
Source: Reports of the Reputation Institute.

The improvement in the international image of Spain from 2014 was largely due to its economic recovery. Government policy had only a negligible influence on this image, probably because it lacked continuity and insufficient resources.[35] In addition, *Marca España*'s promotional campaigns were severely criticised by some experts who believed they adopted the wrong approach, lacked credibility, and were uncoordinated.[36] Ideological factors have also prompted attacks. For example, it was claimed that the campaigns only promoted the interests of multinationals, or sought to homogenise and politically instrumentalise the country's cultural heritage. [37]

Spanish fashion

Contemporaneously with *Proyecto Marca España*, the government launched the *Plan Global de la Moda* (Global Fashion Plan), which sought to promote Spanish fashion abroad, thereby increasing this industry's exports. Compared to other countries in the European Union, Spanish clothing manufacturers were less engaged with exports. The major obstacles which confronted exports included Spain's weak international image as a creator of fashion, lack of knowledge of Spanish brands, and the failure of companies with international exposure to identify with the Made in Spain initiative.[38] To promote Spanish fashion in foreign markets, a diverse range of activities were undertaken, including advertisements in the most influential international fashion magazines; tours were organised for overseas fashion experts, journalists, and major buyers; Spanish fashion shows were promoted, principally Gaudí, in Barcelona, and Cibeles, in Madrid; major Spanish brands were sponsored to attend leading international fairs and shows; ICEX company programmes were adapted to the fashion sector; specialists in the foreign trade of fashion products were employed, and an electronic portal of Spanish fashion was created.

When the Global Fashion Plan ended, many of its activities were sustained by ICEX. Furthermore, the clothing sector was also supported by Spain's regional governments where the fashion industry was concentrated – Galicia, Catalonia, and Valencia. In Catalonia, for example, the Generalitat (the Regional Government) implemented the *Pla de Dinamització de la Moda Catalana* between 2007 and 2010, which created the 080 Barcelona Fashion show.

However, these initiatives had a limited impact on the international recognition of Spanish brands. An Interbrand study in 2009 showed that in foreign countries, Spanish fashion remained largely unknown: more than 40% of those surveyed did not relate the fashion sector to Spain; in the United States, this figure was 56%.[39] Spanish fashion articles benefited from the prestige that their European origin conferred, but their rating was much lower compared to similar products that originated from France or Italy. According to the Interbrand study, even the few brands that were internationally prominent were not recognised by consumers as Spanish.

Marked improvement in the international recognition of Spanish brands occurred later in the second decade of the twenty-first century. A 2019 report by the market research company, GFK, based on a total of 6,000 interviews conducted in China, France, Germany, Mexico, the UK, and the United States, reported that Spanish fashion brands ranked second among all Spanish brands. This report also showed that among the 25 Spanish brands that most respondents remembered spontaneously, four were the fashion brands: *Bershka*, *Desigual*, *Mango*, and *Zara*. Even so, only 19% of the interviewees impulsively associated Spain with fashion products; in Europe, this figure did not exceed 13%.[40] Overall, data from this report suggested that the image of Spain as a fashion-producing country was still very weak, particularly in Europe, even though some Spanish brands had gained considerable international recognition.

The success of Spain's leading fashion companies in the twenty-first century has improved Spanish export performance. The World Trade Organisation ranked Spain eighth in the world, and third in Europe, according to the value of its clothes exports.[41] In terms of sales, the largest companies were Inditex, Punto Fa (parent company of *Mango*), and Tendam (which owns

Springfield, Women's Secret, Fifty, and *Cortefiel*). The annual turnover of these three companies in 2019, was 28, 2, and 1 billion Euros, respectively. Behind these leaders were approximately 12 companies that also have international repute, each with annual sales of around 100m Euros, including *Pepe Jeans, Desigual, Mayoral, Purificación García, Bimba y Lola, Pronovias, Inside, Adolfo Domínguez,* and *Punt Roma.* The majority of the latter companies specialised in the design and sale of the product, but they do not possess their own manufacturing capacity, or it is small in relation to the volume of products marketed. Many of these companies began as manufacturers but, from the 1980s, they off-shored production to countries with lower labour costs. All Spanish clothing companies found it beneficial to expand their exports because per capita consumption of clothing in Spain was less than half that of other countries in Western Europe and because domestic demand declined during the economic crisis of 1993.

All of Spain's leading clothing companies manufacture products in the low-medium price and quality category, but with innovative designs. Furthermore, they have all adopted or approached the fast fashion model, which is characterised by the continuous launch of new garments on the market, and the rapid adaptation of production to retailer demand. This strategy necessitated substantial investment in logistics. Another important aspect of business strategy was the creation or franchising of international chain stores which facilitated the global expansion of company brands. However, this trend has been changing in recent years because of the boom in electronic commerce.

Inditex led the development of Spanish fast fashion, and it has been the country's most internationally successful clothing company. Its strategies of managing demand, making production flexible, and logistics agile, have provided benchmarks for the world's fast fashion companies. Currently, Inditex is the world's largest clothes retail company, with almost 180,000 workers, and approximately 7,500 stores located in more than 200 countries.[42] Its principal brand, *Zara*, is the most valuable of all Spanish brands. According to Brand Finance, *Zara* is ranked second among the world's 50 most-valued clothing brands. Furthermore, within the 'top 50' are *Bershka* (ranked thirty-eighth) and *Massimo Dutti* (ranked forty-fifth), both of which are also owned by Inditex.[43] Inditex accounts for more than three-quarters of Spain's fashion exports. Its business model has been imitated by other Spanish companies in the clothing industry because they have all benefited from the favourable attitudes generated by this type of fashion. Consequently, it is no exaggeration to state that the international success of the Spanish clothing sector can be attributed to Inditex. It is appropriate, therefore, to provide a brief overview of how this company promoted its brands without referencing Spain, its country of origin.

Established in 1963, Inditex began as a small family-run clothing business, with the *Zara* retail chain, which was highly focused on the Spanish market. From the outset, it based its competitive strategy on just-in-time production to reduce the stock of unsold items to a minimum and used its stores to capture information about changes in demand and to promote its articles. Additionally, it supplied garments that followed the latest fashion trends, at medium-low prices. As sales increased, more production was outsourced, first to cooperatives and companies in Galicia, and northern Portugal, and then to other countries with lower labour costs. International expansion, which began in the 1990s, was very fast: in 2000, with a turnover of 2.6 billion Euros, the company had stores in 33 countries and exports accounted for more than half of the group's sales. Eleven years later, with a turnover of almost 14 billion Euros, the group had stores in more than 80 countries, and exports represented 75% of total sales.[44]

In the early 1990s, Inditex created new chains of stores to target different segments of demand, although *Zara*, the most popular brand of clothing for women, men, and children, remained the principal chain store, accounting for approximately 70% of sales and profits. In 1991, Inditex founded *Pull & Bear*, and acquired 65% of the shares issued by *Massimo Dutti* (purchasing the rest in 1995). Both of these brands were initially dedicated to young men's fashion. In 1993, the company launched *Kiddy's Class*, a children's fashion chain, and this was followed in 1998 by the establishment of the *Bershka* brand, a casual young fashion brand. Over the following years, Inditex acquired *Stradivarius*, a clothes chain for teenage girls; it created *Lefties*, a low-cost version of *Zara*; it promoted the lingerie chain *Oysho*, the house linen chain *Zara Home* and *Often*, and in 2008, it launched *Uterqüe*, a brand for accessories and clothes in the medium-to-high price bracket.[45]

However, none of the Inditex brands have features that identify them as Spanish. On the contrary, two of the brands have names that suggest they are Italian (*Massimo Dutti* and *Stradivarius*), four have English names (*Pull&Bear, Kiddy's Class, Lefties*, and *Often*), and four other brands – *Bershka, Oysho, Uterqüe*, and *Zara* – have exotic connotations, unidentifiable with a specific country, although the first two brands resemble Slavic and Japanese terms, respectively. Similar observations can be made for two other large Spanish retailers. For example, Punto Fa uses the word *Mango* as its principal brand, but this name is common to several languages and it does not indicate Spanish origin. Although this company incorporated the city of Barcelona into its brand (*Mango Barcelona*), this connection, which was not explicitly related to Spain, is now rarely seen. Similarly, Tendam retained some Spanish brands inherited from the past (*Cortefiel* and *Pedro del Hierro*), but all the brands created were given English names: *Springfield, Women's Secret*, Fifty, *Slowlove*, and *High Spirits*. Because recognition of a brand's country of origin depends principally on consumers associating the brand name with the language of the country,[46] it is evident that the most successful Spanish clothes brands have tended to conceal their Spanish identity and, therefore, their association with Spanish fashion.

Neither of the above companies sought to associate themselves with the image of Spain, either through logos, slogans, advertising campaigns, or other forms of brand promotion. In fact, until recently, these brands were not recognised as Spanish by many consumers in other countries. The Interbrand report of 2009, was emphatic that not even *Zara* and *Mango*, the best-known brands, were identified as Spanish by many consumers.[47] Indeed, most large Spanish fashion companies have never used images of Spain or indicated Spanish origin on their brands. Proof of this disdain is that none of these companies participated in the Spanish Confederation of Fashion Companies. This institution was established to distinguish Spanish fashion products in the market, and to enable consumer identification of the precise origin of the design and manufacture of products.

Conclusion

More than half a century of research on the country-of-origin effect has shown that the country with which consumers associate a product, or brand influences their purchasing decision, although this influence is moderated by several factors. Products that benefit from a positive association with their country of origin enjoy a further resource with which to compete.

Fashion is an industry that is particularly sensitive to the influence of country-of-origin effects. Consequently, many fashion brands associate with particular countries. France and Italy, in particular, and the UK and United States, are countries which have achieved high repute in the fashion world, and this enhances the competitiveness of domestic companies in this industry. This is not the case for Spain. The positive image of this country relies on its exceptional tourism industry and leisure facilities, and not the economic and technological progress achieved since the 1980s. Spanish brands and products are rarely appreciated by overseas consumers. In addition to tourism and leisure, Spain is most famous for its agricultural and horticultural produce, which accounts for a substantial share of its exports.

Despite the efforts made to modernise the image of Spain, and to promote the external image of its brands and products, the country-of-origin effect remains weak for many sectors of the Spanish economy. In the fashion industry, several international promotion plans have been implemented, but with little success. The global expansion of a group of Spanish fashion companies, which began in the 1990s, and has continued since, was not underpinned by a strong country brand. These companies did not derive any advantage from indicating their Spanish origin. Instead, they created global brands.

Paradoxically, the absence of a strong country-of-origin effect enhanced the international competitiveness of these companies from the 1990s, for the following reasons. First, they manufactured products in the low-medium quality and price range. Such products are much less sensitive to the influence of the country of origin than high-end products. Second, the principal consumers of this type of fashion are young people who are knowledgeable of the product, and directly involved in its purchase. This category of consumers is largely unconcerned by country of origin. Finally, the creation of strong brands, which are recognised as global brands, negated the need to rely on indicia such as Made in Spain, or 'Spanish'. Moreover, the type of product in which these companies specialised did not enhance the general image of Spanish fashion, which continues to be held in low regard.

It is only recently that the principal brands of Spanish fashion companies have become known as Spanish by overseas consumers. The formation of the image of a country, and its products is a historical process, which usually evolves in a gradual manner. The expansion of Spanish fashion companies has been impressive because of its speed, and because the leading company, Inditex, is now a world leader in clothes sales. Nonetheless, the number of Spanish fashion companies with a significant share of the international market continues to be low when compared with other countries.

Notes

1 Higgins, *Brands.*
2 Usunier, 'Relevance'.
3 Magnusson, Westjohn, and Zdravkovic, 'What?'.
4 Samiee, Shimp, and Sharma, 'Brand'; Magnusson, Westjohn, and Zdravkovic, 'What?'.
5 Dholakia, Zhao, and Duan, 'The COO'.
6 Donze, 'National'.
7 Higgins. 'Its made in the USA', this volume.
8 Pegan, Vianelli, and De Luca, *International.*
9 Darling and Puetz, 'Analysis'.
10 Ercan, 'Country'.
11 Hornikx et al., 'How'.
12 Hornikx et al., 'How'.
13 Alden, Steenkamp, and Batra, 'Brand'.
14 For Italian fashion, see Belfanti, 'Made in Italy', this volume.
15 Kim, Shin, Cheng, Lennon, and Liu, 'Influence'.
16 Krupka, Ozretic-Dosen, and Previsic, 'Impact'; Salciuviene et al., 'Do brand'.
17 Rosendorf, *Franco.*
18 Aronczyk, *Branding.*
19 Gilmore, 'A country'.
20 Lamo de Espinosa, 'La Imagen'.
21 Futurebrand, *Country Brand Index 2009*, p. 6.
22 Morello, 'The "made in"'.
23 Noya, *La imagen.*
24 González and Casilda, 'La Marca'.
25 Cerviño and Rivera, 'La Globalización'.
26 Bolin and Miazhevich, 'The soft'.
27 Hao et al., 'Two decades'.
28 ICEX, Real Instituto Elcano, FMRE and Dircom, 2003. *Informe Proyecto Marca España.* ICEX, Real Instituto Elcano, FMRE and Dircom, https://media.realinstitutoelcano.org/wp-content/uploads/2021/11/informe-proyecto-marca-espana.pdf.
29 Reputation Institute, *La reputación de España.*
30 S. Daley, "Spain recoils, as its hungry forage trash bins for a next meal," *The New York Times*, 25 September 2012. https://www.nytimes.com/2012/09/25/world/europe/hunger-on-the-rise-in-spain.html.

31 Futurebrand, *Country Brand Index 2007. Insights, Findings & Country Rankings*, n.d., p. 6, https://cupdf.com/document/future-brand-2007-country-brand-index.html?page=1; and Country Index 2014–15," n.d., p. 53, https://cupdf.com/document/future-brand-2007-country-brand-index.html?page=1; https://www.futurebrand.com/uploads/Country-Brand-Index-2014-15.pdf.
32 Press release from the Ministry of Industry, Tourism and Trade of the Government of Spain, 28 March 2011, https://www.mincotur.gob.es/es-es/gabineteprensa/notasprensa/documents/npplanmadeinrusia280311.pdf.
33 Borzova and Nikolashvili, 'Marca España'.
34 Oficina de Información Diplomática, *Plan Anual de Acción Exterior de La Marca España 2013*. http://bases.cortesaragon.es/bases/NdocumenVIII.nsf/e86600a24e054a61c12576d2002e551c/be05bfb20ca29176c1257c60002f5891/$-FILE/PLAN%20ANUAL%20DE%20ACCION%20EXTERIOR2013.pdf.
35 Corbacho, Mínguez, and Valderrama, 'Percepción'.
36 Vangehuchten and Crespo, 'Reinventar'.
37 Ramiro, *Marca España*; Rius and Martin, 'Spain's'.
38 Montes, "La Promoción'.
39 Interbrand, *Análisis del Sector de la Moda Española. Informe de Resultados*. Observatorio Industrial Del Sector Textil y de La Confección. Consejo Intertextil Español, CCOO y UGT, 2009, pp. 25–28. http://aipclop.com/fotos/1278597566_Gue8.pdf.
40 GFK, *Las Marcas Españolas y el Efecto País de Origen. Un Estudio sobre su Conocimiento y Percepción en Seis Mercados Prioritarios para la Empresa Española*. GFK and Foro de Marcas Renombradas Españolas, 2019. https://www.icex.es/icex/es/navegacion-principal/todos-nuestros-servicios/informacion-de-mercados/estudios-de-mercados-y-otros-documentos-de-comercio-exterior/DOC2019819241.html.
41 2019 data from the WTO online database on international trade statistics, https://stats.wto.org/.
42 Inditex, *Memoria anual 2019*, p. 12.
43 Brand Finance, *Apparel*, p. 12.
44 Miranda and Roldán, 'Inditex', pp. 161–163.
45 Miranda and Roldán, 'Inditex', pp. 165–166.
46 Samiee, Shimp, and Sharma, 'Brand'.
47 Interbrand, *Análisis Del Sector de La Moda Española. Informe de Resultados*. Observatorio Industrial Del Sector Textil y de La Confección. Consejo Intertextil Español, CCOO y UGT, 2009, p. 9. http://aipclop.com/fotos/1278597566_Gue8.pdf.

Bibliography

Alden, D.L., Steenkamp, J.B.E.M., and Batra, R., 'Brand positioning through advertising in Asia, North America, and Europe: the role of global consumer culture', *Journal of Marketing*, 63 (1999), pp. 75–87.

Aronczyk, M., *Branding the Nation: The Global Business of National Identity*. New York: Oxford University Press, 2013.

Bolin, G., and Miazhevich, G., 'The soft power of commercialised nationalist symbols: using media analysis to understand nation branding campaigns', *European Journal of Cultural Studies*, 21 (2018), pp. 527–542.

Borzova, A.Y., and Nikolashvili, N.D., 'Marca España': development of Spanish government policy on the implementation of "soft power", *Bulletin of the Russian State University of the Humanities: Political Science, History, and International Relations, Series*, 2 (2020), pp. 77–93.

Brand Finance, *Apparel 50 2019. The Annual Report on the World's Most Valuable and Strongest Apparel Brands*. N.p.: Brand Finance, 2019.

Cerviño, J., and Rivera, J., 'La Globalización de las marcas españolas: liderazgo y notoriedad internacional', *Información Comercial Española, ICE: revista de Economía*, 839 (2007), pp. 121–139.

Corbacho, J.M., Mínguez, M.I., and Valderrama, M., 'Percepción interna y externa de la imagen de la marca España: análisis de métodos de evaluación', *Sphera Publica*, June (2014), pp. 82–99. https://sphera.ucam.edu/index.php/sphera-01/article/view/201.

Darling, J.R., and Puetz, J.E., 'Analysis of changes in consumer attitudes toward the products of England, France, Germany and the USA, 1975–2000', *European Business Review*, 14 (2002), pp. 170–183.

Dholakia, R.R., Zhao, M., and Duan, J., 'The COO construct: methodological and related issues in a globalized world', *Journal of Global Marketing*, 33 (2020), pp. 3–17.

Donzé, P., 'National labels and the competitiveness of European industries: the example of the "Swiss Made" law since 1950', *European Review of History*, 26 (2019), pp. 855–870.

Ercan, E., 'Country of origin and consumers' willingness to purchase an apparel', *Journal of Textile and Apparel, Technology and Management*, 6 (2010), pp. 1–15.

Gilmore, F., 'A country – can it be repositioned? Spain – the success story of country branding,', *Journal of Brand Management*, 9 (2002), pp. 281–293.

González, E., and Casilda, R., 'La Marca País como Ventaja Competitiva. El Valor de la Marca España', *Información Comercial Española, ICE: Revista de Economía*, 799 (2002), pp. 101–114.

Hao, A.W., Paul, J., Trott, S., Guo, C., and Wu, H., 'Two decades of research on nation branding: a review and future research agenda', *International Marketing Review*, 38 (2021), pp. 46–69.

Higgins, D.M., *Brands, Geographical Origin, and the Global Economy: A History from the Nineteenth Century to the Present*. Cambridge: Cambridge University Press, 2018.

Hornikx, J., Van Meurs, F., Van Den Heuvel, J., and Janssen, A., 'How brands highlight country of origin in magazine advertising: a content analysis', *Journal of Global Marketing*, 33 (2020), pp. 34–45.

Inditex, *Memoria anual 2019*. Arteixo: Dirección General de Comunicación y Relaciones Institucionales de Inditex, 2020.

Kilduff, K., and Núñez-Tabales, J.M., 'Country image management: brand Spain in the United States (U.S.)', *Regional and Sectoral Economic Studies*, 14 (2014), pp. 1–16. http://www.usc.es/economet/reviews/eers1421.pdf.

Kim, H., Shin, E., Cheng, A., Lennon, S.J., and Liu, W., 'Influence of design, workmanship, and familiarity on perceptions of country-of-origin apparel brands: a study of consumers in the US, China and Japan', *Journal of Global Fashion Marketing*, 6 (2015), pp. 265–277.

Krupka, Z., Ozretic-Dosen, D., and Previsic, J., 'Impact of perceived brand name origin on fashion brand's perceived luxury', *Acta Polytechnica Hungarica*, 11 (2014), pp. 153–216.

Lamo de Espinosa, E., 'La Imagen de España en el Exterior: Conclusiones de una Investigación', *Estudios Agrosociales y Pesqueros*, 189 (2000), pp. 243–268.

Magnusson, P., Westjohn, S.A., and Zdravkovic, S., '"What? I thought Samsung was Japanese": accurate or not, perceived country of origin matters', *International Marketing Review*, 28 (2011), pp. 454–472.

Miranda, J.A., and Roldán, A., 'Inditex y la ventaja competitiva de la fast fashion española, 1985–2019', *Dimensioni e Problemi della Ricerca Storica*, 2 (2021), pp. 155–178.

Montes, V.J., 'La Promoción de la Moda Española en los Mercados Internacionales', *Boletín Económico de ICE*, no. 2768 (2003), pp. 55–65.

Morello, G., *The 'Made in' Issue: A Comparative Research on the Image of Domestic and Foreign Products*. Amsterdam: Serie Research Memoranda from VU University Amsterdam. Faculty of Economics, Business Administration and Econometrics, 1983.

Noya, J., *La imagen de España en el Exterior: Estado de la Cuestión*. Madrid: Real Instituto Elcano, 2020.

Pegan, G., Vianelli, D. and De Luca, P., *International Marketing Strategy: The Country of Origin Effect on Decision-Making in Practice*. Cham: Springer, 2020.

Ramiro, P., *Marca España. ¿A quién beneficia?* Barcelona: Icaria, 2013.

Reputation Institute, *La reputación de España en el mundo*. Madrid: Instituto de Análisis de Intangibles, 2009.

Rius, J., and Martín, M., 'Spain's nation branding project Marca España and its cultural policy: the economic and political instrumentalization of a homogeneous and simplified cultural image', *International Journal of Cultural Policy*, 21 (2015), pp. 20–40.

Rosendorf, N.M., *Franco Sells Spain to America: Hollywood, Tourism and Public Relations as Postwar Spanish Soft Power*. Basingstoke: Palgrave Macmillan, 2014.

Salciuviene, L., Ghauri, P.N., Streder, R.S. and De Mattos, C., 'Do brand names in a foreign language lead to different brand perceptions?', *Journal of Marketing Management*, 26 (2010), pp. 1037–1056.

Samiee, S., Shimp, T.A., and Sharma, S., 'Brand origin recognition accuracy: its antecedents and consumers' cognitive limitations', *Journal of International Business Studies*, 36 (2005), pp. 379–397.

Usunier, J., 'Relevance in business research: the case of country-of-origin research in marketing', *European Management Review*, 3 (2006), pp. 60–73.

Vangehuchten, L., and Crespo, M., 'Reinventar la Marca España en tiempos de crisis, un análisis comunicativo de la campaña española de nation branding', *Ámbitos. Revista Internacional de Comunicación*, 24 (2019), pp. 1–14.

10 From the 'yellow peril' to 'cool Japan'

Country's image and global competitiveness of the Japanese manufacturing industry since the Meiji period

Pierre-Yves Donzé

Introduction

This chapter discusses the evolution of the dialectic relation between Japan's image and the competitiveness of its manufacturing sector from the late nineteenth century. The rapid economic development of Japan during the last 150 years – from being the last country to open up to global trade to becoming one of the most competitive nations in the world – is well known. The central argument of this chapter is that the characteristics associated with Made in Japan were constructed outside Japan, mainly in the West, and in the context of the globalization of consumption. Foreign consumers and manufacturers developed narratives about what Japanese manufactured goods were, what they represented, and what they meant.

Over time, this narrative changed: a positive image of traditional crafts during the last third of the nineteenth century (Japonisme); a negative image during the industrialization and catch-up phase (cheap and nasty), and a new era, following the collapse of the bubble economy,[1] when Made in Japan was viewed positively (cool Japan). These epochs are shown in Table 10.1.

Although external perceptions of Made in Japan varied over time, one message remained constant: positive images of Japan and its products were not linked to a *place*, but to a *culture* and an *identity*. This association provided a competitive advantage to Japanese manufacturers. To illustrate this argument, consider, first, the cultural identity of products. According to J. Rius-Ulldemolins, 'the cultural dimension of products distinguishes them and allows one territory to gain a competitive advantage over others'.[2] Japan's traditional goods such as sake, kimonos, and ceramics are neither manufactured nor consumed abroad. They embody a specific (Japanese) culture and manufacturers of these products are protected from foreign competition. The situation is, however, completely different for manufacturing with a low cultural identity – cotton yarn, steel, and steamships. These goods are manufactured and consumed throughout the world.[3]

DOI: 10.4324/9781003166184-10

Table 10.1 'Made in' narratives and global competition

	1860–1890 Japonisme	*1890–1940 Yellow Peril I*	*1950–1990 Yellow Peril II*	*Since 2000 Cool Japan*
Image of "Made in Japan"	Positive	Negative	Positive and negative	Positive
Industrial sectors	Traditional	Light industries	High-tech	Creative industries
Competition towards foreign goods	None	Strong	Strong	Weak
Japanese promotion policy	International exhibitions	None	JETRO and industrial associations (1950s)	Advertisement
Definition of the image	From abroad	From abroad	From abroad	From abroad and domestic

Sources: The author.

Next, consider the international competitiveness of Japanese manufacturing. Japan was the first non-Western country to achieve industrial development and thereby challenge the global domination of European and American companies. Trade frictions – and Japanese imperial expansion in Asia-Pacific until 1945 – influenced deeply narratives of Made in Japan throughout the twentieth century. Moreover, Japanese economic development relied on the mass production and export of products possessing low cultural identity – matches, toys, and basic textile fabrics in the early twentieth century, and cars and electronics later in that century. The 1930s, and the period encompassing the 1970s and 1980s, were periods of major trade friction with the West.[4] These two periods correspond to substantial changes in the volume of references to Made in Japan (Figure 10.1).

What, then, of the domestic Japanese market? Ensuring that consumers and manufacturers were protected from imports embossed with misleading indications of geographical origin – including country of origin – was a notable feature of national, and international legislation during the nineteenth century, and is arguably best exemplified by the British Merchandise Marks Act of 1887, and the US McKinley Tariff, 1890.[5] In the post-1945 period, the rapid growth of international trade in intermediate products, and the continued expansion of multinational companies, meant that indications of the country of origin became a major issue. Some countries, such as Switzerland, implemented specific regulations to protect the reputation of its manufacturing sector and to preserve its manufacturing base.[6] However, in this regard, Switzerland was unusual. In Japan, and, indeed, many other countries (excluding the US), there are no specific statutes protecting Made in Japan. In common with many countries, there are laws prohibiting unfair

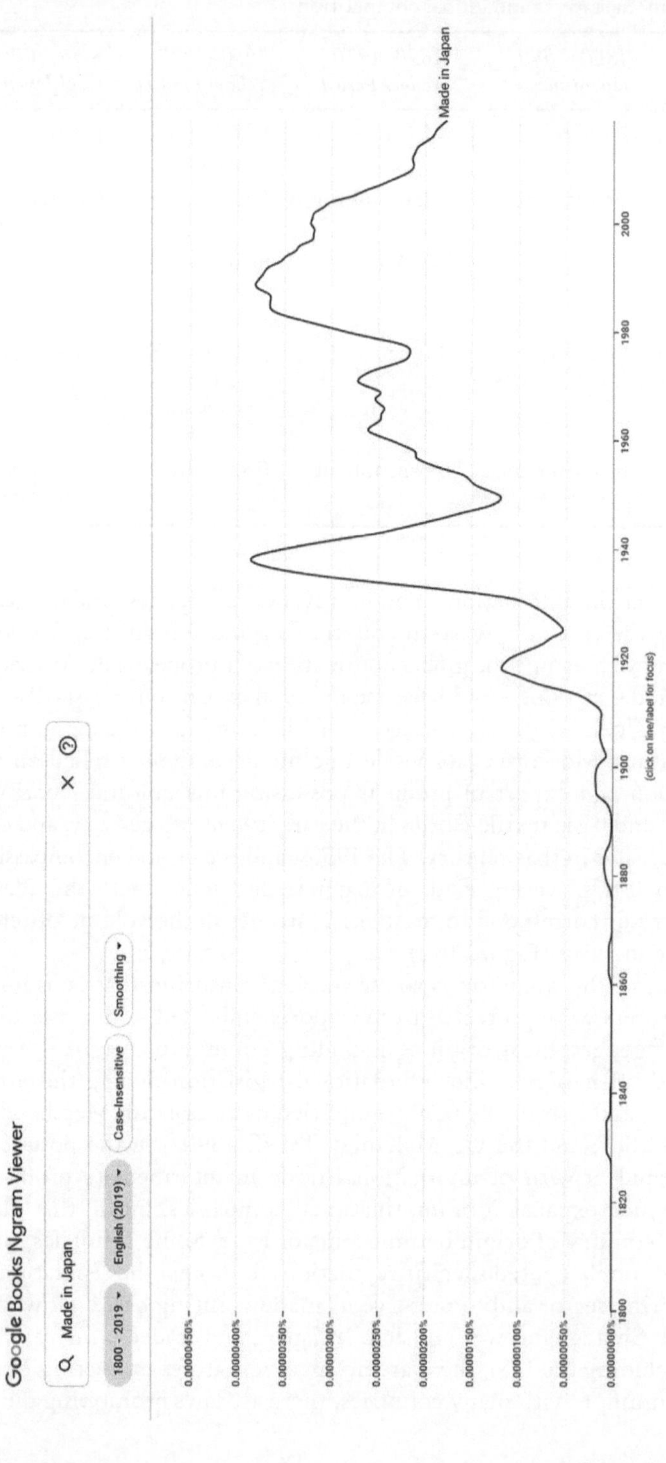

Figure 10.1 'Made in Japan' in Google Books, 1850–2019
Source: https://books.google.com/ngrams. Accessed 5 July 2021.

competition, and Customs regulations prohibiting the import of products falsely indicating Made in Japan. However, there is no legal definition of Made in Japan.

This chapter has a chronological structure incorporating four major periods between 1850 and today, during which external perceptions of Made in Japan changed. The discussion is organized as follows. The next section focuses on the period between 1850 and 1890, and explains how traditional Japanese products, such as ceramics, kimonos, and prints, were sought by Western consumers precisely because they reflected Japanese culture. This is followed by a discussion of Japanese industrialization between 1890 and 1930, and its adverse effects on external perceptions of Made in Japan. Next, Japan's remarkable economic growth between 1950 and 1990 is contrasted with ambiguous views about Japanese products, which improved towards the end of this period. Conversely, the penultimate section explains how the declining international competitiveness of Japanese manufacturing helped to resurrect the positive international image of Made in Japan. Conclusions are then presented.

The era of *Japonisme*, 1850–1890

Although there was some trade between Japan and foreign countries during the Edo period (1603–1867), the expansion of Japanese products on world markets was a consequence of the forced opening-up of Japan, and the adoption of unequal treaties during the 1850s and early 1860s.[7] During the first decades following this liberalization, Japanese exports consisted mostly of two agricultural commodities: silk and tea. Between 1868 and 1895, silk was Japan's principal export, with a share constantly above 30%, while tea accounted for approximately 20% of exports between 1868 and 1880, after which it declined to less than 10% in the early 1890s, due to competition from rival tea producers.[8] Consequently, Japanese exports did not challenge the dominant position of Western manufactured goods on world markets, and neither did they compete with European agricultural products, such as cereals and wine; Japanese silk and tea were not a threat. However, during this period, no specific discourse emerged about the Japanese origin of these products.

Instead, the European and American bourgeoisie focused on Japanese decorative arts and fashions. Kimonos, ceramics, and woodblock prints became popular. Although they were negligible in Japanese trade (ceramics, never accounted for more than 2% of Japanese exports between 1880 and 1895), these items benefited from a strong demand from Western countries following the opening-up of Japan. Moreover, these products influenced artists, notably French impressionists, and craftsmen, generating the artistic movement, *Japonisme*.[9] Such articles were consumed because they were different:

Their strong association with Japanese culture created a positive external image, which enabled these products to secure a competitive advantage.

This advantage was important because ceramics was a heavily export-oriented industry: During the 1880s, exports averaged 51% of domestic production.[10] Initially, Europe was the main market for exports which supported the growth of craft-based workshops in traditional clusters, such as Kyoto. After 1890, there was less European interest in traditional Japanese manufacturing which led to an industrial transformation of the ceramics industry, characterized by the industrialization of production, the development of Western-style products, and a shift towards the American mass market.[11]

The promotion of traditional Japanese goods in European markets was mainly confined to international exhibitions.[12] The first presentation of Japanese decorative arts occurred in London in 1862, hosted by the British diplomat Rutherford Alcock. Subsequently, the Japanese authorities organized their own displays, beginning with the Paris exhibition of 1867, followed by Vienna in 1873, Philadelphia in 1876, and Paris in 1878. To improve the export promotion of decorative art products, Japanese entrepreneurs and the government founded the semi-public trading company, Kiriu Kosho Kaisha, in 1873.[13] This company was particularly successful in the US. Kiriu Kosho's representative at the 1878 Paris exhibition, Tadamasa Hayashi, remained in France, as an independent art merchant. He founded a company in 1883, and introduced Japanese art to French collectors and artists.[14]

Success at international exhibitions, and the work of entrepreneurs such as Hayashi, meant that Japanese products enjoyed an excellent reputation on Western markets between the 1860s and 1880s. Although Japanese officials and businessmen collaborated to promote the export of traditional Japanese artefacts, they did not create a brand image associated with Made in Japan. Instead, this image was created externally, by the consumers of these artefacts. The zenith of *Japonisme* occurred in the 1880s. Kiriu Kosho was dissolved in 1891 and the share of the national production of ceramics exported dropped to 36% in 1900.[15] Thereafter, the Japanese economy became more industrialized, and a greater volume of Japanese manufactured products was exported to international markets. This transformation dramatically altered external perceptions of Made in Japan, and the popularity of Japanese decorative arts.

Industrialization and the Yellow Peril, 1890–1930

Industrialisation and imperialism adversely affected the external image of Japanese manufacturing from the 1890s. Such products no longer communicated an attractive, exotic culture; instead, they were associated with an aggressive country which simultaneously posed an industrial threat to manufacturers in Western countries, and a military challenge to countries in Asia, and beyond. Japan's share of global exports of manufactured goods grew from 1.5% in 1899, to 3.9% in 1929, and reached 6.9% in 1937.[16] The main exported items were no longer tea and silk, but cotton textiles and light industrial goods.

The development of a competitive cotton textile industry, the result of technology transfer from Britain, enabled Japan to become the world's leading exporter of cotton fabrics by 1933.[17] Turning to the products of 'light' industries, these were diverse and included brushes, umbrellas, clocks, and toys, all produced by a multitude of small and medium-sized enterprises (hereafter, SMEs) for which competitiveness relied on cheap labour and modern technology.[18] These industries were organized as small workshops clustered in the main cities of Tokyo and Osaka.[19] In 1933, there were approximately 100 small toy manufacturers located in Tokyo, all exporting to Western markets. By 1934, US imports of Japanese toys exceeded those from Germany.[20] Similar trends can be observed for other light industrial products. In 1898, for example, a French newspaper reported that 'everywhere too, from the Amur River to the Straits of Malacca and even to India, the words Made in Japan are written on all matchboxes'.[21]

The increase in Japanese manufacturing exports was supported by many private and public organizations that gathered market intelligence. In 1882, large companies in the cotton textile industry established the Japan Cotton Spinners Association, which was required to distribute a monthly report providing information on competitors, and markets to its members.[22] The foreign subsidiaries of general trading companies, such as Mitsui, and Mitsubishi played a similar role.[23] Public organizations at the level of local and central government were also involved. As early as 1898, the Kyoto Ceramic Experimental Centre was providing advice on design.[24] Experiment centres, (*shikenjo*), were also established to evaluate the quality of manufacturing , and to help entrepreneurs improve design and production methods. By 1934, there were more than 80 such centres throughout Japan.[25] Moreover, in 1928, the Ministry of Commerce and Industry opened a national centre which disseminated information on the design of industrial products (*Kogei shidojo*).[26] It employed 66 persons by 1934 and played a major role in supporting manufacturers to adapt their products to foreign markets.[27] Unlike the earlier period, Japanese culture did not facilitate export growth; it was a liability that had to be overcome if Western markets were to be accessed.

Porcelain products provide an exemplar of this problem. This industry experienced considerable success in Europe and the US during the era of *Japonisme*, precisely because traditional art expressed Japanese culture. However, to compete in the mass market, porcelain manufacturers needed to adapt their products to the tastes and incomes of Western consumers, especially the urban middle class in the US. Consequently, 'Western' tableware – plates, cups, tea sets – was sold at price-quality ratios that allowed Japanese manufacturers to compete with established producers in France, Germany, and Britain. The company, Japan Ceramics (*Nihon Toki*), founded in Nagoya in 1904, organized the mass production of Western-style porcelain. Between 1904 and 1937, over 90% of production was exported. This company launched a Western-style dinner set on the US market in 1914, under the Noritake China brand, and benefited from rapid sales growth: 2,000 of these dinner sets were produced in 1914, rising to nearly 50,000 by 1927. This dinner set quickly became the firm's main product.[28] In fact, Japan Ceramics provided a model of how Japanese manufacturers adapted to foreign markets, and its example was followed by many other SMEs in this industry.[29]

The reaction in Western countries against this competition was twofold. First, motivated by the belief that domestic consumers preferred US products, the McKinley Tariff Act of 1890, required that US imports indicate their country of origin.[30] Imports from Japan were labelled 'Nippon', and then, from 1921, and subsequently, 'Japan'. However, this requirement had little impact on Japanese exports: Their price-quality characteristics made them popular among US consumers, as demonstrated by the success of the Noritake porcelain brand. For Japanese silk products exported to the US, in 1904, some merchants passed-off Chinese silk products as Made in Japan in an attempt to secure higher prices.[31] In 1919, the *New York Times* reported that US manufacturers used, 'the marks of an imported article [as] the word 'imported' infers better quality than domestic make'.[32] This report continued, '"Made in Germany" of course is no longer popular, so "Made in Japan" has been substituted'.[33]

Similarly, in Britain, the Standing Committee appointed by the Board of Trade to examine whether imported knitted products and hosiery should be compelled to indicate their country of origin, reported opposition from prominent manufacturers. However, other producers, such as Alfred Stern, opined: 'Japan had now obtained a high standing in the hosiery trade, and he had made a label "Made in Japan" which he affixed to underwear from that country because it was such a good quality'.[34] The Standing Committee decided that imported hosiery and knitted products were required to indicate their country of origin when sold in the UK.[35]

Second, there was an emotional reaction that became important during the interwar years. Low wages and long working hours enabled Japanese manufacturers to undercut, significantly, US textile prices, which threatened the ruination of this industry. In 1914, the Commercial Museum of Philadelphia, which provided market intelligence to the local textile industry, argued that 'if the present duties were maintained, a great majority of American citizens will be wearing Japanese hosiery before 1920'.[36] Some US companies sought to create a positive narrative surrounding Japanese exports. In 1934, the department store, Macy's, advertised the portmanteau word 'Japanama', which referred to a new hat for the summer season. Macy's described the construction of this hat as follows: 'it's a fine pliant paper which was made in Japan. After the paper is made, it is sent in twisted strips to the Island of Okinawa, where it is woven, by hand, in the homes of the farmers, by weavers who are skilled specialists'.[37] However, such narratives were exceptional.

More common were the views of the manager of a Swiss watch company: 'Made in Japan [has] a nice little reputation of cheap and nasty'.[38] Japanese watches were mere copies of Swiss products, of lower quality, manufactured by underpaid workers, and sold for less than a quarter of the common price. European and American merchants, and politicians made very similar statements about a broad range of Japanese products during this period. All shared a common fear of the invasion of world markets by cheap and low-quality Japanese products that challenged their economic hegemony. The discourse on Made in Japan at that time was negative, and it was developed by actors outside of the country.

It was not the bad quality of Japanese products that was feared, but their relatively low prices. Violins, toys, matches, and glassware, arrived in significant quantities on American and European markets, during the 1930s. These exports were too competitive, threatened Western manufacturers, and hence provoked strong reactions. The discourse on Japanese products that evolved during the interwar years increasingly focused on unfair competition. Japan's military expansion in China provided an opportunity to denounce the dangers of Made in Japan – which was now associated with Japanese imperialism. The French communist newspaper *L'Humanité*, called for a boycott of Japanese products in December 1937; it argued that Japan's military capabilities were financed from the profits obtained by its global manufacturing exports.[39] In East Liverpool, Ohio, Japanese products were publicly burned to protest against the destruction of the USS Panay in China.[40]

How did consumers react to the threats posed by Japan? Although intellectuals and politicians in the US and in Panama, organized a boycott of Japanese goods to protest against Japan's invasion of China, not all consumers shared these sentiments. In January 1938, the *New York Times* reported that in Panama stores, 'the pre-Christmas rush cleared the shelves of Japanese merchandise'.[41] In other words, Japanese products remained popular among Western consumers at the beginning of the twentieth century.

The global expansion of Made in Japan during the high-growth years, 1950–1990

Japanese products almost disappeared from world markets during World War II, and in the decade following 1945. Thus, Japan's share of world exports had fallen to 0.4% in 1948 and grew only slightly to 1.5% in 1953, and 3.5% in 1963.[42] During this period, Japanese products were not perceived as a major threat to Western companies because their quality was below US standards. Because of this perception of Japanese products, Akio Morita, co-founder of Sony, explained in his memoires that, during the 1950s, his company printed Made in Japan on Sony products in the smallest size allowed by US Customs in an attempt to conceal their origin.[43] Such views were a throwback to the interwar period. In 1948, the *New York Times* printed a picture of young girls in Tokyo testing ballpens prior to export.[44] This image conveyed the message that Japanese products were technically underdeveloped and that their price competitiveness relied on the mass use of low-wage workers. Two years later, the managing director of the National Association of Variety Stores explained that, despite the growing US import of Japanese toys, American manufacturers had nothing to fear because such toys were of inferior quality: 'Mechanical toys made in Japan do not last and are highly unsatisfactory'.[45] Similar opinions were expressed in Western Europe. In 1958, a Swiss magazine stated, 'Japan has started to flood the market with low-cost souvenir jewellery'.[46]

However, such perceptions changed significantly during the 1960s. Japanese exports accelerated over subsequent decades and reached a peak of 9.8% of world exports by 1993.[47] Of particular importance, this growth was underpinned by a major shift in the composition of exports, from light industrial goods to electronics, cars, and other high-tech products. Large Japanese corporations, such as Toyota and Sony were in the vanguard of this expansion, but such companies did not highlight Japanese origin in their advertisements. The explanation for this reticence is that the yen appreciated during the 1970s, and this encouraged Japanese companies to relocate their factories to low wage countries, particularly in South-East Asia, and Latin America. Thus, in 1977, Matsushita Electric (Panasonic), had 56 foreign subsidiaries that assembled radios, televisions, and other electric consumer goods, with a value of USD 884 million.[48] Such products were not Made in Japan, but they were manufactured by a company with headquarters in Japan. Such practices were apparent in other leading Japanese companies.

The situation was different for SMEs in the precision instrument industries – cameras, watches, and medical instruments. These firms benefited from the activities of a semi-public organization, the Japan Export Trade Research Organization (hereafter, JETRO), founded in 1951.[49] Its main objectives were to gather market intelligence about foreign countries, and to foster the global promotion of Japanese manufacturing. JETRO opened its first Japan Trade Centre (hereafter, JTC) in New York in November 1953, followed by San Francisco in November 1954, and others, which included: Cairo in February 1955; Toronto in March 1956; Bangkok in March 1959, and Hamburg in March 1959.[50] By 1970, there existed 19 JTCs.[51] These centres were important for Japanese exporters because they supplied essential logistics, and sometimes hosted the offices of industrial associations. Moreover, from 1954 onwards, JETRO had offices around the world, each staffed by a few representatives. Their number reached 26 in 1960 and 41 in 1970. In total, JTC and foreign offices employed 3 persons in 1953, 119 in 1960, and 255 in 1970.[52]

In addition to JETRO, some trade associations organized their own trade centres and fairs in foreign countries. The Japanese Camera Industry Association opened an information and service centre in New York in 1956, which offered repair services for any type of camera made in Japan. This centre cooperated with the local JETRO office, and it was partially funded by the government.[53] Consequently, these organizations collectively promoted Japanese products and emphasized their high quality-price ratio.

The rapid growth of Japanese exports generated friction between Japan and Western countries.[54] Japanese products had an ambiguous image on world markets: Their high quality-cost ratio made them popular among consumers, but their image was tarnished by accusations of unfair competition. Referring to Japanese exports of textile products, in 1960, the *New York Times* opined that 'Japan's own attitude presents a formidable block to trade benevolence by others. Ironically this nation that is so successfully invading foreign markets maintains tariffs, quotas, and other import restrictions that are among the world's most rigorous'.[55] The following year, one of the largest trade unions in the US apparel industry, the Amalgamated Clothing Workers of America, initiated a boycott against imported Japanese cotton fabrics. Its 385,000 members decided to 'refuse to cut Japanese cloth'.[56]

Subsequently, similar discourses and actions in relation to Japanese machine tools, cars, and electronics, became widespread.[57] Nonetheless, the high quality of Japanese products was gaining recognition. An excellent illustration of this transition was provided in Morita's memoires. Having explained how Sony became one of the world's leading consumer electronics firms, Morita concluded that:

> we in the free world can do great things. We proved it in Japan by changing the image of the words 'Made in Japan' from something shoddy to something fine. But for a single nation or a few nations to have accomplished this is not enough. My vision of the future is of an exciting world of superior goods and services, where every nation's stamp of origin is a symbol of quality, and where all are competing for the consumers' hard-earned money at fair prices that reflect appropriate rates of exchange.[58]

For Morita, the capabilities of large corporations took precedence over the specificities of nations. Many US scholars visited Japan to determine the competitiveness of its leading companies during the 1970s and 1980s.[59] The common message that appeared from these studies was that Japan was strong because of its culture, aspects of which included long-term oriented management, the predominance of the group over the individual, and because Japan, unlike Western countries, did not follow the rules of free-market capitalism. However, it was the perspective of Western countries that Made in Japan no longer signalled low quality, but instead, it signalled unfair trade practices. For example, during the early 1980s, Japanese manufacturers were accused of dumping, and of forcing US partners to leave joint ventures.[60] The closure of the Japanese domestic market, and the imposition of non-tariff barriers were also major issues in relations with European countries.[61]

Contemporaneously, more attention was also being devoted to Japan's cultural influence. When Sony purchased Columbia Pictures in 1989, *Newsweek* dressed the statue of Liberty with a kimono, and titled one of its issues, 'Japan invades Hollywood'.[62] The fear of cultural invasion was perfectly epitomized by the discourse against Japanese cartoons (*anime*) in France during the 1980s. Japanese cartoon producers began their foreign expansion during this decade, and France was a major market, accounting for 33 and 35% of exports in 1986 and 1990, respectively.[63] French film producers purchased Japanese cartoons because of limited domestic supply, and because US cartoons were too expensive.[64] Dragon Ball, Goldorak, and other anime were shown on French television. Despite their popularity among children and teenagers, the cartoons received severe criticism by official bodies, such as the Superior Council of Audiovisual (which controls the content of television programmes), the media, leftwing politicians, and artists. Japanese *anime* were considered violent and unsuitable for young audiences. Moreover, there was a willingness to protect French children's literature from this cultural invasion. In 1989, Ségolène Royal, a Socialist MP, claimed in her book: 'our ambition is to call on French authors; they know how to tell lovely stories which are extremely entertaining while having an educative power. … It is easy to make a program for children, there are kilometers of cartoons, notably in Far East, mostly very violent. This is not our intention'.[65]

Post-bubble stagnation and the birth of 'cool Japan' from 1990

Although Japanese *anime* were severely criticized by French elites, they became popular with youngsters. In 1993, the French publisher Glénat Editions released a translation of the manga Dragon Ball, which sold rapidly more than 100,000 copies. Based on this success, Glénat acquired the rights to other Japanese cartoons.[66] Subsequently, several French companies published manga and produced anime which were sold in video cassettes. As a result of these activities, France promoted Japanese culture in Europe, which remains one of the largest markets for manga.

The success of manga and anime in France reflects a fundamental, favourable, and global change of perception towards Japanese products during the 1990s. This transition was simultaneous with the stagnation of the Japanese economy following the financial bubble, and the decline in Japan's manufacturing competitiveness: Japan's share of world exports declined from 9.8% in 1993 to 6.4% in 2003, and reached 3.7% in 2018.[67] Contemporaneously, other Asian nations, particularly China, emerged as large exporters, so Japanese products are no longer considered a threat to Western markets. In 2009, the *New York Times* reported that stores in that city were selling the world's finest denim for a few hundred dollars, and commented: 'a fabric made in Japan with shuttle looms used in the good old days of classic American jeanmaking'.[68] This quotation indicates that apparel produced in Japan is not viewed as a threat to the US clothing industry; instead, such articles are viewed favourably as the embodiment of artisanal excellence that meets the needs of a new generation of US urban dwellers.

Moreover, it is also necessary to explain how the transformation of Asian manufacturing exerted a positive impact on the perception of Japanese products. Since 2000, the dissemination of new production architecture (from integral to modular), the expansion of global value chains, and digitalization have changed the sources of competitive advantage in electronics, and related sectors of manufacturing, except automobiles.[69] The division of work made possible by these developments encouraged Japanese firms to refocus their manufacturing towards the development of electronic components and materials. Japanese companies no longer manufacture *complete* products; consequently, Japan is not considered a threat. Consider Panasonic, which dominated the global market for consumer electronics. In 2010, this company began the mass production of lithium batteries for electric vehicles. By 2019, its automotive and industrial systems divisions represented 33% of Panasonic's gross sales, compared to the 31% accounted for by appliances.[70]

A second major change was the geographical refocusing of Japanese exports towards Asian markets. Between 1990 and 2019, North America's share of Japanese exports declined from 34 to 21%; conversely, exports to East Asia and the Pacific increased from 27 to 48%.[71] The image of Japanese products in Asia is different to that in Western countries. In the former, Japanese manufacturing is perceived to embody high quality excellent design. In these countries, this sector is held up as a role model for their own industrial development.

In a global context, from about the 1990s, the image of Japanese products has been transformed: once they were seen as the embodiment of the 'yellow peril', but, during the later twentieth century, they are viewed more positively – an incarnation of 'cool Japan' – which combines a unique traditional culture with technological creativity. The expression 'cool Japan' was coined by the American journalist Douglas McGray. One of his articles published by *Foreign Policy* in 2002, presented the argument that anime, video games, and manga had enabled Japan to strengthen its global cultural influence; that Japan's Gross National Cool had to be considered a 'soft' power or, 'a reminder that commercial trends and products, and a country's knack for spawning them, can serve political and economic ends'.[72] Foreign sales of the Japanese animation industry, including movies and television, increased faster than domestic market sales in the early twenty-first century. The former grew from 373 billion to 522 billion yen between 2002 and 2005. After a period of stagnation following the global financial crisis, foreign sales, largely focused on China, peaked at 1,009 billion yen in 2018.[73]

Food is another product which reflects the global success of cool Japan. The export of a diverse range of foodstuffs, including green tea, sake, Kobe beef, instant noodles, and soy sauce has increased since 2000 – a direct consequence of growing health concerns and the positive reputation of Japanese food culture. Sake illustrates how, after 2000, a traditional alcoholic beverage was able to find niche export markets.[74] The production of Sake had been in decline since around the 1970s, because of declining domestic sales, and a shift in consumer preferences towards beer and wine.[75] Yet, the situation changed in the early twenty-first century.

Exports of Sake increased from 3 billion to 8.5 billion yen, between 2000 and 2010, and reached 15.5 billion yen in 2016. Contemporaneously, the share of production sold abroad increased from 1 to 4.1% This growth was even more remarkable because the average price per litre of Sake doubled between 2000 and 2016. This expansion was supported by the fast growth of consumption in the US (the largest export market), Korea, and, more recently, mainland China. Another factor which contributed to this growth was the rapid expansion of Japanese restaurants overseas, for which the Ministry of Agriculture, Forestry, and Fisheries introduced a certification system in 2016, following the inclusion of Japanese traditional food (*washoku*) on UNESCO's Intangible Cultural Heritage list. Many Sake brewers focused on this expanding restaurant market. Thus, Takara Shuzo, the largest producer of Sake, established a sales subsidiary in the US in 1983, following which gross sales accounted for by its overseas operations grew from 13 to 33% between 2013 and 2017.[76]

The external promotion of anime, sake, and other cultural products, received official support. The Ministry of Foreign Affairs initiated a programme for cultural diplomacy in 2003, and five years later made the anime character, Doreamon, a cultural ambassador. The Ministry of Economy, Trade, and Industry, opened a Cool Japan Bureau in 2010, to promote exports, and in 2013, it created the Cool Japan Fund to co-invest with private companies in the promotion of Japanese fashion, food, and anime products overseas.

Conclusion

This chapter has discussed the transformation of the global, external image Made in Japan from the Meiji Restauration (1868) until today. The cultural identity of products, and the international competitiveness of Japanese manufacturing, were the two major factors that impacted the transformation of this image. Table 10.1 shows that the positive image of Made in Japan was clearly related to periods when Japan's manufacturing sector was weak – between 1860 and 1890, and since 2000. Conversely, periods of trade expansion, between 1890 and 1940, resulted in highly negative views of Made in Japan. The period between 1950 and 1990 was characterized by a balanced image of Made in Japan: the threat posed by cheap, high-quality goods was offset by the attractiveness, and innovativeness of such products.

Internationally, Japan's experience looks odd: there was no relationship between a competitive industry and a positive country of origin image. In contrast, French, and Italian fashion, or Swiss watches, benefited from strong and positive external images, conveyed by 'Made in', which facilitated their international competitiveness. Japan's experience was different because narratives about Made in Japan were largely defined outside the country. The Japanese government, trade associations, and enterprises did not actively collaborate to protect and promote indications of Japanese origin. The current cool Japan policy may be seen as an important step in this deirection.

Notes

1 This refers to the financial bubble between 1985 and 1991 which marked a turning point in economic growth.
2 Rius-Ulldemolins, 'Barcelona', p. 816.
3 Miyamoto and Kasuya, 'Soron', pp. 1–48.
4 Ishii, *Cotton-Textile*; Ikeda, *Japan in Trade*; Abe, 'The Japan problem', pp. 13–35.
5 Higgins, *Brands*, pp. 157–164; Higgins, 'Its made in the USA', this volume.
6 Donzé, 'National labels'.
7 Francks, *Japanese Economic*, pp. 41–72.
8 Sugiyama, 'Kokusai kankyo', pp. 196–197.
9 Lambourne, *Japonisme*.
10 In value. *Nihon toki 70 shunen shi*, pp. 461–468.
11 Hidetoshi, *Kindai nihon*.
12 Teramoto, *Pari bankoku hakurankai*.
13 Hida, *Meiji no yushutsu*.
14 Koyama-Richard, *Yumemita Nihon*.
15 Miyaki, *Kindai nihon*, p. 49.
16 Howe, *The Origins*, p. 121.
17 Miyamoto, 'The products', pp. 117–159; Abe and Hirano, *Seni sangyo*, p. 71.
18 Tanimoto, *The Role*.
19 Tanimoto, *The Role*.
20 Tanimoto, 'From peasant', pp. 167, 170.
21 *Journal des débats*, 26 February 1898. https://en.wikipedia.org/wiki/Journal_des_d%C3%A9bats.
22 Miles, 'The Japan', pp. 49–75.
23 Shogyo Gakkai, *Kaigai*.
24 Hidetoshi, *Kindai nihon*, p. 94.
25 Sawai, *Kindai nihon*, pp. 55–56.
26 *Dezain no yoran jidaiten*, Matsudo, Matsudo-shi kyoiku iinkai, p. 10.
27 Sawai, *Kindai nihon*, p. 51.
28 *Nihon toki 70 nenshi*, p. 226.
29 *Nihon toki 70 nenshi*.
30 Taussig, 'The McKinley', pp. 326–350; Higgins. 'Its Made in the USA', this volume.
31 *New York Times*, 12 February 1904, p. 11.
32 *New York Times*, 11 June 1919, p. 21.
33 *New York Times*, 11 June 1919, p. 21.
34 *Financial Times*, 24 July 1929, p. 8.
35 Board of Trade. Merchandise Marks Act, 1926. *Report of the Standing Committee, respecting hosiery, knitted goods and fabrics*. Parliamentary Papers, XVI.41, 1929–1930.
36 *New York Times*, 5 April 1914, p. 12.
37 *New York Times*, 13 May 1934, p. 11.
38 Musée international d'horlogerie, La Chaux-de-Fonds, Switzerland, papers of the Chambre suisse d'horlogerie, 197, *Concurrence japonaise*, 5 October 1933.
39 *L'Humanité*, 19 December, 1937, p. 3.
40 *La Sentinelle*, 27 December 1937, p. 1.
41 *New York Times*, 3 January 1938, p. 1.
42 General Agreement on Tariffs and Trade (GATT), *International Trade*. Geneva: GATT, 1963.
43 Morita, *Made in Japan*, p. 77.
44 *New York Times*, 27 July 1948, p. 15.
45 *New York Times*, 15 March 1950, p. 40.
46 *Pour Tous*, 15 April 1958, p. 40.

47 World Bank, https://wits.worldbank.org. Accessed 14 February 2022.
48 *Sengo nihon no gijutsu kakushin*, 1979, p. 208.
49 Japan External Trade Organisation (JETRO) *40 nen no ayumi*, Tokyo: JETRO, 2000, p. 11.
50 JETRO *40 nen no ayumi*, Tokyo: JETRO, 2000, pp. 68–70.
51 JETRO *40 nen no ayumi*, Tokyo: JETRO, 2000, p. 600.
52 JETRO *40 nen no ayumi*, Tokyo: JETRO, 2000, p. 600.
53 Nelson, *Rivalry*, pp. 98–99.
54 Sato and Nelson, *Beyond trade.*
55 *New York Times*, 12 June 1960, p. 208.
56 *New York Times*, 15 March 1961, p. 7.
57 Schröter, 'Japanese-European', pp. 5–12.
58 Morita, *Made in Japan*, p. 309.
59 Vogel, *Japan*; Johnson, Chalmers. *MITI*; Abegglen and Stalk, *Kaisha.*
60 *New York Times*, 22 August 1981, p. 31; 16 December 1981, p. 4. See also Tsurumi, 'US-Japanese'.
61 Abe, 'The "Japan problem"'.
62 *Newsweek*, 9 October 1989.
63 Kawabe, "Anime bijinesu', p. 162.
64 *Le Figaro*, 30 August 2012.
65 Laffont, Ségolène Royal, *Le ras-le-bol des bébés zappeurs.* p. 44. Translation by the author.
66 *Le Figaro*, 30 August 2012.
67 World Bank, https://wits.worldbank.org. Accessed 14 February 2022.
68 *The New York Times*, 16 August 2009, p. 2.
69 Kikkawa, 'Beyond product', pp. 89–97.
70 Other divisions are eco solutions (23%), and connected solutions (13%). Panasonic, *Annual Report*, 2019, p. 52.
71 World Bank, https://wits.worldbank.org. Accessed 20 July 2021.
72 McGray, 'Japan's gross national', p. 53.
73 Anime Industry Report 2019, https://aja.gr.jp/download/anime_ind_rpt2019_summary_en. Accessed 30 September 2020.
74 Shohei and Yasuyuki, 'Kaigai seichu', pp. 107–127.
75 Qing and Donzé, 'Surviving'.
76 *The Japan Times*, 1 August 2018. Retrieved from: https://www.japantimes.co.jp/news/2018/08/01/business/japans-largest-sake-exporter-eyes-even-larger-slice-international-market/. Accessed 14 February 2022.

Bibliography

Abe, T., and Hirano, K., *Seni sangyo.* Tokyo: Nihon keieishi kenkyujo, 2013.

Abe, T., 'The "Japan problem": the trade conflict between the European countries and Japan in the last quarter of the 20th century', *Entreprises et histoire*, 80 (2015), pp. 13–35.

Abegglen, G., and Stalk, J.C., *Kaisha: The Japanese Corporation.* New York: Basic Books, 1985.

Chalmers, J., *MITI and the Japanese Miracle: The Growth of Industrial Policy, 1925–1975.* Redwood, CA: Stanford University Press, 1982.

Dezain no yoran jidaiten, Matsudo, Matsudo-shi kyoiku iinkai, 1996.

Donzé, P.-Y., 'National labels and the competitiveness of European industries: the example of the "Swiss Made" law since 1950', *European Review of History*, 26 (2019), pp. 855–870.

Francks, P., *Japanese Economic Development: Theory and Practice*. London: Routledge, 2015.

Hida, T., *Meiji no yushutsu kogei zuan: Kiriu kosho kaisha no rekishi*. Kyoto: Kyoto shoin, 1998.

Hidetoshi, M., *Kindai nihon no tojikigyo: sangyo hatten to seisan soshiki no fukuzosei*. Nagoya: Nagoya University Press, 2008.

Higgins, D.M., *Brands, Geographical Origin, and the Global Economy: A History from the Nineteenth Century to the Present*. Cambridge: Cambridge University Press, 2018.

Howe, C., *The Origins of Japanese Trade Supremacy: Development and Technology in Asia from 1540 to the Pacific War*. Chicago: University of Chicago Press, 1996.

Ikeda, M., *Japan in Trade Isolation, 1926–1937 & 1948–1985*. Tokyo: I-House Press, 2008.

Ishii, O., *Cotton-Textile Diplomacy: Japan, Great Britain, and the United States: 1930–1936*. New York: Arno Press, 1981.

Kawabe, N., 'Anime bijinesu no kaigai tenkai: toei animeshon no jirei kenkyu', in Sawako K., Ayse, A.N., and Vassileva, M. (eds), *Manga anime ni miru nihon bunka*. Tokyo: Bunkyo University, 2016.

Kikkawa, T., 'Beyond product lifecycle and flying geese: international competitiveness of East Asian region and the Japanese position within', *Hitotsubashi Journal of Commerce and Management*, 45 (2011), pp. 89–97.

Koyama-Richard, B., *Yumemita Nihon: Edomon do Gonkuru to Hayashi Tadamasa*. Tokyo: Heibonsha, 2006.

Lambourne, L., *Japonisme: Cultural Crossings between Japan and the West*. London: Phaidon, 2005.

McGray, D., 'Japan's gross national cool', *Foreign Policy*, 130 (2002), pp. 44–54.

Miles, F.W., 'The Japan spinners association: creating industrial policy in Meiji Japan', *Journal of Japanese Studies*, 22 (1996), pp. 49–75.

Miyamoto, M., 'The products and market strategies of the Osaka Cotton Spinning Company: 1883–1914', *Japanese Yearbook on Business History*, 5 (1989), pp. 117–159.

Miyamoto, M., and Kasuya, M., 'Soron', in Miyamoto, M., and Kasuya, M. (eds), *Kôza nihon keieishi I: Keieishi edo no keiken, 1600–1882*, Kyoto: Minerva, 2009, pp. 1–48.

Morita, A., *Made in Japan: Akio Morita and Sony*. London: Penguin, 1988.

Nelson, P.A., *Rivalry and Cooperation: How the Japanese Photography Industry Went Global*. Unpublished PhD thesis, University of Warwick, 1998.

Nihon toki 70 nenshi. Nagoya: Nihon Tôki, 1974.

Rius-Ulldemolins, J., 'Barcelona and SEAT, a history of lost opportunity: corporate marketing, nation branding, and consumer nationalism in the automotive industry', *Enterprise & Society*, 16 (2015), pp. 811–846.

Royal, S., *Le ras-le-bol des bébés zappeurs*. Paris: R. Laffont, 1989.

Sato, R., and Nelson, J. (eds), *Beyond trade friction: Japan-US Economic Relations*. Cambridge: Cambridge University Press, 2006.

Sawai, M., *Kindai nihon no kenkyu kaihatsu taisei*. Nagoya: Nagoya University Press, 2012.

Schröter, H.G., 'Japanese-European business encounters during the second half of the 20th century', *Entreprises et histoire*, 3 (2015), pp. 5–12.

Shohei, H., and Yasuyuki, K., 'Kaigai seichu shijo no jittai haaku; nihonshu no yushutsu to kaigai seisan no kankei', *Seikei daigaku keizaigakubu ronshu*, 49 (2018), pp. 107–127.

Shôgyô Gakkai, N. (ed.), *Kaigai maketingu*. Tokyo: Chikura, 1963.

Sugiyama, S., 'Kokusai kankyo to gaikoku boeki', in Umemura, M., and Yamamoto, Y. (eds), *Nihon keizaishi 3: kaiko to isshin*. Tokyo: Iwanami shoten, 1989, pp. 196–197.

Tanimoto M. (ed.), *The Role of Tradition in Japan's Industrialization: Another Path to Industrialization*. Oxford: Oxford University Press, 2006.

Tanimoto, M., 'From peasant economy to urban agglomeration: the transformation of 'labour-intensive industrialization' in modern Japan', in Austin, G., and Sugihara, K., *Labour-Intensive Industrialization in Global History*, London: Routledge, 2013, pp. 153-189.

Taussig, F.W., 'The McKinley tariff act', *Economic Journal*, 1 (1891), pp. 326–350.

Teramoto, N., *Pari bankoku hakurankai to japonizumu no tanjo*. Kyoto: Shibunkaku, 2008.

Tsurumi, Y., 'US-Japanese relations: From brinkmanship to statesmanship', *World Policy Journal*, 7 (1989), pp 1–33.

Vogel, E.F., *Japan as Number One*. Cambridge, MA: Harvard University Press, 1979.

Xia, Q., and Donzé, P.-Y., 'Surviving in a declining industry: a new entrepreneurial history of Nihonsakari since the 1970s', *Business History*, 2021, online prepublication.

11 Crisis and continuity

The promotion of Made in New Zealand in the export and domestic markets

Felicity Barnes and Jim McAloon

Introduction

The structure of the economy was influential in the branding of New Zealand products. From the 1790s, merchandise exports predominantly consisted of food, fibres, and beverages. Until the islands were incorporated into the British Empire, in 1840, indigenous Māori indicia featured in New Zealand exports to complex Asian, Pacific, and Atlantic networks. From the 1850s, the settler economy, based largely on sheep and later dairy cattle, displaced the thriving Maori economy. With the development of refrigerated shipping from the 1880s, Britain was, until the 1960s, the principal export market for New Zealand sheep meat, butter, cheese, and wool.

Throughout this period, New Zealand's population was small: one million in 1911 and two million in 1952. This population, combined with the country's relative remoteness, meant that manufacturing industries were usually oriented to local markets. From the late nineteenth century, governments adopted a range of protective measures. For example, tariffs were imposed until 1938, when a balance of payments crisis prompted the government to introduce quantitative import and exchange controls as well. These controls lasted in some form until the 1980s.

Branding campaigns had two entirely distinct constituencies and purposes. Export campaigns sought to persuade overseas audiences that New Zealand food (and, more recently, beverage) exports were superior compared to the products offered by rival exporters. Conversely, campaigns focused on the domestic market were intended to persuade consumers to favour New Zealand-made goods over imported. While there is a surprising degree of continuity in overseas campaigns, because New Zealand remains an export-led economy, domestic efforts have varied according to national economic conditions.

This chapter proceeds as follows. The next section discusses the promotional campaigns of New Zealand food and beverage exporters between the 1880s and 1970s, which sought to emphasise cultural affinity with Britain, by far New Zealand's biggest export market during this period. Subsequently, we explain how, from the late twentieth century, the promotion of New Zealand food and beverages, and merino wool in foreign markets increasingly

DOI: 10.4324/9781003166184-11

utilized Maori culture, and New Zealand's 'green' credentials. The penultimate section is largely devoted to the development of Made in New Zealand campaigns for the domestic market during the twentieth century, after which conclusions are presented.

Food and beverage exports, 1880s–1970s

The branding of New Zealand food and, more recently, beverage exports has consistently emphasized themes of nature, rurality, and nutritional quality. Because refrigeration was a novel technology in the 1880s, British consumers had to be persuaded that frozen meat and imported dairy products were not only nutritious, but safe, and palatable, and that New Zealand produce was superior to Australian and Argentinian produce. For branding to be successful, consumers need to be confident in the brand. However, British consumers were suspicious of frozen New Zealand meat which undermined the reputation of the product. Exacerbating matters, inadequate freezing – a consequence of faulty conditions on board the ship – and deficiencies in the processing and transport of carcasses on either side of the long voyage, meant that New Zealand meat did not appear attractive to retail consumers. This reputational damage could be very costly: one meat freezing company maintained it had lost £20,000 over four shipments.[1] Similar concerns applied to dairy exports.

Producers, too, had to be persuaded of the importance of reputation. From the early 1890s, the New Zealand government required butter and cheese exports to be factory-made, thereby ruling out farm-made produce, and it mandated inspection and grading. Some farmers who wished to export farm-made produce maintained that grading was useful for them, but not for consumers.[2] However, the head of the department of agriculture argued that grading was in the national interest because poor-quality produce inflicted lasting reputational damage:

> landing of produce, whether meat, butter, or cheese, in an improper state, or, in other words, "out of condition," ... hurts and checks the trade all round, and competitors immediately experience a benefit, and probably gain permanent ground from which it may be found it is impossible to dislodge them.[3]

Simultaneously, it was alleged that English butchers sold the best New Zealand meat as British meat and inferior meat of whatever origin, as colonial.[4] One New Zealand politician and sheep farmer thought that exporters benefited from this practice.[5] This argument did not find favour with New Zealand's Agent-General, William Pember Reeves who insisted that whatever the short-term gain some exporters might realize, the long-term result of passing off, and exporting inferior produce would be to damage the brand New Zealand.[6]

Use of country of origin was part of a product differentiation strategy. The target market for New Zealand was not the wealthy, who could afford to pay a premium for British meat and regarded it as a social obligation to support domestic producers. Retailers serving this class of consumer insisted that their customers were not 'th[e] sort of people' who would eat frozen meat, and their reputation would die if they were known to even look at frozen meat.[7] However, poorer consumers would take whatever they could afford, in a part of the market which New Zealand producers should avoid. Instead, the 'ideal' market segment for New Zealand's meat producers was the middle class, who could afford to be conscious of quality and to pay a little extra for New Zealand meat. Strict quality control was essential to attract and hold such consumers.[8]

Maintaining quality was not the only concern confronting New Zealand producers. The image of New Zealand had to be carefully constructed. A London butcher emphasized that ordinary Londoners possessed little knowledge of New Zealand or its products. Such consumers had, 'only a vague notion of where on the face of the globe New Zealand is situated', and while possessed of 'some sort of hazy notion that all the British colonies have fertile soils, fine climates, plenty of sheep and cattle that have no great value where they are grown', they would also have absorbed messages about high colonial debt, unemployment, earthquakes, and active volcanoes, not to mention lurid stereotypes of Māori cannibals.[9] New Zealand's Britishness was therefore emphasized. As early as 1882, the Agent-General, Dillon Bell, suggested that it was far better that Britain's food be produced by 'kith and kin' rather than potential enemies such as the US. Bell also noted the extensive area of New Zealand land already sown with 'English' grasses compared to the Australian colonies; this provided a means by which New Zealand could differentiate the scale and reliability of its farming products.[10]

In an age of rapid technological change, sourcing edible meat from the antipodes was presented as a fruit of the march of science. In 1889, a two-page spread in *Pictorial World* – commissioned by a shipping company, and Nelson Brothers, meat processors, and merchants – was reprinted and widely circulated. Entitled 'New Zealand frozen meat trade; history of a sheep from a New Zealand sheep station to the Central Meat Market, London', the large-format poster consisted of a series of woodcut illustrations with accompanying text. The poster sought to inform consumers of, 'this wonderful revolution in our food supply'. A New Zealand sheep station was presented in an attractive landscape, with 'breeds of sheep' in a similarly bucolic setting. Views of the Tomoana works, near Hastings, on the east coast of the North Island, portrayed thoroughly attractive, modern factories; carcasses being wrapped for shipping; the latest freezing machinery; a modern steamship, and views of passengers sitting in the comfort of the saloon while carcasses were being unloaded. Carcasses on display for inspection and sale at a London market were accompanied by happy workers and dignified gentlemen in bowler and top hats looking on. The whole impression was of modernity, progress, and cleanliness; needless to say, the poster did not depict the slaughterhouse (Figure 11.1).

Figure 11.1 History of a sheep from a New Zealand sheep station to the Central Meat Market, London, 1887

Source: Maclean, E W (Mr), active 1937. New Zealand frozen meat trade; history of a sheep from a New Zealand sheep station to the Central Meat Market, London. Reprinted by permission from 'The Pictorial World', 21 July 1887. Ref: Eph-E-MEAT-1887-01. Alexander Turnbull Library, Wellington, New Zealand /records/22765621.

From the 1880s, then, a sense of 'cultural affinity was carefully constructed in advertising'.[11] This attachment was facilitated by the nature of New Zealand's commodities: 'Butter and lamb were the familiar products of British farms, not the exotic produce of colonial plantations'.[12] There was a remarkable continuity in these themes for the next several decades, even as New Zealand meat exporting came under the oversight of a statutory authority, the Meat Board, from 1922. The Board insisted that the 'New Zealand' brand be prominently displayed on carcasses, even as it promoted the meat as 'British from New Zealand'.[13]

Similar nomenclature was used by the Empire Marketing Board, established in 1926 to encourage British consumers to buy the produce of the dominions and colonies.[14] One poster, advertising generic New Zealand butter in the late 1920s or early 1930s, showed a 'British Empire Butter Cheese Dairy Factory', in New Zealand, juxtaposed with a road crowded with horses and wagons delivering cans of milk and cream. In the background was a peaceful rural landscape, with the modern touch of telegraph poles, and in the far distance a conical mountain, no doubt derived from popular images of Taranaki Mountain (or Mount Egmont as it was known).[15] One of the best-known New Zealand brands, *Anchor* butter, incorporated similar themes in its advertising. Thus, a 1935 image highlighted 'Anchor Butter Direct from New Zealand' and depicted a packet of butter being carried by a jolly-looking sailor, surrounded by cows grazing peacefully in a green and sun-drenched rural landscape.[16]

By the 1930s, 'New Zealand Lamb' was a sufficient guarantee of quality on the international market. The usual line in advertisements was 'the best in the world'. This message, and others, appeared with a reminder to 'look for the brand on the joints – it's your guarantee of genuine New Zealand'.[17] The slogan 'New Zealand Lamb: The Best in the World' lasted at least into the 1950s. One such advertisement showed a forequarter ready to be roasted, against a green-coloured map of New Zealand, with the information that 'The housewife looks to NEW ZEALAND confident in the knowledge that while production increases, the traditional high quality of New Zealand lamb is being rigidly maintained'.[18]

Such images and messages continued into the 1970s. A contemporary campaign in Britain continued to emphasize quality, taste, nutritional value, and versatility. The fundamental task was to, 'reduce the differential in consumer attitudes between New Zealand and home-killed lamb by correcting any perceptions of the New Zealand product as a cheap "substitute" meat'.[19] Print and television advertising featured 'an ordinary housewife; authoritative and knowledgeable about New Zealand lamb; a New Zealander'. One image conveyed the message of value and quality, with the housewife holding a heaped plate of sliced roast lamb. Originally, it appears that the advertisement intended to use Colin Meads, the renowned All Black, but a panel of housewives thought that rugby players were given to profanity and drinking, whereas a housewife was taken to present a more wholesome image.[20]

Similarly, rural landscapes persisted in New Zealand butter advertisements for many decades. In the 1960s, this butter was described as, 'the cream and sunshine butter'. In one poster, an image of plenty was reinforced by the improbably thick spread of butter on toast, but again an idealized rural landscape was featured. Another advertisement on the same theme told consumers that, 'there's sunshine in New Zealand butter, even in mid-winter, from New Zealand's sunny skies'.[21] In the 1970s, with British demography rapidly changing, an *Anchor* advertisement appealed to tradition when promoting 'Britain's favourite butter … The flavour, the rich dairy creaminess are just the way we like it in Britain … That's why Anchor is consistently the best'.[22] Reflecting the changing demography, this advertisement depicted a small Black girl enjoying a buttered bun.

Food and beverage marketing in the twenty-first century

New Zealand's primary sector changed markedly from the 1960s. The classic trinity of meat, wool, and dairy was complemented by forest products, seafood, wine, and an increasing range of horticultural products, notably kiwifruit. In 2003, the government established New Zealand Trade and Enterprise (hereafter, NZTE) to, 'support the development of internationally competitive New Zealand business'.[23] By the early twenty-first century, marketing increasingly emphasized a comprehensive 'New Zealand' brand across different categories of food and beverages. Such promotions focused on better-off consumers, in the context of growing concern about health, climate, animal welfare, and food safety.

The New Zealand meat industry faced significant challenges after 2000. One report in 2011 noted, 'the climate change lobby, and their "food miles" argument and debates over relative carbon footprints of differing forms and locations of production', as well as reputational issues surrounding animal welfare, and debates on the consumption of red meat.[24] It was argued that New Zealand producers were, 'well positioned for a world that is becoming increasingly health conscious, wealthy aging populations able and willing to pay for premium meat products'.[25] To appeal to these consumers, it was necessary to better communicate the New Zealand story.[26] The clothing manufacturer Icebreaker was cited as an exemplar.[27]

Icebreaker produced a range of casual outdoor clothing made of merino wool. Merino sheep, noted for the fineness of their wool, were the original basis of New Zealand's wool industry. By the 1990s, wool accounted for a greatly diminished share of New Zealand export revenue, and merino was a small proportion of the national flock. In 1994, merino farmers broke away from the marketing organization, the New Zealand Wool Board, and established the New Zealand Merino Company.[28] Merino was to be promoted as a high-quality fibre. In contrast to wool, which was perceived to be heavy, itchy, and unfashionable, merino was marketed as light, fashionable, comfortable, and easy to care for. Until the mid-1990s, New Zealand merino was often blended with fibre from other countries.[29] Differentiation not merely as merino, but as New Zealand merino, was the first task of the Merino Company.[30] Marketing focused on New Zealand's 'unspoilt, natural' landscape, with the result that merino was transformed from a graded commodity to a national brand, generating complex emotional brand associations'.[31] Advertising by Icebreaker emphasized, 'the heritage and history of the high country ... This gave meaning ... in terms of provenance and a story that could be readily communicated'.[32]

Similar trends were apparent in the meat industry. It was acknowledged that as New Zealand meat had become a niche article, it could no longer compete in mass markets, and would 'never feed the world, and nor does it have to, to be profitable'.[33] Instead it was important to, 'leverage New Zealand's international identity, cultural differences and reputation for producing quality products'. To communicate this message, the industry relied on images of New Zealand as an unspoilt paradise, and explicit reference was made to the New Zealand tourism sector's international '100% Pure' marketing campaign.[34]

Seven years later, in 2018, the meat industry's co-ordinating group addressed the challenge of alternative (plant-based) forms of protein. Influential celebrity voices were, 'starting to push the performance benefits of plant protein diets, with the conversation moving from being focused around niche animal ethics to a mainstream dialogue about sustainability and health benefits'.[35] The red meat industry needed to respond to this if it was to maintain its premium consumers.[36] This meant emphasizing the meat's grass-fed qualities and dissociating New Zealand meat from debates on climate change and negative animal welfare.[37]

Samantha Cassetty, a high-profile dietitian, was engaged to extol the virtues of New Zealand meat to US consumers. The pitch was explicitly tied to Earth Day, and was placed on a website aimed at well-off, health-conscious consumers. The dietician averred that she always, 'look[ed] for New Zealand grass-fed beef and lamb because it is humanely raised and the animals graze freely on open pastures 365 days a year, ensuring the healthiest and most naturally flavourful meat you can find'.[38] The fundamental message was that in New Zealand, natural beauty and animal welfare were symbiotic: 'NZ farmers have prioritized soil health and regenerating native forestry on sheep and cattle farms which helps sequester carbon, slowing the accumulation of greenhouse gases … shipping miles are off-set by the small production footprint'.[39] Similarly,

> Our animals graze freely and happily here, on wide open spaces brimming with lush, green grasses year-round. Our farmers work hand in hand with nature and are committed to raising animals humanely while also preserving biodiversity, reducing carbon emissions, and protecting the water, soil, and air.[40]

The most recent NZTE campaign relating to the export of food and beverages, launched in 2020, was based on the slogan 'Made With Care: New Zealand.'[41] This crusade reiterated the central message that New Zealand was uniquely placed to meet the varied characteristics that consumers were increasingly demanding from their food: 'more than ever, consumers are looking for safe, nutritious and premium quality food and beverage that is ethically produced and tastes good too. New Zealand's combination of exceptional natural resources and experienced food producers sets us apart and perfectly positions us to meet the needs of consumers'.[42] This message was also communicated by a brand made available to firms if their products were, 'made, grown, raised or harvested in New Zealand' and 'owned by a registered New Zealand business'.[43] The brand was provided in a large variety of languages.[44]

The Made with Care campaign thus distinguished New Zealand produce by 'the unique connection our people have with the land and sea'. In Māori culture this connection is described by 'the principle of taiao, which acknowledges the interconnectedness of people and the natural world – if the natural world is healthy, so too are the people'. Māori terminology was further deployed by the core values of manaakitanga ('we care for others and always show hospitality, kindness, generosity, support and respect'),[45] and kaitiakitanga: 'we work to protect and safeguard the land, the sea and our people'.[46] Other characteristics emphasized in this campaign included biodiversity, sustainability, and the avoidance of genetically modified organisms in fresh produce.[47] There was continued emphasis on reassuring consumers that the contribution of livestock farming to climate change was less than might be supposed: 'sheep and beef cattle numbers have declined significantly, along with absolute greenhouse gas emissions from sheep and beef farms – they are 30 percent below 1990 levels – while the sector's contribution to GDP has more than doubled'.[48]

Finally, campaign images were carefully curated. Colour, balance, and saturation were adjusted to make the scenery more impactful and bountiful. For example, the depicted landscape had to include a food production element, and images of 'F&B People' (workers employed in food and beverages) were used to 'show the diversity of our people'. All the sample images were of people in bucolic landscapes. Similarly, images of fruit, vegetables, meat, and fish should be 'perfect. No marks or blemishes'.[49]

Currently, New Zealand's food and beverage producers are working in an international environment which is very different from that which existed between the 1880s and 1960s. Even so, there are significant continuities, and one major discontinuity in advertising campaigns. In the former, there was always competition from rival producers. Consequently, New Zealand produce had to be constantly positioned as safe and nutritious. In common with earlier promotions, idealized images of the New Zealand landscape featured prominently in advertisements. For example, during the last two decades or so, public concern about climate change has escalated, and this has been reflected in marketing campaigns which have positioned New Zealand produce as premium quality, sustainable, and wholly natural.

The major discontinuity between previous and current promotional campaigns is the greater prominence now given to Māori imagery. Earlier branding strategies emphasized New Zealand's Britishness; a Britishness which was at least implicitly contrasted with a 'savage' past. Māori were thus usually made invisible, as indeed were most distinctively New Zealand flora and fauna. Even the Fernleaf brand for New Zealand butter, introduced for the British market in 1926, was not a stylized Māori image, such as presently adorns the tails of Air New Zealand planes. The emphasis on the 'Britishness' of New Zealand producers, which only slowly faded, implied trustworthiness. By the early twenty-first century, however, branding New Zealand food and beverage exports increasingly involved an appeal to Māori concepts, expressed in the Māori language. As one Māori agribusiness consultant suggested, 'New Zealand has a unique selling point, the one advantage we have over the rest of the world is Māori culture'.[50]

The evolution of made in New Zealand

The first attempts at persuading domestic consumers to buy New Zealand products began in the midst of a recession. New Zealand's economy boomed in the 1860s and 1870s, fuelled by booms in gold and wool, the stimulating effects of mass migration, large-scale borrowing, and public works schemes. But, by the 1880s, the boom had imploded. In 1886, the newly-formed New Zealand Industrial Association (hereafter, NZIA), began agitating for tariffs that favoured, 'New Zealand manufactured goods in preference to imported goods', to 'drag our industries out of the doldrums'.[51] Appeals to consumer patriotism featured prominently in this agitation. When it inaugurated the first 'Buy New Zealand Made' consumer campaign in 1887, the NZIA referred to it as a 'great patriotic movement', designed to 'clear away the depression scare that with darkly brooding wings has so long darkened the hopes of easily discouraged colonists'.[52] 'Ignorant' shoppers – especially women – were instructed it was their 'duty' to choose locally made goods to ease unemployment, especially amongst their 'own kin'.[53] Within two years the association's membership had grown to 400, and they called for tariffs on an extensive range of imports including agricultural implements, furniture, brush-ware, boots, paints, and engines. However, this association collapsed in 1891, partly as a result of imprudent budgeting, and, more importantly, a general improvement in economic conditions, together with a substantial free trade constituency, especially amongst farmers.

Other manufacturers' organizations replaced the NZIA, and by 1908, supported by the Department of Industries and Commerce, they had begun a series of 'New Zealand Industries' weeks.[54] Because considerable anti-protectionism sentiment remained, these promotions could have shifted from tariff debates towards coherent campaigns focused on 'New Zealand' brand values.[55] However, the onset of World War One meant domestic manufacturers had a protected market; consequently, interest in promoting New Zealand products receded. But market instability after the war prompted manufacturers to reprise their calls for protection with 'Buy New Zealand Made'. Led by the Auckland Industrial Association, manufacturers coalesced in the 'Forward' movement to campaign for import substitution policies and the promotion of New Zealand's manufacturing exports. Their publicity campaign included lantern shows and brave, if ill-advised, advertisements stating: 'No country ever became great because of its agriculture'.[56] In view of this claim it is, perhaps, unsurprising that this campaign met with little success. Another campaign, run in 1925, by an allied organization, the Industrial Corporation of New Zealand, also urged consumers to 'Buy New Zealand Made Goods', but this initiative did not last.[57] In any event, government support was confined to the slogan, 'Always ask for New Zealand products' which appeared on post marks.[58]

Buy New Zealand campaigning continued sporadically throughout the interwar period; it appeared as a slogan at industrial fairs, in window displays and in political speeches.[59] The strategy gained greater traction as the depression of the 1930s hardened. Between 1929 and 1932, Auckland manufacturers published weekly advertisements, supplemented by radio broadcasts, exhorting consumers to insist on 'New Zealand goods' to support employment.[60] Wellington hosted a 'Made in New Zealand' week, the Dunedin Manufacturers Association asked for 'pledges' to 'Ask first for New Zealand-made goods', and Canterbury mobilized a women's auxiliary to support 'propaganda work'.[61] In 1931, Auckland woman Esther James generated considerable propaganda when she walked the length of the country promoting New Zealand goods. Wearing a 'wholly feminine New Zealand wool costume', James promised to 'eat only New Zealand food', on her journey, although she drew the line at promoting the domestic alcohol and tobacco industries.[62] Shopping weeks, window displays, parades, more advertisements, and even the odd sermon kept the Buy New Zealand made message before the public as the depression continued.[63]

In common with the nineteenth century, generalized patriotic appeals, which conflated national and personal well-being, suffused campaigns throughout the 1920s and 1930s. The Industrial Corporation urged consumers to think of the 'welfare of their homeland'.[64] The New Zealand Preference League determined to persuade the public of the 'wisdom' of preferring New Zealand goods with a laundry list of effects, from reducing unemployment to supporting primary producers.[65] Such appeals only increased in intensity over the depression years, with advertisements run by the Auckland Manufacturers' Association exhorting shoppers to 'Ask for New Zealand Goods. Make Our Stores Busy. Keep Our Workers Busy. Help Find Jobs For All.'[66]

Tangible political support arrived late and it, too, was also a response to crisis. In 1938, reduced export earnings and a foreign exchange emergency forced the government to hastily impose import licensing and currency controls. Although this new regime sometimes impeded the flow of essential materials, it also protected domestic industries. A national campaign to increase the sale of New Zealand goods under the banner, 'Let's Build a Nation', began, promoted by the Governor General, the Prime Minister, and the president of the New Zealand Manufacturers Association. With a budget of NZ $3,000, the campaign featured trains painted with slogans,[67] two films, and publicity material distributed in railway stations and post offices.[68] Some businesses adopted the slogans in their advertising, notably the enterprising film company, Dominion Productions, whose nation-building plans included 'PROPER SCREEN TESTS, VOICE TESTS and DEPORTMENT TESTS' for aspiring stars of stage and screen.[69] Combined, these activities marked the high point in interwar Buy New Zealand campaigns.

Research has discounted the effectiveness of patriotic appeals because patriotism is but one of the many factors that affect purchasing decisions.[70] During the interwar period, the imperial context brought into sharp relief the tensions between promoting New Zealand and supporting the empire. At the same time as consumers were being asked to buy New Zealand made, empire trade and empire shopping were also widely promoted as patriotic activities. Indeed, though it has been argued that the dominions 'focused quickly on national protectionism rather than imperial cooperation', in New Zealand, the intricacies of imperial citizenship played out in rather more nuanced ways.[71] In one small indication of that nuance, the Auckland Industrial Association was also home to the Empire League.[72] In another, politicians in this era regularly repeated the mantra of 'buy New Zealand first, then British', in line with rhetoric espoused by the Imperial Economic Committee. Even as the depression deepened, former Prime Minister Gordon Coates tempered his 'Buy New Zealand goods' message by adding 'these thoughts in no way contravene our duty to the Motherland or our Empire' for where local goods could not be selected, 'our next duty is to purchase British-made goods ....'[73] The first Labour government was more committed to economic nationalism, but understood the necessity of maintaining access to the British foodstuffs market, and to British loans. Minister of Industries and Commerce, Dan Sullivan, in response to numerous requests from newspapers for messages

Figure 11.2 The problem of promoting buying local in an imperial context: billboard advertisement for Crockett & Jones, boots and shoes

Source: Head, Samuel Heath, 1868–1948:Negatives. Ref: 1/1–007267-G. Alexander Turnbull Library, Wellington, New Zealand.

to support local shopping weeks provided messages highlighting 'the necessity for specifying firstly "New Zealand Made" and secondly "British made" for our purchases'.[74] Even the Governor General joined the appeals for this version of 'true patriotism'.[75] Retailers also put a dollar each way on 'New Zealand' and 'British made'. In 1931, for example, Waipukurau ran a 'New Zealand and British Empire' shopping week, while the *Napier Telegraph* ran a 'Buy New Zealand Week' in October 1937, and it supported a 'Buy British Empire-made Goods' week in time for Empire Day in May 1938.

Even manufacturers found it difficult to reconcile their imperial and local identities. By the late 1920s, it seemed the 'consensus of local manufacturers is undoubtedly towards the adoption of the brand Made in New Zealand.[76] But this was by no means universal. Some claimed a New Zealand 'British' identity, marking locally made products as 'British made' and then arguing products actually made in Britain should be marked 'Made in the United Kingdom.' Others played both sides: one manufacturer advertised their premium line as British made and their cheaper line as Made in New Zealand.[77]

> 'the brand "British made" or "empire made" is as correctly applied to [New Zealand] goods as to goods manufactured in the United Kingdom or in any of the British Dominions, and that in a great many cases locally-made articles are more distinctly British than goods which may be merely designed or partly manufactured in other parts of the Empire.'[78]

Import restrictions were imposed between 1938 and 1984. Such measures effectively ended the crisis-led deployment of domestic 'Made in' schemes for more than 40 years. In the meantime, local manufacturing expanded under protection, and despite the later reference to 'Polands of the Pacific', it was not necessarily inefficient.[79] As import substitution developed, consumers often particiapted in 'buy New Zealand' by default. Shielded from the competition, Auckland, a city with less than half a million inhabitants, sported nine pantyhose factories. 'Copy cat' local manufacturers emerged to satisfy demand when imports were priced out of the market. 'Screwdriver' operations meant that products which were manufactured overseas ended up 'Made in New Zealand': 'At one stage there were seven companies assembling televisions that had already been assembled elsewhere, usually in Japan, and then pulled apart to be exported to New Zealand.'[80]

However, from the 1980s, the government abolished import restrictions to accelerate industrial restructuring. Exposed to intense international competition 'insolvencies reached record levels'.[81] After the global stock market crash in 1987, economic conditions deteriorated,[82] and manufacturers returned to a 'Made in' strategy. In 1988, the New Zealand Manufacturers Federation, and the Council of Trade Unions formed a new 'Buy New Zealand Made' (BNZM) organization, with local packaging giant Printpac UEB as lead sponsor.[83] This organization launched a 23-week television advertising campaign which continued into the early 1990s; it was complemented by initiatives such as New Zealand Purchasing Awards, resource kits for schools, and 'Make It Here' seminars.[84] BNZM also lobbied the public sector, with some success, to direct its procurement toward domestic industry, and in 1991, the Ministry of Commerce introduced the New Zealand Industrial supplies office to provide information on domestic products and services. Perhaps the most powerful innovation was the development of a brand and logo to help consumers identify domestic products (and, increasingly, services). However, use of these indicia is restricted to BNZM members.[85]

BNZM laid the foundation for an enduring 'Made in' campaign, and it continued to promote New Zealand business. During the 1990s, for example, advertisements featured a cartoon character, 'Kenny the Kiwi' whose message was 'Buy New Zealand Made and Keep Your Country Working'.[86] Consumers were enrolled through shopping weeks repackaged as 'Kiwi Pride Festivals'. Like earlier Buy New Zealand campaigns, with their scout parades and sermons, these festivals reached beyond retailers to the wider community. The festival handbook enthused 'you can do almost anything you like' provided 'your activities fit within the concept of generating pride in New Zealand, its products, services, people and achievements …'.[87] Helpful suggestions included gala openings, playing New Zealand music, including the 'Kiwi Pride' festival jingle, scavenger hunts or treasure hunts to locate or identify domestic products from shop window displays, celebrity store visits, consumer competitions, plant tours, and school visits.[88] Later campaigns, while claiming a 'fresh, modern approach', reanimated the same ideas. Global trade regulations which increasingly proscribed non-tariff trade barriers meant domestic product lines could not explicitly be promoted, thereby continuing the generic tone of the campaigns.[89]

A relaunch of 'Buy New Zealand' in 2000, which attracted modest government funding, sought to 'kick start the campaign out of its maintenance mode' but it appears to have made little headway.[90] Still, 'Made in' schemes retained some allure. In 2007, driven by ideology rather than crisis, a new 'Made in' scheme was launched. As part of a parliamentary agreement with the Green Party to promote sustainability, the Labour government initiated a 'Buy Kiwi Made' programme which collaborated with BNZM.[91] This time, government support was generous, and over NZ $11 million was committed to the programme.[92] But it was short-lived: a change of government in 2008 brought the campaign to an end.

Subsequently, though BNZM continues, there have been no further ambitious campaigns, even though there has been no shortage of crises. New Zealand's 'Made in' promotions appear to have passed their zenith. One explanation for this decline is that the increasingly globalized nature of business has exacerbated the problems associated with defining 'made in New Zealand', especially for consumers. For example, The Bank of New Zealand is owned by an Australian bank. Similarly, Icebreaker began manufacturing in China in 2003, and it was acquired by an American company in 2017. Another explanation is that analyses of 'Made in' campaigns in New Zealand, as elsewhere, have consistently concluded that while they may be warmly received by consumers, they rarely translate into changing purchasing decisions.[93] Also, there was a failure to create a cohesive set of brand values associated with New Zealand's identity. Finally, and in contrast to the export of produce and beverages, manufacturing was not subject to sustained campaigning which compromised the development of buying domestic.

Conclusion

The story of 'Made in New Zealand' has two parts. First, exporters responded to opportunity and competition by creating long-running campaigns centred on a set of 'New Zealand' values. Aspects of these campaigns have changed over time: New Zealand meat and butter are no longer 'British' products from 'British" farms', and the range of produce that is exported has diversified and now encompasses merino and wine. Nonetheless, images of quality, rurality, and nature have remained pervasive throughout. Produce exporters focused less on 'Made in', and more on 'New Zealand': their emphasis on provenance created a durable set of values for consumers. For domestic manufacturers, who make up the second part of the story, the emphasis was reversed. They generally only adopted such campaigns in periods of economic crisis when 'Made in' mattered much more than any qualities conveyed by 'New Zealand' produce. In fact, it was not until the late twentieth century that New Zealand's manufacturers made a sustained effort to promote their products in the domestic market. It remains to be seen if, in the future, they can convert consumers with an approach based on continuity rather than crisis.

Though the imperial context led exporters to emphasize a distinctively British New Zealand brand identity, that same context had a markedly different effect domestically, especially during the interwar period. Use of 'Made in Britain' or 'Empire' reflected New Zealanders' imperial allegiance, but also concealed New Zealand origins, and, implicitly, New Zealand values. Ironically, perhaps, when, in the 1990s, BNZM developed a label to identify New Zealand products, manufacturers noted a 'prejudice against home products.[94]

For more than 100 years, 'Buy New Zealand' campaigns were more preoccupied with how consumers might help manufacturers, than with how buying domestic would help consumers. Unlike export advertising, no regular suite of brand values around 'New Zealand' appeared, and even a shared mark was delayed until the late twentieth century. This may be a critical factor in their overall lack of success. Recent research has suggested there might be some benefit in appealing to patriotism 'where all other things are equal (including price and quality)'.[95] But in the case of New Zealand, all things were not equal and campaigns did not respond to consumer desires. Externally focused campaigns such as those in food and beverage exports, on the other hand, have been able to articulate – if inaccurately – a set of values that remain widely applicable yet still persuasive for consumers. Domestic 'Made in' campaigns lack such promise. Born out of crises and then shaped by them, they have struggled to emulate the success of their export counterparts.

Notes

1 Appendices to the Journals of the House of Representatives, (hereafter, AJHR),1896, I-9, pp. 41–49.
2 AJHR,1896, I-9, pp. 89–95.
3 AJHR, 1896, I-9, p. 97.
4 Higgins, '"Mutton', pp. 161–184.
5 AJHR,1896, I-9, p. 88.
6 AJHR, 1898, H-17. In this context, the term 'brand' was similar to a trade mark because it indicated trade origin. Blanco-White, *Kerly's Law*, p. 36.
7 *Lyttleton Times*, 21 November 1888, p. 5.
8 AJHR, 1898, H-17, p. 2.
9 *Lyttleton Times*, 11 October 1889, p. 3.
10 *Lyttleton Times* LT, 20 July 1882, p. 6.
11 Barnes and Higgins, 'Brand image', p. 82.
12 Barnes, and Higgins, 'Brand image', p. 82.
13 Hayward, *Golden Jubilee*, pp. 31, 90.
14 The latest research suggests that the Empire Marketing Board did not substantially alter British imports of produce from its colonies or dominions. Higgins and Varian, 'Britain's Empire'.
15 https://www.empire.amdigital.co.uk/FurtherResources/VisualResources/Image/Empire%20Marketing%20Board%20Posters/14.
16 The New Zealand Co-operative Dairy Company, *New Zealand Dairy Group*, 1919–2001, Hamilton, 2001, n.p.
17 Press Advertisement: New Zealand Lamb. Print Advertising/27 May 1939. Colin McArthur Collection of consumer magazine tearsheets. History of Advertising Trust, Reference HAT20/2/45/26/3. https://www.hatads.org.uk/catalogue/record/54964882-92d3-48e0-a76f-8660836f732c, accessed 16 November 2022.
18 https://www.advertisingarchives.co.uk/index.php?service=search&action=do_quick_search&language=en&q=zealand: item 30533171.
19 https://www.warc.com/content/article/new_zealand_meat_producers_board__a_case_history/4078.
20 *Auckland Star*, 30 March 1976, see https://natlib.govt.nz/records/30709871?-search%5Bi%5D%5Bcentury%5D=1900&search%5Bi%5D%5Bsubject%5D=-Blade%2C+Raewyn&search%5Bpath%5D=items.
21 https://www.advertisingarchives.co.uk/index.php?service=search&action=do_quick_search&language=en&q=zealand: items 30583815 and 30567868.
22 https://www.advertisingarchives.co.uk/index.php?service=search&action=do_quick_search&language=en&q=zealand item 30556337.
23 http://www.nzlii.org/nz/legis/hist_act/nztaea20032003n27321/.
24 Red Meat Sector Strategy Report Beef + Lamb New Zealand Limited, Meat Industry Association of New Zealand Limited. Hereafter, Meat Industry Association, 2011, p. 48.
25 Red Meat Sector, p. 12.
26 Red Meat Sector, p. 48.
27 Red Meat Sector, p. 62.
28 Pawson and Perkins, 'Worlds of wool'.

29 Pawson and Perkins, 'Worlds of wool'. Before the mid-1990s, identification of 'merino', or 'New Zealand merino', was weak. Subsequently, even if blending sometimes occurred, the identification of 'New Zealand merino' was strong. See, for example, 'how and why we use both natural and synthetic materials': https://www.icebreaker.com/en-nz/our-story/product.html.
30 Pawson and Perkins, 'Worlds of wool'.
31 Mitchell, Smith, and Dana, 'The international', pp. 111–122.
32 Pawson and Perkins, 'The merino story'.
33 Red Meat Sector, p. 71.
34 Red Meat Sector, p. 98.
35 Future of Meat: How Should New Zealand's Red Meat Sector Respond to Alternative Protein Advancements? Summary Report. Beef + Lamb New Zealand, 2018, p. 5.
36 Future of Meat: How Should, p. 5.
37 Future of Meat: How Should, p. 7.
38 https://www.realsimple.com/food-recipes/shopping-storing/food/foods-to-splurge-and-save-on. Accessed 19 May 2021.
39 https://beeflambnz.com/news-views/taste-pure-nature-celebrates-earth-day. Accessed 19 May 2021.
40 https://beefandlambnz.com/. Accessed 19 May 2021.
41 New Zealand Trade and Enterprise, Made with Care Campaign Toolkit, 2020, available at https://www.nzstory.govt.nz/assets/PDF/MADE-WITH-CARE-NZ-STORY-FB-campaign-toolkit-Version-3.0.pdf. Downloaded 16 November 2022 from https://www.nzstory.govt.nz/about-us/news/made-with-care-sharing-our-food-and-beverage-stories-with-the-world/.
42 New Zealand Trade and Enterprise (NZTE), *Made With Care New Zealand: Campaign Toolkit, Sharing our food and beverage stories with the world, version 2.0.* Wellington: NZTE 2020, p. 4. Downloaded 19 May 2021 from https://www.nzstory.govt.nz/about-us/news/made-with-care-sharing-our-food-and-beverage-stories-with-the-world/.
43 New Zealand Trade and Enterprise (NZTE), *Made With Care New Zealand: Campaign Toolkit, Sharing our food and beverage stories with the world, version 2.0.* Wellington: NZTE 2020, p. 5. Downloaded 19 May 2021 from https://www.nzstory.govt.nz/about-us/news/made-with-care-sharing-our-food-and-beverage-stories-with-the-world/.
44 New Zealand Trade and Enterprise (NZTE), *Made With Care New Zealand: Campaign Toolkit, Sharing our food and beverage stories with the world, version 2.0.* Wellington: NZTE 2020, p. 12-13. Downloaded 19 May 2021 from https://www.nzstory.govt.nz/about-us/news/made-with-care-sharing-our-food-and-beverage-stories-with-the-world/.
45 New Zealand Trade and Enterprise (NZTE), *Made With Care New Zealand: Campaign Toolkit, Sharing our food and beverage stories with the world, version 2.0.* Wellington: NZTE 2020, p. 5. Downloaded 19 May 2021 from https://www.nzstory.govt.nz/about-us/news/made-with-care-sharing-our-food-and-beverage-stories-with-the-world/.
46 New Zealand Trade and Enterprise (NZTE), *Made With Care New Zealand: Campaign Toolkit, Sharing our food and beverage stories with the world, version 2.0.* Wellington: NZTE 2020, pp. 15-22. Downloaded 19 May 2021 from https://www.nzstory.govt.nz/about-us/news/made-with-care-sharing-our-food-and-beverage-stories-with-the-world/.
47 New Zealand Trade and Enterprise (NZTE), *Made With Care New Zealand: Campaign Toolkit, Sharing our food and beverage stories with the world, version 2.0.* Wellington: NZTE 2020, p. 19. Downloaded 19 May 2021 from https://www.nzstory.govt.nz/about-us/news/made-with-care-sharing-our-food-and-beverage-stories-with-the-world/.
48 New Zealand Trade and Enterprise (NZTE), *Made With Care New Zealand: Campaign Toolkit, Sharing our food and beverage stories with the world, version 2.0.* Wellington: NZTE 2020, p. 22. Downloaded 19 May 2021 from https://www.nzstory.govt.nz/about-us/news/made-with-care-sharing-our-food-and-beverage-stories-with-the-world/.

49 New Zealand Trade and Enterprise (NZTE), *Made With Care New Zealand: Campaign Toolkit, Sharing our food and beverage stories with the world, version 2.0.* Wellington: NZTE 2020, p. 44. Downloaded 19 May 2021 from https://www.nzstory.govt.nz/about-us/news/made-with-care-sharing-our-food-and-beverage-stories-with-the-world/.
50 Stephen Thomson, Indigenous Branding – Creating a point of difference to the New Zealand Primary Sector. Kellogg Rural Leadership Course, 2015, p. 2.
51 Parker, *Wealthmakers*, p. 33.
52 See, for example, *Auckland Star*, 22 June 1887, p. 55; *Auckland Star*, 16 July 1887, p. 6.
53 Parker, *Wealthmakers*, p. 35. Generally, see for example, Garland and Coy, 'Buying New Zealand', p. 2.
54 Ulrich, *A Century*, p. 2.
55 Parker, *Wealthmakers*, p. 37.
56 Parker, *Wealthmakers*, p. 96.
57 Industrial Corporation of New Zealand, and Dunedin Manufacturers' Association. *"New Zealand Made"*. Christchurch, NZ: Edward H. Marriner, 1925.
58 Post Master General to Minister of Industries and Commerce, 29 December 1924, IC1 782 31/75/1 Miscellaneous – Advertising NZ made goods – general file, ANZ.
59 *New Zealand Herald*, 23 March 1927, p. 10; Otago Daily Times, 1 June 1927, 5; *Star* (Christchurch), 30 March 1927, p. 15.
60 Urlich, *A Century*, p. 5; Thirteenth Annual Report of Department of Industries and Commerce, 1931, *Appendices to the Journals of the House of Representatives*, p. 12.
61 Thirteenth Annual Report of Department of Industries and Commerce, 1931, *Appendices to the Journals of the House of Representatives*, p. 12; Eleventh Annual Report of Department of Industries and Commerce, 1929, *Appendices to the Journals of the House of Representatives.*
62 'Walk Around Dominion', press clipping, IC1 782 31/75/1 Miscellaneous – Advertising NZ made goods – general file, ANZ.
63 Urlich, *A Century*, p. 6; District Officer to Secretary Industries and Commerce, 2 June 1931, IC1 782 31/75/1 Miscellaneous – Advertising NZ made goods – General File, ANZ.
64 *Otago Daily Times*, 26 December 1925, p. 2.
65 *Otago Daily Times*, 18 March 1927, p. 5.
66 *New Zealand Herald*, 28 May 1931, p. 17.
67 Urlich, *A Century*, p. 6.
68 Twenty-first Annual Report of Department of Industries and Commerce, 1939, *Appendices to the Journals of the House of Representatives*, pp. 19–20.
69 *New Zealand Herald*, 28 April 1939, p. 15.
70 Insch, Mather, and Knight, 'Buy-national campaigns', p. 243.
71 Thackeray, *Forging*, p. 80.
72 *AS*, 29 April 1922, p. 8.
73 *Poverty Bay Herald*, 10 March, 1930, p. 7.
74 Sullivan to Editor, 19 August 1938, IC1 1321 31/75/1 Pt 2 Miscellaneous – Advertising and Buying of NZ made goods throughout the Country – General File regarding 1937–1951, ANZ.
75 *Star,* (Christchurch), 10 November 1930, p.11.
76 AJHR, 1928, p. 12.
77 The Department of Industries and Commerce did little to clarify matters, instead suggesting.
78 AJHR, 1928, p. 12. See also *Otago Daily Times*, 15 November 1921, p. 10.

79 McAloon, 'Long slow boom', pp. 49–52.
80 Parker, *Wealthmakers*, p. 315.
81 Carlyon and Morrow, *Changing Times*, p. 295.
82 Fenwick, and Wright, 'Effect', p. 137.
83 *Kiwilink: The Buy New Zealand Made Campaign Newsletter*, No. 1 (July) 1995.
84 *Kiwilink: The Buy New Zealand Made Campaign Newsletter*, No. 1 (July) 1995.
85 Jenkins, *Buy Kiwi*, p. 13.
86 Urlich, *A Century*, p. 7.
87 Kiwi Pride Festival, *Kiwi Pride Festival Handbook: A Reference Guide for Use in Putting Together Activities for the Kiwi Pride Festival, 16–28 March 1992* (Auckland, 1992), pp. 2–3.
88 Kiwi Pride Festival, *Kiwi Pride Festival Handbook*, 5.
89 Ministry of Economic Development Evaluation Team, 'Buy Kiwi Made Campaign Evaluation report', September 2009, https://www.mbie.govt.nz/dms-document/2267-buy-kiwi-made-campaign-evaluation-report-pdf. Accessed 15 September 2021, p. 17.
90 Buy NZ Made Campaign, Newsletter, Buy NZ Made, Winter (2000).
91 Urlich, *A Century*, p. 10.
92 Jenkins, *Buy Kiwi*, p. 12.
93 Insch, Mather, and Knight, 'Buy-national Campaigns'; Garland, and Coy, 'Buying New Zealand'; Insch, Prentice, and Knight, 'Retail Buyers'; Fenwick and Wright, 'Effect', pp. 135–145; Ministry of Economic Development Evaluation Team, 'Buy Kiwi Made Campaign Evaluation report', September 2009, https://www.mbie.govt.nz/dmsdocument/2267-buy-kiwi-made-campaign-evaluation-report-pdf. Accessed 15 September 2021.
94 Parker, *Wealthmakers*, p. 34; Fenwick and Wright, 'Effect', p. 136.
95 Jenkins, *Buy Kiwi*, pp. 27–28.

Bibliography

Barnes, F., and Higgins, D.M., 'Brand image, cultural association, and marketing: 'New Zealand' butter and lamb exports to Britain, c.1920–1938'. *Business History*, 62 (2020), pp. 70–97.

Blanco White, T.A., *Kerly's Law of Trade Marks and Trade Names*. London: Sweet & Maxwell, 1966.

Carlyon, J., and Morrow, D., *Changing Times: New Zealand since 1945*. Auckland: Auckland University Press, 2013.

Fenwick, G.D., and Wright, I.C., 'Effect of a buy-national campaign on member firm performance', *Journal of Business Research*, 47 (2000), pp. 135–145.

Garland, R., and Coy, D., 'Buying New Zealand made groceries: does behaviour match attitude?', *New Zealand Journal of Business*, 15 (1993), pp. 1–18.

Hayward, D., *Golden Jubilee: The Story of the First Fifty Years of the New Zealand Meat Products Board, 1922–1972*. Wellington: Meat Producers Board, 1972.

Higgins, D.M., '"Mutton dressed as lamb?" The misrepresentation of Australian and New Zealand meat in the British market, c. 1890–1914', *Australian Economic History Review*, 44 (2004), pp. 161–184.

Higgins, D.M., and Varian, B.D., 'Britain's empire marketing board and the failure of soft trade policy, 1926–33', *European Review of Economic History*, 25 (2021), pp. 780–805.

Insch, A., Prentice, R.S., and Knight, J., 'Retail buyers' decision-making and buy national campaigns: AMJ', *Australasian Marketing Journal*, 19 (2011), pp. 257–266.

Insch, A., Mather, D., and Knight, J., 'Buy-national Campaigns: congruence determines premiums for domestic products', *International Marketing Review*, 34 (2017), pp. 239–253.

Jenkins, M., *Buy Kiwi Made Evaluative Report*. Wellington: Ministry of Economic Development, 2009.

McAloon, J., 'Long slow boom'? Manufacturing in New Zealand, 1945–70', *Australian Economic History Review*, 46 (2006), pp. 45–69.

Mitchell, J.D., Smith, L.J., and Dana, L.P., 'The international marketing of New Zealand merino wool: past, present and future', *International Journal of Business and Globalisation*, 3 (2009), 111–122.

Parker, S., *Wealthmakers: A History of the Northern Employers' and Manufacturers' Associations*. Auckland, NZ: Employers' & Manufacturers' Association (Northern), 2005.

Pawson, E., and Perkins, H.C., 'Worlds of wool: recreating value off the sheep's back', *New Zealand Geographer*, 69 (2013), pp. 208–220.

Pawson, E., and Perkins, H.C., 'The merino story', in E. Pawson and the Biological Economies Team, *The New Biological Economy: How New Zealanders Are Creating Value from the Land*, Auckland: Auckland University Press, 2018, pp. 41–60.

Thackeray, D., *Forging a British World of Trade: Culture, Ethnicity, and Market in the Empire-Commonwealth, 1880–1975*. Oxford: Oxford University Press, 2019.

Ulrich, J., *A Century of Buying New Zealand Made: A Short History*. Wellington, NZ: Ministry of Economic Development, 2008.

12 Made in Australia

Supporting primary products and import substitution

Simon Ville

Introduction

Today, support for Australian made products remains important at both the corporate and national levels, as the following examples amply demonstrate:

> "Twiggy Forrest's purchase of RM Williams shows Australian consumers want to buy local, experts say.
>
> Iconic outfitter RM Williams is back in Australian hands, with its new owner vowing the company will manufacture more of the brand's footwear and clothing locally as support grows for Australian-made products."
>
> [https://www.abc.net.au/news/2020-10-20/twiggy-forrest-buying-rm-williams-could-create-australian-jobs/12782024. 20.10.2020]
>
> "The Australian Made Campaign (AMCL) has announced the launch of the first ever Australian Made Week.
>
> It will be running from 24–30 May 2021, and will encourage shoppers to actively focus their buying activities on genuine, Aussie products while celebrating and supporting local makers and growers around the country."
>
> [https://retailworldmagazine.com.au/first-ever-australian-made-week/]

The above extracts indicate the continued appeal of supporting Australian made products at both the corporate and national levels. Such campaigns as these have been a recurrent theme in Australia's struggle to assert a distinctive and independent image on the global economic and political stage since the decades leading up to Federation in 1901. However, the desire for political sovereignty was curtailed by continued links to the British Commonwealth.[1] Marketing and promotional campaigns have nonetheless drawn heavily upon appeals to patriotism, and the unique, attractive, and high-quality products grown and manufactured in Australia.[2]

A series of key but overlapping episodes in the country's economic and political trajectory determined the evolution of Made in Australia. For example, Australia developed with a strong comparative advantage in the

DOI: 10.4324/9781003166184-12

primary sector. Furthermore, successive Australian governments confronted the dilemma of determining economic policy against the backdrop of a changing neo-colonial relationship with Britain.[3] Finally, the powerful position of many foreign multinationals owning global brands and located in Australia, has sometimes constrained Australia's sense of economic independence. Together, these three factors largely shaped the distinctive nature of the Made In movement in Australia. Prior to Federation, the focus was promoting Australian primary exports. After 1901, the newly-federated nation, supported by industry associations, placed greater emphasis on the development of a broader economic base to improve the viability of import-substituting consumer industries which confronted severe competition from European and US manufacturers. Nonetheless, the promotion of primary products remained important. By the 1960s, governments were becoming more proactive in Made in Australia campaigns to promote economic development and stability, higher employment, improved trade balances, and lower debt. During the final decades of the twentieth century, the reduction in trade barriers fostered the belief that domestic industries needed more support, but this time against new manufacturing nations in Asia. More recently, growing concerns about public health, well-being, and the environment were fundamental in the refocusing of national and corporate marketing strategies.

The remainder of this chapter is organised as follows. In the next section, there is a review of the broad trends in Australian economic development which provide the context within which Made in Australia campaigns were effected. Subsequently, for export markets, the limited efforts to promote 'Australian' or 'Made in Australia' in meat, are contrasted with more successful initiatives for dairy produce and fruit, and the highly successful campaigns for Australian wool, which became synonymous with the international *Woolmark* logo. This is followed in the next two sections by a discussion of initiatives to promote Made in Australia as an import substitution policy during the interwar period, and after 1945. There then follows two brief sections which review the growing importance of sustainability and environmentalism in promoting the image of products Made in Australia, and provide an assessment of the effectiveness of Made in Australia, before conclusions are presented.

Australian economic development

Marketing and advertising expenditure by American and European manufacturers expanded rapidly in the second half of the nineteenth century, supporting the growth of consumer markets and the expansion of multinational enterprises with their global brands.[4] During this period foreign manufacturers confidently applied their overseas marketing strategies to culturally similar Australian consumers. For example, in 1901, Lever's advertised their range of soap brands, including *Lux*, *Lifebuoy*, and *Sunlight*, in Australia,[5] while an issue of *Punch* (Melbourne), in 1910, contained many advertisements for multinational brands: Cadbury's *Bourneville*, *Pears* (soap), *Dewars* ('Imperial Whisky'), *Dunlop* (tyres), *Cerebos* (foods), *Lamson Paragon* (stationery), and *Continental Rubber* (tyres).[6] By contrast, contemporaneous marketing by Australian manufacturers was generally restricted, perhaps reflecting the importance of the primary sector.

The economic development of Australia in the nineteenth century was concentrated on the extraction, production, and export of natural resources and primary produce. Australia has been one of a small group of successful resource-based economies that achieved modern economic growth without significant manufacturing sectors. Other countries that benefited from similar development include New Zealand, Norway, and, to some extent, Canada. These economies have defied the conventional wisdom of economic history – that primary industries are a transition to economic modernisation – and the resource curse hypothesis of development economists – that nations with large primary sectors are destined to experience limited economic growth.[7]

Gold, wool, wheat, meat, and dairy products accounted for approximately 90% of the visible exports of Australia before 1901, most of which were destined for Britain.[8] In the first half of the twentieth century, Australia sought to broaden its economy by stimulating manufacturing behind increasing tariff barriers. Trade policy varied among the colonies that constituted Australia, but after 1901 the new nation unified around protectionism, beginning with the 1907 Customs Tariff Act – the Lyne Tariff – followed by regular revisions in duties in subsequent decades.[9] The share of production accounted for by manufacturing grew in the first half of the twentieth century (Table 12.1), as the country's economic base diversified. However, it was increasingly recognised that this diversification was harmful to efficient resource allocation because it protected inefficient, high-cost domestic manufacturers.[10]

The government recognised the shortcomings of this strategy, and from the 1960s national policy was reoriented toward free trade, which probably accelerated the decline of the manufacturing sector. Microeconomic reforms in factor and product markets were insufficient to offset the superior competitiveness of newly industrialising Asian nations; this prompted a revival of the mining sector, particularly coal and iron ore, but increasingly a broad range of minerals.[11] Subsequently, the range and technological sophistication of the primary sector's products developed to include large-scale aquaculture, the export of liquid natural gas, and the extraction of a range of precious metals

Table 12.1 Manufacturing's share of GDP (%), 1900–1990

1900	*1910*	*1920*	*1930*	*1939*	*1950*	*1960*	*1970*	*1980*	*1990*
12	12	11	18	19	25	29	25	19	15

Sources: Butlin, M., Dixon, R., and Lloyd, P.J., 'Statistical Appendix: selected data series, 1800–2010', in Ville, S., and Withers, G., (eds), *The Cambridge Economic History of Australia*. Melbourne: Cambridge University Press, 2015, Table A1, pp. 557–559.

including rutile and lithium.[12] Complementing these trends, a generous reserve price scheme for wool led to a substantial increase in output during the 1970s and 1980s. Finally, the economic expansion of China, especially from the 1990s, reignited overseas demand for a wide range of Australian food and mining products.

Promoting Australia's staple exports

The previous section provided a distinctive context for understanding Made in Australia strategies. The branding and marketing strategies of American and British multinationals had little relevance to Australian primary producers; their operations, mostly restricted to family farms, were too small to generate the resources needed for prolonged, large-scale investment in advertising and brand promotion. Larger enterprises existed in mining, but their products were perceived as standardised, with limited opportunities to promote the unique qualities of their country of origin. Such companies produced raw materials or intermediate goods in the supply chain destined for other businesses that were closer to final consumers. Nonetheless, Made in perspectives still mattered.

Australian farm products, the majority of which were exported to Britain, faced growing competition in this market from the later nineteenth century. On British markets, frozen meat from the antipodes and Argentina was sometimes compared unfavourably with local, fresh produce, and concerns were expressed that some British butchers passed-off cheaper Australian meat as British produce.[13] There was considerable debate in the late nineteenth century on the benefits and disadvantages of requiring that British meat imports indicated their country of origin.[14] The British Merchandise Marks Act of 1887 criminalised the application of false trade descriptions, and it mandated that in specific circumstances imports needed to indicate their geographical origin.[15] Ironically, the New Zealand and Australian Agents' Association strongly resisted proposals in 1933 to introduce compulsory origin marking on British meat imports.[16] Unlike the primary producers in many other countries, the Australian meat producers were poorly organised and it was not until 1936 that the Australian Meat Producers Board was established.[17] Ross Duncan attributes this laggardness to the vast distances confronting meat producers, particularly across northern Australia, which provided little opportunity to harmonise opinions on farming matters.[18]

Australia was much more successful in promoting the sale of other food products to British consumers, particularly after World War One. The orderly and cooperative marketing of dairy and fruit during the 1920s was made possible by commodity boards, for example, the Dairy Produce Control Board established in 1925. The Australian Trade Publicity Committee, formed in 1926, and based in London, assumed responsibility for advertising Australian fruit, dairy produce, and wine; its publicity was directed at British wholesalers, retailers, and consumers. A marketing film in which the Australian

Prime Minister, Joseph Lyons, starred, promoted Australian apples as 'British to the core'; it was shown in over 160 British cinemas to an audience that exceeded three million viewers.[19]

Australia dominated the international market for high-quality merino wool by the late nineteenth century (Table 12.2). This product was vital to the Australian economy because it accounted for at least 50% of Australian exports by value.[20] By the mid-nineteenth century, Australian wool competed on the London market with established European producers, such as Spain, but by the 1890s, most Australian wool was sold within Australia prior to export.[21] In contrast to the meat producers, the wool industry was well-organised from an early stage. Brokers in each of the major wool-selling centres organised themselves into industry associations in the 1890s, and in 1919 they established a national body – the National Council of Wool-Selling Brokers of Australia – to which each was affiliated. Contemporaneously, industry associations emerged among wool growers and buyers. Much attention was devoted to organisation and coordination which underpinned the success of the Australian wool trade. In contrast, institutional development was much slower in several other major wool producing countries, particularly South Africa, Argentina, and Uruguay.[22]

Wool buyers and their agents arrived in Australia confident of the high quality of Australian wool, and keen to secure supplies from regions and farms whose reputation was advancing. However, some of the major overseas wool buying firms, such as Masurel Brothers from France, also transacted in other major wool markets, particularly the countries previously mentioned. Consequently, the marks of individual producers branded onto wool bales were a valuable way by which high-quality merino wool producers in Australia connected with overseas buyers and their agents. In 1889, George Augustus Burgoyne published a list of over 3,000 Australian wool marks; many were simple identifiers that included the grower's name, address, and the wool district in which the sheep were farmed. Burgoyne noted:

> The European manufacturer, ever desirous of improvement, can ... study the advantages resulting from knowing the pastoral district in which his favourite wools are grown - some districts being celebrated for the uniform excellence of their wool.[23]

In the more challenging markets after World War One, which were characterised by the interwar depression, the growth of new producers, and the expansion of wool substitutes, the principal bodies in the industry played an increasingly important role in promoting Australian wool brands by focussing on the qualities, natural properties, and even the fashionable final products that used fine, Australian-grown wool. As a precursor to the modern pursuit of product provenance, the Australian Woolgrowers Council brought

Table 12.2 Apparel raw wool production by main exporting countries, 1909–1944 (million lbs, 5 year av.)

	Australia	*New Zealand*	*South Africa*	*Argentina*	*Uruguay*
1909/10–1913/14	757	220	154	341	112
1919/20–1923–24	700	229	186	326	108
1929/30–1933–34	981	275	305	361	122
1939/40–1943–44	1112	324	258	457	126

Sources: Blau, G., "Wool in the World Economy", *Journal of the Royal Statistical Society*, 109 (1946), p. 184.

Australian wool to the attention of Paris fashion houses and, in cooperation with Bradford woollen manufacturers, participated in a Wembley Exhibition in 1931, at which, 'attractive goods were displayed, not only in the piece but in the made-up article and exhibited on live mannequins'.[24] Similarly, the Graziers Federal Council produced a detailed advertising campaign in 1929 that promoted Australian wool, which was encountering severe competition from rayon production in Europe and North America: between 1918 and 1926, it was estimated that rayon output had increased from 35 million to over 200 million pounds (weight).[25] This campaign included plans to enlist the services of Sir Basil Clarke who was a pioneer British public relations specialist with a long list of esteemed clients.[26]

In 1936, the Australian Wool Broad was established to undertake research and promote Australian wool. In the following year, the International Wool Secretariat (hereafter, IWS) was formed. Its members – Australia, New Zealand, and South Africa – accounted for nearly two-thirds of raw apparel wool exports. The IWS sought to promote the international use of wool and the distinctive qualities of wool from the three principal producers. The impact of the IWS was constrained by limited funds and by the lack of engagement from other bodies such as the International Wool Textile Organisation. Operating from offices in Bush House, central London, the IWS focused on promotion and education, which included: the development of showrooms, attendance at exhibitions, and the distribution of information to manufacturers, retailers, and media outlets. After 1945, its range of activities and target countries became much more extensive as it disseminated its promotion across Europe, North America, and Asia.[27]

As a new generation of synthetic substitutes – acrylic, nylon, and polyester – undermined the demand for wool, the IWS introduced the renowned *Woolmark* logo in 1964 – the result of an international competition won by Italian graphic artist, Franco Grignani. The logo certified that a product was made of new wool possessing specific qualities. Reflecting the enduring success of the logo, the IWS was reformed in 1997 as the Woolmark Company, and in 2015 the British magazine *Creative View* designated *Woolmark* the most globally recognised logo.[28] Australia was likely to have been the main beneficiary of this certification trade mark: it was responsible for nearly half of global apparel wool production and export, and it was particularly dominant in high-quality merino.[29] Further, *Woolmark* provides an interesting example of international cooperation in the promotion of a *national* product.

In the twenty-first century, Australian wool continues to be promoted. The Campaign for Wool reports the connection between fine merino and its use in high-fashion products.[30] In London, Savile Row tailors championed their 'Made in England' credentials, but also promoted the provenance of the raw material. Simon Cundey, managing director of bespoke tailor Henry Poole and Company observed, 'Australian wool weaves through Savile Row and has done for generations'.[31]

Import substitution

True to the law of comparative advantage, Australian natural resource exports paid for the import of manufactured goods.[32] Although Australia lacked the low labour costs and a large domestic population that were prerequisites of most industrialised countries, regular debates ensued about the desirability and practicability of developing domestic industries to reduce imports and counter the growing influence of foreign firms on Australian soil.[33] Victoria, the principal manufacturing colony before Federation, imposed tariffs to protect local industry, while New South Wales remained free trade. After Federation, tariffs were introduced across the new nation. In 1904, the promotion of local manufacturing was supported by a Made in Australia movement which was established by various groups advocating the protection of domestic manufacturers. These groups included the Associated Chamber of Manufacturers (established in 1904), the Victorian Chamber of Commerce, and the The Australian Natives' Association, all of which advocated that domestic consumers purchase more Australian goods.[34] The movement expanded rapidly and within two years it attracted an audience of 600,000 to its annual exhibition. David Thackeray commented:

> By 1914 annual Made in Australia exhibitions and weeks were a common feature of civic life in towns and cities across the country, promoting the message that industrial development was the key for the future health and prosperity of the nation.[35]

The use of 'Made in Australia', 'Australian Made', or 'Australians First' juxtaposed on a map of Australia became an increasingly common characteristic of advertising by companies in the manufacturing and primary industries. Examples of this practice appear in Kate Dilanchian's study of the visual qualities of the Australian flag, which included steel maker BHP, manufacturer Hugo Wertheim, and Sydney fruit dealer, W. E. Lever.[36] A more coordinated approach emerged with the formation in 1924 of the Australian-Made Preference League, to defend local manufacturing. Its promotional activity included the twenty carriage Great White Train that travelled through New South Wales promoting Australian made products.[37]

The continued progress of the Made in Australia movement after World War One revealed the tensions between growing national self-confidence and loyalty to empire. The concurrent Buy Empire Goods movement was believed to promote British goods and employment at Australia's expense. Organisations, including the Australian Chamber of Manufacturers and the Housewives Association, increasingly boycotted Empire shopping weeks, and promoted 'Australia Week' initiatives, particularly as economic conditions deteriorated with the onset of the interwar depression.[38] While Australian produce exporters would have seen value in closer imperial connections to boost sales to the United Kingdom,[39] the best interests of domestic manufacturers were likely to have been quite different.

Exacerbating matters, tensions existed between choosing the cheapest, or best value Japanese manufactured products, and a sense that Australian business achievements owed much to the country's British origins. Moreover, domestic manufacturers faced their most intense competition from American and Japanese multinationals who located in Australia to avoid rising tariff barriers. Doubtless, lingering White Australia perspectives also coloured attitudes to Asian products. In 1939 the Australia Association of British Manufacturers and the Made in Australia Council jointly supported both Australian and Empire goods.

In this environment, firms developed brands that signalled national identity by portraying unique Australian conditions. Susie Khamis argued that 'certain brands have consistently invoked and articulated key nationalist discourses'.[40] Khamis used *Kiwi* Shoe Polish and *Bushells* tea as examples of how brands, 'harness verbal and visual props to bolster and buttress their purported Australianness'. Leveraging the image of the brave and noble Australian digger, sales of *Kiwi* accelerated during World War One.[41] Contemporaneously, Bushell focused on modernising Australian consumer culture, but decades later responded to a changed national imagery which emphasised nostalgia and the Australian countryside.[42] Bert Appleroth's *Aeroplane Jelly* brand was introduced in 1927 and promoted a series of stunts foregrounding iconic scenes such as deliveries to outback areas by a Tiger Moth plane. Ten years later, five-year-old Joy King recorded The Aeroplane Jelly Song to accompany the firm's saturation advertising; the song became a cultural icon of Australia and was used in advertising for many decades.[43]

Development of a national policy

After World War Two, Made in Australia became more proactive as it responded to the changing international environment, particularly the weakened links between Britain and Australia. National policy was stimulated by the wartime experience, especially the belief that Australia needed to be strategically more secure with a larger manufacturing base that produced a diverse range of products. Such a policy would also create employment opportunities for an expanding population. A key component of this policy was the development of the domestic car industry.

The notion of producing a fully manufactured motor vehicle in Australia had been broached earlier, largely with the intention of attracting British manufacturers to build locally. Concerns about the size of the Australian market, and its considerable distance from UK head office control, together with the onset of World War Two, terminated such plans. However, after 1945, pent-up demand for vehicles, and the problems generated by the shortage of US dollars, created more favourable conditions for the production of an Australian-made vehicle. In return for fiscal concessions, GM-Holden successfully tendered for Australian production. Its model 48–215 commenced production in 1948 as the first car model completely made in Australia.[44] Although a product of the joint efforts of General Motors and Holden, it epitomised the direction of Australian industrial policy. Pictures of Prime Minister Ben Chifley standing proudly in front of the new vehicle symbolised the postwar national development policy. However, the domestic automobile industry did not survive: tariff reductions from the 1970s (discussed below), exposed domestic firms to higher-volume, lower-cost Asian carmakers. Despite periodic subsidies, Australian car production ceased with the closure of the remaining factories of Ford in 2016, and Toyota and Holden in 2017.[45]

The decline of the Sterling Area by the 1960s weakened the economic and financial ties between Australia and the UK.[46] Overtures by the latter for membership of the Common Market during the early 1960s sent a clear message to Australian policy makers, and galvanised Australia's economic self-determination independent of the UK. Two British applications to join the Common Market in 1961 and 1964 were unsuccessful, but the direction of policy was clear, and the UK became a member of the European Economic Community in 1973.

Given these major policy developments, the 1960s witnessed an orchestrated national approach to support local products, and the concept of Made in Australia was increasingly appropriated by political leaders. In May 1961, only three months before the UK's first application to join the Common Market, a national campaign was promoted by the Associated Chambers of Manufacturers of Australia, which brought together earlier initiatives by individual States. It was launched by Prime Minister Robert Menzies and received extensive media coverage. This campaign, known as *Operation Boomerang* promoted the purchase of domestic products by attaching to them a quintessential Australian image (Figure 12.1). This image continued the patriotic connotations of campaigns launched earlier in the twentieth century, which depicted company brands against the background of a map of Australia. Quality and loyalty were emphasised as reasons to buy domestic

Figure 12.1 Logo of the Operation Boomerang campaign
Source: © Australian Chamber of Commerce and Industry. Reproduced by permission of the Australian Chamber of Commerce and Industry.

products. Prime Minister Menzies expressed the hope that manufacturing as a proportion of exports would increase from their current 14% to 50%. Noting the cyclicality of the climate, he concluded, 'We will have periodical problems of balance of payments so long as our exports are almost entirely of primary products'.[47] The general intention was not only to increase import substitution but to help domestic products become more competitive in export markets. Further, to the extent efficiency improved, higher wages would mitigate industrial unrest.

Prime Minister Menzies' statement was part of a long debate about the alleged instability of resource-based economic development. During the second half of the twentieth century, many economists supported the resource curse theory.[48] Despite the optimistic tone at the launch of Operation Boomerang, and subsequent praise for the initiative,[49] manufacturing's share of GDP was already on the decline in the 1960s *before* tariff reductions commenced (Table 12.1). Nonetheless, Prime Minister Menzies' thinking was echoed a quarter of a century later by Prime Minister Bob Hawke, who believed that buying Australian products would strengthen Australian industry and reduce the country's overseas debt.[50]

As discussed earlier, in the final decades of the twentieth century, Australian economic policy changed from providing broad macroeconomic stimuli through trade policy and infrastructural investments, toward targeted microeconomic reform which emphasised improved production efficiency.[51] National and international research reported that Australian manufacturing was becoming less competitive because tariffs protected its industry from global competition. A major part of Australian policy, therefore, was to reduce tariffs on manufacturing. The effective rate of protection fell from 22% in 1984–1985 to 4% in 2009–2010.[52] The strengthening of competition policy, financial deregulation, and labour market reform were other aspects of the drive for increased competitiveness. These initiatives were designed to foster greater efficiency in manufacturing, but the greater exposure to international competition raised concerns about Australia's relative productivity.

To address this problem there was a renewed effort to use buy Australian policies to foster consumer loyalty and patriotism. While earlier Made in Australia policies complemented tariffs, the former policy was now an antidote to the possible negative effects of trade liberalisation. Indeed, it might be viewed as a surreptitious, or 'soft', form of protection. *Buy Australia Made* was launched by Prime Minister Bob Hawke in 1986 by appealing to the national pride of citizens to choose domestic products. The Australian Made certification trade mark consisted of a gold kangaroo on a triangular green background; it certified that products originated primarily within Australia (Figure 12.2). A product could use this trade mark if 75% of the factory or work costs were incurred in Australia. This ratio could be as low as 50% in special cases where the benefits to the Australian economy were viewed as substantial.[53] This campaign was relaunched by Prime Minister John Howard in 1999, in consort with the Australian Chamber of Commerce and Industry, and the Commonwealth Department of Industry Science and Resources. In 2002, responsibility for the logo was transferred to a not-for-profit company – Australian Made Campaign Limited (https://www.australianmade.com.au/).

Complementing the Made in Australia policy was a push by advertising agencies and the Confederation of Australian Industry, to foster a sense of modern, assertive Australian values that were differentiated from 'traditional' British and Empire values. This type of strategy, which was similar to campaigns in the early twentieth century, was epitomised by the 'ocker' mannerisms of Paul Hogan (of Crocodile Dundee fame), in a series of advertisements in the 1980s, to promote *Foster's* Lager in Britain.[54]

Campaigns which emphasised domestic content were policed by various organisations to ensure compliance with the relevant legislation. For example, the Food Standards Authority of Australia was established as an independent statutory authority under the *Food Standards Australia New Zealand Act* of 1991. Its responsibilities included monitoring the origin labelling of food products. Made in Australia, however, proved to be an ambiguous definition

Figure 12.2 Logo of the Buy Australia Made campaign
Source: © Australian Made. Reproduced by permission of the Australian Made organisation.

of Australian origin. It has been claimed that 'The "Made in Australia" designation can be legally used only if the essential processing has taken place in Australia, but the decisions of the Federal Court say nothing about all components having to emanate from Australia.'[55] After various government inquiries, the *Trade Practices Amendment (Country of Origin Representations) Act* of 1998, removed some of the ambiguity by introducing additional definitions. Most important of which was the stricter definition of 'Product of Australia', which now indicated that a product did not contain imported components and that all processing had been undertaken in Australia. In contrast, Australian Made means that the last 'substantial transformation'[56] of a product occurred in Australia – irrespective of the origin of materials and components used in that product. These definitions continue to the present day.

Globalisation, sustainability, and the environment

Definitions of Australian grown or made have evolved over recent decades and in response to growing consumer concerns, particular emphasis is now placed on the environment and sustainable production. Australia's unique natural environment and its products are particularly well suited to meet these concerns. Rapid globalisation and the growth of international sourcing have required that national policies address the question of what it means to be Australian grown, made, or produced. In most cases, businesses advertise that Australian produce and its manufactured products are of high quality, made from natural products derived from a single, verifiable geographical source. The earlier examples of merino wool used in Savile Row suits, and the boots and clothing of *R M Williams* reinforce such characteristics. In addition, sustainable and ethical farming practices have been embraced and leveraged to present a wholesome or 'woke' face to Australian capitalism.

The green credentials of domestically sourced produce and materials have been a source of competitive advantage to Australian firms which have recognised that consumers increasingly prefer products embodying such characteristics. Consequently, there has been a plethora of domestic 'eco labels' which expound the green credentials of products; a minimum of 57 such labels have been identified. While some received strong backing from industry and environmental groups, others are believed to be examples of 'greenwashing' and lack credibility.[57] Similarly, organic farming practices have been adopted to reflect green credentials, and producers can seek certification from the National Standard for Organic and Biodynamic Produce, administered by the Department of Agriculture, Water, and the Environment.

Guidelines and legislation provided by the independent Australian Competition and Consumer Commission, established in 1995, have reinforced these approaches by providing appropriate definitions, and more effective labelling requirements covering a wide range of business practices. In 2016, the Australian Government changed food labelling laws to ensure that they indicated the percentage of local ingredients, and provided more details about foreign ingredients used in Australian made products. Businesses are also permitted to indicate the origin of produce, which may provide a greater appeal to consumers when that location is highly reputed, for example, Tasmanian seafood or Hunter Valley wines.[58]

Effectiveness of made in Australia strategies

The relevant literature has evaluated country of origin effects and compared them with other intrinsic and extrinsic considerations such as price, quality, and brand.[59] However, there does not appear to be any consensus on the relative importance of each. Made In campaigns can invoke a specific bias toward domestic products, but again, the literature is inconclusive. Some Australian studies have surveyed consumer opinion and concluded that although there was awareness of, and support for, such campaigns, and that consumers considered the country of origin when making purchases, they only exercised a preference in favour of Australian products when their price and quality were comparable with imports. Some consumers were prepared to pay slightly more for Australian products of comparable quality.[60] Older Australians were more likely to commit to domestic products; food and clothing bearing the Made in Australia trade mark were the products most commonly purchased.[61] However, the shortcomings of these surveys should be noted: they were based on small samples, and respondents' positive intentions provide no guarantee that these translated into purchases.

While individual firms may have benefited from Made in Australia campaigns, their broader economic impact remains debatable. Prime Ministers Menzies, and Hawke, and others believed that a preference for domestic products would improve the international competitiveness of Australian industry, raise employment, and improve the Balance of Payments. However, by encouraging investment in sectors where Australia did not possess a comparative advantage, Made in Australia campaigns may have adversely affected allocative efficiency and shielded individual firms from international competition. Terry Black provided a powerful, if slightly polemical, criticism of Made in Australia. According to Black, such campaigns lowered exports, leading to a reduction in aggregate demand; Australian consumers paid more for domestic products, and it was highly likely that foreign multinationals based in Australia were the major beneficiaries.[62]

Conclusion

What distinguishes Australia from the other countries in this volume is its development as a successful, resource-based economy. The periodic support provided to domestic manufacturers helped diversify the economy during the early twentieth century and provided some assistance to domestic firms when tariffs were subsequently reduced. However, the more consistent focus of Made in Australia was to support the export of primary products, which have been crucial to Australia's long-term economic development and the maintenance of high standards of living.

For all groups involved in promoting Australian exports – governments, statutory bodies, industry associations, and individual firms – the challenge was to identify distinctive characteristics. While this was rarely possible for mining products, there was substantial investment in the promotion of Australian wool, meat, fruit, dairy, and wine. For some products, this promotion involved concrete signifiers of quality, arguably best epitomised by the reputation of fine merino wool for which Australia has been the leading producer for many decades. For this product, certification trade marks were applied by individual regions and farms. Similarly, Australian wines have developed a reputation for high quality in international markets, with origination again reaching down to individual areas and specific producers such as *Penfolds* in South Australia's Barossa Valley. For other domestically manufactured products, emotional cues were often substituted for concrete signifiers. Initially, such cues drew upon empire connections, but were subsequently replaced by logos reflecting Australian national identity. Indeed, it might be argued that discursive constructs using Australian symbols – boomerangs, wildlife, and pioneer settlers – have helped to shape this identity.

In recent decades, concrete identifiers and social constructs have become intermingled as the bounteous Australian landscape, which generated high-quality Australian produce, became a battleground in the debate on environmental sustainability. The critical role of government in distinguishing true from false claims, particularly in relation to food standards, product origin, and farming practices, has been enshrined in the work of the Australian Competition and Consumer Commission.

Notes

1 Magee and Thompson, *Empire*; Crough and Wheelwright, *Australia*.
2 Note should be made of the work of the trade commissioners service promoting Australian products. Formed initially by colonial governments, the service was taken over by the Commonwealth in the 1920s. In 1986, the various activities of the service were subsumed into Austrade. Schedvin, *Emissaries of Trade*.
3 Wilson, 'Government'; Keating, 'The evolution'.
4 Fox, *The Mirror*, p. 39; Silvuka, *Soap*: chapters two and three; Godley, 'Selling'; Boyce and Ville, *The Development*, pp. 175–176.
5 *The Australian Star*, 8 April 1901, p. 3.
6 *Punch* (Melbourne), 14 July 1910.
7 Wright, 'The origins'; Sachs and Warner, 'The curse'; Barbier, *Scarcity*; Ville and Wicken, 'The dynamics'.
8 Dyster and Meredith, *Australian*, p. 66; Ville and Wicken, 'The dynamics', Table 2, p. 11.
9 Lloyd, '100 years'.
10 Forsyth, 'A perspective'.
11 Pomfret, 'Reorientation'; Lee, *The Second*; McLean, *Why Australia*, chapter nine.
12 Ville and Wicken, 'The dynamics'; Ville, Wicken, and Dean, 'Dynamic'.
13 Higgins, 'Mutton'.
14 See, for example, *Select Committee of House of Lords on Marking of Foreign Meat*. Parliamentary Papers XII.341. London: HMSO, 1893.
15 50 & 51 Vict. Ch.28, Merchandise Marks Act, 1887, s.3; s.16 (1); s.16 (4).
16 Merchandise Marks Act, 1926. *Report of the Standing Committee on Meat*. Parliamentary Papers, XIV.167. London: HMSO, 1933.
17 For a discussion of the marketing and branding practices used in the principal countries that exported foodstuffs to Britain, see, for example, Higgins, *Brands*, pp. 57–123.
18 Duncan, 'The Australian'.
19 Barnes, *Selling*, chapter one.
20 Ville, 'The relocation', p. 75.
21 Ville, 'The relocation'.
22 Merrett and Ville, 'Accounting'.
23 Burgoyne, *The Wool*, preface.
24 Australian National University (ANU), Noel Butlin Archives Centre (NBAC), Australian Woolgrowers Council E246/1, correspondence – Walter Devereux to Chairman, 4 June, 1930, p. 6.
25 ANU, NBAC, Australian Woolgrowers Council E266/30. World Rayon Production.
26 Evans, *From*; ANU, NBAC, Australian Woolgrowers Council E266/30. Report entitled, 'A Broad Outline of an Advertising Campaign that might be termed, "The truth about wool"'.

27 Abbott, 'Promoting', pp. 269–273.
28 https://www.creativereview.co.uk/landing-page/top-logos-of-all-time/
29 A certification mark is 'a mark which indicated that certain characteristics of goods … in connection with which the mark is used, are certified'. Belson, *Certification*, p. 1.
30 http://www.campaignforwool.org/about-wool/.
31 Sinott, 'Street'.
32 *Commonwealth Yearbook*, 1912, pp. 623–624.
33 Merrett and Ville, 'Tariffs', pp. 51–52.
34 Blackton, 'Australian', p. 37.
35 Thackeray, *Forging*, p. 39.
36 Dilanchian, *The Graphic*, pp. 5–11.
37 Crawford, *But Wait*, p. 48.
38 Thackeray, *Forging*, p. 92.
39 Recent research suggests that the promotional activities of the Empire Market Board did not result in greater UK imports of Australian produce. Higgins and Varian, 'Britain's Empire'.
40 Khamis, 'Buy', pp. 121–122.
41 Khamis, 'Buy', p. 123.
42 Khamis, 'Buy', pp. 124–125.
43 Boyce and Ville, *The Development*, p. 190.
44 Conlon and Perkins, *Wheels*, p. 119.
45 Pomfret, 'Reorientation', pp. 415–418.
46 Schenk, 'The Sterling'.
47 *The Canberra Times*, 18 May 1961, p. 1. https://trove.nla.gov.au/newspaper/article/133980297/15106825
48 Sachs and Warner, 'The curse'.
49 'Australian Made Campaign has five objectives' *The Canberra Times* 26 November, 1963, p. 33. https://trove.nla.gov.au/newspaper/article/104289124.
50 Cameron and Elliott, 'The country', p. 40.
51 Borland, 'Microeconomic'.
52 Productivity Commission, *Submission*, p. 19.
53 Fischer and Byron, 'Buy', p. 90.
54 Thackeray, *Forging*, pp. 166–167. See also Lopes, *Global*, p. 153, and illustration 8.
55 Fischer & Byron, 'Buy', p. 94.
56 Substantial transformation is determined either by a change in tariff classification, or value-added, or a specific processing requirement, or some combination of these. For a further discussion of this term, see Higgins, 'Made in Britain', and Higgins, 'Its made in the USA', this volume.
57 Choice, 'Eco-labels'.
58 Australian Competition and Consumer Commission (2021) *Country of Origin Food Labelling* https://www.accc.gov.au/system/files/Country%20of%20origin%20food%20labelling.pdf. Accessed 7 January 2022.
59 Cameron and Elliott, 'The country', p. 40.
60 Fischer and Byron, 'Buy'; Cameron and Elliott, 'The country'.
61 Baker and Ballington, 'Country', p. 163.
62 Black, 'Buy'.

Bibliography

Abbott, M.J., 'Promoting wool internationally: the formation of the International Wool Secretariat', *Australian Economic History Review*, 38 (1998), pp. 258–279.

Australian Made, 'Frequently asked questions', https://www.australianmade.com.au/why-buy-australian-made/faqs/. Accessed 7 January 2002.

Baker, M.J., and Ballington, L., 'Country of origin as a source of competitive advantage', *Journal of Strategic Marketing*, 10 (2002), pp. 157–168.

Barbier, E.B., *Scarcity and Frontiers: How Economies have Developed through Natural Resource Exploitation*. Cambridge: Cambridge University Press, 2011.

Barnes, F., *Selling Britishness: The Dominions, Commodity Culture and Empire, 1926–1939*. Montreal: McGill-Queens University Press, 2022.

Belson, J.B., *Certification Marks*. London: Sweet & Maxwell, 2002.

Black, T., Buy Australian? *Policy*, 10/1 (1994), pp. 8–10.

Blackton, C.S., 'Australian nationality and nativism: The Australian Natives' Association, 1885–1901', *Journal of Modern History*, 30 (1958), pp. 37–46.

Borland, J., 'Microeconomic reform', in Ville, S., and Withers, G., (eds), *The Cambridge Economic History of Australia*, Melbourne: Cambridge University Press, 2015, pp. 419–437.

Boyce, G., and Ville, S., *The Development of Modern Business*. Houndmills: Palgrave, 2002.

Burgoyne, G.A., *The Wool Marks Directory of Australia, Containing an Alphabetical Classification of Wool Marks, with the Name of Owner, Station, Postal Address, and Pastoral District in Australia and Tasmania*. Sydney: John Sands, 1889.

Butlin, M., Dixon, R., and Lloyd, P., 'A statistical narrative: Australia, 1800–2010', in Ville, S., and Withers, G., (eds), *The Cambridge Economic History of Australia*, Melbourne: Cambridge University Press, 2015, pp. 465–488.

Cameron, R.C., and Elliott, G.R., '"The 'country-of-origin effect" and consumer attitudes to "buy local" campaigns: Australian evidence', *Australasian Marketing Journal*, 6 (1998), pp. 39–50.

Choice (2021), 'Eco labels – too many, and too confusing', https://www.choice.com.au/shopping/packaging-labelling-and-advertising/labelling/articles/greenwashing-eco-labels.

Commonwealth Yearbook. Melbourne: Commonwealth Bureau of Census and Statistics (various years).

Conlon, R., and Perkins, J., *Wheels and Deals: The Automotive Industry in Twentieth-Century Australia*. Aldershot: Ashgate, 2001.

Crawford, R., *But Wait There's More: A History of Australian Advertising, 1900–2000*. Melbourne: Melbourne University Press, 2008.

Crough, G., and Wheelwright, T., *Australia: A Client State*. Ringwood: Penguin Books, 1982.

Dilanchian, K., *The Graphic Gift: A Study of the Map of Australia's Visual Qualities*. Unpublished thesis, University of Technology Sydney, 2011.

Duncan, R., 'The Australian beef export trade and the origins of the Australian meat board', *Australian Journal of Politics and History*, 5 (1959), pp. 191–201.

Dyster, B., and Meredith, D., *Australian in the Global Economy: Continuity and Change*. Melbourne: Cambridge University Press, 2012.

Evans, R., *From the Frontline: The Extraordinary Life of Sir Basil Clarke*. Cheltenham: The History Press, 2013.

Fischer, W.C., and Byron, P., 'Buy Australian made', *Journal of Consumer Policy*, 20 (1997), pp. 89–97.

Forsyth, P., 'A perspective on microeconomic reform', in Forsyth, P., (ed.), *Microeconomic Reform in Australia*. Sydney: Allen and Unwin, 1992, pp. 3–23.

Fox, S., *The Mirror Makers: A History of American Advertising and Its Creators*. New York: William Morrow & Co, 1984.

Godley, A., 'Selling the sewing machine around the world: Singer's international marketing strategies, 1850–1920', *Enterprise & Society*, 7 (2006), pp. 266–314.

Higgins, D.M., 'Mutton dressed as lamb? the misrepresentation of Australian and New Zealand meat in the British market, c.1890–1914', *Australian Economic History Review*, 44 (2004), pp. 161–184.

Higgins, D.M., *Brands, Geographical Origin, and the Global Economy*. Cambridge: Cambridge University Press, 2018.

Higgins, D.M., and Varian, B., 'Britain's Empire Marketing Board and the failure of soft trade policy, 1926–33', *European Review of Economic History*, 25 (2021), pp. 780–805.

Keating, M., 'The evolution of Australian macroeconomic strategy since World War 2', in Ville, S., and Withers, G., (eds), *The Cambridge Economic History of Australia*. Melbourne: Cambridge University Press, 2015, pp. 438–462.

Khamis, S., 'Buy Australiana: diggers, drovers and vegemite', *Journal of Australian Studies*, 27 (2003), pp. 121–130.

Lee, D., *The Second Rush: Mining and the Transformation of Australia*. Redland Bay, Qld: Connor Court, 2016.

Lloyd, P., '100 years of tariff protection in Australia', *Australian Economic History Review*, 48 (2008), pp. 99–145.

Lopes, T. Da Silva, *Global Brands: The Evolution of Multinationals in Alcoholic Beverages*. Cambridge: Cambridge University Press, 2007.

McLean, I., *Why Australia Prospered: The Shifting Sources of Economic Growth*. Princeton, NJ: Princeton University Press, 2013.

Magee, G., and Thompson, A., *Empire and Globalisation: Networks of People, Goods and Capital in the British World, 1850–1914*. Cambridge: Cambridge University Press, 2010.

Merrett, D., and Ville, S., 'Tariffs, subsidies and profits: a re-assessment of structural change in Australia, 1901–1939', *Australian Economic History Review*, 51 (2011), pp. 46–70.

Merrett, D., and Ville, S., (2015), 'Accounting for non-convergence in global wool marketing before 1939: the iron cage unlocked', *Business History Review*, 89 (2015), pp. 229–253.

Pomfret, R., 'Reorientation of trade, investment and migration', in Ville, S., and Withers, G., (eds), *The Cambridge Economic History of Australia*. Melbourne: Cambridge University Press, 2015, pp. 397–418.

Productivity Commission, *Submission to the House of Representatives Standing Committee on Economics: Inquiry into Raising the Level of Productivity Growth in Australia*. Canberra: Australian Government, 2009.

Sachs, J.D., and Warner, A.M., 'The curse of natural resources', *European Economic Review*, 45 (2001), pp. 827–838.

Schedvin, C.B. (2008), *Emissaries of Trade. A History of the Australian Trade Commissioner Service*. Barton, ACT: Department of Foreign Affairs and Trade.

Schenk, C., 'The sterling area 1945–1972', in Battilossi, S., Cassis, Y., and Yago, K., (eds), *Handbook of the History of Money and Currency*, Singapore: Springer, 2020, pp. 771–790.

Silvuka, J., *Soap, Sex and Cigarettes: A Cultural History of American Advertising*. Boston, MA: Wadsworth, 2012.

Sinott, A. 'Street Cred', *Ag Journal*, March 2021, pp. 18–19.

Thackeray, D., *Forging a British World of Trade: Culture, Ethnicity, and Market in the Empire-Commonwealth, 1880–1975*. Oxford: Oxford University Press.

Ville, S., 'The relocation of the international market for Australian wool', *Australian Economic History Review*, 45 (2005), pp. 73–95.

Ville, S., and Wicken, O., 'The dynamics of resource-based economic development: evidence from Australia and Norway', *Industrial and Corporate Change*, 22 (2013), pp. 1341–1371.

Ville, S., Wicken, O., and Dean, J., 'Dynamic paths of innovation in natural resource industries in Australia and Norway since World War Two', *Scandinavian Economic History Review*, 67 (2019), pp. 90–109.

Wilson, J., 'Government and the evolution of public policy', in Ville, S., and Withers, G., (eds), *The Cambridge Economic History of Australia*, Melbourne: Cambridge University Press, 2015, pp. 330–350.

Wright, G., 'The origins of American industrial success, 1879–1940', *American Economic Review*, 80 (1990), pp. 651–668.

13 'Made in Britain' or Made in Britain?

David M. Higgins

Introduction

Attempts to develop a Made in Britain trade mark can be traced to the late nineteenth century when British manufacturers became irate at the success of Made in Germany.[1] This latter indicia represented a spectacular 'own goal' following the Merchandise Marks Act of 1887. Indeed, so far as can be determined, the first proposals to develop a Made in Britain trade mark originated in Sheffield in the same year.[2] Move forward 127 years, and in 2014, the trade mark 'Made in Britain' was registered. This trade mark is a collective mark[3] owned by the organisation Made in Britain (hereafter, MiB), which was formed to, 'unite, support and promote British Manufacturers … to help them leverage provenance marketing of such British Products as a business advantage. We also aim to raise awareness of British manufacturing and communicate this in a positive way to businesses and consumers in the UK and overseas'.[4]

Debates on the merits of a Made in Britain trade mark involved business, consumers, and government, though the relative importance of each varied over time. In general terms, prior to 1945, consumers barely featured in trade mark debates. Thereafter, organisations representing consumer interests proliferated. The Consumer's Association was established in 1956, and in 1957 it began publishing *Which?* In 1959, the Advertising Inquiry Council was formed, and in 1960, the Molony Committee began taking evidence on consumer protection.[5] Subsequently, major legislation protecting consumers was enshrined in the Trade Descriptions Acts of 1968 and 1972.[6]

In contrast, business and trade associations always featured in debates surrounding Made in Britain. Members of these organisations appeared prominently in the earliest official investigations into this subject.[7] Proponents of Made in Britain argued that consumers preferred domestic, or empire products, and in order to exercise this preference, it was imperative that products indicated their provenance. This argument was used to support claims for 'Empire' or 'Foreign' marking throughout the interwar period.[8] From this perspective, protectionist motives underlying business views on country of origin marking could be made more acceptable to the government if presented as

DOI: 10.4324/9781003166184-13

a means to protect consumers. In the post-1945 period, firms and employer organisations gave evidence before the Molony Committee, and they were crucial to the deliberations which resulted in the Trade Descriptions (Origin Marking) (Miscellaneous Goods) Order of 1981.[9] Finally, of course, businessmen established MiB.

Inevitably, the government was substantially involved in these debates because it provided legislation on trade marks, and government departments, such as the Board of Trade, shaped and enforced legislation. However, the latitude available to the UK government on Made in Britain varied significantly during the twentieth century. Before 1945, UK governments, unrestricted by Treaty obligations or international protocols, were at liberty to promote British and British empire interests, as demonstrated by the Empire Marketing Board (hereafter, EMB), between 1926 and 1933, and the buy British campaign of 1931.[10] After 1945, international restrictions on the official promotion of domestic products increased, beginning with the General Agreement on Tariffs in 1947, and culminating with the UK's accession to the European Economic Community (subsequently EU) in 1973.

The interaction of consumers, business, and government, generated themes which are possibly unique to the UK. Until the post-1945 period, the 'British World', that is, the networks of trade and communication between the UK, Australia, Canada, New Zealand, and South Africa, was vital to the UK and the Dominions.[11] This World also generated strong social and cultural affinities between the white settlers in the Dominions and the 'Mother' country. Dominion discourse, 'emphasised the familiar, white and "British" nature of the former colonies of settlement ... In doing so, the white dominions stressed ... their similarity to Britain'.[12] One theme stressed in official debates on a Made in Britain trade mark was the interchangeability of 'British' and 'British Empire'.[13] But, did consumers in Britain and the British Empire, share the same perceptions of, and preferences for British products?

John Benson suggested a potent relationship existed between consumption and national identity which extended to the British Empire. For example, the 'Britishness' of Dominion produce was emphasised in advertising campaigns centred on the British market. However, as acknowledged by Benson, the relationship between national identity and national consumption was sometimes contradictory.[14] During the interwar period, the EMB promoted intra-empire trade in the belief that a symbiotic relationship existed between Britain and the Dominions, but, '...Canada was also by the 1920s a manufacturing nation with an industrial sector which in its home market at least was often competing with British products'.[15] Felicity Barnes argued that the advertising campaigns of the EMB elided industrial development in Australia and New Zealand.[16] Similarly, in the early 1930s, the Indian Merchants' Chamber argued that 'Buy British' was designed to support British industrial strength, and that the best way to facilitate domestic industrial development was for Indians to buy Indian products.[17]

Another observation on the UK experience is that from the late nineteenth century many companies traded on the British image. Robert Opie claimed this practice emerged in a spirit of patriotism and pride in British achievements which appealed to domestic and empire consumers.[18] Thus, images of Britannia were used in the promotion of Lever Brother's Sunlight Soap; Horniman's advertised their tea with the slogan 'A right royal drink', accompanied by an image of Edward VII; John Bull was used to advertise Cadbury's Cocoa Essence, Colman's Mustard, and England's Glory matches; images of Britain's armed forces were used in publicity for Peak Frean biscuits, while other quintessential British images were used on Beecham medicines, Ryvita crispbread, Whitbread, and Worthington beers, and Ogden's, and John Player (Player's) tobacco and cigarettes.[19] One possible explanation for this observation is that images of nobility, the royal family, and famous explorers and sportsmen, were far more effective in signalling archetypal British qualities than Made in Britain.

A final set of issues that need to be considered (some of which are discussed in more detail later), is what does Made in Britain mean? In one sense, this term signals economic nationality, but this conflicts with the historical reality: only a few manufactured products have ever been wholly produced from inputs sourced entirely within the UK. Alternatively, was Made in Britain synonymous with British identity – in the same way that, for example, Cool Britannia in the 1990s, symbolised domestic pride in British fashion and music? Indeed, it has been argued that 'Britishness is a powerful and long standing marker of authenticity, quality and tradition in fashion brands'.[20]

This chapter discusses two interrelated themes: Made in Britain as a trade description, and 'Made in Britain' as a registered trade mark. Historically, adoption of either legend was limited: many UK manufacturers did not adopt the former even though they were at liberty to do so,[21] and attempts to register the latter in the nineteenth and early twentieth centuries, encountered severe opposition, and ultimately failed. If companies were unwilling, voluntarily, to adopt Made in Britain as a trade description, how likely was it they would agree to be bound by the regulations governing a registered collective trade mark? There have been long-standing concerns about descriptions of origin applied to UK products.[22] Moreover, survey evidence has failed to provide definitive proof that UK consumers were influenced by Made in Britain. The Made in Britain trade mark was an attempt to address some of these problems.

The central argument of this chapter is that the trade description, Made in Britain, is not protected as rigorously as the trade mark, 'Made in Britain'. The former is available to all manufacturers to use on a voluntary basis. Consequently, individual firms have little incentive (or ability) to determine whether this description is being used to mislead consumers. In contrast, the latter is the intellectual property of MiB. This organisation has the same incentive to protect its collective trade mark as do individual companies with their own trade marks. However, unlike individual trade marks, 'Made in

Britain' confers benefits to many manufacturers and it helps to ensure that consumers can accurately express a preference for British products.

This chapter proceeds as follows. The next section explains why early attempts to register a British, or British Empire trade mark, were unsuccessful. Section III discusses the problems of defining 'British' products when Britain abandoned its commitment to free trade during the interwar period. The general unwillingness of UK manufacturers to voluntarily use indications of origin, and the problems this posed for government policy in the post-1945 period, are examined in Section IV. The penultimate section provides the first analysis of MiB and explains why its ownership of the Made in Britain trade mark was integral to its activities and future growth. Conclusions are presented in section VI.

Made in Britain as a trade mark: the early campaign

In a UK context, it was impossible for trade bodies to register a trade mark for members' use until the early twentieth century. This omission was rectified by the 1905 Trade Marks Act which permitted the registration of 'standardisation' (certification) trade marks[23] To be registered as such, the following criteria had to be met: an association or person had to examine the products with respect to mode of manufacture, origin, or some other characteristic; following a successful examination, the association certified the use of the mark by the applicant for a specific class of products, and the Board of Trade had to determine that such marks were to the public advantage.[24] There was a rapid uptake of such trade marks by a variety of associations, including the Cutlers Company of Sheffield, for 'Sheffield', the Irish Industrial Development Association, and the Scottish Woollen Trade Mark Association. Between 1906 and 1938, over 1,100 applications were made for such marks.[25]

Prior to 1914, two organisations sought to promote British exports using standardisation trade marks: The Register of British Manufacturers (hereafter, RBM), was incorporated in 1910 to secure registration of 'British Made', and the British Empire Trade Marks Association (hereafter, BETMA), was established around the same time for the registration of a trade mark consisting of a circle, the legend, 'The British Empire Mark. British product', and an indication of the specific Dominion, such as Canada, in the middle of the circle (Figure 13.1).[26] Despite their apparent similarities, important differences existed between the RBM and the BETMA, which meant that both organisations were in conflict.[27]

The RBM's scheme – motivated by the desire to prevent foreign products from being sold as British – applied only to British manufacturers. Ireland was excluded from this scheme because it already possessed the certification trade mark, Déanta i nÉirinn, which was owned by the Irish Industrial Development Association.[28] The focus on manufacturing meant the RBM excluded agricultural produce from its scheme and, therefore, most Dominion exports. To be eligible for the RBM mark, the maximum proportion of foreign *manufactured*

Figure 13.1 British empire origin mark
Source: Merchandise Marks Committee, Minutes of Evidence, London: HMSO, 1920, p. 231.
Note: This mark was never registered as a trade mark.

inputs in a British product was 10%; no restrictions were imposed on the proportion of foreign raw materials. It was acknowledged that these requirements raised anomalies: a car manufactured in Britain with an imported, expensive, technologically advanced engine, might not be entitled to the RBM mark, whereas a car with a cheaper, less-advanced engine was eligible. Nonetheless, the RBM claimed that, when compared to the BETMA scheme, the main advantages of its proposals were simplicity and workability.[29]

In common with the Register of British Manufacturers, BETMA sought to prevent the sale of foreign products as British or British Empire.[30] Unlike the former organisation, BETMA's proposals encompassed the empire, not just Britain. Consequently, BETMA's mark was available to manufacturers, produce originating within the British Empire, and retailers selling empire produce. In BETMA's scheme, Britain and the British Empire were synonymous. BETMA recognised that many foreign products were exported to the Dominions without an indication of origin, thereby benefitting from the preferential treatment the Dominions afforded British exports; consequently, use of its trade mark ensured that preferential treatment would only apply to British exports.[31] A further difference between BETMA and the RBM was that the former did not specify limits on the proportion of foreign inputs that could be used in products bearing its trade mark. Instead, products were eligible if they 'can fairly be described as of British origin'.[32]

Why, then, did the RBM and BETMA proposals fail? There was a belief that fraudulent imitation of company trade marks was facilitated when more marks appeared on a product, and that national trade marks received limited protection overseas. There was also a concern that national trade marks might become compulsory by default: products not bearing these marks might be perceived as being not British. Such a perception threatened esteemed British trade marks which indicated and/or included English provenance, for example, 'Gossage's

Fine Primrose', 'Bass, Burton-on-Trent', and 'Platt Brothers, Oldham'. Fears were expressed that the proposed trade marks created the impression of official endorsement. Furthermore, manufacturers were already at liberty to use 'Made in Britain', or 'Product of British Empire', as descriptive marks.[33] Finally, there was opposition to any scheme that restricted the use of descriptive trade marks to licensed members.[34] Further official investigations raised more doubts about the merits of a national or empire trade mark, and the RBM and BETMA schemes fell into abeyance.[35]

'British made' during the interwar period

After 1919, there was a resurgence of interest in marks of origin to combat unfair competition. A Merchandise Marks Committee was appointed in 1919, to assess, *inter alia*, the merits of promoting a British national trade mark.[36] Much of the evidence given before this Committee by the British Empire League (hereafter, BEL), repeated that made by its sub-body, BETMA, before the Dominions Royal Commission in 1912.[37] Nonetheless, supporters argued that their earlier case now had greater merit because of the establishment in 1915 of the French organisation, Union Nationale Inter-Syndicate des Marques Collectives, (UNIS). This body licensed the *UNIS* mark to French manufacturers provided they satisfied various criteria, which included: the mark was not to be used on inferior products, and products bearing this mark had to be made in France using French capital, or labour, under the supervision of one of the syndicates comprising the Union.[38] Finally, and in contrast to its earlier position, BEL provided a quantitative definition of a British product: To be eligible to use its proposed trade mark, British costs had to exceed 25% of the export value of a product.[39]

Once again, famous manufacturers reiterated their long-established arguments against BEL's proposals.[40] However, unlike in 1912, opponents appear to have emphasised the distinction between 'British' or 'British Empire' as *descriptive* trade marks, compared to their use as *registered* trade marks. Concerns were again expressed that registration of a national or empire trade mark empowered the owner to reject applications.[41] Such an interpretation was correct; in any event, manufacturers were free to use origin marks descriptively. Doubts were also expressed about whether consumers had favourable views toward the trade mark proposed by BEL.[42]

Given the diversity of views on the merits of adopting a national trade mark, the Merchandise Marks Committee concluded:

> … no proposal which has been so far put forward for a national mark in this country has secured anything approaching general acceptance … in the absence of agreement among the bulk of traders concerned, we see grave objections to the institution of a British national or Empire mark, particularly one which is to be under the control and administration of a private Association.[43]

The issue of what constituted a British product, and whether, therefore, 'British made' could be legally applied to products made in the UK from imported components, remained a cause for concern between 1919 and 1939. Prior to the First World War, the UK was a free trade nation; Customs did not impose tariffs to 'protect' domestic industry or to give preference to particular countries.[44] But after the war, Britain abandoned its commitment to free trade.[45] This change in policy presented problems for UK manufacturers who imported foreign components. In 1925, the engineering firm, Cooper-Stewart, requested advice from the Board of Trade on how to determine the lawful use of 'British made'. The Board replied that, '... there are no regulations governing the percentage of foreign material which may be employed in the manufacture of speedometers, described as of British manufacture, and the Board of Trade have no authority to give any ruling on the matter'.[46] Similar problems affected imported saxophones which were subsequently marked 'British made' because 40–50% of the total cost of the finished instrument was incurred in the UK.[47] Such issues persisted into the 1930s. The Federation of British Industries reported it had received a, 'considerable volume of correspondence ... related to questions concerning the use of the word "British Made" in relation to goods made up in this country of imported materials'.[48] This ambiguity was particularly damaging for intra-empire trade: US companies located in Canada were exporting products to the UK duty free, provided that a minimum of 25% of the product was obtained in the empire.[49]

Exacerbating matters were two separate categories of legislation. In 1919, the Finance Act specified the proportion of UK or empire costs which enabled a product to be classed as 'British made' and thereby obtain preferential treatment.[50] In contrast, the Merchandise Marks Act of 1887, and its successors, prohibited the application of any form of false trade description which might mislead consumers. However, the latter Acts never specified the proportion of a product's costs that had to be incurred in the UK, or the British Empire, to justify 'British made'. The Merchandise Marks Act of 1926, stipulated that imported products did not include, 'goods which since the date of their importation have undergone in the United Kingdom any treatment or process resulting in a substantial change in the goods'.[51] But this Act did not specify what constituted 'substantial change'. Consequently, concerns were expressed that 'British Made' and 'Empire Made' were being applied to products which were not comprised substantially of UK, or British Empire, labour and/or materials.[52] Thus, it was the established practice to stamp 'British made' on briar pipes imported from foreign countries provided fitting and finishing in the UK exceeded 25% of the total cost of the pipe.[53] Similarly, firms producing toys and Christmas crackers were accustomed to marking their products 'British made', even when some of the component parts were from foreign manufacturers. Such practices were so entrenched that even the Board of Trade was unwilling to launch a prosecution.[54]

The conflict between the Finance, and Merchandise Marks Acts soon became evident.[55] It was brought into stark relief in 1933 when the Board of Trade prosecuted Marks & Spencer. The Board claimed that foreign pencils and pencil cases were sold under a banner bearing the legend 'British made'. This trade description misled consumers into believing that the pencils were British. The defendant, and its supplier claimed that a false trade description was not applied because the Finance Acts stipulated that if an article was composed of 25% British work, it was entitled to be classed as 'British'. In fact, the pencils and pencil cases were composed of 80–85% British materials. Nonetheless, the magistrate ruled: 'if you want to say a thing is "British made", the whole article and not part of it must be British'. Marks & Spencer was found guilty and ordered to pay costs of 15 guineas (equivalent to £15.75).[56]

Why bother with origin marking?

In the 1950s, there were growing doubts about the effectiveness of the Merchandise Marks Acts, and concern, 'about the inequality between consumers on the one hand and well organised business interests on the other'.[57] The Molony Committee was appointed in 1959 to 'consider and report what changes if any in the law and what other measures, if any, are desirable for the protection of the consuming public'.[58] Consumer interest groups that gave evidence before this Committee included the Consumers Association, the Consumers Advisory Council of the British Standards Institute, and the National Citizens Advice Bureau Committee. In its final report, published in 1962, the Committee was scathing of the belief that the Merchandise Marks Acts, especially the Act of 1926, protected consumers; their interests were only 'incidental' to this Act, which was primarily designed to afford protection to UK agricultural and industrial producers.[59] However, the Committee was unwilling to alter the 'substantial change' regulation in the 1926 Merchandise Marks Act,[60] and it was unsympathetic to claims that consumer protection required that all imported products be marked with an indication of origin:

> we are confident that if the county of origin is a good-selling point in public repute … it will … be shown on the article … If the manufacturer …[does] not think it expedient to mention the actual country of origin, the consumer may draw the conclusion that it is one of low or indifferent reputation.[61]

Following the Committee's recommendations, the Merchandise Marks Acts were replaced by the Trade Descriptions Acts, of 1968 and 1972.[62]

Arguments that the onus of indicating country of origin rested with manufacturers was reiterated in debates on the Trade Descriptions Bill, 1972:

> if a country was proud of the value of its goods, it might be in the interests of manufacturers in that country to mark the origin of its goods ... it would be ... of dubious value if goods were sold in the shops without any mark.[63]

Similar claims resurfaced prior to the introduction of the Trade Descriptions (Origin Marking) (Miscellaneous Goods) Order 1981, which required compulsory indications of origin on a range of manufactured products. The fundamental issue raised in all of these debates was why UK manufacturers were unwilling *voluntarily* to mark their products with country of origin: 'There has of course been nothing to stop British manufacturers voluntarily marking their goods – but their seeming reluctance to do so ... must raise a considerable question mark over their expectations from ... marking'.[64]

Was the general unwillingness of UK manufacturers to use Made in Britain based on the belief that domestic consumers perceived little value in this indication? Hard survey evidence of consumer perceptions was absent until the Labour government commissioned a confidential survey by Marplan in 1978. This was followed in 1979 with similar surveys conducted by the National Consumer Council and the National Union of Townswomen's Guilds – both at the behest of the Conservative government. In broad terms, the surveys indicated that UK consumers were, at best, ambivalent about the country of origin. The main determinants of consumer expenditure decisions were, in descending order: good quality; style/design; well-known make; good guarantee; well-known store, and cheap price.[65]

Another possible explanation for UK consumer indifference to Made in Britain might have been growing disillusionment about the general performance of UK manufacturing. Judging by the trends in UK trade, this explanation looks plausible. Between 1950 and 1980, the UK's share of world trade in manufacturing declined from 25.5 to 10.2%, and between 1955 and 1980, UK import penetration increased by a factor of 3.75.[66] Exacerbating these trends were cross-border mergers and acquisitions which involved famous British marques: Nanjing Automobile acquired MG Rover in 1985: Lotus cars was bought by General Motors in 1986. Other famous brands, such as HP Sauce (owned by Heinz) and Smarties (owned by Nestlé) are no longer produced in the UK.[67] To the extent that Made in Britain does have cachet, it is restricted to the, '... highly fashionable, highly desirable and sometimes highly expensive – goods'.[68]

Made in Britain: more than provenance?

A number of organisations exist to promote British products. The Walpole Group, founded in 1992, acts as 'the voice of British luxury'. In 2005, it developed its mission policy from, 'promoting British excellence to promoting, protecting and developing British luxury'.[69] Similarly, Make it British, 'promotes ... British-made brands and helps businesses get their products manufactured in the UK'.[70] MiB shares some of these aims and objectives. For example, 'it brings together the British manufacturing community', it encourages, buyers, contract-specifiers, and consumers to procure British-made goods, and it is, 'a fast-growing community of like-minded manufacturers'.[71]

However, in other respects, MiB is different. Unlike the Walpole Group, MiB does not focus on luxury brands such as Laurent Perrier and Rolex – which are not British. Indeed, to be eligible for membership of MiB, applicants must be British, which requires that they have manufacturing facilities in Britain. Another difference is that MiB defined 'British products'. Such products, '... are deemed to have been manufactured or produced in Great Britain, as a result of Great Britain being the place where all labour/human resources, manufacturing, or producing the finished Physical Product is provided'. In turn, 'finished' products are those, 'where raw materials/components have undergone a substantial and transformative change as a result of your manufacturing processes in Great Britain'.[72] The 'substantial transformation' criterion is a Custom's procedure for determining the economic nationality of a product.[73] Undoubtedly the biggest difference between MiB and other organisations is that MiB owns the collective trade mark 'Made in Britain'.

A collective trade mark is, 'a mark distinguishing the goods or services of members of the association which is the proprietor of the mark from those of other undertakings'.[74] Collective trade marks generate a number of advantages. Such marks combine the production and management capacities of member firms without diluting their identity. Consequently, members have an incentive to foster the collective reputation of the mark. Further, to the extent that collective marks are used in advertising, they help to reinforce

MADE IN BRITAIN ®

Figure 13.2 Registered trade mark belonging to *Made in Britain*
Source: © Made in Britain. Reproduced by permission of Made in Britain.

the appeal of individual member's brands. Viewed from another perspective, use of 'Made in Britain' provides a double warranty: it conveys MiB to non-members and consumers, and members would not use the mark if they believed it was disadvantageous. Clearly, only members of MiB obtain these benefits.[75] Although MiB is the proprietor of 'Made in Britain', it is not entitled to prohibit other organisations, or non-members from using signs or indications which designate the geographical provenance of products, such as Made in Britain, provided such indicia are used honestly, and do not infringe the MiB trade mark. Further, a collective mark cannot be used against a third party entitled to use a geographical name.[76] One feature of the MiB trade mark which deserves recognition is that it should be placed in proximity to a member's trade mark with the 'arrow' pointing to the latter (Figure 13.2). This arrangement overcomes nineteenth-century concerns that Made in Britain would obfuscate a company's trade mark.

The origins of MiB can be dated to 2011, when one of its founder members, Denver Hewlett, of Stoves, a Liverpool-based oven maker, commissioned a survey on consumer understanding of the provenance of iconic British products. This survey reported that 43% of the respondents believed that Royal Doulton was made in the UK when, in fact, most of its products are made in China. The survey also revealed that 48% of consumers were unsure about which UK companies actually manufactured their products in Britain, and 67% supported the introduction of a mark indicating UK-made.[77] Initially, Hewlett thought that his emphasis on British provenance would be restricted only to Stoves appliances, but when this initiative was picked up on social media, Hewlett received enquiries from over 900 manufacturers who believed Made in Britain would help their own marketing efforts.[78]

From its inception, the MiB campaign received enthusiastic backing from Gavin Williamson and Shaun Edwards, Members of Parliament, who represented South Staffordshire and St Helens, respectively. This political support was inevitable: the pottery industry is located in Staffordshire, and Stoves (now Glen Dimplex plc) was based in Edwards' constituency. The campaign also received support from many firms, precisely because of the perceived benefits of using a Made in Britain trade mark:

> ... [we] strongly support the campaign for a standardised 'Made In Britain' marque to be used on British-made products. Manufacturers in the UK provide a level of reassurance that can't be offered elsewhere because of the provenance of their products and the sustainability of their manufacturing processes. Further transparency, when it comes to labelling products as British, can therefore only help to raise standards and make things clearer for the consumer.[79]

Some of the founding members of MiB were already using Made in Britain indicia, but the launch of MiB gave them, 'the opportunity to join something that was … policed in a way that gave us the right sort of recognition and the right sort of accreditation'.[80] Many companies belonging to MiB are small-medium sized enterprises; they reported that membership enhanced their ability to, 'work with or complement each other in a supply chain to the big tier one contractors'.[81] By facilitating collaboration via the Members' Directory, and social media, MiB helps its members share best practice which benefits all members, irrespective of whether they are vertically or horizontally related. Neil Ansell, non-executive director of Tratos, stated:

> We like to network with other businesses … so we can learn from what they actually do … we feel its very important in terms of moving our business forward that we're at the forefront of technology in terms of what's going on in industry in general … many organisations who are in Made in Britain … helped in terms of creating our views moving forward into the future.[82]

Subsequently, MiB was registered as a non-profit limited company in 2013, and its collective trade mark was first registered in 2014. MiB was legally obliged to specify the conditions that governed use of its trade mark. This requirement ensured that MiB's trade mark distinguished the products of its members from those of non-members. MiB's terms and conditions stipulated that:

> By submitting an application form for the MiB Membership Programme, you warrant that you are eligible … and you are able to provide us with evidence to support your eligibility. Your application to join MiB and your business transparency included within your MiB Directory page serves as a declaration of provenance.[83]

Further safeguards are provided because members must allow an appointed representative of MiB to inspect their manufacturing facilities, products, and show how they have used the 'Made in Britain' trade mark. Moreover, members need to be willing to demonstrate how their products are made and publish evidence to support the claim that their 'British' products are manufactured in Britain. If MiB obtains evidence that a member is misusing its trade mark, it reserves the right to suspend or terminate a company's membership.[84]

Currently, MiB has almost 2,000 members covering a diverse manufacturing base: building and construction, clothing and apparel, engineering, and transport. Many of the companies belonging to MiB are of considerable repute and lineage, for example ESSE Engineering Ltd, Carradice of Nelson, Ltd, Marshalls, Naylor Industries, and Roach Bridge Tissues.

In 2019, MiB commissioned a survey of 2,000 consumers and 1,000 purchasing and procurement decision-makers, to assess the determinants of buy British. Some of the responses are shown in Table 13.1, from which it is apparent that a substantial proportion of consumers and businesses wanted to

Table 13.1 Response of a sample of British consumers and businesses to a survey on Made in Britain

	Consumers Number	*%*	*Business Number*	*%*
Would you like to buy more British products than you already do?				
Yes	1587	79.0	728	73.0
No	412	21.0	272	27.0
How important is it to try and buy British products?				
Very important	755	38.0	475	48.0
Somewhat important	964	48.0	398	40.0
Not very important	208	10.0	79	8.0
Not at all important	73	4.0	48	5.0
Why don't you buy as many British products as you would like to?				
I don't know when a product is or isn't made in Britain	562	35.0	272	37.0
Its too expensive	707	45.0	376	52.0
I don't know where to buy them/ Where to shop	303	19.0	244	34.0
It's confusing	317	20.0	212	29.0
I don't know which brands are actually made in Britain, even If it's a registered brand	670	42.0	291	40.0
Why do you prefer to buy products made in Britain?				
It's better for the environment	448	53.0	337	53.0
It boosts the British economy	579	69.0	377	59.0
It supports British jobs	561	67.0	355	56.0
I like buying British	433	51.0	310	49.0
I prefer to know where things come from	323	39.0	267	42.0
It will be of better quality	300	36.0	274	43.0
The business I work for likes to support British businesses	n.a	n.a	302	48.0

(*Continued*)

	Consumers *Number*	%	*Business* *Number*	%
The business I work for produces British goods and we need support	n.a.	n.a.	242	38.0
British manufacturers have higher ethical standards	307	36.0.	260	41.0
Do you think you will buy more or fewer products Made in Britain after Brexit?				
Plan to buy more British Products	720	36.0	459	46.0
Plan to buy fewer British Products	140	7.0	131	13.0
Don't plan to change	647	32.0	218	22.0
I don't know	493	25.0	192	19.0

Source: Made in Britain : Buying British Survey Results, 2019, supplied by John Pearce, CEO of MiB.
Notes: Percentages are rounded.
n.a. denotes not available.

buy more British products (79 and 73%, respectively), and thought it very, or somewhat important, to buy more British products (86 and 88%, respectively). Another observation from Table 13.1 is that both consumers and businesses ranked climate considerations, support for the British economy, and British jobs, as the three most important determinants of their decision to buy British-made products. Table 13.1 also indicates that expense was the biggest obstacle to buying British (45 and 52%, respectively). Furthermore, among the least important factors which made British products 'better' than imports were quality (36 and 43%, respectively), and ethical standards (36 and 41%, respectively). Another observation is that both consumers and, perhaps surprisingly, firms, were uncertain about the geographical origin of products and whether brands were a sufficient indicator of this origin. Finally, Table 13.1 shows that Brexit has had a noticeable impact on the inclination of consumers and firms to purchase British products.[85]

Intrinsically, the MiB trade mark cannot allay concerns about the image, price, and quality of British products. Nor can this mark redress the problems caused by unscrupulous vendors selling imported products as 'British' or 'Made in Britain'. The solution to this latter problem depends on the rigour with which Trading Standards prosecute consumer protection legislation. Nonetheless, consumers and producers can be assured that products bearing the MiB trade mark are genuinely made in Britain.

Conclusion

The campaign for a trade mark indicating British provenance on manufactured products dates back to the late nineteenth century. And yet, surprisingly, it was not until 2014 that 'Made in Britain' was registered. This chronology seems counterintuitive: we might have anticipated that registration would have been secured much earlier – when Britain was the 'workshop of the world'. But, when Britain was the workshop of the world, many of its leading manufacturers opposed compulsory and voluntary use of Made in Britain. How paradoxical it appears, then, that it was only after a period of severe deindustrialisation in the later twentieth century that MiB obtained registration of its trade mark?

Explaining this conundrum is not easy. For example, substantial transformation remains central to UK Customs' decisions on the economic nationality of imports; it is also an integral part of MiB's membership regulations. But most consumers are unaware of Custom's decisions and, as noted earlier in the chapter, MiB cannot prevent non-members from using the legend Made in Britain. Moreover, throughout the period covered by this chapter, consumer attitudes to British products and Made in Britain were lukewarm. Generally, consumers were aware of the benefits of buying British, but this recognition did not always translate into purchasing decisions.[86] In any event, the substantial presence of multinational enterprises, the foreign ownership of once famous British companies – Cadbury, Bentley, DAKS, Rowntree, and Rolls Royce – and the growth of increasingly complex global supply chains, means that consumers and, indeed, companies, cannot be certain that they can accurately exercise their preference for buying British (Table 13.1).

Perhaps the most plausible explanation for this paradox is that MiB, and its trade mark, were never intended to act as *blunt* instruments to promote Buy British. Certainly, MiB supports members in four key areas – sales, marketing, exports and communications/public relations. But, 'Made in Britain' does more than simply convey provenance. One feature of the MiB strategy which is becoming especially important is its Green Growth Programme which seeks to foster sustainable business development and help members achieve a net-zero carbon footprint by 2050. A key component of this strategy is to reduce the demand for scarce resources through greater recycling. This approach has obvious benefits for society – there are growing public concerns about climate change – and it helps improve the competitiveness of businesses which are keen to advertise their 'green' credentials. For example, MiB member, Carradice of Nelson Ltd, has developed their fabric recycling capabilities to such an extent that its established consumers are now switching to the company's recycled products. Carradice recycles firehoses and lorry tarpaulins within a radius of 10 and 40 miles, respectively.[87] The emphasis on local sourcing helps to strengthen supply chains in the regional economy, and it dissociates MiB from the historical association in the UK between nationalism and Made in Britain.

Notes

1 Williams, *Made in*.
2 Dominions Royal Commission, *Minutes of Evidence*, Part II, Q.2874. Hereafter, *Dominions Royal Commission*.
3 Such marks are owned by an organisation, usually a trade association, to indicate membership and to distinguish the products and services of members from non-members.
4 Made in Britain, Terms and Conditions: https://0ad76616978651e5edb7-aa1506af7ba9a7abaaa3b03255ff4fc2.ssl.cf3.rackcdn.com/Documents/MiB%20TCs%20V4_Final.pdf.
5 For the growth of consumerism in Britain see, Hilton, *Consumerism*; *Final Report of the Committee on Consumer Protection*, pp. 507–515.
6 *Trade Descriptions Act*, 1968, Ch.29, s.2; *Trade Descriptions Act*, 1972, C.34. The 1968 Act was replaced by the *Consumer Protection from Unfair Trading Regulations*, S.I. 1277, 2008.
7 *Dominions Royal Commission*, pp. 132–146, 173–180, 194–224; *Merchandize Marks Committee*, Minutes of Evidence (hereafter, *Merchandize Marks Committee*), pp. 215–257.
8 Use of the terms 'Empire' or 'Foreign', were provided for in *16 & 17 Geo.5*, Merchandise Marks Act, 1926, s.10. For an analysis of this legislation, see Higgins, *Brands*, pp. 124–156.
9 Clayton and Higgins, '"Buy British"'.
10 Constantine, 'The buy', pp. 44–59.
11 Thackeray, *Forging*.
12 Barnes, 'Bringing'.
13 *Dominions Royal Commission*, pp. 132–133; QQ. 2341–2342.
14 Benson, *The Rise*, pp. 144–146.
15 Constantine, 'Anglo', p. 371.
16 Barnes, *Selling*, pp. 160–161.
17 Thackeray, *Forging*, p. 78.
18 Opie, *Rule*, p. 6.
19 Opie, *Rule*, p. 11, 16, 30–32, 71, 73, 148–150, 153.
20 Pike, *Origination*, p. 113.
21 Provided the description was not false.
22 Bragg, *Trade Descriptions*.
23 5 EDW.7. CH.15, Trade Marks Act, 1905, s.62.
24 Trade Marks Act, 1905, 5 EDW 7. Ch.15, s.62. Subsequently, section 62 was amended: the requirement to examine was removed, and the Board of Trade had to be satisfied that the association was 'competent to certify'. Trade Marks Act, 1919, 9 & 10 Geo.5 Ch.79, Second Schedule. However, collective trade marks, where not recognised as such in UK law until the 1994 Trade Marks Act, C.26, s.49.
25 Calculated from Dawson, *Certification*, p. 23.
26 *Dominions Royal Commission*, Q.241. I have not been able to determine the precise date when BETMA was formed, but it had its first meeting in 1912. *Times*, 17 October, 1912, p. 12.
27 *Dominions Royal Commission*, QQ.2887–2889.
28 See Adams, 'Made in Ireland', this volume.
29 *Dominions Royal Commission*, Q.2874; Q.2878; QQ.2896–2897; Q.2937; Q.2918; QQ.2936–2937.
30 BETMA was established under the auspices of the British Empire League, which sought to secure permanent unity of the British empire.
31 *Dominions Royal Commission*, Q.2217; QQ.2243–2245.

32 *Dominions Royal Commission*, Q.2717.
33 Descriptive marks consist, 'exclusively of signs or indications which may serve, in trade, to designate the kind, quality, quantity, intended purpose, value, geographical origin, the time of production of goods or of rendering of services, or other characteristics of goods or services'. Kitchin, Llewelyn, Mellor, Meade, Moody-Stuart, and Keeling, Kerly's Law, p. 180. For example, 'Monobrut' champagne; 'Old London Dock' gin.
34 *Dominions Royal Commission*, pp. 201–211, 225–227; p. 213, 215, 220, 222.
35 *Dominions Royal Commission*, Second Interim Report, p. 54; *Dominions Royal Commission* Third Interim Report, p. 52.
36 Merchandise Marks Committee: *Report to the Board of Trade*, p. iii.
37 *Merchandise Marks Committee*, pp. 132–146. The RBM did not give evidence before the 1919 Committee.
38 *Merchandise Marks Committee*, Q.4559; Q.4565; Q.4765; Q.4793. For a further discussion of UNIS and the opposition it encountered when registering *UNIS* in Britain, see Higgins, *Brands*, pp. 49–52.
39 *Merchandise Marks Committee*, Q.4690; Q.4823; Q.4833; Q.4871.
40 *Merchandise Marks Committee*, Q.4892; Q.4901; Q.4942; Q.5087; QQ.5251–5252; Q.5296; Q.5301.
41 *Merchandise Marks Committee*, Q. 830.
42 *Merchandise Marks Committee*, QQ.5055–5057.
43 Merchandise Marks Committee: *Report to the Board of Trade*, p. x.
44 McGuire, *The British*, pp. 231–253. I am grateful to Brian Varian for this reference.
45 Mace and Adam, 'Imperial', pp. 226–228.
46 The National Archives (hereafter, TNA), BT 11/33, Cooper Stewart to Board of Trade, 29 August 1925; Board of Trade to Cooper Stewart, 3 September 1925.
47 TNA, BT 11/27, Board of Trade to Messrs. Besson & Co Ltd., 17 November 1925.
48 Modern Records Centre, University of Warwick (hereafter, MRC). MSS200/F/4/2/14.
49 Guildhall Library, London (hereafter, Guildhall) Association of British Chambers of Commerce MS 14487 (3), Meeting of the Overseas Committee, 6 July 1932.
50 Finance Act, 1919 'Imperial Preference', s.1. London: HMSO, 1919. For a review of British tariff policy during the inter war years, see, Mace and Adam, 'Imperial'.
51 16 & 17 Geo.5. Merchandise Marks Act, 1926, s.10. The principal Act – the Merchandise Marks Act, 1887, did not specify the percentage of foreign and British components governing the use of 'British made'.
52 Guildhall, Association of British Chambers of Commerce, MS 14482, Meeting of the Home Affairs and Transport Committee, 14 June 1933.
53 Guildhall, London Chamber of Commerce, MS 1659, Meeting of the Briar Pipe Trade Section, 20 February, 1924; 24 March 1925; 9 July 1925.
54 Guildhall, London Chamber of Commerce, MS 16775, Minutes of the Annual General Meeting of the British Toy Manufacturers Association, 24 February 1931.
55 'Prosecution under the Merchandise Marks Act'. MRC, *The United Manufacturers Journal*, June 1922, pp. 126–127.
56 Guildhall, London Chamber of Commerce, MS 16775, Minutes of a General Meeting of the British Toy Manufacturers' Association, 30 May 1933.
57 *Review of the Trade Descriptions Act* 1968. A Report by the Director General of Fair Trading, p. 10.
58 Board of Trade, *Interim Report*, p. 3.
59 *Final Report of the Committee on Consumer Protection* (hereafter, *Final Report*). pp. 231–232.

60 *Final Report*, p. 234.
61 *Final Report*, p. 233.
62 Trade Descriptions Act, C.29, 1968; Trade Descriptions Act, C.34 1972. These were subsequently replaced by The Consumer Protection from Unfair Trading Regulations, 2008. In some cases, the EEC intervened in the UK marked to prohibit 'screwdriver' operations– where Japanese subsidiaries in the UK assembled mainly Japanese components to avoid the import duties charged on finished goods imported from Japan. *Times*, 8 March 1988, p. 23.
63 *Times,* 26 February 1972, p. 5.
64 TNA, FV 73/190, 'Secretary of State's Dinner -28 April: Country of origin marking on clothing and textiles', 24 April 1980.
65 Clayton and Higgins, 'Buy British'.
66 Williams, Williams, and Thomas, *Why Are the British*, pp. 116–119.
67 *Times*, 16 March,1996 (Car supplement), p. 1; *Times*, 28 March 2007, p. 40.
68 'The cachet of Made in Britain', *Times*, 9 February 2011. GALE document number: IF0504184387.
69 https://www.thewalpole.co.uk/about#Discover. Accessed 4 January 2021.
70 https://makeitbritish.co.uk/about/. Accessed 5 January 2021.
71 https://www.madeinbritain.org/about/made-in-britain. Accessed 5 January 2021.
72 *Made in Britain*, Terms and Conditions. https://0ad76616978651e5edb7-aa1506af7ba9a7abaaa3b03255ff4fc2.ssl.cf3.rackcdn.com/Documents/MiB%20TCs%20V4_Final.pdf.
73 Substantial transformation is determined either by a change in tariff classification, or value-added, or a specific processing requirement, or some combination of these.
74 Belson, *Special*, p. 35.
75 Crucially, *Made in Britain* can prevent non-members using the mark.
76 I am grateful to Dev Gangjee for bringing this point to my attention.
77 I am grateful to Adrian Johnson of UMPF for supplying the original press release.
78 Obtained from *Made in Britain* website: case studies.
79 UPMF press release.
80 Phillip Kalli, MD of Ideal Manufacturing. Downloaded from *Made in Britain* Case Studies: https://www.madeinbritain.org/about/case-studies/why-these-members-joined-made-in-britain-videos.
81 Dave Oswin, business development manager, Hutchinson Engineering. Downloaded from MiB Case Studies: https://www.madeinbritain.org/about/case-studies/why-these-members-joined-made-in-britain-videos. Members are required to, 'explore all reasonable options to trade with fellow members and other British suppliers and manufacturers'. The Made in Britain Code of Conduct, point 11.
82 Downloaded from *Made in Britain* Case Studies: https://www.madeinbritain.org/about/case-studies/tratos-world-class-manufacturing-business.
83 *Made in Britain*, Terms and Conditions: https://0ad76616978651e5edb7-aa1506af7ba9a7abaaa3b03255ff4fc2.ssl.cf3.rackcdn.com/Documents/MiB_Terms_Conditions_July2022.pdf, article 2.2.
84 *Made in Britain*, Terms and Conditions: https://0ad76616978651e5edb7-aa1506af7ba9a7abaaa3b03255ff4fc2.ssl.cf3.rackcdn.com/Documents/MiB%20TCs%20V4_Final.pdf.
85 A survey conducted by Make it British, reported that 69% of consumers were more likely to buy UK-made products after Brexit and the pandemic. https://makeitbritish.co.uk/uncategorized/madeinuk-survey-2022/?inf_contact_key=3870403e75d8c70339bffd7144cb2ff7b7af0999dac2af6212784c39e-

05d2aef&utm_campaign=mibnewsletter&utm_medium=email&utm_source=email_list.

86 Table 13.1; Clayton and Higgins, 'Buy British'.

87 David Chadwick, MD, Carradice of Nelson Ltd. Downloaded from *Made in Britain* Case Studies: https://www.madeinbritain.org/about/case-studies/why-these-members-joined-made-in-britain-videos.

Bibliography

Barnes, F., 'Bringing another empire alive: the empire marketing board and the construction of dominion identity, 1926–1933', *Journal of Imperial and Commonwealth History*, 42 (2014), pp. 61–85.

Barnes, F., *Selling Britishness: The Dominions, Commodity Culture and Empire, 1926–1939.* Montreal: McGill-Queens University Press, 2022.

Belson, J., *Special Report on Certification and Collective Marks.* London: Edward Elgar, 2017.

Benson, J., *The Rise of Consumer Society in Britain, 1880–1980.* London: Longman, 1994.

Board of Trade, *Interim Report of the Committee on Consumer Protection*, Cmnd.1011. London: HMSO, 1960.

Bragg, R.J., *Trade Descriptions.* Oxford: Clarendon Press, 1991.

Clayton, D., and Higgins, D.M., '"Buy British": an analysis of UK attempts to turn a slogan into government policy during the 1970s and 1980s', *Business History*, forthcoming.

Constantine, S., 'The buy British Campaign of 1931', *Journal of Advertising History*, 10 (1987), pp. 44–59.

Constantine, S., 'Anglo-Canadian relations, the empire marketing board and Canadian national autonomy between the wars', *Journal of Imperial and Commonwealth History*, 21 (1993), pp. 357–384.

Dawson, N., *Certification Trade Marks.* London: Intellectual Property Publishing, 1988.

Dominions Royal Commission, *Minutes of Evidence*, Part II, PP, XVI.393. London: HMSO 1912.

Dominions Royal Commission, *Second Interim Report*, PP, XVIII.137. London: HMSO, 1914.

Dominions Royal Commission, *Third Interim Report*, PP, XVIII.447. London, HMSO, 1914.

Final Report of the Committee on Consumer Protection, Cmnd. 1781, London: HMSO, 1972.

Higgins, D.M., *Brands, Geographical Origin, and the Global Economy.* Cambridge: Cambridge University Press, 2018.

Hilton, M., *Consumerism in 20th Century Britain.* Cambridge: Cambridge University Press, 2003.

Kitchin, D., Llewelyn, D., Mellor, J., Meade, R., Moody-Stuart, T., and Keeling, D., *Kerly's Law of Trade Marks and Trade Names.* London: Sweet & Maxwell, 2005.

Mace, B.M., and Adam, T.R., 'Imperial preference in the British Empire', *The Annals of the American Academy of Political and Social Science*, 168 (1933), pp. 226–234.

McGuire, E.B., *The British Tariff System.* London: Methuen, 1939.

Merchandize Marks Committee, *Minutes of Evidence.* London: HMSO, 1920.

Merchandise Marks Committee: *Report to the Board of Trade of the Merchandise Marks Committee*, PP.XVI.615, London: HMSO, 1920.
Opie, R., *Rule Britannia: Trading on the British Image*. London: Viking, 1985.
Pike, A., *Origination*. Oxford: Wiley-Blackwell, 2015.
Review of the Trade Descriptions Act 1968. A Report by the Director General of Fair Trading, PP.IX.907, 1976.
Thackeray, D., *Forging a British World of Trade*. Oxford: Oxford University Press, 2019.
Williams, E.E., *Made in Germany*. London: Heinemann, 1896.
Williams, K., Williams, J., and Thomas, D., *Why Are the British Bad at Manufacturing?* London: Routledge & Kegan Paul, 1983.

Index

Note: **Bold** page numbers refer to tables and *italic* page numbers refer to figures.